~ 700~

Easy to make and delicious low-carb,
high fat recipes, #2020 edition.

Includes a 365 diet meal plan,
nutritional facts and grocery shopping tips

STELLA RAY

TABLE OF CONTENTS

INTRODUCTION

The keto diet is the shortened term for ketogenic diet and it is basically a high-fat and low-carb diet that helps you lose weight, thereby reaping various health benefits. Essentially, the diet drastically restricts your carb intake and fat intake is increased; this then, pushes your body to go into a state of ketosis. We will tackle ketosis in a bit.

The body actually uses glucose from carbs to fuel metabolic pathways—meaning various bodily functions like digestion, breathing—essentially anything that needs energy. Even when you are resting, the body needs fuel or energy for you to continue leaving. If you think about it, when have you ever stopped breathing, or your heart stopped breathing or your liver from cleansing the body or your kidneys from filtering blood? Not unless, you're dead that's the only time the body doesn't need energy. So, glucose is the primary pathway when it comes to sourcing the body's energy.

But the body has another pathway, it can make use of fats to fuel the various bodily processes. And this is what we call ketosis or the ketosis. And the body can only enter the ketosis when there is no glucose available, thus the reason why eating a low-carb diet is essential in the keto diet. Since no glucose is available, the body is pushed to use fats—it can either come from the food you consume or from your body's fat reserves—the adipose tissue or from the flabby parts of your body. This is how the keto diet helps you lose weight, by burning up all those stored fats that you have and using it to fuel bodily processes.

BREAKFAST

01. Coconut Green Smoothie

Preparation time: 5 minutes
Cooking time: 0 minutes
Servings: 2

Ingredients:

- 1 tablespoon coconut oil
- 1 cup kale, torn
- 1 cup spinach leaves
- ½ cup coconut milk
- 1 tablespoon coconut ,shredded and unsweetened
- 2 tablespoons walnuts, chopped

Directions:

1. In your blender, combine the kale with the spinach and the other ingredients, pulse well, divide into glasses and serve.

Nutrition: calories 274, fat 26.6, fiber 2.9, carbs 8.5, protein 4.8

02. Pesto Tomato Bowls

Preparation time: 10 minutes
Cooking time: 10 minutes
Servings: 2

Ingredients:

- 1 tablespoon avocado oil
- 1 pound cherry tomatoes, halved
- 3 scallions, chopped
- 1 tablespoon basil, chopped
- 1 tablespoon Italian seasoning
- 1 tablespoon coconut cream
- 1 tablespoon basil pesto
- Salt and black pepper to the taste

Directions:

1. Heat up a pan with the oil over medium high heat, add the tomatoes and the scallions and sauté for 2 minutes.
2. Add the cream and the other ingredients, toss, cook over medium heat for 8 minutes, divide into bowls and serve for breakfast.

Nutrition: calories 97, fat 5.3, fiber 3.8, carbs 12.1, protein 2.8

03. Scallions Zucchini Bake

Preparation time: 10 minutes
Cooking time: 35 minutes
Servings: 4

Ingredients:

- 1 tablespoon avocado oil
- 4 scallions, chopped
- 2 garlic cloves, minced
- 1 teaspoon nutmeg, ground
- 1 teaspoon cumin, ground
- 1 pound zucchinis, sliced
- 1 cup cashew cheese, shredded
- 1 cup coconut cream
- Salt and black pepper to the taste
- 2 tablespoons oregano, chopped

Directions:

1. Heat up a pan with the oil over medium heat, add the scallions and the garlic and sauté for 5 minutes.
2. Add the zucchinis and cook them for 5 minutes more.
3. Add the cheese mixed with the cream and the remaining ingredients, spread well, introduce the pan in the oven and bake at 360 degrees F for 25 minutes.
4. Divide the bake between plates and serve for breakfast.

Nutrition: calories 260, fat 13.2, fiber 1, carbs 6, protein 4.5

04. Leeks and Arugula Salad

Preparation time: 5 minutes
Cooking time: 0 minutes
Servings: 4

Ingredients:

- 2 tablespoons coconut cream
- 4 leeks, sliced
- 1 cup baby arugula
- ½ cup kalamata olives, pitted and halved
- Salt and black pepper to the taste
- A pinch of chili flakes
- 1 tablespoon capers, drained

- 1 tablespoon cilantro, chopped
- 1 tablespoon olive oil

Directions:

1. In a salad bowl, combine the leeks with the arugula, olives and the other ingredients, toss and serve for breakfast.

Nutrition: calories 160, fat 2, fiber 1, carbs 2, protein 6

05. Spinach Salad

Preparation time: 5 minutes
Cooking time: 0 minutes
Servings: 2

Ingredients:

- 2 cups baby spinach
- 1 red bell pepper, roughly chopped
- 1 green bell pepper, roughly chopped
- ½ cup cherry tomatoes, halved
- 2 tablespoons olive oil
- 1 teaspoon rosemary, dried
- 1 teaspoon basil, dried
- ½ teaspoon chili powder
- Salt and black pepper to the taste

Directions:

1. In a bowl, combine the spinach with the peppers, tomatoes and the other ingredients, toss and serve for breakfast.

Nutrition: calories 180, fat 12, fiber 4, carbs 5, protein 7

06. Zucchini Butter

Preparation time: 10 minutes
Cooking time: 0 minutes
Servings: 6

Ingredients:

- 3 tablespoons coconut oil, melted
- 1 pound zucchinis, grated
- 2 tablespoons coconut butter
- A pinch of salt and black pepper
- 2 garlic cloves, minced
- 1 tablespoon chives, chopped

Directions:

1. In a blender, combine the zucchinis with the coconut oil, butter and the other ingredients, pulse well, divide into bowls and serve as a breakfast.

Nutrition: calories 140, fat 9, fiber 2, carbs 3, protein 4

07. Basil Zucchini and Cucumber Noodle Salad

Preparation time: 10 minutes
Cooking time: 0 minutes
Servings: 2

Ingredients:

- 2 tablespoons avocado oil
- 4 zucchinis, cut with a spiralizer
- 1 cucumber, cut with a spiralizer
- 1 tablespoon balsamic vinegar
- Salt and black pepper to the taste
- 1 teaspoon chili powder
- 1 teaspoon turmeric powder
- Juice of 1 lime
- 1 tablespoon basil, chopped

Directions:

1. In a bowl, combine the combine the zucchinis with the cucumber and the other ingredients, toss, divide into smaller bowls and serve for breakfast.

Nutrition: calories 296, fat 13.6, fiber 3.3, carbs 10.6, protein 3.7

08. Avocado Oatmeal

Preparation time: 10 minutes
Cooking time: 0 minutes
Servings: 2

Ingredients:

- 2 avocados, peeled, pitted and roughly mashed
- 1 cup almond milk
- 2 dates, pitted
- 1 teaspoon vanilla extract
- 1 cup coconut flesh, unsweetened and shredded
- 1 tablespoon chia seeds

Directions:

1. In a bowl, combine the avocados with the milk, dates and the other ingredients, toss, leave aside for 10 minutes and serve for breakfast.

Nutrition: calories 451, fat 25.1, fiber 9.9, carbs 55.4, protein 9.3

09. Oregano Peppers Bake

Preparation time: 10 minutes
Cooking time: 40 minutes
Servings: 4

Ingredients:

- ½ cup coconut milk
- 2 tablespoons flaxseed mixed with 3 tablespoons water
- Salt and black pepper to the taste
- 1 teaspoon oregano, dried
- 1 red bell pepper, cut into strips
- 1 orange bell pepper, cut into strips
- 1 green bell pepper, cut into strips
- ½ cup chives, chopped
- 2 cups baby spinach
- Cooking spray

Directions:

1. In a bowl, combine the peppers with the milk, flaxseed mix and the other ingredients except the cooking spray and stir.
2. Grease a baking pan with the cooking spray, pour the peppers mix, spread and bake at 390 degrees F for 40 minutes.
3. Divide the bake between plates and serve for breakfast.

Nutrition: calories 259, fat 20.2, fiber 1, carbs 4.4, protein 16.3

10. Asparagus and Avocado Bowls

Preparation time: 5 minutes
Cooking time: 6 minutes
Servings: 4

Ingredients:

- 1 tablespoon avocado oil
- 1 pound asparagus, trimmed and roughly sliced
- 2 avocados, peeled, pitted and sliced
- 2 tablespoons lemon juice
- 1 tablespoon basil, chopped
- 2 teaspoons Dijon mustard
- 1 cup baby spinach
- Salt and black pepper to the taste

Directions:

1. Heat up a pan with the oil over medium-high heat, add the asparagus, avocado, lemon juice and the other ingredients, toss, cook for 6 minutes, divide into bowls and serve for breakfast.

Nutrition: calories 323, fat 21, fiber 10.9, carbs 24.8

11. Avocado Smoothie

Preparation time: 5 minutes
Cooking time: 0 minutes
Servings: 2

Ingredients:

- 3 cups kale, torn
- 2 avocados, peeled, pitted and chopped
- 2 tablespoons chia seeds
- 1 teaspoon stevia
- 2 cups coconut water

Directions:

1. In your blender, combine the kale with the avocados, chia and the other ingredients, pulse well, divide into 2 glasses and serve for breakfast.

Nutrition: calories 168, fat 10.1, fiber 6, carbs 21, protein 2.1

12. Avocado and Pomegranate Bowls

Preparation time: 10 minutes
Cooking time: 0 minutes
Servings: 2

Ingredients:

- 1 tablespoon avocado oil
- 2 avocados, peeled, pitted and roughly cubed
- 2 cups baby spinach
- Juice of 1 lime
- A pinch of salt and black pepper
- 1 fennel bulb, thinly sliced
- 2 tablespoons pomegranate seeds

Directions:

1. In a bowl, combine the avocados with the spinach, pomegranate seeds and the other ingredients, toss, divide into 2 smaller bowls and serve for breakfast..

Nutrition: calories 148, fat 20.8, fiber 12.3, carbs 38.7, protein 7.1

13. Zucchini Muffins

Preparation time: 5 minutes
Cooking time: 30 minutes
Servings: 6

Ingredients:

- 4 scallions, chopped
- 1 tablespoon olive oil
- 2 zucchinis, chopped
- 1 yellow bell pepper, chopped
- Salt and black pepper to the taste
- 2 tablespoons flaxseed mixed with 3 tablespoons water
- 1 cup almond flour
- 1 cup almond milk
- 1 teaspoon baking powder
- 2 tablespoons chives, chopped

Directions:

1. Heat up a pan with the oil over medium heat, add the scallions, zucchini is and the bell pepper and sauté for 5 minutes.
2. In a bowl, combine the scallions mix with the rest of the ingredients, stir well, divide into a muffin tray and bake at 390 degrees F for 25 minutes.
3. Divide the muffins between plates and serve them for breakfast.

Nutrition: calories 258, fat 21.8, fiber 4.9, carbs 11.9, protein 6.6

14. Berry and Dates Oatmeal

Preparation time: 5 minutes
Cooking time: 0 minutes
Servings: 2

Ingredients:

- ½ cup coconut flesh, unsweetened and shredded
- 1 cup coconut milk
- ¼ cup dates, chopped
- 1 teaspoon vanilla extract
- 1 tablespoon stevia
- 1 cup berries, mashed

Directions:

1. In a bowl, combine the coconut flesh with the coconut milk, the dates and the other ingredients, whisk well, divide into 2 bowls and serve.

Nutrition: calories 572, fat 47.2, fiber 11.5, carbs 38.8, protein 5.8

15. Tomato Oatmeal

Preparation time: 5 minutes
Cooking time: 20 minutes
Servings: 4

Ingredients:

- 3 cups water
- 1 cup coconut milk
- 1 tablespoon avocado oil
- 1 cup coconut flesh, unsweetened and shredded
- ¼ cup cherry tomatoes, chopped
- A pinch of red pepper flakes
- 1 teaspoon chili powder

Directions:

2. Meanwhile, heat up a pan with the oil over medium-high heat, add the tomatoes, chili powder and pepper flakes and sauté for 5 minutes
3. Add the coconut and sauté for 5 minutes more.
4. Add the remaining ingredients, toss, bring to a simmer, cook over medium heat fro 10 minutes more, divide into bowls and serve for breakfast.

Nutrition: calories 170, fat 17.8, fiber 1.5, carbs 3.8, protein 1.5

16. Mushroom Muffins

Preparation time: 10 minutes
Cooking time: 30 minutes
Servings: 8

Ingredients:

- 1 cup cauliflower rice
- 2 tablespoons flaxseed mixed with 3 tablespoons water
- Salt and black pepper to the taste
- 1 cup cashew cheese, grated
- 4 scallions, chopped
- 1 red bell pepper chopped
- 1 cup white mushrooms, sliced
- Cooking spray

Directions:

1. In a bowl, combine the cauliflower rice with the flaxseed mix, scallions and the

other ingredients, and whisk well.

2. Grease a muffin pan with the cooking spray, divide the mushrooms mix, bake at 350 degrees F for 30 minutes and serve for breakfast.

Nutrition: calories 123, fat 5.6, fiber 1.3, carbs 10.8, protein 7.5

17. Bell Pepper and Cauliflower Rice Pan

Preparation time: 5 minutes
Cooking time: 20 minutes
Servings: 4

Ingredients:

- 1 tablespoon olive oil
- 4 scallions, chopped
- 1 red bell pepper, chopped
- 1 green bell pepper, chopped
- 1 cup cauliflower rice
- 1 cup vegetable stock
- 1 teaspoon oregano, dried
- 1 teaspoon turmeric powder
- 1 tablespoon chives, chopped
- Salt and black pepper to the taste

Directions:

1. Heat up a pan with the oil over medium heat, add the scallions and sauté for 5 minutes.
2. Add the cauliflower rice and the other ingredients, toss, cook over medium heat for 15 minutes more, divide into bowls and serve for breakfast.

Nutrition: calories 304, fat 14, fiber 3.8, carbs 27.5, protein 17.8

18. Chives Stuffed Tomatoes

Preparation time: 10 minutes
Cooking time: 20 minutes
Servings: 4

Ingredients:

- 2 tablespoons olive oil
- 8 tomatoes, insides scooped
- 1 cup chives, chopped
- ½ cup cashew cheese, grated
- Salt and black pepper to the taste
- 4 tablespoons rosemary, chopped

Directions:

1. Grease a pan with the oil and arrange the tomatoes inside.
2. Divide the chives and the other ingredients in each tomato, introduce the pan in the oven and bake at 375 degrees F for 20 minutes.
3. Divide the mix between plates and serve for breakfast.

Nutrition: calories 276, fat 20.3, fiber 4.7, carbs 13.2, protein 13.7

19. Capers Cauliflower Rice and Avocado

Preparation time: 10 minutes
Cooking time: 12 minutes
Servings: 2

Ingredients:

- 2 spring onions, chopped
- 1 tablespoon olive oil
- 1 tablespoon capers, drained
- 1 cup cauliflower rice
- 1 teaspoon chili powder
- 2 tablespoons black olives, pitted and sliced
- A pinch of salt and black pepper
- ¼ teaspoon oregano, dried
- 1 tablespoon parsley, chopped

Directions:

Heat up a pan with the oil over medium-high heat, add the spring onions and sauté for 2 minutes.
Add the cauliflower rice, capers and the other ingredients, toss, cook over medium heat for 10 minutes more, divide into bowls and serve for breakfast.

Nutrition: calories 249, fat 17, fiber 3.2, carbs 13.3, protein 13.5

20. Mint Watermelon Bowl

Preparation time: 5 minutes
Cooking time: 0 minutes
Servings: 2

Ingredients:

- 2 cups watermelon, peeled and cubed
- 6 kalamata olives, pitted and sliced
- 1 teaspoon avocado oil
- ½ tablespoon balsamic vinegar
- 1 tablespoon mint, chopped

Directions:

1. In a bowl, combine the watermelon with the olives and the other ingredients, toss, divide into smaller bowls and serve.

Nutrition: calories 90, fat 3, fiber 1, carbs 7, protein 2

21. Roasted Peppers Muffins

Preparation time: 10 minutes
Cooking time: 15 minutes
Servings: 6

Ingredients:

- 2 tablespoons flaxseed mixed with 3 tablespoons water
- 1/3 cup spinach, chopped
- ½ cup coconut cream
- ¼ cup cashew cheese, grated
- ½ cup roasted red peppers, chopped
- A pinch of salt and black pepper
- 2 tablespoons oregano, chopped
- 1 teaspoon chili powder
- Cooking spray

Directions:

1. In a bowl, combine the spinach with the flaxseed mix, the cream and the other ingredients except the cooking spray, and whisk well.
2. Grease a muffin pan with the cooking spray, divide the peppers mix, bake at 400 degrees F for 15 minutes and serve for breakfast.

Nutrition: calories 209, fat 16.7, fiber 1.8, carbs 6.8, protein 9.3

22. Tomato and Avocado Pizza

Preparation time: 20 minutes
Cooking time: 20 minutes
Servings: 2

Ingredients:

- 2 cups almond flour
- A pinch of salt and black pepper
- 1 and ½ cups water
- 2 tablespoons avocado oil
- 1 teaspoon chili powder
- 1 tomato, sliced
- 1 avocado, peeled, pitted and sliced
- ¼ cup tomato passata
- 2 tablespoons chives, chopped

Directions:

1. In a bowl, mix the flour with salt, pepper, water, the oil and chili powder, stir well until you obtain a dough, knead a bit, put in a bowl, cover and leave aside for 20 minutes.
2. Transfer the dough to a working surface, shape a circle, transfer it to a baking sheet lined with parchment paper and bake at 400 degrees F for 10 minutes.
3. Spread the tomato passata over the pizza crust, also add the rest of the ingredients and bake at 400 degrees F for 10 minutes more.
4. Cut and serve for breakfast.

Nutrition: calories 416, fat 24.5, fiber 9.6, carbs 36.6, protein 15.4

23. Sweet Cauliflower Rice Casserole

Preparation time: 10 minutes
Cooking time: 1 hour
Servings: 8

Ingredients:

- 1 and ½ cups blackberries
- 1 cup coconut cream
- 1 tablespoon cinnamon powder
- 2 teaspoons vanilla extract
- 1 teaspoon ginger, ground
- 1 cup cauliflower rice
- ¼ cup walnuts, chopped
- 2 cups almond milk

Directions:

1. In a baking dish, combine the cauliflower rice with the berries, the cream and the other ingredients, toss and bake at 350 degrees F for 1 hour.
2. Divide the mix into bowls and serve for breakfast.

Nutrition: calories 213, fat 4.1, fiber 4, carbs 41, protein 4.5

24. Spicy Bowls

Preparation time: 10 minutes
Cooking time: 15 minutes
Servings: 4

Ingredients:

- 1 cup baby spinach
- ½ cup cherry tomatoes, halved
- ¼ teaspoon cardamom, ground
- 1 teaspoon turmeric powder
- 1 tablespoon olive oil
- A pinch of salt and black pepper
- ½ cup coconut cream
- ½ cup green olives, pitted and halved
- ½ cup cucumbers, sliced
- 1 tablespoon parsley, chopped

Directions:

1. Heat up a pan with the oil over medium heat, add the olives and the tomatoes, toss and cook for 5 minutes.
2. Add the spinach and the other ingredients, toss, cook over medium heat fro 10 minutes, divide into bowls and serve.

Nutrition: calories 116, fat 11.3, fiber 1.6, carbs 4.2, protein 1.3

25. Keto Pumpkin Pancakes

Preparation Time: 10 minutes
Cooking Time: 6 minutes
Servings: 8

Ingredients:

- 2 tablespoons butter
- 1 teaspoon pumpkin spice
- 1 teaspoon baking powder
- 2 large eggs
- ¼ cup sour cream
- 1 cup almond meal
- ¼ cup pumpkin puree
- 1/4 teaspoon salt

Directions:

1. First in a mixing bowl combine your eggs, sour cream and butter. In another mixing bowl, combine salt, almond meal, spice, baking powder. Now slowly add your wet ingredients to your dry ingredients, while stirring to blend. This will give you a sweet, smooth batter. Over medium-heat warm up a cast-iron frying pan and grease it with butter. Pour about 1/3 of your mixture into the skillet. When bubbles begin to form on top of the batter, allow it to cook for about another minute, then flip it over. Cook on the other side for an additional minute or so. Repeat the previous last two steps until your batter is done. Serve up your keto pumpkin pancakes with your favorite toppings.

Nutritional Values (Per Serving):

Calories: 150, Fat: 11 g, Carbs: 1.5 g, Protein: 5.5 g

26. Scrambled Eggs with Cheddar & Spinach

Preparation Time: 8 minutes
Cooking Time: 10 minutes
Servings: 1

Ingredients:

- 1 tablespoon heavy cream
- 1 tablespoon olive oil
- 1 pinch of sea salt and pepper
- 4 large eggs
- ½ cup cheddar cheese, shredded
- 4 cups spinach, chopped

Directions:

1. Crack eggs into mixing bowl, along with heavy cream, salt, and pepper. Mix. Heat a large pan over medium-high heat, adding olive oil. When it is hot, add the spinach and let it sizzle and wilt adding some salt and pepper to it. When the spinach is fully cooked, reduce heat to medium-low and add in the egg mixture. Stir the eggs slowly and cook. When the eggs have set, add in the cheese on top and allow it to melt.

Nutritional Values (Per Serving):
Calories: 700, Fat: 55 g, Carbs: 7 g, Protein: 42 g

27. Waffle/Cinnamon Roll

Preparation Time: 5 minutes
Cooking Time: 6 minutes
Servings: 1

Ingredients:

- Waffle:
- ½ teaspoon vanilla extract
- ½ teaspoon cinnamon
- ¼ teaspoon baking soda

- 2 large eggs
- 1 tablespoon erythritol
- 6 tablespoons almond flour
- Frosting:
- 2 teaspoons batter from waffles
- 2 tablespoons cream cheese
- 1 tablespoon heavy cream
- ¼ teaspoon of cinnamon
- 1 tablespoon erythritol
- ¼ teaspoon vanilla extract

Directions:

1. Add all the dry waffle ingredients in a mixing bowl. In another mixing bowl, mix your wet ingredients. Ensure that they are combined well. Add your wet ingredients to the dry ingredients and blend well. Heat your waffle iron. When waffle iron is hot, add your batter. Remember to reserve 2 teaspoons of your waffle batter for the frosting. While the waffle is cooking, add your cream cheese and erythritol to a small bowl. Now add heavy cream, cinnamon, and batter. Mix until smooth. Once the waffle is finished cooking, remove it from iron, place on serving the dish and spread frosting on top. Enjoy!

Nutritional Values (Per Serving):

Calories: 545
Fat: 52 g
Carbs: 6 g
Protein: 25 g

28. Creamy Zucchini Noodles

Preparation Time: 10 minutes
Cooking Time: 5 minutes
Servings: 4

Ingredients:

- 3 medium zucchinis, use spiralizer to make noodles
- 1 tablespoon arrowroot powder
- ¼ teaspoon ground nutmeg
- Black pepper to taste
- 1 teaspoon butter
- 2 garlic cloves, minced
- ½ cup almond milk, unsweetened
- ¾ cup parmesan cheese, grated

Directions:

1. In a pan over medium-high heat melt butter. Add in the garlic and cook for about 1 minute or until garlic softens. Decrease the heat to medium-low. Add heavy cream, almond milk, nutmeg and stir well, bringing to a simmer. In a mixing bowl, whisk 2 tablespoons of water and arrowroot powder until smooth. Pour mixture into the pan and stir well. Add black pepper and grated cheese and stir until cheese melts. Pour sauce into a bowl, cover and set aside. Heat pan over medium-high heat. Once the pan is hot adding in zucchini noodles and stir until they soften, for about 5 minutes. Now stir in the prepared sauce and serve.

Nutritional Values (Per Serving):

Calories: 307
Fat: 21.9 g
Carbohydrates: 9.2 g
Sugar: 3.6 g
Protein: 20.6 g
Cholesterol: 33 mg

29. Vegetarian Keto Breakfast Frittata

Preparation Time: 10 minutes
Cooking Time: 5 minutes
Servings: 4

Ingredients:

- 4 organic eggs
- ¼ teaspoon sea salt
- 1 avocado, peeled, sliced
- 2-ounces cheddar cheese, shredded
- 10 olives, pitted
- 1 teaspoon herb de Provence
- 2 tablespoons olive oil
- 2 tablespoons butter

Directions:

1. In a mixing bowl, add herb de Provence, eggs, olives, sea salt and whisk until frothy. Melt the butter in a pan over high heat. Add avocado slices to pan and cook until lightly golden brown. Remove from pan and set aside. Pour the egg mixture

into the pan and sprinkle cheese on top over the top of egg mixture. Cover pan with lid and cook for 3 minutes. Flip over to other side and cook for another 2 minutes. Transfer the frittata to serving plate and top with avocado slices. Enjoy!

Nutritional Values (Per Serving):

Calories: 346
Fat: 32.8 g
Carbohydrates: 5.5 g
Sugar: 0.7 g
Protein: 10.2 g
Cholesterol: 194 mg

30. Creamy Cheese Soufflés

Preparation Time: 10 minutes
Cooking Time: 25 minutes
Servings: 8

Ingredients:

- 6 organic eggs, separated
- 1 teaspoon salt
- ½ cup almond flour
- 1 teaspoon mustard, ground
- ½ teaspoon pepper
- ½ teaspoon xanthan gum
- ¼ teaspoon cayenne pepper
- ¾ cup heavy cream
- 2 cups cheddar cheese, shredded
- 4 tablespoons chives, fresh, chopped
- ¼ teaspoon cream of tartar

Directions:

1. Preheat your oven to 350°Fahrenheit. Spray 8 ramekins with cooking spray and place them onto a cookie sheet. In a mixing bowl, whisk together pepper, mustard, cayenne, xanthan gum, salt and almond flour. Slowly add in the cream and mix until well combined. Whisk your egg yolks, cheese, chives until well blended. In another mixing bowl, beat the egg whites with the cream of tartar until stiff peaks are formed. Gently fold egg whites into the cheese and almond flour mixture. Pour the mixture into prepared ramekins. Bake in preheated oven for 25 minutes or until your soufflés are lightly golden brown. Serve and enjoy!

Nutritional Values (Per Serving):

Calories: 214
Fat: 17.9 g
Carbohydrates: 1.6 g
Sugar: 0.5 g
Protein: 11.6 g
Cholesterol: 168 mg

31. Keto Zucchini Fritters

Preparation Time: 25 minutes
Cooking Time: 6 minutes
Servings: 8

Ingredients:

- 1 lb. zucchini, grated and squeezed
- 1 teaspoon salt
- 2 organic eggs
- 1 ½ ounces onion, minced
- 1 teaspoon lemon pepper
- ½ teaspoon baking powder
- ½ cup almond flour
- ¼ coconut flour
- ¼ cup Parmesan cheese, grated

Directions:

1. Add your zucchini, eggs, and onion in a mixing bowl and mix until well combined. Add all the remaining ingredients into another mixing bowl, and stir well. Add your dry ingredients to the zucchini mixture and mix well. Pour enough oil into the pan to cover the bottom surface of it. Heat the oil over medium-high heat. Once the oil becomes hot, pour ¼ cup zucchini batter into pan and cook for 3 minutes then flip and cook the other side for another 3 minutes. Place your fried zucchini fritters on a paper towel to soak up the excess oil. Serve and enjoy!

Nutritional Values (Per Serving):

Calories: 81
Fat: 6 g
Carbohydrates: 5 g
Sugar: 0 g
Protein: 5 g
Cholesterol: 58 mg

32.Avocado Spinach Cucumber Breakfast

Smoothie

Preparation Time: 10 minutes
Servings: 1

Ingredients:

- 1 scoop protein powder
- 1 ½ cups almond milk
- 1-ounce spinach, fresh, chopped
- 1.8-ounces cucumber, chopped
- 1.8-ounce celery, chopped
- 1.8-ounce avocado
- 1 tablespoon coconut oil
- 10 drops liquid Stevia

Directions:

1. Add all the ingredients into a blender and blend until smooth. Serve and enjoy!

Nutritional Values (Per Serving):

Calories: 385
Fat: 26.6 g
Carbohydrates: 12.9 g
Sugar: 2.7 g
Protein: 26.1 g
Cholesterol: 65 mg

33. Keto Flax Cinnamon Muffins

Preparation Time: 10 minutes
Cooking Time: 20 minutes
Servings: 12

Ingredients:

- 4 organic eggs, beaten
- 1/8 teaspoon salt
- 1 cup flax seed, ground
- ½ cup olive oil
- ½ cup coconut sugar
- ¼ cup coconut flour
- 2 teaspoons vanilla
- 2 teaspoons cinnamon
- 1 teaspoon lemon juice
- ½ teaspoon baking soda
- 1 cup walnuts, chopped

Directions:

1. Preheat your oven to 350°Fahrenheit. Spray muffin pan with cooking spray and set aside. Add all ingredients into a mixing bowl and mix well to combine. Pour the batter into prepared muffin pan—filling each about ¾ full of mixture. Bake for about 20 minutes. Serve and enjoy!

Nutritional Values (Per Serving):

Calories: 219
Fat: 20 g
Carbohydrates: 6 g
Sugar: 1 g
Protein: 6 g
Cholesterol: 55 mg

34. Healthy Keto Pancakes

Preparation Time: 10 minutes
Cooking Time: 2 minutes
Servings: 6

Ingredients:

- 1 large banana, mashed
- 2 organic eggs
- 1/8 teaspoon baking powder
- 2 tablespoons vanilla protein powder

Directions:

1. Heat your pan over medium heat. In a mixing bowl add all your ingredients and mix well to combine. Spray pan with cooking spray. Pour 3 tablespoons of batter into the hot pan to make the pancake. Cook the pancake for no more than 1 minute and flip onto other side and cook for an additional minute. Serve with sugar-free syrup. Enjoy!

Nutritional Values (Per Serving):

Calories: 78
Fat: 1.6 g
Carbohydrates: 5.5 g
Sugar: 3 g
Protein: 11.1 g
Cholesterol: 55 mg

35. Keto Protein Breakfast Muffins

Preparation Time: 12 minutes
Cooking Time: 25 minutes
Servings: 12

Ingredients:

- 8 organic eggs
- 8-ounces cream cheese
- 4 tablespoons butter, melted
- 2 scoops protein powder

Directions:

1. Mix cream cheese and melted butter in a mixing bowl. Add eggs and protein powder and mix well. With the use of a hand mixer mix until well combined and spray your muffin pan with cooking spray. Fill each muffin cup ¾ full of mixture. Bake for 25 minutes in preheated oven at 350˚Fahrenheit. Serve and enjoy!

Nutritional Values: (Per Serving):

Calories: 148
Fat: 12.3 g
Carbohydrates: 2 g
Sugar: 0.4 g
Protein: 7.8 g
Cholesterol: 116 mg

36. Coconut Waffles

Preparation Time: 12 minutes
Cooking Time: 5 minutes
Servings: 4

Ingredients:

- 1/3 cup coconut flour
- ½ teaspoon salt
- 4 tablespoons butter, melted
- 6 organic eggs
- 1/8 teaspoon Stevia drops
- ½ teaspoon baking powder

Directions:

1. Add eggs along with butter into your blender and blend until well combined. Pour egg mixture into mixing bowl. Add coconut flour, Stevia, baking powder and salt, mix well. Set aside for 5 minutes. Heat your waffle iron, once it is hot pour batter and cook for 5 minutes or according to your waffle iron instructions. Serve and enjoy!

Nutritional Values (Per Serving):

Calories: 247
Fat: 19 g
Carbohydrates: 6 g
Sugar: 1 g
Protein: 11 g
Cholesterol: 309 mg

37. Coconut Pecan Porridge

Preparation Time: 5 minutes
Cooking Time: 5 minutes
Servings: 2

Ingredients:

- ½ teaspoon cinnamon
- ¼ cup pecans, chopped
- ¼ cup coconut, unsweetened, toasted
- 2 tablespoons chia seeds
- ¼ cup coconut milk
- ¾ cup almond milk, unsweetened
- ¼ cup almond butter
- 1 tablespoon coconut oil
- 2 tablespoons hemp seeds

Directions:

1. Add almond butter, coconut oil, almond milk, coconut milk into a saucepan and simmer over medium heat for 5 minutes or so. Once your mixture has reached the point of becoming hot, remove it from heat. Add toasted coconut, hemp seeds, chia seeds, cinnamon, and pecans, mix well. Set aside for 5 minutes. Serve and enjoy!

Nutritional Values (Per Serving):

Calories: 489
Fat: 47.9 g
Carbohydrates: 15.1 g
Sugar: 3.9 g
Protein: 11.2 g
Cholesterol: 0 mg

38. Vanilla Chia Breakfast Pudding

Preparation Time: 10 minutes
Servings: 2

Ingredients:

- ½ cup blueberries for topping
- 6 tablespoons chia seeds
- 2 cups coconut milk, unsweetened
- ½ teaspoon vanilla extract

Directions:

1. Add the coconut milk, chia seeds, vanilla to a glass jar. Seal the jar and shake well. Place the jar in the fridge overnight. The next morning pour the chia breakfast pudding into serving bowls and top with blueberries. Serve and enjoy!

Nutritional Values (Per Serving):

Calories: 223
Fat: 12 g
Carbohydrates: 18 g
Sugar: 2 g
Protein: 10 g
Cholesterol: 0 mg

39. Almond Cinnamon Smoothie

Preparation Time: 10 minutes
Servings: 1

Ingredients:

- ¾ cup almond milk, unsweetened
- ¼ cup coconut oil
- 1 tablespoon almond butter, unsweetened
- 1 tablespoon vanilla protein powder
- 1/8 teaspoon cinnamon

Directions:

1. Add into your blender all the ingredients, blend them until they are nice and smooth. Serve and enjoy!

Nutritional Values (Per Serving):

Calories: 500
Fat: 43 g
Carbohydrates: 10 g
Sugar: 2 g
Protein: 14.6 g
Cholesterol: 0 mg

40. Almond Flour Waffles

Preparation Time: 10 minutes
Cooking Time: 5 minutes
Servings: 2

Ingredients:

- Pinch of xanthan gum
- Pinch of salt
- 1 tablespoon butter, melted
- 1 large organic egg
- 2 tablespoons sour cream
- 1 teaspoon vinegar
- 2 teaspoons arrowroot flour
- 1/8 teaspoon baking powder
- 1/8 teaspoon baking soda
- ¼ cup almond flour

Directions:

1. In a mixing bowl combine vinegar, butter, sour cream, and egg mix well. Add dry ingredients into wet and mix until well blended. Heat your waffle iron and cook waffle for 5 minutes or to your waffle iron instructions. Serve and enjoy!

Nutritional Values (Per Serving):

Calories: 208
Fat: 18 g
Carbohydrates: 4.83 g
Sugar: 2.1 g
Protein: 6.52 g
Cholesterol: 114 mg

41. Healthy Breakfast Porridge

Preparation Time: 5 minutes
Cooking Time: 5 minutes
Servings: 2

Ingredients:

- 1/8 teaspoon salt
- 4 tablespoons coconut, unsweetened, shredded
- 1 tablespoon oat bran
- 1 tablespoon flaxseed meal
- ½ tablespoon butter
- ¾ teaspoon Truvia
- ½ teaspoon cinnamon
- ½ cup heavy cream
- 1 cup water

Directions:

1. Add all your ingredients into a saucepan over medium-low heat. Once the mixture comes to a boil remove from heat. Serve warm and enjoy!

Nutritional Values (Per Serving):

Calories: 222
Fat: 21 g
Carbohydrates: 3.90 g
Sugar: 3.9 g
Protein: 2.68 g, Cholesterol: 49 mg

42. Parsley Spread

Preparation time: 5 minutes
Cooking time: 0 minutes
Servings: 8

Ingredients:

- 1 cup parsley leaves
- 1 cup coconut cream

- 1 tablespoon sun-dried tomatoes, chopped
- 2 tablespoons lime juice
- ¼ cup shallots, chopped
- 1 teaspoon oregano, dried
- A pinch of salt and black pepper

Directions:

1. In a blender, combine the parsley with the cream, the tomatoes and the other ingredients, pulse well, divide into bowls and serve for breakfast.

Nutrition: calories 78, fat 7.2, fiber 1, carbs 3.6, protein 1.1

43. Baked Cheesy Artichokes

Preparation time: 10 minutes
Cooking time: 45 minutes
Servings: 6

Ingredients:

- 1 cup spinach, chopped
- 1 cup almond milk
- 12 ounces canned artichokes, halved
- 2 garlic cloves, minced
- ½ cup cashew cheese, shredded
- 1 tablespoon dill, chopped
- A pinch of salt and black pepper
- teaspoons olive oil

Directions:

1. Heat up a pan with the oil over medium heat, add the garlic, artichokes, salt and pepper, stir and cook for 5 minutes.
2. Transfer this to a baking dish, add the spinach, almond milk and the other ingredients, toss a bit, bake at 380 degrees F for 40 minutes, divide between plates and serve for breakfast.

Nutrition: calories 149, fat 12.2, fiber 4.3, carbs 9.7, protein 3.5

44. Oatmeal with Berries

Preparation Time: 25 MIN | Serves: 1

Ingredients:

- 1 2/3 cups water
- 1 cup quick oats
- 1 cup frozen berries
- 1 banana, chopped
- 1-2 tbsp brown sugar
- 1/4 cup soy milk or almond milk
- 1-2 tbsp brown sugar
- For Garnishing (Optional):
- Almonds, chopped
- Coconut flakes

Directions:

1. Add water and oats directly to Instant Pot and cover it.
2. Switch on manual button for 6 minutes over high pressure. When the timer goes off allow the pressure to release naturally for about 10 minutes. After 10 minutes, change the steam handle to 'venting'.
3. Open the lid and transfer the oats to a bowl and top it with mixed berries, banana, non-dairy milk and brown sugar.

45. Pumpkin and Oats Recipe

Preparation Time: 30 Minutes
Servings: 1

Ingredients:

- 1 cup steel cut oats
- 1 2/3 cups water
- 1 frozen banana
- ½ cup pumpkin purée
- 3 medjool dates, chopped
- 1 tbsp of buckwheat groats
- 1 tbsp of coconut flakes

Directions:

1. Add 1 cup steel cut oats to Instant Pot, along with water, pumpkin purée, banana, and chopped dates.
2. Stir it once and set steam release handle to 'sealing'. Switch on manual button for 10 minutes.
3. Once time is up, allow it for natural release for 10 minutes. Switch on 'Keep Warm/Cancel' button and change steam release handle to 'venting'.
4. Using a spoon, mix it around. Make sure to mash banana and dates together with oatmeal.
5. Serve it topped with some buckwheat groats and coconut flakes.

46. Strawberries and Cream Oatmeal

Preparation Time: 15 Minutes
Servings: 4

Ingredients:

- 1 cup steel-cut oats
- 3 cups water
- 1 teaspoon strawberry extract
- Vanilla-flavored nondairy milk
- 1 cup fresh strawberries, chopped

Directions:

1. Spray the instant pot with nonstick spray. Stir in the oats and water, then seal the lid and cook on high 3 minutes.
2. Let the pressure release naturally, then stir in the vanilla milk and fresh strawberries.

47. Pecan Pumpkin Spice Oatmeal

Preparation Time: 15 Minutes
Servings: 2

Ingredients:

- 1/2 cup steel-cut oats
- 1/2 cup pumpkin purée
- 1 1/2 cups unsweetened almond milk
- 1/2 teaspoon cinnamon
- 1/8 teaspoon nutmeg
- 1 teaspoon vanilla extract
- 1/8 teaspoon of ground cloves
- 1/8 teaspoon ginger
- 1/4 cup brown sugar
- Chopped pecans, for serving

Directions:

1. Spray the instant pot with nonstick spray.

Combine everything except for the brown sugar and pecans.
2. Seal the lid and cook on high 3 minutes, then let the pressure release naturally.
3. Stir in the brown sugar and top with chopped pecans.

48. Carrot Cake Oatmeal with Cream Cheese Frosting

Preparation Time: 20 Minutes
Servings: 2

Ingredients:

- 1 small white sweet potato, peeled and steamed
- 1 small carrot, grated
- 1/4 small zucchini, grated
- 1/2 cup steel-cut oats
- 1 1/2 cups nondairy milk
- 1/2 teaspoon lemon juice
- 1/2 teaspoon apple cider vinegar
- 1/8 teaspoon of salt
- 1/8 teaspoon ground cloves
- 1/8 teaspoon nutmeg
- 1/2 teaspoon cinnamon
- 2 tablespoons brown sugar
- 2 tablespoons maple syrup
- 1 1/2 tablespoons coconut oil
- 1 tablespoon water

Directions:

1. To make the cream cheese frosting, puree half of the steamed sweet potato in a food processor. Add the maple syrup, water, coconut oil, lemon juice, and apple cider vinegar and puree until smooth. Add more sweet potato if the mixture is not thick enough.
2. Spray the instant pot with nonstick spray. Combine the rest of the ingredients, then seal the lid and cook on high 3 minutes.
3. Let the pressure release naturally. Add additional milk to the oatmeal if needed, and top each serving with a dollop of the cream cheese frosting.

49. Chocolate Walnut Oatmeal

Preparation Time: 15 Minutes
Servings: 2

Ingredients:

- 1/2 cup steel-cut oats
- 2 tablespoons cocoa powder
- 1 teaspoon brown sugar
- 1 tablespoon agave nectar
- 1 teaspoon vanilla extract
- 1/2 cup unsweetened almond milk
- 1 1/2 cups water
- Semi-sweet chocolate chips, for topping
- Walnuts for topping

Directions:

1. Spray the instant pot with nonstick spray. Combine the oats, cocoa powder, water, vanilla, brown sugar, and agave nectar.
2. Cook on high 3 minutes, then let the pressure release naturally. Stir in the almond milk.
3. Top with chocolate chips and walnuts.

50. Breakfast Burrito Filling

Preparation Time: 15 Minutes
Servings: 4

Ingredients:

- 15 ounces tofu, drained and crumbled
- 1/2 cup water
- 1 clove garlic, minced
- 1/2 bell pepper, chopped
- 1/2 teaspoon chili powder
- 1/4 teaspoon chipotle chili powder
- 1/4 teaspoon sriracha sauce
- 1 teaspoon lime juice
- Salt and pepper, to taste
- 1/4 cup shredded vegan cheddar cheese, for serving
- Warm tortillas, for serving
- Salsa, for serving

Directions:

1. Combine all the ingredients in the instant pot. Seal the lid and cook on high 4 minutes, then let the pressure release naturally.
2. If the mixture is too wet, drain off some of the water. Stir in the cheese to melt it. Serve wrapped warm tortillas with salsa.

51. Tofu Breakfast Custard and Potatoes

Preparation Time: 25 Minutes
Servings: 4

Ingredients:

- 12 ounces frozen hash browns
- 1 shallot, chopped
- 2 tablespoons vegan chicken-flavored bouillon
- 10 ounces silken tofu
- 1/2 cup shredded vegan cheddar cheese
- 1/2 cup nondairy milk
- 1/4 teaspoon onion powder
- 1/8 teaspoon garlic powder
- 1/2 teaspoon seasoned salt
- 1/4 teaspoon freshly ground pepper
- 1 tablespoon olive oil
- Hot sauce, for serving

Directions:

1. Puree the tofu, milk, bouillon, garlic powder, onion powder and seasoned salt in a food processor.
2. Heat the oil in the instant pot on the sauté setting and cook the shallot for 3 minutes.
3. Spread the hash browns on top of the cooked shallots, and top with the cheese. Pour the tofu puree over the top, then sprinkle with fresh ground pepper.
4. Cook on high 5 minutes, then quick release the pressure.
5. The tofu mixture should be a jiggly custard texture. If it is too moist, return the instant pot to the sauté setting and cook longer with the lid on but vented.
6. Serve with hot sauce!

52. Apple and Sausage French Toast Casserole

Preparation Time: 25 Minutes
Servings: 4

Ingredients:

- 4 links vegan breakfast sausages, chopped into coins
- 2 apples, peeled and chopped
- Juice of 1/2 lemon
- Zest of 1/2 lemon
- 1/2 loaf whole wheat bread, chopped into cubes
- 1 1/2 cups water
- 1 teaspoon vanilla extract
- 3 tablespoons unsweetened applesauce
- 1/2 teaspoon cinnamon
- 1 tablespoon olive oil
- Maple syrup, for serving

Directions:

1. Heat olive oil in the instant pot using the sauté setting. Add the sausage and cook for 10 minutes.
2. Add the water, applesauce, vanilla extract, lemon juice, and cinnamon to the instant pot. Add the apples, then the bread cubes. Push the bread down to make sure it is all coated with the mixture.
3. Seal the lid and cook on high 4 minutes, then let the pressure release naturally. Dust with powdered sugar and lemon zest and serve.

53. Granola.

Preparation Time: 25 Minutes
Servings: 8 cups

Ingredients:

- 5 cups old-fashioned rolled oats
- 1 cup slivered blanched almonds
- ⅔ cup pure maple syrup
- ½ cup wheat germ
- ½ cup unsweetened shredded coconut
- ½ cup sunflower seeds
- ½ cup golden raisins or sweetened dried cranberries
- ½ cup chopped dates or dried apricots
- ¼ cup vegetable oil
- ¼ cup packed light brown sugar
- 3 tablespoons water
- 1 teaspoon pure vanilla extract

Directions:

1. Spray the Instant Pot insert with cooking spray and set to high.
2. Add the maple syrup, oil, water, sugar, and vanilla.
3. In a bowl combine the oats, wheat germ, almonds, sunflower seeds, coconut, and dates.
4. Mix the oats into the syrup mix in the Instant Pot.

5. Seal and cook on Meat for 12 minutes.
6. Release the pressure and cook with the lid open until your granola is crisp.

54. Granola Oats.

Preparation Time: 50 Minutes
Servings: 4

Ingredients:

- 4½ cups water
- 1¼ cups old-fashioned rolled oats or steel-cut oats
- 1 cup granola
- 1½ teaspoons ground cinnamon
- ½ teaspoon salt

Directions:

1. Lightly oil your Instant Pot insert with cooking spray.
2. Combine the oats, water, cinnamon, and salt.
3. Seal and cook on Stew for 40 minutes.
4. Release the pressure naturally and stir in the granola.

55. Spiced Apple Oats.

Preparation Time: 50 Minutes
Servings: 4

Ingredients:

- 3 cups water
- 2 cups apple juice
- 2 apples, peeled, cored, and chopped
- 1¼ cups steel-cut oats
- ½ cup golden raisins or dried cranberries
- ¼ cup packed light brown sugar or granulated natural sugar, or more to taste
- 1 tablespoon ground flaxseed
- 1 teaspoon ground cinnamon
- ½ teaspoon salt

Directions:

1. Lightly oil your Instant Pot insert with cooking spray.
2. Combine the ingredients.
3. Seal and cook on Stew for 40 minutes.

56. PB&J Oats.

Preparation Time: 50 Minutes
Servings: 6

Ingredients:

- 5½ cups water
- 1½ cups steel-cut oats
- ½ cup strawberry jam
- ½ cup creamy peanut butter, at room temperature
- 1 teaspoon ground cinnamon
- ¾ teaspoon salt

Directions:

1. Lightly oil your Instant Pot insert with cooking spray.
2. Combine the oats, water, cinnamon, and salt.
3. Seal and cook on Stew for 40 minutes.
4. Release the pressure naturally and stir in the peanut butter and jam.

57. Amish Oats.

Preparation Time: 15 Minutes
Servings: 6

Ingredients:

- 3 cups unsweetened almond milk or other non-dairy milk
- 2½ cups old-fashioned rolled oats
- 2/3 cup sweetened dried cranberries
- ½ cup packed light brown sugar or maple syrup
- ½ cup toasted slivered blanched almonds or chopped walnuts
- 2 tablespoons vegan butter, melted
- 2 teaspoons pure vanilla extract
- 1½ teaspoons ground cinnamon
- 1½ teaspoons baking powder
- ½ teaspoon salt

Directions:

1. Lightly oil your Instant Pot insert with cooking spray.
2. In a bowl mix the almond milk, butter, vanilla, sugar, baking powder, salt, and cinnamon.
3. Stir in the oats, cranberries, and nuts.
4. Seal and cook on Beans for 12 minutes.

58. Sweet Pumpkin Quinoa.

Preparation Time: 45 Minutes
Servings: 4

Ingredients:

- 4 cups unsweetened almond milk
- 1 cup quinoa, rinsed and drained
- ½ cup canned solid-pack pumpkin
- ¼ cup pure maple syrup
- 1 teaspoon pure vanilla extract
- 1 teaspoon ground cinnamon
- ½ teaspoon salt
- ¼ teaspoon ground ginger
- ¼ teaspoon ground allspice
- ¼ teaspoon ground nutmeg

Directions:

1. Spray the insert of your Instant Pot with cooking oil.
2. Add the ingredients.
3. Seal and cook on Stew for 38 minutes.
4. Depressurize naturally and serve.

59. Breakfast Polenta.

Preparation Time: 50 Minutes
Servings: 4

Ingredients:

- 4 cups water
- 1 cup medium- or coarse-ground polenta
- 1 tablespoon vegan butter
- 2 tablespoons pure maple syrup
- 1 teaspoon salt

Directions:

1. Combine the polenta, water and salt in your Instant Pot.
2. Seal and cook on Stew for 40 minutes.
3. Release the pressure naturally and stir in vegan butter and maple syrup.

60. Molasses Polenta.

Preparation Time: 50 Minutes
Servings: 6

Ingredients:

- 3½ cups unsweetened almond milk
- 2/3 cup chopped dates
- ½ cup medium-ground cornmeal
- ¼ cup packed light brown sugar
- ¼ cup molasses
- 2 tablespoons vegan butter
- 1 teaspoon pure vanilla extract
- ½ teaspoon salt
- ½ teaspoon baking powder
- ½ teaspoon ground cinnamon
- ½ teaspoon ground ginger
- ¼ teaspoon ground nutmeg

Directions:

1. Spray your Instant Pot insert with cooking spray.
2. Warm 2 cups of the almond milk, the cornmeal, and some salt.
3. When boiling add the sugar, molasses, cinnamon, nutmeg, ginger, and dates.
4. Add another cup of almond milk, vanilla, and baking powder and mix well.
5. Add the remaining almond milk and seal.
6. Cook on Stew for 40 minutes.

61. Congee.

Preparation Time: 35 Minutes
Servings: 6

Ingredients:

- 6 cups hot vegetable broth
- 1 cup uncooked Arborio rice
- 1 small yellow onion, minced
- 1 tablespoon soy sauce
- 2 teaspoons grated fresh ginger
- 1 teaspoon salt

Directions:

1. Mix the ingredients in your Instant Pot.
2. Seal and cook on Rice.
3. Release the pressure naturally.

62. French Toast Pudding.

Preparation Time: 15 Minutes
Servings: 4

Ingredients:

- 8 cups stale white Italian bread cubes
- 6 ounces soft or silken tofu, drained
- 2 cups non-dairy milk
- ½ cup packed light brown sugar
- ¼ cup pure maple syrup, plus more for serving
- ¼ cup coarsely chopped pecans or walnuts
- 1 tablespoon vegan butter
- 2 teaspoons pure vanilla extract
- 1 teaspoon ground cinnamon
- ¼ teaspoon ground nutmeg

- ¼ teaspoon salt
- ⅛ teaspoon ground allspice

Directions:

1. Oil a pan that will fit in your Instant Pot steamer basket.
2. Add the bread to the pan.
3. Blend together the tofu, vanilla, cinnamon, allspice, nutmeg, sugar, and salt. Stir in the milk and maple syrup.
4. Pour the tofu over the bread.
5. Add the minimum water to the Instant Pot and put the tray in the steamer basket.
6. Cook on Steam for 10 minutes.

63. Bananas Foster French Toast.

Preparation Time: 15 Minutes
Servings: 4

Ingredients:

- 8 cups stale cubed white bread
- 6 ounces firm silken tofu
- 3 ripe bananas
- 1 cup nondairy milk
- 1 cup pecan pieces
- ½ cup packed light brown sugar
- ½ cup pure maple syrup
- ⅓ cup dried banana chips
- 3 tablespoons dark rum or brandy
- 2 tablespoons vegan butter
- 2 tablespoons cornstarch
- 1 teaspoon pure vanilla extract
- ½ teaspoon salt

Directions:

1. Oil a pan that will fit in your Instant Pot steamer basket.
2. Add the bread to the pan.
3. Blend together the maple syrup, butter, sugar, rum, bananas, tofu, milk, cornstarch, vanilla, and salt.
4. Sprinkle bananas and pecans over the bread.
5. Pour the tofu over the bread.
6. Add the minimum water to the Instant Pot and put the tray in the steamer basket.
7. Cook on Steam for 10 minutes.

64. Vegan Sausage Scramble.

Preparation Time: 15 Minutes
Servings: 6

Ingredients:

- 1 pound firm tofu, drained, crumbled, and squeezed dry
- 6 cups cubed French or Italian bread
- 2 cups sliced white mushrooms
- 2 cups crumbled cooked vegan sausage
- 1½ cups plain unsweetened nondairy milk
- 1 medium-size yellow onion, minced
- 1 red or green bell pepper, seeded and chopped
- 3 garlic cloves, minced
- 2 teaspoons olive oil
- ½ teaspoon ground fennel seed
- ½ teaspoon dried basil
- ¼ teaspoon red pepper flakes, or more to taste
- 3 tablespoons nutritional yeast
- 1 tablespoon cornstarch
- 1 teaspoon yellow mustard
- 1 teaspoon smoked paprika
- Salt and freshly ground black pepper

Directions:

1. Warm the oil in your Instant Pot and soften the onion for 5 minutes in it.
2. Add the garlic, mushrooms, and pepper and cook another 2 minutes.
3. Add the basil, fennel, and red pepper.
4. Pulse the tofu, milk, cornstarch, nutritional yeast, mustard, and paprika.
5. Put the bread in your Instant Pot and mix with the vegetables.
6. Pour the tofu over the bread.
7. Seal and cook on Stew for 12 minutes.

65. Chorizo Frittata.

Preparation Time: 20 Minutes
Servings: 4

Ingredients:

- 1 pound firm tofu, well drained and lightly pressed
- 8 ounces white mushrooms, chopped
- 5 scallions, minced
- 1 cup crumbled vegan chorizo
- 1 cup shredded vegan cheese of your choice

- ½ cup vegetable broth
- ¼ cup nutritional yeast
- 2 teaspoons olive oil
- 1 tablespoon cornstarch or tapioca starch
- ½ teaspoon onion powder
- ½ teaspoon dried basil
- ½ teaspoon garlic powder
- ½ teaspoon smoked paprika
- Salt and freshly ground black pepper

Directions:

1. Blend the tofu, nutritional yeast, cornstarch, garlic powder, onion powder, basil, paprika, broth, salt and pepper.
2. Warm the oil in the base of your Instant Pot.
3. Add the scallions, chorizo, mushrooms, and some salt and pepper and cook 5 minutes.
4. Stir the chorizo and tofu mixes together.
5. Top with cheese.
6. Seal and cook on Stew for 15 minutes.
7. Remove and cut into slices.

66. Artichoke Frittata.

Preparation Time: 22 Minutes
Servings: 4

Ingredients:

- 1 pound firm tofu, well drained and lightly pressed
- 2 cups canned or thawed frozen artichoke hearts, chopped
- 8 ounces white mushrooms, thinly sliced or chopped
- 5 scallions, minced
- 1 cup vegetable broth
- ½ cup shredded vegan cheese of your choice
- ⅓ cup chopped sun-dried tomatoes
- 3 tablespoons nutritional yeast
- 1 tablespoon cornstarch or tapioca starch
- 2 teaspoons olive oil
- 1 teaspoon capers, rinsed and drained
- ½ teaspoon dried thyme
- ½ teaspoon dried basil
- ½ teaspoon onion powder
- Salt and freshly ground black pepper

Directions:

1. Blend the tofu, nutritional yeast, cornstarch, onion powder, salt and pepper with 1 tablespoon tomatoes.
2. Warm the oil in the base of your Instant Pot.
3. Add the scallions, mushrooms, thyme, basil, and some salt and pepper and cook 5 minutes.
4. Stir the veg and tofu mixes together.
5. Top with cheese.
6. Seal and cook on Stew for 18 minutes.
7. Remove and cut into slices.

67. Greek Frittata.

Preparation Time: 20 Minutes
Servings: 4

Ingredients:

- 1 pound firm tofu, well drained and lightly pressed
- 3 cups lightly packed fresh baby spinach
- ½ cup pitted kalamata olives, coarsely chopped
- 1 small yellow onion, chopped
- 3 large garlic cloves, crushed
- 1 jarred roasted red bell pepper, chopped
- 3 tablespoons nutritional yeast
- 1 tablespoon freshly squeezed lemon juice
- 2 teaspoons olive oil
- 1 teaspoon dried basil
- 1 teaspoon dried oregano
- Salt and freshly ground black pepper

Directions:

1. Warm the oil in the base of your Instant Pot.
2. Add the onion and cook 5 minutes.
3. Add the basil, oregano, and garlic and cook another minute.
4. Blend the tofu, nutritional yeast, onion mix, lemon juice, and salt and pepper.
5. Stir the veg and tofu mixes together in the Instant Pot.
6. Seal and cook on Stew for 15 minutes.
7. Remove and cut into slices.

68. Stewed Fall Fruits.

Preparation Time: 25 Minutes
Servings: 8

Ingredients:

- 3 large apples, peeled, cored, and cut into 1-inch dice
- 2 just-ripe pears, peeled, cored, and cut into 1-inch dice
- 1 cup dried apricots, quartered
- ½ cup pitted prunes, halved
- ½ cup sweetened dried cranberries
- ¼ cup water
- ¼ cup granulated natural sugar
- 1 cinnamon stick
- Grated zest and juice of 1 lemon or orange

Directions:

1. Combine all the ingredients in your Instant Pot and mix well.
2. Seal and cook on Stew for 22 minutes.
3. Release the pressure naturally.
4. If it is not thick enough, simmer with the lid off a while.

39. Chai Breakfast Loaf.

Preparation Time: 15 Minutes
Servings: 10

Ingredients:

- 1¾ cups unbleached all-purpose flour
- ¾ cup organic sugar
- ¾ cup non-dairy milk mixed with ½ teaspoon apple cider vinegar
- ½ cup double-strength brewed black tea
- ¼ cup vegan butter, melted and cooled
- 2 tablespoons unsweetened applesauce
- 2 tablespoons sunflower seeds
- 2 teaspoons baking powder
- 2 teaspoons pure vanilla extract
- ½ teaspoon salt
- ½ teaspoon baking soda
- ¾ teaspoon ground cinnamon
- ½ teaspoon ground cardamom
- ¼ teaspoon ground nutmeg
- ⅛ teaspoon ground cloves

Directions:

1. Lightly oil a baking tray that will fit in the steamer basket of your Instant Pot.
2. In a bowl, combine the flour, baking powder, baking soda, salt and spices.
3. In another bowl cream the sugar and butter.
4. Stir the applesauce, milk, tea, and vanilla into the butter.
5. Stir the wet mixture into the dry mixture slowly until they form a smooth mix.
6. Fold in the seeds.
7. Pour the batter into your baking tray and put the tray in your steamer basket.
8. Pour the minimum amount of water into the base of your Instant Pot and lower the steamer basket.
9. Seal and cook on Steam for 10 minutes.
10. Release the pressure quickly and set to one side to cool a little.

70. Granola Apples.

Preparation Time: 25 Minutes
Servings: 6

Ingredients:

- 6 Granny Smiths, washed
- 1½ cups granola
- ½ cup apple juice
- Juice of 1 lemon
- 2 tablespoons light brown sugar or granulated natural sugar
- 1½ tablespoons vegan butter, cut into 6
- ½ teaspoon ground cinnamon

Directions:

1. Core the apples most of the way down, leaving a little base so the stuffing stays put.
2. Stand your apples upright in your Instant Pot. Do not pile them on top of each other! You may need to do two batches.
3. In a bowl combine the sugar, granola, and cinnamon.
4. Stuff each apple with the mix and top with butter.
5. Pour the apple juice around the apples.
6. Seal and cook on Stew for 20 minutes.
7. Depressurize naturally.

71. Vegan Frittata

Preparation time: 10 minutes
Cooking Time: 10 minutes
Servings: 3

Ingredients

- ½ vegan sausage, sliced
- 2 tablespoons flax meal mixed with 3 tablespoons water
- 4 cherry tomatoes, halved
- 1 tablespoon parsley, chopped
- 1 tablespoon olive oil
- Salt and black pepper to the taste

Preparation

1. Put oil, tomatoes and vegan sausage in your Air Fryer's pan, preheat at 360 ° F and bake for 5 minutes.
2. Add flax meal, parsley, salt and pepper, toss, spread in the pan, cover and cook at 360 ° F for 5 minutes more.
3. Slice, divide between plates and serve.

Nutrition facts per serving

Calories 150, Fat 8g, Fiber 3g, Carbs 13g, Protein 2g

72. Scrambled Tofu

Preparation time: 10 minutes
Cooking Time: 30 minutes
Servings: 4

Ingredients

- 2 tablespoons coconut aminos
- 1 block firm tofu, cubed
- 1 teaspoon turmeric powder
- 2 tablespoons olive oil
- ½ teaspoon onion powder
- ½ teaspoon garlic powder
- 2½ cup red potatoes, cubed
- ½ cup yellow onion, chopped
- Salt and black pepper to the taste

Preparation

1. In a bowl, mix tofu with 1 tablespoon oil, salt, pepper, coconut aminos, garlic and onion powder, turmeric and onion and toss to coat.
2. In another bowl, mix potatoes with the rest of the oil, salt and pepper and toss.
3. Put potatoes in preheated Air Fryer at 350 ° F and bake for 15 minutes, shaking them halfway
4. Add tofu and the marinade and bake at 350 ° F for 15 minutes.
5. Divide between plates and serve.

Nutrition:

Calories 150, Fat 4.5g, Fiber 4g, Carbs 11g, Protein 14g

73. Vegan Cheese Sandwich

Preparation time: 10 minutes
Cooking Time: 8 minutes
Servings: 1

Ingredients

- 2 slices vegan bread
- 2 slices cashew cheese
- 2 teaspoons cashew butter

Preparation

1. Spread cashew butter on bread slices, add vegan cheese on one slice, top with the other, cut into halves diagonally, put in your Air Fryer, cover and cook at 370 ° F for 8 minutes, flipping the sandwiches halfway.
2. Serve them right away.

Nutrition facts per serving

Calories 144, Fat 3g, Fiber 2g, Carbs 7g, Protein 2g

74. Breakfast Beans Burrito

Preparation time: 10 minutes
Cooking Time: 10 minutes
Servings: 2

Ingredients

- 2 cups baked black beans
- Cooking spray
- ½ red bell pepper, sliced
- 1 small avocado, peeled, pitted and sliced
- 2 tablespoons vegan salsa
- Salt and black pepper to the taste
- ⅛ cup cashew cheese, grated
- Vegan tortillas for serving

Preparation

1. Grease your Air Fryer with the cooking spray, add black beans, bell pepper, salsa, salt and pepper, cover and cook at 400 ° F for 6 minutes.
2. Arrange tortillas on a working surface, divide beans mix on each, also add avocado and cashew cheese, roll burritos, put them in your Air Fryer, cover and cook at 300 ° F for 3 minutes more.

3. Divide burritos between plates and serve for breakfast.

Nutrition facts per serving

Calories 249, Fat 3g, Fiber 7g, Carbs 2g, Protein 5g

75. Cinnamon Toast

Preparation time: 10 minutes
Cooking Time: 5 minutes
Servings: 6

Ingredients

- A drizzle of vegetable oil
- 12 vegan bread slices
- ½ cup coconut sugar
- A pinch of black pepper
- 1½ teaspoon vanilla extract
- 1½ teaspoon cinnamon powder

Preparation

1. In a bowl, mix oil with cinnamon, sugar, vanilla and a pinch of pepper and stir well.
2. Spread this over bread slices, put them in your Air Fryer, cook at 400 ° F for 5 minutes, divide them between plates and serve for breakfast.

Nutrition facts per serving

Calories 120, Fat 2g, Fiber 2g, Carbs 15g, Protein 2g

76. Onion and Tofu Mix

Preparation time: 10 minutes
Cooking Time: 15 minutes
Servings: 2

Ingredients

- 2 tablespoons flax meal mixed with 3 tablespoons water
- 1 yellow onion, sliced
- 1 teaspoon coconut aminos
- Cooking spray
- A pinch of black pepper
- ¼ cup firm tofu, cubed

Preparation

1. In a bowl, mix flax meal with coconut aminos and black pepper and whisk well.
2. Grease your Air Fryer with the cooking spray, preheat at 350 ° F, add onion slices and cook for 10 minutes.
3. Add flax meal and tofu, cook for 5 minutes more, divide between 2 plates and serve for breakfast.

Nutrition facts per serving

Calories 170, Fat 3g, Fiber 1g, Carbs 7g, Protein 2g

77. Tomato Frittata

Preparation time: 10 minutes
Cooking Time: 30 minutes
Servings: 2

Ingredients

- 2 tablespoons flax meal mixed with 3 tablespoons water
- ½ cup cashew cheese, shredded
- 2 tablespoons yellow onion, chopped
- Salt and black pepper to the taste
- ¼ cup coconut milk
- ¼ cup tomatoes, chopped

Preparation

1. In a bowl, mix flax meal with milk, cheese, salt, pepper, onion and tomatoes, stir well, and pour this into your Air Fryer's pan, cover and cook at 340 ° F for 30 minutes.
2. Divide frittata between plates and serve for breakfast.

Nutrition:

Calories 150, Fat 3g, Fiber 2g, Carbs 12g, Protein 10g

78. Greek Potatoes Mix

Preparation time: 10 minutes
Cooking Time: 20 minutes
Servings: 4

Ingredients

- 1½ pound potatoes, peeled and cubed
- 2 tablespoons olive oil
- Salt and black pepper to the taste
- 1 tablespoon hot paprika
- 3½ ounce coconut cream

Preparation

1. Put potatoes in a bowl, add water to cover, leave them aside for 10 minutes, drain them, mix with half of the oil, salt, pepper and the paprika and toss them.
2. Put potatoes in your Air Fryer's basket

and cook at 360 ° F for 20 minutes.

3. In a bowl, mix coconut cream with salt, pepper and the rest of the oil and stir well.
4. Divide potatoes between plates, add coconut cream on top and serve for breakfast

Nutrition:

Calories 230, Fat 3g, Fiber 2g, Carbs 10g, Protein 5g

79. Breakfast Mushroom Cakes

Preparation time: 2 hours and 10 minutes
Cooking Time: 8 minutes
Servings: 8

Ingredients

- 3½ ounce mushrooms, chopped
- 1 small yellow onion, chopped
- Salt and black pepper to the taste
- ¼ teaspoon nutmeg, ground
- 2 tablespoons olive oil
- 1 tablespoon breadcrumbs
- 14 ounces coconut milk

Preparation

1. Heat up a pan with half of the oil over medium-high heat, add onion and mushrooms, stir and cook for 3 minutes.
2. Add coconut milk, salt, pepper and nutmeg, stir, take off heat and leave aside for 2 hours.
3. In a bowl, mix the rest of the oil with breadcrumbs and stir well.
4. Take 1 tablespoon mushroom filling, roll in breadcrumbs and put them in your Air Fryer's basket.
5. Repeat with the rest of the mushroom mix and cook cakes at 400 ° F for 8 minutes.
6. Divide mushroom cakes between plates and serve them for breakfast.

Nutrition:

Calories 212, Fat 2g, Fiber 1g, Carbs 10g, Protein 6g

80. Breakfast Bell Peppers

Preparation time: 10 minutes
Cooking Time: 10 minutes
Servings: 8

Ingredients

- 1 yellow bell pepper, halved
- 1 orange bell pepper, halved
- Salt and black pepper to the taste
- 3½ ounces firm tofu, crumbled
- 1 green onion, chopped
- 2 tablespoons oregano, chopped

Preparation

1. In a bowl, mix tofu with onion, salt, pepper and oregano and stir well.
2. Place bell pepper halves in your Air Fryer's basket and cook at 400 ° F for 10 minutes.
3. Leave bell pepper halves to cool down, peel, divide tofu mix on each piece, roll, arrange on plates and serve right away for breakfast.

Nutrition:

Calories 170, Fat 1g, Fiber 2g, Carbs 8g, Protein 5g

81. Green Breakfast Salad

Preparation time: 10 minutes
Cooking Time: 10 minutes
Servings: 4

Ingredients

- 1 tablespoon lemon juice
- 4 red bell peppers
- 1 lettuce head, cut into strips
- Salt and black pepper to the taste
- 3 tablespoons coconut cream
- 2 tablespoons olive oil
- 1 ounces rocket leaves

Preparation

1. Place bell pepper in your Air Fryer's basket, cook at 400 ° F for 10 minutes, transfer to a bowl, leave them aside to cool down, peel, cut them in strips and put them in a bowl.
2. Add rocket leaves and lettuce strips and toss.
3. In a bowl, mix oil with lemon juice, coconut cream, salt and pepper, whisk well, add over the salad, toss to coat, divide between plates and serve for breakfast.

Nutrition:

Calories 170, Fat 0.5g, Fiber 0.7g, Carbs 7g, Protein 6g

82. Breakfast Spinach Quiche

Preparation time: 10 minutes
Cooking Time: 15 minutes
Servings: 4

Ingredients

- 7 ounces whole wheat flour
- 7ounces spinach, torn
- 2 tablespoons olive oil
- 2 tablespoons flax meal mixed with 3 tablespoons water
- 2 tablespoons almond milk
- 3 ounces soft tofu, crumbled
- Salt and black pepper to the taste
- 1 yellow onion, chopped

Preparation

1. In your food processor, mix flour with half of the oil, flax meal, milk, salt and pepper and pulse well.
2. Transfer to a bowl, knead a bit, cover and keep in the fridge for 10 minutes.
3. Heat up a pan with the rest of the oil over medium-high heat, add onion, spinach, tofu, salt and pepper, stir, cook for a few minutes and take off heat.
4. Divide dough in 4 pieces, roll each piece, place on the bottom of a ramekin, divide spinach mix into the ramekins, place all ramekins in your Air Fryer's basket and cook at 360 °F for 15 minutes.
5. Leave quiche aside to cool down a bit and then serve them for breakfast.

Nutrition:

Calories 250, Fat 12g, Fiber 2g, Carbs 13g, Protein 9g

83. Tomatoes Breakfast Salad

Preparation time: 10 minutes
Cooking Time: 20 minutes
Servings: 2

Ingredients

- 2 tomatoes, halved
- Cooking spray
- Salt and black pepper to the taste
- 1 teaspoon parsley, chopped
- 1 teaspoon basil, chopped
- 1 teaspoon oregano, chopped
- 1 teaspoon rosemary, chopped
- 1 cucumber, chopped
- 1 green onion, chopped

Preparation

1. Spray tomato halves with cooking oil, season with salt and pepper, place them in your Air Fryer's basket and cook at 320 ° F for 20 minutes.
2. Transfer tomatoes to a bowl, add parsley, basil, oregano, rosemary, cucumber and onion, toss and serve for breakfast.

Nutrition:

Calories 100, Fat 1g, Fiber 3g, Carbs 8g, Protein 1g

84. Pear Oatmeal

Preparation time: 10 minutes
Cooking Time: 15 minutes
Servings: 3

Ingredients

- 2 cup coconut milk
- ½ cup steel cut oats
- ½ teaspoon vanilla extract
- 1 pear, chopped
- ½ teaspoon maple extract
- 1 tablespoon stevia

Preparation

1. In your Air Fryer's pan, mix coconut milk with oats, vanilla, pear, maple extract and stevia, stir, cover and cook at 360 ° F for 15 minutes.
2. Divide into bowls and serve for breakfast.

Nutrition:

Calories 200, Fat 5g, Fiber 7g, Carbs 14g, Protein 4g

85. Pumpkin Oatmeal

Preparation time: 10 minutes
Cooking Time: 20 minutes
Servings: 4

Ingredients

- 1½ cup water
- ½ cup pumpkin puree
- 1 teaspoon pumpkin pie spice

- 3 tablespoons stevia
- ½ cup steel cut oats

Preparation

1. In your Air Fryer's pan, mix water with oats, pumpkin puree, pumpkin spice and stevia, stir, cover and cook at 360 ° F for 20 minutes
2. Divide into bowls and serve for breakfast.

Nutrition:

Calories 211, Fat 4g, Fiber 7g, Carbs 8g, Protein 3g

86. Breakfast Pizza

Preparation Time: 10 minutes
Cooking time: 15 minutes
Servings: 4

Ingredients:

- 1 cup cauliflower, shredded
- 3 tablespoon almond flour
- ¼ teaspoon salt
- 2 eggs, beaten
- 1 cup spinach, chopped
- 1 oz Parmesan

Directions:

1. Whisk the eggs and combine them together with almond flour, salt, and shredded cauliflower.
2. Stir the mixture until smooth.
3. Line the pizza mold with the baking paper and transfer the cauliflower dough inside it.
4. Flatten the cauliflower crust gently.
5. Place the spinach over the pizza crust.
6. Grate the cheese and sprinkle the spinach.
7. Preheat the oven to 365F.
8. Put the pizza in the oven and cook for 15 minutes or until cooked.

Nutrition: calories 182, fat 14.3, fiber 3.1, carbs 6.5, protein 10.3

87. Donuts

Preparation Time: 15 minutes
Cooking time: 25 minutes
Servings: 4

Ingredients:

- 1 egg, beaten
- 1 cup almond flour
- 1 teaspoon vanilla extract
- 2 tablespoon butter
- 1 teaspoon baking powder
- 1 tablespoon ground cinnamon
- 3 tablespoon swerve

Directions:

1. Make the donut dough: mix up together beaten egg, almond flour, vanilla extract, butter, and baking powder.
2. Knead the soft and non-sticky dough.
3. Let it rest for 10 minutes.
4. Meanwhile, preheat oven to 365F.
5. Line the tray with the parchment.
6. Roll up the dough and make the donuts with the help of the cutter.
7. Transfer the donuts on the tray and put in the oven.
8. Cook the donuts for 25 minutes or until light brown.
9. Meanwhile, mix up together swerve and ground cinnamon.
10. Coat the hot cooked donuts in the cinnamon mixture.

Nutrition: calories 119, fat 10.4, fiber 1.7, carbs 5.2, protein 3

88. Crepes

Preparation Time: 10 minutes
Cooking time: 10 minutes
Servings: 7

Ingredients:

- 1 cup coconut flour
- 1/3 cup almond milk
- 1 teaspoon swerve
- 1 teaspoon vanilla extract
- 1 egg, beaten
- 2 tablespoon flax meal

Directions:

1. Mix up together all the ingredients in the mixing bowl.
2. Whisk the mixture until homogenous and smooth. The mixture should have sour cream texture.
3. Preheat the non-stick pan.
4. Ladle the 1 ladle of the crepe mixture in the pan. Cook every crepe for 1 minute from each side over the medium-high

heat.

Nutrition: calories 115, fat 5.8, fiber 7.7, carbs 13.1, protein 3.8

89. Waffles

Preparation Time: 8 minutes
Cooking time: 10 minutes
Servings:4

Ingredients:

- 3 egg whites
- 4 tablespoon almond flour
- 1 tablespoon swerve
- ½ teaspoon baking powder
- 1 teaspoon vanilla extract
- 2 teaspoon butter
- 1 tablespoon heavy cream

Directions:

1. Whisk the egg whites until soft peaks.
2. Then add almond flour, swerve, baking powder, vanilla extract, and heavy cream.
3. Stir the mixture well.
4. Melt the butter and add in the batter. Stir it well until smooth.
5. Preheat the waffle maker and pour the mixture inside it.
6. Cook the waffles according to the directions of waffle maker manufacturer or until they are golden brown.

Nutrition: calories 208, fat 17.3, fiber 3, carbs 7.2, protein 8.8

90. Herbed Eggs

Preparation Time: 10 minutes
Cooking time: 5 minutes
Servings:4

Ingredients:

- 8 eggs
- 1 tablespoon butter
- 1 teaspoon olive oil
- 1 teaspoon chili flakes
- 1 teaspoon dried oregano
- ½ teaspoon salt
- 1 teaspoon garlic powder

Directions:

1. Boil the eggs in the saucepan for 5 minutes.
2. Meanwhile, melt the butter and combine it together with olive oil.
3. Add chili flakes, dried oregano, salt, and garlic powder.
4. Whisk the mixture.
5. When the eggs are cooked – chill them in the ice water and peel.
6. Then place the eggs in the serving plates and sprinkle with the herbed butter mixture.

Nutrition: calories 165, fat 12.9, fiber 0.2, carbs 1.5, protein 11.3

91. Noatmeal

Preparation Time: 5 minutes
Cooking time: 2.5 minutes
Servings:3

Ingredients:

- 4 tablespoon coconut shred
- 2 tablespoon chia seeds
- 2 tablespoon hemp seeds
- 1 tablespoon almond flour
- 1 teaspoon vanilla extract
- 1 tablespoon swerve
- 1 cup almond milk
- 1 tablespoon almonds, crushed

Directions:

1. Take the glass bowl and combine together all the ingredients in it.
2. Stir until homogenous.
3. Cook the noatmeal in the microwave oven for 2 minutes.
4. Then stir the meal and cook it for 30 seconds more.
5. Chill the noatmeal until warm.

Nutrition: calories 362, fat 33.1, fiber 6.7, carbs 12.6, protein 8.1

92. Chia Pudding

Preparation Time: 8 minutes
Cooking time: 5 hours
Servings:2

Ingredients:

- ½ cup almond milk
- 4 teaspoon chia seeds
- 1 teaspoon vanilla extract
- 1 tablespoon swerve

- 1 oz blackberries

Directions:

1. In the food processor blend together almond milk, vanilla extract, swerve, and blackberries.
2. When the mixture is smooth – pour it in the serving glasses.
3. Add chia seeds and stir gently.
4. Transfer the glasses in the fridge and let them rest for 5 hours.
5. Stir the pudding well before serving.

Nutrition: calories 256, fat 20.9, fiber 9.4, carbs 14.9, protein 5.1

93. Granola

Preparation Time: 10 minutes
Cooking time: 15 minutes
Servings:2

Ingredients:

- 2 tablespoons walnuts, chopped
- 1 tablespoon almond, chopped
- 1 tablespoon macadamia nuts, chopped
- 3 tablespoon coconut shred
- 2 teaspoon chia seeds
- 1 tablespoon almond flour
- 2 tablespoon swerve
- 1 tablespoon coconut butter

Directions:

1. Preheat the oven to 360F.
2. Meanwhile, mix up together all the ingredients in the big bowl.
3. Stir the ingredients until you get a homogenous mixture.
4. Line the baking tray with parchment and place the granola mixture on it.
5. Flatten it well and put in the oven.
6. Cook the granola for 15 minutes.
7. Cut the cooked granola into bars.

Nutrition: calories 253, fat 22.7, fiber 6.2, carbs 11.5, protein 5

94. Yogurt Bowl

Preparation Time: 5 minutes
Cooking time: 20 minutes
Servings: 2

Ingredients:

- 1 cup almond yogurt
- 2 tablespoon coconut shreds
- 1 tablespoon swerve
- ½ cup blackberries
- 1 oz raspberries
- 1 oz almond flakes

Directions:

1. Whisk the almond yogurt and freeze it for 20 minutes.
2. Freeze the blackberries.
3. Then combine together frozen yogurt, swerve, and blackberries in the food processor.
4. Blend the mixture until smooth.
5. Transfer the yogurt mixture in the serving bowls.
6. Sprinkle the yogurt with the raspberries, coconut shred, and almond flakes.

Nutrition: calories 165, fat 11.4, fiber 4.3, carbs 12.7, protein 3.8

95. Morning Coffee Shake

Preparation Time: 8 minutes
Servings:2

Ingredients:

- 1 cup brewed coffee
- 1 cup almond milk
- 1 tablespoon butter
- 1 teaspoon vanilla extract
- 4 ice cubes

Directions:

1. Put the brewed coffee, almond milk, butter, and vanilla extract in the food processor.
2. Blend the liquid until smooth.
3. Pour the coffee shake in the serving glasses and add ice cubes.

Nutrition: calories 334, fat 34.4, fiber 2.6, carbs 6.9, protein 3

96. Tofu Scramble

Preparation Time: 5 minutes
Cooking time: 10 minutes
Servings:2

Ingredients:

- 10 oz firm tofu
- 1 teaspoon turmeric
- ½ white onion, diced

- 1 teaspoon garlic powder
- 1 tablespoon coconut oil
- 1 teaspoon salt
- ½ cup spinach, chopped

Directions:

1. Pour coconut oil in the frying pan.
2. Add white onion and start to cook it.
3. Then place the firm tofu over the onion and scramble it with the help of potato mash.
4. Stir the ingredients.
5. Add salt, turmeric, garlic powder, and spinach.
6. Close the lid and cook the meal for 5 minutes over the medium-high heat.

Nutrition: calories 179, fat 12.9, fiber 2.4, carbs 7, protein 12.5

97. Kale and Spinach Muffins

Preparation time: 10 minutes
Cooking time: 25 minutes
Servings: 8

Ingredients:

- 2 tablespoons flaxseed mixed with 3 tablespoons water
- 1 leek, chopped
- 1 cup coconut milk
- 1 cup kale, torn
- 1 tablespoon coconut oil, melted
- 1 cup baby spinach
- Salt and black pepper to the taste
- ½ teaspoon baking soda
- ½ cup almond flour
- Cooking spray

Directions:

1. In a bowl, combine the kale with the leeks, spinach and the other ingredients except the cooking spray and whisk well.
2. Grease a muffin tray with the cooking spray, pour the kale mix, introduce in the oven at 360 degrees F and bake for 25 minutes.
3. Divide the muffins between plates and serve them for breakfast.

Nutrition: calories 200, fat 7, fiber 4, carbs 7, protein 5

98. Lime Cabbage Muffins

Preparation time: 10 minutes
Cooking time: 20 minutes
Servings: 8

Ingredients:

- 1 cup cabbage, shredded
- Salt and black pepper to the taste
- ½ cup coconut oil, melted
- 3 cups coconut flour
- 1 teaspoon baking powder
- 2 tablespoons flaxseed mixed with 3 tablespoons water
- 2 teaspoons lime zest, grated

Directions:

1. In a bowl, combine the cabbage with the oil, salt, pepper and the other ingredients and stir really well.
2. Divide this into a muffin pan lined with parchment paper, introduce in the oven at 350 degrees F and bake for 20 minutes.
3. Leave muffins to cool down a bit, divide between plates and serve for breakfast.

Nutrition: calories 213, fat 7, fiber 2, carbs 9, protein 8

99. Creamy Oregano Cabbage Bowls

Preparation time: 5 minutes
Cooking time: 15 minutes
Servings: 4

Ingredients:

- 2 tablespoons olive oil
- 1 green cabbage head, shredded
- ¼ cup coconut cream
- ½ teaspoon oregano, dried
- Salt and black pepper to the taste
- 1 tablespoon chives, chopped

Directions:

1. Heat up a pan with the oil over medium heat, add the cabbage, the cream and the other ingredients, toss, cook over medium heat for 15 minutes, divide into bowls and serve for breakfast.

Nutrition: calories 160, fat 3, fiber 2, carbs 6, protein 10

100. Coconut Pudding

Preparation time: 10 minutes
Cooking time: 20 minutes
Servings: 4

Ingredients:

- 1 cup coconut, unsweetened and shredded
- 1 cup cauliflower florets, riced
- 4 scallions, chopped
- 2 tablespoons coconut oil, melted
- 2 tablespoons chives, chopped
- Salt and black pepper to the taste

Directions:

1. Heat up a pan with the oil over medium heat, add the scallions and sauté for 5 minutes.
2. Add the coconut, cauliflower rice and the other ingredients, toss, cook over medium heat for 15 minutes more, divide into bowls and serve for breakfast.

Nutrition: calories 135, fat 7, fiber 2, carbs 4, protein 10

101. Herbed Salad

Preparation time: 10 minutes
Cooking time: 0 minutes
Servings: 4

Ingredients:

- 1 tablespoon olive oil
- 1 teaspoon garlic powder
- 1 tablespoon rosemary, chopped
- 1 tablespoon oregano, chopped
- 1 teaspoon onion powder
- 1 pound cherry tomatoes, halved
- 1 cucumber, sliced
- 1 avocado, peeled, pitted and cubed
- 1 tablespoon cilantro, chopped
- Salt and black pepper to the taste

Directions:

1. In a salad bowl, combine the tomatoes with the cucumber, avocado and the other ingredients, toss and serve for breakfast.

Nutrition: calories 280, fat 12, fiber 4, carbs 7, protein 1.4

102. Radish and Kale Pan

Preparation time: 10 minutes
Cooking time: 15 minutes
Servings: 4

Ingredients:

- 1 tablespoon avocado oil
- 4 scallions, chopped
- ½ pound kale, torn
- 1 cup radishes, cubed
- 2 garlic cloves, minced
- Salt and black pepper to the taste
- 1 tablespoon lime juice
- 1 tablespoon cilantro, chopped

Directions:

1. Heat up a pan with the oil over medium high heat, add the scallions and the garlic and sauté for 5 minutes.
2. Add the kale, radishes and the other ingredients, toss, cook over medium heat for 10 minutes more, divide into bowls and serve for breakfast.

Nutrition: calories 240, fat 7, fiber 3, carbs 12.4, protein 1.5

103. Brussels Sprouts and Tomato Mix

Preparation time: 10 minutes
Cooking time: 15 minutes
Servings: 4

Ingredients:

- 1 pound Brussels sprouts, trimmed and halved
- 1 cup cherry tomatoes, halved
- 2 tablespoons avocado oil
- 1 tablespoon lime juice
- 1 tablespoon balsamic vinegar
- Salt and black pepper to the taste
- 2 shallots, minced
- 2 garlic cloves, minced
- 1 tablespoon chives, chopped

Directions:

1. Heat up a pan with the oil over medium heat, add the shallots and the garlic and sauté for 2 minutes.
2. Add the Brussels sprouts, tomatoes and the other ingredients, toss, cook over medium heat for 13 minutes more, divide into bowls and serve.

Nutrition: calories 240, fat 7, fiber 4, carbs 7,

protein 12

104. Chia and Avocado Pudding

Preparation time: 20 minutes
Cooking time: 0 minutes
Servings: 4

Ingredients:

- 2 tablespoons coconut cream
- ½ cup chia seeds
- 1 cup coconut milk
- 1 avocado, peeled, pitted and cubed
- 1 tablespoon vanilla extract
- 2 tablespoons coconut oil
- 1 tablespoon stevia

Directions:

1. In a bowl, combine the coconut milk with the avocado, chia seeds and the other ingredients, toss well, leave aside for 20 minutes and serve for breakfast.

Nutrition: calories 245, fat 12, fiber 12, carbs 2, protein 9

105. Coffee Almond Pudding

Preparation time: 10 minutes
Cooking time: 30 minutes
Servings: 4

Ingredients:

- 2 tablespoons coffee, brewed
- 2 cups almond milk
- ½ cup coconut cream
- 1/3 cup almonds, chopped
- 1 tablespoon swerve
- 1 tablespoon vanilla extract

Directions:

1. Heat up a small pot with the milk over medium heat, add the coffee, coconut cream and the other ingredients, toss, cook for 30 minutes, divide into bowls and serve for breakfast.

Nutrition: calories 100, fat 0.4, fiber 4, carbs 3, protein 3

106. Mushroom Porridge

Preparation time: 5 minutes
Cooking time: 25 minutes
Servings: 4

Ingredients:

- 2 cups coconut cream
- ½ pound mushrooms, sliced
- 1 cup coconut, unsweetened and shredded
- 1 tablespoon hemp hearts
- A pinch of salt and black pepper
- 1 teaspoon rosemary, dried

Directions:

1. In a pan, combine the cream with the mushrooms, coconut and the other ingredients, toss, cook over medium heat for 25 minutes, divide into bowls and serve.

Nutrition: calories 230, fat 12, fiber 7, carbs 3, protein 12

107. Nuts and Berries Bowls

Preparation time: 10 minutes
Cooking time: 0 minutes
Servings: 4

Ingredients:

- ½ cup strawberries, halved
- ½ cup blackberries
- 1 cup coconut cream
- 1 tablespoon stevia
- 1/3 cup macadamia nuts, chopped
- 1/3 cup walnuts, chopped

Directions:

1. In a bowl, combine the berries with the cream and the other ingredients, toss, leave aside for 10 minutes and serve for breakfast.

Nutrition: calories 296, fat 29.1, fiber 4.3, carbs 9, protein 5.1

108. Cinnamon Porridge

Preparation time: 10 minutes
Cooking time: 12 minutes
Servings: 4

Ingredients:

- 1 avocado, peeled, pitted and cubed
- 1 cup coconut, unsweetened and shredded
- 1 tablespoon stevia
- 1/3 cup coconut cream
- 2 tablespoons coconut oil, melted
- 1 teaspoon cinnamon powder

Directions:

1. Heat up a pan with the oil over medium heat, add the cream, coconut and the other ingredients, toss, cook for 12 minutes, divide into bowls and serve.

Nutrition: calories 278, fat 28.1, fiber 5.6, carbs 8.5, protein 2.1

109. Almond Pancakes

Preparation time: 5 minutes
Cooking time: 12 minutes
Servings: 4

Ingredients:

- 1 teaspoon vanilla extract
- ½ cup almonds, chopped
- 1 teaspoon stevia
- 2 tablespoons flaxseed mixed with 3 tablespoons water
- Cooking spray
- 2 ounces coconut cream

Directions:

1. In your blender, combine the flaxseed with the cream and the other ingredients except the cooking spray and pulse well.
2. Heat up a pan over medium heat, grease with cooking spray, pour ¼ of the batter, spread well, cook for 3 minutes on each side and transfer to a plate.
3. Repeat the action with the rest of the batter and serve the pancakes right away.

Nutrition: calories 126, fat 10.7, fiber 2.8, carbs 4.7, protein 3.6

110. Almond and Avocado Salad

Preparation time: 5 minutes
Cooking time: 0 minutes
Servings: 4

Ingredients:

- 2 avocados, peeled, pitted and roughly cubed
- 1 teaspoon almond extract
- ½ teaspoon vanilla extract
- ¼ cup almonds, toasted
- 1 cup coconut cream

Directions:

1. In a bowl, combine the avocados with the almonds and the other ingredients, toss and serve for breakfast.

Nutrition: calories 266, fat 13, fiber 8, carbs 10, protein 4.1

111. Zucchini Pancakes

Preparation time: 10 minutes
Cooking time: 15 minutes
Servings: 6

Ingredients:

- 2 ounces almond flour
- 3 tablespoons flaxseed mixed with 3 tablespoons water
- 1 teaspoon baking powder
- 1 cup coconut cream
- 1 cup zucchinis, grated
- 1 tablespoon coconut oil, melted

Directions:

2. In a bowl, combine the flour with the flaxseed and the other ingredients except the oil and stir really well.
3. Heat up a pan with the oil over medium high heat, pour 1/6 of the batter, spread, cook for 3 minutes on each side and transfer to a plate.
4. Repeat with the rest of the batter and serve the pancakes right away for breakfast.

Nutrition: calories 200, fat 12.3, fiber 4, carbs 5, protein 1.2

112. Asparagus Salad

Preparation time: 5 minutes
Cooking time: 0 minutes
Servings: 2

Ingredients:

- 1 bunch asparagus, trimmed, blanched and halved
- 1 tablespoon avocado oil
- 1 cup cherry tomatoes, halved
- 1 avocado, peeled, pitted and cubed
- 1 tablespoon lime juice
- A pinch of salt and black pepper

Directions:

1. In a bowl, combine the asparagus with the tomatoes and the other ingredients, toss and serve for breakfast.

Nutrition: calories 200, fat 12, fiber 1, carbs 1, protein 7

113. Walnuts Waffles

Preparation time: 10 minutes
Cooking time: 20 minutes
Servings: 4

Ingredients:

- 3 tablespoons flaxseed mixed with 3 tablespoons water
- ¼ cup coconut milk
- 1 teaspoon baking soda
- 3 tablespoons stevia
- 4 tablespoons almond flour
- 2 teaspoon vanilla
- 4 ounces coconut oil, melted

Directions:

1. In a bowl, combine the flaxseed with the milk, baking soda and the other ingredients and whisk well.
2. Pour some of the mix into your waffle iron and cook for about 5 minutes.
3. Repeat with the rest of the batter and serve your waffles right away.

Nutrition: calories 240, fat 23, fiber 2, carbs 4, protein 7

114. Coconut Almond Granola

Preparation time: 10 minutes
Cooking time: 45 minutes
Servings: 4

Ingredients:

- 1 cup almonds, chopped
- 1 cup coconut, flaked and unsweetened
- ¼ cup flax meal combined with 4 tablespoons water
- 1 cup coconut milk
- ¼ cup coconut cream
- ½ cup stevia
- ¼ cup coconut oil, melted
- 1 teaspoon cinnamon powder

Directions:

1. In a bowl, combine the almonds with the coconut, flaxmeal and the other ingredients and stir well.
2. Line a baking sheet with parchment paper, spread the granola mix, press well, introduce in the oven at 250 degrees F and bake for 45 hour.
3. Leave the granola aside to cool down, cut into squares and serve for breakfast.

Nutrition: calories 340, fat 32, fiber 12, carbs 20, protein 12

115. Spinach and Walnuts Smoothie

Preparation time: 5 minutes
Cooking time: 0 minutes
Servings: 2

Ingredients:

- 1 cup coconut milk
- ¼ cup almonds, chopped
- 2 cups spinach leaves
- 1 tablespoon psyllium seeds
- ½ cup water

Directions:

1. In your blender, combine the coconut milk with the spinach and the other ingredients, pulse well, divide into 2 glasses and serve.

Nutrition: calories 340, fat 30, fiber 7, carbs 7, protein 12

116. Ginger Cucumber Smoothie

Preparation time: 5 minutes
Cooking time: 0 minutes
Servings: 4

Ingredients:

- 1 cup baby spinach
- 2 cups water
- 1 cup almond milk
- 1 tablespoon ginger, grated
- 1 tablespoon swerve
- 2 cucumbers, sliced
- 1 avocado, pitted and peeled

Directions:

1. In your blender, combine the spinach with the water, the milk and the other ingredients, pulse well, divide into glasses and serve for breakfast.

Nutrition: calories 60, fat 2, fiber 3, carbs 3, protein 1

117. Cherries and Watermelon Salad

Preparation time: 5 minutes
Cooking time: 0 minutes
Servings: 2

Ingredients:

- 1 cup baby spinach
- ¼ cup cherries, pitted and halved
- 1 cup watermelon, peeled and cubed
- 1 small avocado, pitted, peeled and cubed
- ¼ teaspoon turmeric powder
- 1 tablespoon lime juice
- A pinch of cayenne pepper

Directions:

1. In a bowl, combine the spinach with the cherries and the other ingredients, toss and serve for breakfast.

Nutrition: calories 100, fat 3, fiber 2, carbs 3, protein 5

118. Fennel and Olives Bowls

Preparation time: 5 minutes
Cooking time: 0 minutes
Servings: 4

Ingredients:

- 2 fennel bulbs, shredded
- 1 cup black olives, pitted and halved
- 1 cup kalamata olives, pitted and halved
- ½ cup cherry tomatoes, halved
- 1 teaspoon oregano, dried
- 1 tablespoon lime juice
- 1 tablespoon olive oil
- 1 tablespoon basil, chopped

Directions:

1. In a bowl, combine the fennel with the olives, cherry tomatoes and the other ingredients, toss and serve for breakfast.

Nutrition: calories 300, fat 23, fiber 3, carbs 4, protein 18

119. Green Beans and Tomato Bowls

Preparation time: 10 minutes
Cooking time: 12 minutes
Servings: 4

Ingredients:

- 2 cups baby spinach
- 1 small avocado, pitted, peeled and sliced
- 1 tablespoon avocado oil
- 4 scallions, chopped
- ½ pound green beans, trimmed and halved
- 1 cup tomatoes, cubed
- 1 tablespoon balsamic vinegar
- Salt and black pepper to the taste

Directions:

1. Heat up a pan with the oil over medium heat, add the scallions, stir and cook for 2 minutes.
2. Add the green beans, the avocado and the other ingredients, toss, cook over medium heat for 10 more minutes, divide into bowls and serve for breakfast.

Nutrition: calories 200, fat 4, fiber 10, carbs 3, protein 10

120. Seeds and Tomato Bowls

Preparation time: 10 minutes
Cooking time: 0 minutes
Servings: 4

Ingredients:

- ½ pound cherry tomatoes, halved
- 1 tablespoon pine nuts, toasted
- 1 tablespoons sunflower seeds
- 1 tablespoon pumpkin seeds
- 1 small avocado, pitted, peeled and cubed
- 1 tablespoon lime juice
- 1 tablespoon avocado oil
- Salt and black pepper to the taste

Directions:

1. In a bowl, combine the cherry tomatoes with the nuts, seeds and the other ingredients, toss and serve for breakfast.

Nutrition: calories 200, fat 32, fiber 6, carbs 4, protein 2

MAINS

121. Creamy Brussels Sprouts Bowls

Preparation time: 10 minutes
Cooking time: 30 minutes
Servings: 4

Ingredients:

- 1 tablespoon olive oil
- 1-pound Brussels sprouts, trimmed and halved
- 1 cup coconut cream
- ½ teaspoon chili powder
- ½ teaspoon garam masala
- ½ teaspoon garlic powder
- A pinch of salt and black pepper
- 1 tablespoon lime juice

Directions:

2. In a roasting pan, combine the sprouts with the cream, chili powder and the other ingredients, toss, introduce in the oven at 380 degrees F and bake for 30 minutes.
3. Divide into bowls and serve for lunch.

Nutrition: calories 219, fat 18.3, fiber 5.7, carbs 14.1, protein 5.4

122. Green Beans and Radishes Bake

Preparation time: 10 minutes
Cooking time: 25 minutes
Servings: 4

Ingredients:

- 2 tablespoons olive oil
- 1 pound green beans, trimmed and halved
- 2 cups radishes, sliced
- 1 cup coconut cream
- 1 teaspoon sweet paprika
- 1 cup cashew cheese, shredded
- Salt and black pepper to the taste
- 1 tablespoon chives, chopped

Directions:

1. In a roasting pan, combine the green beans with the radishes and the other ingredients except the cheese and toss.
2. Sprinkle the cheese on top, introduce in the oven at 375 degrees F and bake for 25 minutes.
3. Divide the mix between plates and serve.

Nutrition: calories 130, fat 1, fiber 0.4, carbs 1, protein 0.1

123. Avocado and Radish Bowls

Preparation time: 10 minutes
Cooking time: 0 minutes
Servings: 4

Ingredients:

- 2 cups radishes, halved
- 2 avocados, peeled, pitted and roughly cubed
- 2 tablespoons coconut cream
- 2 tablespoons balsamic vinegar
- 1 tablespoon green onion, chopped
- 1 teaspoon chili powder
- 1 cup baby spinach
- Salt and black pepper to the taste

Directions:

1. In a bowl, combine the radishes with the avocados and the other ingredients, toss, divide into smaller bowls and serve for lunch.

Nutrition: calories 340, fat 23, fiber 3, carbs 6, protein 5

124. Celery and Radish Soup

Preparation time: 10 minutes
Cooking time: 20 minutes
Servings: 4

Ingredients:

- ½ pound radishes, cut into quarters
- 2 celery stalks, chopped
- 2 tablespoons olive oil
- 4 scallions, chopped
- 1 teaspoon fennel seeds, crushed
- 1 teaspoon coriander, dried
- 6 cups vegetable stock
- Salt and black pepper to the taste
- 6 garlic cloves, minced
- 1 tablespoon chives, chopped

Directions:

1. Heat up a pot with the oil over medium heat, add the celery, scallions and the garlic and sauté for 5 minutes.
2. Add the radishes and the other ingredients, bring to a boil, cover and simmer for 15 minutes.
3. Divide into soup bowls and serve.

Nutrition: calories 120, fat 2, fiber 1, carbs 3, protein 10

125. Lime Avocado and Cucumber Soup

Preparation time: 5 minutes
Cooking time: 0 minutes
Servings: 4

Ingredients:

- 2 avocados, pitted, peeled and roughly cubed
- 2 cucumbers, sliced
- 4 cups vegetable stock
- Salt and black pepper to the taste
- ¼ teaspoon lemon zest, grated
- 1 tablespoon white vinegar
- 1 cup scallions, chopped
- 1 tablespoon olive oil
- ¼ cup cilantro, chopped

Directions:

1. In a blender, combine the avocados with the cucumbers and the other ingredients, pulse well, divide into bowls and serve for lunch.

Nutrition: calories 100, fat 10, fiber 2, carbs 5, protein 8

126. Avocado and Kale Soup

Preparation time: 5 minutes
Cooking time: 7 minutes
Servings: 4

Ingredients:

- 4 cups kale, torn
- 1 teaspoon turmeric powder
- 1 avocado, pitted, peeled and sliced
- 4 cups vegetable stock
- Juice of 1 lime
- 2 garlic cloves, minced
- 1 tablespoon chives, chopped
- Salt and black pepper to the taste

Directions:

2. In a pot, combine the kale with the avocado and the other ingredients, bring to a simmer, cook over medium heat for 7 minutes, blend using an immersion blender, divide into bowls and serve.

Nutrition: calories 234, fat 12, fiber 4, carbs 7, protein 12

127. Spinach and Cucumber Salad

Preparation time: 5 minutes
Cooking time: 0 minutes
Servings: 4

Ingredients:

- 1 pound cucumber, sliced
- 2 cups baby spinach
- 1 tablespoon chili powder
- 2 tablespoons olive oil
- ¼ cup cilantro, chopped
- 2 tablespoons lemon juice
- Salt and black pepper to the taste

Directions:

3. In a large salad bowl, combine the cucumber with the spinach and the other ingredients, toss and serve for lunch.

Nutrition: calories 140, fat 4, fiber 2, carbs 4, protein 5

128. Avocado Soup

Preparation time: 10 minutes
Cooking time: 0 minutes
Servings: 4

Ingredients:

- 2 avocados, pitted, peeled and chopped
- 4 cups vegetable stock
- 2 scallions, chopped
- Salt and black pepper to the taste
- 2 tablespoons coconut oil, melted
- 2/3 cup coconut cream

Directions:

1. In a blender, combine the avocados with the stock and the other ingredients, pulse well, divide into bowls and serve.

Nutrition: calories 332, fat 23, fiber 4, carbs 6, protein 6

129. Avocado, Spinach and Kale Soup

Preparation time: 10 minutes
Cooking time: 0 minutes
Servings: 4

Ingredients:

- 2 avocados, pitted, peeled and cut in halves
- 4 cups vegetable stock
- 2 tablespoons cilantro, chopped
- Juice of 1 lime
- 1 teaspoon rosemary, dried
- ½ cup spinach leaves
- ½ cup kale, torn
- Salt and black pepper to the taste

Directions:

1. In a blender, combine the avocados with the stock and the other ingredients, pulse well, divide into bowls and serve for lunch.

Nutrition: calories 300, fat 23, fiber 5, carbs 6, protein 7

130. Curry Spinach Soup

Preparation time: 10 minutes
Cooking time: 0 minutes
Servings: 4

Ingredients:

- 1 cup almond milk
- 1 tablespoon green curry paste
- 1 pound spinach leaves
- 1 tablespoon cilantro, chopped
- Salt and black pepper to the taste
- 4 cups veggie stock
- 1 tablespoon cilantro, chopped

Directions:

1. In your blender, combine the almond milk with the curry paste and the other ingredients, pulse well, divide into bowls and serve for lunch.

Nutrition: calories 240, fat 4, fiber 2, carbs 6, protein 2

131. Arugula and Artichokes Bowls

Preparation time: 5 minutes
Cooking time: 0 minutes
Servings: 4

Ingredients:

- 2 cups baby arugula
- ¼ cup walnuts, chopped
- 1 cup canned artichoke hearts, drained and quartered
- 1 tablespoon balsamic vinegar
- 2 tablespoons cilantro, chopped
- 2 tablespoons olive oil
- Salt and black pepper to the taste
- 1 tablespoon lemon juice

Directions:

1. In a bowl, combine the artichokes with the arugula, walnuts and the other ingredients, toss, divide into smaller bowls and serve for lunch.

Nutrition: calories 200, fat 2, fiber 1, carbs 5, protein 7

132. Minty Arugula Soup

Preparation time: 5 minutes
Cooking time: 10 minutes
Servings: 4

Ingredients:

- 3 scallions, chopped
- 1 tablespoon olive oil
- ½ cup coconut milk
- 2 cups baby arugula
- 2 tablespoons mint, chopped
- 6 cups vegetable stock
- 2 tablespoons chives, chopped
- Salt and black pepper to the taste

Directions:

1. Heat up a pot with the oil over medium high heat, add the scallions and sauté for 2 minutes.
2. Add the rest of the ingredients, toss, bring to a simmer and cook over medium heat for 8 minutes more.
3. Divide the soup into bowls and serve.

Nutrition: calories 200, fat 4, fiber 2, carbs 6, protein 10

133. Spinach and Broccoli Soup

Preparation time: 10 minutes
Cooking time: 20 minutes
Servings: 4

Ingredients:

- 3 shallots, chopped
- 1 tablespoon olive oil
- 2 garlic cloves, minced
- ½ pound broccoli florets
- ½ pound baby spinach
- Salt and black pepper to the taste
- 4 cups veggie stock
- 1 teaspoon turmeric powder
- 1 tablespoon lime juice

Directions:

1. Heat up a pot with the oil over medium high heat, add the shallots and the garlic and sauté for 5 minutes.
2. Add the broccoli, spinach and the other ingredients, toss, bring to a simmer and cook over medium heat for 15 minutes.
3. Ladle into soup bowls and serve.

Nutrition: calories 150, fat 3, fiber 1, carbs 3, protein 7

134. Coconut Zucchini Cream

Preparation time: 10 minutes
Cooking time: 25 minutes
Servings: 4

Ingredients:

- 1 pound zucchinis, roughly chopped
- 2 tablespoons avocado oil
- 4 scallions, chopped
- Salt and black pepper to the taste
- 6 cups veggie stock
- 1 teaspoon basil, dried
- 1 teaspoon cumin, ground
- 3 garlic cloves, minced
- ¾ cup coconut cream
- 1 tablespoon dill, chopped

Directions:

1. Heat up a pot with the oil over medium high heat, add the scallions and the garlic and sauté for 5 minutes.
2. Add the rest of the ingredients, stir, bring to a simmer and cook over medium heat for 20 minutes more.
3. Blend the soup using an immersion blender, ladle into bowls and serve.

Nutrition: calories 160, fat 4, fiber 2, carbs 4, protein 8

135. Zucchini and Cauliflower Soup

Preparation time: 10 minutes
Cooking time: 25 minutes
Servings: 4

Ingredients:

- 4 scallions, chopped
- 1 teaspoon ginger, grated
- 2 tablespoons olive oil
- 1 pound zucchinis, sliced
- 2 cups cauliflower florets
- Salt and black pepper to the taste
- 6 cups veggie stock
- 1 garlic clove, minced
- 1 tablespoon lemon juice
- 1 cup coconut cream

Directions:

1. Heat up a pot with the oil over medium heat, add the scallions, ginger and the garlic and sauté for 5 minutes.
2. Add the rest of the ingredients, bring to a simmer and cook over medium heat for 20 minutes.
3. Blend everything using an immersion blender, ladle into soup bowls and serve.

Nutrition: calories 154, fat 12, fiber 3, carbs 5, protein 4

136. Chard Soup

Preparation time: 10 minutes
Cooking time: 25 minutes
Servings: 4

Ingredients:

- 1 pound Swiss chard, chopped
- ½ cup shallots, chopped
- 1 tablespoon avocado oil
- 1 teaspoon cumin, ground
- 1 teaspoon rosemary, dried
- 1 teaspoon basil, dried
- 2 garlic cloves, minced
- Salt and black pepper to the taste
- 6 cups vegetable stock
- 1 tablespoon tomato passata
- 1 tablespoon cilantro, chopped

Directions:

1. Heat up a pan with the oil over medium

heat, add the shallots and the garlic and sauté for 5 minutes.
2. Add the Swiss chard and the other ingredients, toss, bring to a simmer and cook over medium heat for 20 minutes more.
3. Divide the soup into bowls and serve.

Nutrition: calories 232, fat 23, fiber 3, carbs 4, protein 3

137. Avocado, Pine Nuts and Chard Salad

Preparation time: 5 minutes
Cooking time: 15 minutes
Servings: 4

Ingredients:

- 1 pound Swiss chard, roughly chopped
- 2 tablespoons olive oil
- 1 avocado, peeled, pitted and roughly cubed
- 2 spring onions, chopped
- ¼ cup pine nuts, toasted
- 1 tablespoon balsamic vinegar
- Salt and black pepper to the taste

Directions:

1. Heat up a pan with the oil over medium heat, add the spring onions, pine nuts and the chard, stir and sauté for 5 minutes.
2. Add the vinegar and the other ingredients, toss, cook over medium heat for 10 minutes more, divide into bowls and serve for lunch.

Nutrition: calories 120, fat 2, fiber 1, carbs 4, protein 8

138. Grapes, Avocado and Spinach Salad

Preparation time: 10 minutes
Cooking time: 0 minutes
Servings: 4

Ingredients:

- 1 cup green grapes, halved
- 2 cups baby spinach
- 1 avocado, pitted, peeled and cubed
- Salt and black pepper to the taste
- 2 tablespoons olive oil
- 1 tablespoon thyme, chopped
- 1 tablespoon rosemary, chopped
- 1 tablespoon lime juice
- 1 garlic clove, minced

Directions:

1. In a salad bowl, combine the grapes with the spinach and the other ingredients, toss, and serve for lunch.

Nutrition: calories 190, fat 17.1, fiber 4.6, carbs 10.9, protein 1.7

139. Greens and Olives Pan

Preparation time: 10 minutes
Cooking time: 15 minutes
Servings: 4

Ingredients:

- 4 spring onions, chopped
- 2 tablespoons olive oil
- ½ cup green olives, pitted and halved
- ¼ cup pine nuts, toasted
- 1 tablespoon balsamic vinegar
- 2 cups baby spinach
- 1 cup baby arugula
- 1 cup asparagus, trimmed, blanched and halved
- Salt and black pepper to the taste

Directions:

1. Heat up a pan with the oil over medium high heat, add the spring onions and the asparagus and sauté for 5 minutes.
2. Add the olives, spinach and the other ingredients, toss, cook over medium heat for 10 minutes, divide between plates and serve for lunch.

Nutrition: calories 136, fat 13.1, fiber 1.9, carbs 4.4, protein 2.8

140. Mushrooms and Chard Soup

Preparation time: 10 minutes
Cooking time: 30 minutes
Servings: 4

Ingredients:

- 3 cups Swiss chard, chopped
- 6 cups vegetable stock
- 1 cup mushrooms, sliced
- 2 garlic cloves, minced
- 1 tablespoon olive oil
- 2 scallions, chopped
- 2 tablespoons balsamic vinegar

- ¼ cup basil, chopped
- Salt and black pepper to the taste
- 1 tablespoon cilantro, chopped

Directions:

1. Heat up a pot with the oil over medium high heat, add the scallions and the garlic and sauté for 5 minutes.
2. Add the mushrooms and sauté for another 5 minutes.
3. Add the rest of the ingredients, toss, bring to a simmer and cook over medium heat for 20 minutes more.
4. Ladle the soup into bowls and serve.

Nutrition: calories 140, fat 4, fiber 2, carbs 4, protein 8

141. Tomato, Green Beans and Chard Soup

Preparation time: 10 minutes
Cooking time: 35 minutes
Servings: 4

Ingredients:

- 2 scallions, chopped
- 1 cup Swiss chard, chopped
- 1 tablespoon olive oil
- 1 red bell pepper, chopped
- Salt and black pepper to the taste
- 1 cup tomatoes, cubed
- 1 cup green beans, chopped
- 6 cups vegetable stock
- 2 tablespoons tomato passata
- 2 garlic cloves, minced
- 2 teaspoons thyme, chopped
- ½ teaspoon red pepper flakes

Directions:

1. Heat up a pot with the oil over medium heat, add the scallions, garlic and the pepper flakes and sauté for 5 minutes.
2. Add the chard and the other ingredients, toss, bring to a simmer and cook over medium heat for 30 minutes more.
3. Ladle the soup into bowls and serve for lunch.

Nutrition: calories 150, fat 8, fiber 2, carbs 4, protein 9

142. Hot Roasted Peppers Cream

Preparation time: 10 minutes
Cooking time: 30 minutes
Servings: 4

Ingredients:

- 1 red chili pepper, minced
- 4 garlic cloves, minced
- 2 pounds mixed bell peppers, roasted, peeled and chopped
- 4 scallions, chopped
- 1 cup coconut cream
- Salt and black pepper to the taste
- 2 tablespoons olive oil
- ½ tablespoon basil, chopped
- 4 cups vegetable stock
- ¼ cup chives, chopped

Directions:

1. Heat up a pot with the oil over medium heat, add the garlic and the chili pepper and sauté for 5 minutes.
2. Add the peppers and the other ingredients, toss, bring to a simmer and cook over medium heat for 25 minutes.
3. Blend the soup using an immersion blender, divide into bowls and serve.

Nutrition: calories 140, fat 2, fiber 2, carbs 5, protein 8

143. Eggplant and Peppers Soup

Preparation time: 10 minutes
Cooking time: 40 minutes
Servings: 4

Ingredients:

- 2 red bell peppers, chopped
- 3 scallions, chopped
- 3 garlic cloves, minced
- 2 tablespoon olive oil
- Salt and black pepper to the taste
- 5 cups vegetable stock
- 1 bay leaf
- ½ cup coconut cream
- 1 pound eggplants, roughly cubed
- 2 tablespoons basil, chopped

Directions:

1. Heat up a pot with the oil over medium heat, add the scallions and the garlic and sauté for 5 minutes.

2. Add the peppers and the eggplants and sauté for 5 minutes more.
3. Add the remaining ingredients, toss, bring to a simmer, cook for 30 minutes, ladle into bowls and serve for lunch.

Nutrition: calories 180, fat 2, fiber 3, carbs 5, protein 10

144. Eggplant and Olives Stew

Preparation time: 10 minutes
Cooking time: 30 minutes
Servings: 4

Ingredients:

- 2 scallions, chopped
- 2 tablespoons avocado oil
- 2 garlic cloves, chopped
- 1 bunch parsley, chopped
- Salt and black pepper to the taste
- 1 teaspoon basil, dried
- 1 teaspoon cumin, dried
- 2 eggplants, roughly cubed
- 1 cup green olives, pitted and sliced
- 3 tablespoons balsamic vinegar
- ½ cup tomato passata

Directions:

1. Heat up a pot with the oil over medium heat, add the scallions, garlic, basil and cumin and sauté for 5 minutes.
2. Add the eggplants and the other ingredients, toss, cook over medium heat for 25 minutes more, divide into bowls and serve.

Nutrition: calories 93, fat 1.8, fiber 10.6, carbs 18.6, protein 3.4

145. Cauliflower and Artichokes Soup

Preparation time: 10 minutes
Cooking time: 25 minutes
Servings: 4

Ingredients:

- 1 pound cauliflower florets
- 1 cup canned artichoke hearts, drained and chopped
- 2 scallions, chopped
- 2 tablespoons olive oil
- 2 garlic cloves, minced
- 6 cups vegetable stock
- Salt and black pepper to the taste
- 2/3 cup coconut cream
- 2 tablespoons cilantro, chopped

Directions:

1. Heat up a pot with the oil over medium heat, add the scallions and the garlic and sauté for 5 minutes.
2. Add the cauliflower and the other ingredients, toss, bring to a simmer and cook over medium heat for 20 minutes more.
3. Blend the soup using an immersion blender, divide it into bowls and serve.

Nutrition: calories 207, fat 17.2, fiber 6.2, carbs 14.1, protein 4.7

146. Hot Cabbage Soup

Preparation time: 10 minutes
Cooking time: 30 minutes
Servings: 4

Ingredients:

- 3 spring onions, chopped
- 1 green cabbage head, shredded
- 2 tablespoons olive oil
- 1 tablespoon ginger, grated
- 1 teaspoon cumin, ground
- 6 cups vegetable stock
- Salt and black pepper to the taste
- 1 teaspoon hot paprika
- 1 teaspoon chili powder
- 1 tablespoon cilantro, chopped

Directions:

1. Heat up a pot with the oil over medium heat, add the spring onions, ginger and the cumin and sauté for 5 minutes.
2. Add the cabbage and the other ingredients, stir, bring to a simmer and cook over medium heat for 25 minutes more.
3. Ladle the soup into bowls and serve for lunch.

Nutrition: calories 117, fat 7.5, fiber 5.2, carbs 12.7, protein 2.8

147. Grilled Veggie Mix

Preparation time: 10 minutes

Cooking time: 30 minutes
Servings: 4

Ingredients:

- 1 pound cherry tomatoes, halved
- 2 eggplants, roughly cubed
- 2 cups radishes, halved
- 2 green bell peppers, halved, deseeded
- 1 teaspoon chili powder
- 1 teaspoon rosemary, dried
- 1/4 cup balsamic vinegar
- Salt and black pepper to the taste
- 2 tablespoons olive oil
- 1 tablespoon basil, chopped

Directions:

1. In a bowl, combine the tomatoes with the eggplants and the other ingredients except the basil and toss well.
2. Arrange the veggies on your preheated grill and cook over medium heat for 15 minutes on each side.
3. Divide the veggies between plates, sprinkle the basil on top and serve.

Nutrition: calories 120, fat 1, fiber 3, carbs 9, protein 2

148. Vinegar Cucumber, Olives and Shallots Salad

Preparation time: 10 minutes
Cooking time: 0 minutes
Servings: 4

Ingredients:

- 1 pound cucumbers, sliced
- 1 cup black olives, pitted and sliced
- 3 tablespoons shallots, chopped
- ¼ cup balsamic vinegar
- 1 tablespoon dill, chopped
- A pinch of salt and black pepper
- 3 tablespoons avocado oil

Directions:

1. In a bowl, mix the cucumbers with the olives, shallots and the other ingredients, toss well, divide between plates and serve.

Nutrition: calories 120, fat 3, fiber 2, carbs 5, protein 10

149. Tomato and Peppers Pancakes

Preparation time: 10 minutes
Cooking time: 10 minutes
Servings: 4

Ingredients:

- 3 scallions, chopped
- 1 pound tomatoes, crushed
- 1 red bell pepper, chopped
- 1 green bell pepper, chopped
- Salt and black pepper to the taste
- 1 teaspoon coriander, ground
- 2 tablespoons almond flour
- 2 tablespoons flaxseed mixed with 3 tablespoons water
- 3 tablespoons coconut oil, melted

Directions:

1. In a bowl, combine the tomatoes with the peppers and the other ingredients except 1 tablespoon oil and stir really well.
2. Heat up a pan with the remaining oil over medium heat, add ¼ of the batter, spread into the pan, cook for 3 minutes on each side and transfer to a plate.
3. Repeat this with the rest of the batter, transfer all pancakes to a platter and serve.

Nutrition: calories 70, fat 2, fiber 3, carbs 10, protein 4

150. Greens and Vinaigrette

Preparation time: 10 minutes
Cooking time: 0 minutes
Servings: 4

Ingredients:

- 1 cup baby kale
- 1 cup baby arugula
- 1 cup romaine lettuce
- 2 tomatoes, cubed
- 1 cucumber, cubed
- 3 tablespoons lime juice
- 1/3 cup olive oil
- 1 tablespoon balsamic vinegar
- Salt and black pepper to the taste

Directions:

1. In a bowl, combine the oil with the vinegar, lime juice, salt and pepper and whisk well.
2. In another bowl, combine the greens with

the vinaigrette, toss and serve right away.

Nutrition: calories 112, fat 9, fiber 2, carbs 6, protein 2

151. Mushroom and Mustard Greens Mix

Preparation time: 10 minutes
Cooking time: 20 minutes
Servings: 4

Ingredients:

- 1 pound white mushrooms, halved
- 2 cups mustard greens
- 1 tablespoon lime juice
- 3 scallions, chopped
- 2 tablespoons olive oil
- 1 teaspoon sweet paprika
- 1 teaspoon rosemary, dried
- 2 bunches parsley, chopped
- 3 garlic cloves, minced
- Salt and black pepper to the taste

Directions:

1. Heat up a pan with the oil over medium heat, add the scallions, paprika, garlic and parsley and sauté for 5 minutes.
2. Add the mushrooms and the other ingredients, toss, cook over medium heat for 15 minutes, divide between plates and serve.

Nutrition: calories 76, fat 1, fiber 2, carbs 3, protein 3

152. Mustard Greens and Kale Mix

Preparation time: 10 minutes
Cooking time: 10 minutes
Servings: 4

Ingredients:

- 1 pound mustard greens
- ½ pound kale, torn
- 2 celery stalks, chopped
- 2 tablespoons avocado oil
- 1 cup tomatoes, cubed
- 2 avocados, peeled, pitted and cubed
- 1 cup coconut cream
- 2 tablespoons lemon juice
- 2 garlic cloves minced
- 2 tablespoons parsley, chopped
- A pinch of salt and black pepper

Directions:

1. Heat up a pan with the oil over medium heat, add the mustard greens, kale, celery and the other ingredients, toss, cook for 10 minutes, divide between plates and serve warm.

Nutrition: calories 200, fat 4, fiber 8, carbs 16, protein 7

153. Zucchini Fries and Sauce

Preparation time: 10 minutes
Cooking time: 25 minutes
Servings: 4

Ingredients:

- 1 pound zucchinis, cut into fries
- 2 tablespoons olive oil
- ½ teaspoon rosemary, dried
- 3 scallions, chopped
- 2 teaspoons smoked paprika
- A pinch of sea salt and black pepper
- 1 cup coconut cream
- 1 tablespoon balsamic vinegar
- ½ teaspoon garlic powder
- 2 tablespoons cilantro, chopped

Directions:

2. Arrange the zucchini fries on a baking sheet lined with parchment paper, add half of the oil, paprika, garlic powder, salt and pepper, toss and bake in the oven at 425 degrees F for 12 minutes.
3. Heat up a pan with the rest of the oil over medium heat, add the scallions and sauté for 3 minutes.
4. Add the cream and the remaining ingredients, toss, and cook over medium heat for 10 minutes more.
5. Divide the zucchini fries between plates, drizzle the sauce all over and serve.

Nutrition: calories 140, fat 5, fiber 2, carbs 20, protein 6

154. Chard and Garlic Sauce

Preparation time: 10 minutes
Cooking time: 15 minutes
Servings: 4

Ingredients:

- ½ cup walnuts, chopped

- 4 cups red chard, torn
- 3 tablespoons olive oil
- Juice of 1 lime
- 1 celery stalks, chopped
- 1 cup coconut cream
- 4 garlic cloves, minced
- 1 tablespoon balsamic vinegar
- 2/3 cup scallions, chopped
- A pinch of sea salt and black pepper

Directions:

1. Heat up a pan with the oil over medium heat, add the scallions, garlic and the celery and sauté for 5 minutes.
2. Add the chard and the other ingredients, toss, cook over medium heat for 10 minutes more, divide between plates and serve.

Nutrition: calories 374, fat 34.2, fiber 6.7, carbs 15.4, protein 9

155. Parsley Chard Salad

Preparation time: 10 minutes
Cooking time: 0 minutes
Servings: 4

Ingredients:

- 1 pound red chard, steamed and torn
- 1 cup grapes, halved
- 1 cup cherry tomatoes, halved
- 1 celery stalk, chopped
- 3 tablespoons balsamic vinegar
- ½ cup coconut cream
- 1 teaspoon chili powder
- 2 tablespoons olive oil
- ½ cup parsley, minced
- A pinch of sea salt and black pepper

Directions:

1. In a bowl, combine the chard with the grapes, tomatoes and the other ingredients, toss and serve right away.

Nutrition: calories 250, fat 4, fiber 8, carbs 20, protein 6.5

156. Bok Choy Salad

Preparation time: 10 minutes
Cooking time: 20 minutes
Servings: 4

Ingredients:

- 4 scallions, chopped
- 1 pound bok choy, torn
- 2 tablespoons olive oil
- ½ cup veggie stock
- 2 tablespoons balsamic vinegar
- 1 tablespoon chili powder
- 1 cup cherry tomatoes, halved
- 1 tablespoon garlic powder
- ¼ cup chives, chopped
- 1 teaspoon rosemary, dried
- 1 tablespoon thyme, chopped
- A pinch of sea salt and black pepper

Directions:

1. Heat up a pan with the oil over medium heat, add the scallions, garlic powder and rosemary, stir and cook for 5 minutes.
2. Add the bok choy and the rest of the ingredients, toss, cook over medium heat for 15 minutes, divide between plates and serve.

Nutrition: calories 107, fat 8.4, fiber 3.4, carbs 9, protein 3.1

157. Roasted Bok Choy and Sprouts Mix

Preparation time: 10 minutes
Cooking time: 30 minutes
Servings: 4

Ingredients:

- 2 tablespoons olive oil
- 1 pound Brussels sprouts, trimmed and halved
- ½ pound bok choy, torn
- 1 tablespoon garlic powder
- 1 tablespoon chili powder
- 2 tablespoons balsamic vinegar
- 1 tablespoon onion powder
- A pinch of salt and black pepper
- 1 teaspoon sweet paprika

Directions:

1. In a roasting pan, combine the bok choy with the sprouts, the oil and the other ingredients, toss and cook at 390 degrees F for 30 minutes.
2. Divide the mix between plates and serve right away.

Nutrition: calories 100, fat 2, fiber 2, carbs 9, protein 1

158. Bok Choy and Cauliflower Rice

Preparation time: 10 minutes
Cooking time: 20 minutes
Servings: 4

Ingredients:

- 2 tablespoons olive oil
- 2 garlic cloves, minced
- 4 scallions, chopped
- 2 cups cauliflower rice
- 1 cup bok choy, torn
- ½ cup cherry tomatoes, halved
- 2 tablespoons thyme, chopped
- 1 tablespoon lemon juice
- Zest of ½ lemon, grated
- A pinch of sea salt and black pepper

Directions:

1. Heat up a pan with the oil over medium heat, add the scallions and the garlic and sauté for 5 minutes.
2. Add the cauliflower rice and the other ingredients, toss, cook over medium heat for 15 minutes more, divide into bowls and serve.

Nutrition: calories 130, fat 2, fiber 2, carbs 6, protein 8

159. Sweet Kale and Onions Mix

Preparation time: 10 minutes
Cooking time: 12 minutes
Servings: 4

Ingredients:

- 4 cups kale, torn
- 4 spring onions, chopped
- ½ cup tomato passata
- 1 teaspoon stevia
- 2 tablespoons avocado oil
- A pinch of sea salt and black pepper
- 1 teaspoon sweet paprika

Directions:

1. Heat up a pan with the oil over medium high heat, add the spring onions, paprika and stevia, toss and cook for 2 minutes.
2. Add the kale and the other ingredients, toss, cook over medium heat for 10 minutes, divide between plates and serve right away.

Nutrition: calories 150, fat 4, fiber 4, carbs 8.2, protein 5

160. Broccoli, Chard and Kale Mix

Preparation time: 10 minutes
Cooking time: 20 minutes
Servings: 4

Ingredients:

- ½ cup kale, torn
- 2 cups red chard, torn
- 2 cups broccoli florets
- 4 garlic cloves, minced
- 2 tablespoons olive oil
- 1 tablespoon balsamic vinegar
- 1 tablespoon lemon juice
- ½ cup almonds, sliced
- 1 tablespoon chives, chopped

Directions:

1. In a roasting pan, combine the kale with the chard, broccoli and the other ingredients, toss and bake at 400 degrees F for 20 minutes.
2. Divide everything between plates and serve right away.

Nutrition: calories 90, fat 1, fiber 3, carbs 7, protein 2

161. Baked Bok Choy and Tomatoes

Preparation time: 10 minutes
Cooking time: 30 minutes
Servings: 4

Ingredients:

- 1 pound bok choy, torn
- ½ pound cherry tomatoes, halved
- 2 tablespoons olive oil
- 2 teaspoons rosemary, dried
- ½ teaspoon nutmeg, ground
- 1 teaspoon cloves, ground
- 1 teaspoon coriander, ground
- 2 tablespoons balsamic vinegar

Directions:

1. In a roasting pan, combine the bok choy with the cherry tomatoes and the other

ingredients, toss and bake at 400 degrees F for 30 minutes,
2. Divide everything between plates and serve.

Nutrition: calories 220, fat 2, fiber 4, carbs 6, protein 10

162. Italian Bok Choy, Rice and Arugula Salad

Preparation time: 10 minutes
Cooking time: 0 minutes
Servings: 4

Ingredients:

- 2 cups cauliflower rice, steamed
- 1 cup bok choy, torn
- ½ cup baby arugula
- 2 tablespoons pine nuts, toasted
- 1 tablespoon walnuts, chopped
- 2 tomatoes, cubed
- 2 tablespoons avocado oil
- 2 garlic cloves, minced
- 2 tablespoons basil, chopped
- 1 tablespoon Italian seasoning
- 2 tablespoons lime juice
- A pinch of sea salt and black pepper

Directions:

1. In a salad bowl, combine the cauliflower rice with the arugula, bok choy and the other ingredients, toss, divide into smaller bowls and serve.

Nutrition: calories 227, fat 2, fiber 7, carbs 18, protein 11

163. Hot Cranberries and Arugula Mix

Preparation time: 10 minutes
Cooking time: 0 minutes
Servings: 4

Ingredients:

- 1 cup cranberries
- 2 cups baby arugula
- 1 avocado, peeled, pitted and cubed
- 1 cucumber, cubed
- ¼ cup kalamata olives, pitted and sliced
- 1 tablespoon walnuts, chopped
- 2 tablespoons olive oil
- 2 tablespoons lime juice

Directions:

1. In a bowl, combine the arugula with the cranberries and the other ingredients, toss well, divide between plates and serve.

Nutrition: calories 110, fat 4, fiber 2, carbs 10, protein 2

164. Cinnamon Cauliflower Rice, Zucchinis and Spinach

Preparation time: 10 minutes
Cooking time: 10 minutes
Servings: 4

Ingredients:

- 1 cup cauliflower rice
- 2 tablespoons olive oil
- 1 zucchini, sliced
- 1 cup baby spinach
- ½ cup veggie stock
- ½ teaspoon turmeric powder
- ¼ teaspoon cinnamon powder
- A pinch of sea salt and black pepper
- 1/3 cup dates, dried and chopped
- 1 tablespoon almonds, chopped
- ¼ cup chives, chopped

Directions:

1. Heat up a pan with the oil over medium heat, add the cauliflower rice, dates, turmeric and cinnamon and sauté for 3 minutes.
2. Add the zucchini and the other ingredients, toss, cook the mix for 7 minutes more, divide between plates and serve.

Nutrition: calories 189, fat 2, fiber 2, carbs 20, protein 7

165. Asparagus, Bok Choy and Radish Mix

Preparation time: 10 minutes
Cooking time: 12 minutes
Servings: 4

Ingredients:

- ½ pound asparagus, trimmed and halved
- 1 cup bok choy, torn
- 1 cup radishes, halved
- 2 tablespoons balsamic vinegar

- 2 tablespoons olive oil
- 2 teaspoon Italian seasoning
- 2 teaspoons garlic powder
- 1 teaspoon coriander, ground
- 1 teaspoon fennel seeds, crushed
- 1 tablespoon chives, chopped

Directions:

1. Heat up a pan with the oil over medium heat, add the asparagus, bok choy, the radishes and the other ingredients, toss, cook for 12 minutes, divide between plates and serve.

Nutrition: calories 140, fat 1, fiber 10, carbs 20, protein 8

166. Kale and Cucumber Salad

Preparation time: 10 minutes
Cooking time: 0 minutes
Servings: 4

Ingredients:

- 2 cups baby kale
- 2 cucumbers, sliced
- 2 tablespoons avocado oil
- 1 cup coconut cream
- 1 teaspoon balsamic vinegar
- 2 tablespoons dill, chopped

Directions:

1. In a bowl, combine the kale with the cucumbers and the other ingredients, toss and serve.

Nutrition: calories 90, fat 1, fiber 3, carbs 7, protein 2

167. Avocado, Endive and Asparagus Mix

Preparation time: 10 minutes
Cooking time: 10 minutes
Servings: 4

Ingredients:

- 2 avocados, peeled, pitted and sliced
- 2 endives, shredded
- 4 asparagus spears, trimmed and halved
- 2 tablespoons sesame seeds
- 2 tablespoons avocado oil
- Juice of 1 lime
- A pinch of sea salt and black pepper
- Black pepper to the taste
- 1 tablespoon chives, chopped

Directions:

1. Heat up a pan with the oil over medium heat, add the endives, asparagus, avocados and the other ingredients, toss, cook for 10 minutes, divide between plates and serve.

Nutrition: calories 111, fat 2, fiber 5, carbs 8, protein 2

168. Bell Peppers and Spinach Pan

Preparation time: 10 minutes
Cooking time: 12 minutes
Servings: 4

Ingredients:

- 1 tablespoon olive oil
- 1 red bell pepper, cut into strips
- 1 green bell pepper, cut into strips
- 1 orange bell pepper, cut into strips
- 2 cups baby spinach
- 3 garlic cloves, minced
- 2 teaspoons garlic powder
- A pinch of sea salt and black pepper
- 1 teaspoon fennel seeds, crushed
- 1 teaspoon chili powder

Directions:

1. Heat up a pan with the oil over medium high heat, add the peppers and the garlic and sauté for 2 minutes.
2. Add the spinach and the other ingredients, toss, cook over medium heat for 10 minutes more, divide between plates and serve.

Nutrition: calories 125, fat 3, fiber 5, carbs 9, protein 12

169. Mushrooms and Asparagus Mix

Preparation time: 10 minutes
Cooking time: 15 minutes
Servings: 4

Ingredients:

- 1 pound white mushrooms, sliced
- 1 asparagus bunch, trimmed and halved
- 1 teaspoon sweet paprika
- 1 teaspoon coriander, ground
- 1 teaspoon chili powder

- ½ teaspoon thyme, dried
- 2 garlic cloves, minced
- ¼ cup coconut cream
- 1 tablespoon avocado oil

Directions:

1. Heat up a pan with the oil over medium high heat, add the mushrooms, the asparagus and the other ingredients, toss, cook for 15 minutes, divide between plates and serve.

Nutrition: calories 74, fat 4.6, fiber 2.6, carbs 6.9, protein 4.7

170. Kale and Raisins

Preparation time: 10 minutes
Cooking time: 20 minutes
Servings: 4

Ingredients:

- 1 pound kale, torn
- 1 tomato, cubed
- 2 tablespoons avocado oil
- Juice of 1 lime
- ¼ cup raisins
- 1 teaspoon nutmeg, ground
- ½ teaspoon ginger, grated
- ½ teaspoon cinnamon powder
- 1 tablespoon chives, chopped
- A pinch of sea salt and black pepper

Directions:

1. Heat up a pan with the oil over medium heat, add the kale, tomato, lime juice and the other ingredients, toss, cook for 20 minutes, divide into bowls and serve.

Nutrition: calories 102, fat 1.2, fiber 2.7, carbs 21.4, protein 4

171. Collard Greens and Garlic Mix

Preparation time: 10 minutes
Cooking time: 10 minutes
Servings: 4

Directions:

- 2 tablespoons avocado oil
- 4 garlic cloves, minced
- 4 bunches collard greens
- 1 tomato, cubed
- A pinch of sea salt and black pepper
- Black pepper to the taste
- 1 tablespoon almonds, chopped

Directions:

1. Heat up a pan with the oil over medium heat, add the garlic, collard greens and the other ingredients, toss well, cook for 10 minutes, divide into bowls and serve.

Nutrition: calories 130, fat 1, fiber 8, carbs 10, protein 6

172. Veggie Hash

Preparation time: 10 minutes
Cooking time: 20 minutes
Servings: 4

Ingredients:

- 1 bunch asparagus, chopped
- 2 cups radishes, halved
- ½ cup mushrooms, halved
- 3 tablespoons olive oil
- 1 shallot, chopped
- ½ cup roasted bell peppers, chopped
- 2 garlic cloves, minced
- A pinch of salt and black pepper
- 1 tablespoon chives, chopped
- 1 tablespoon sage, chopped

Directions:

1. Heat up a pan with the oil over medium heat, add the shallot and the garlic and sauté for 5 minutes.
2. Add the mushrooms and sauté for 5 minutes more.
3. Add the rest of the ingredients, toss, cook everything over medium heat for another 10 minutes, divide into bowls and serve.

Nutrition: calories 135, fat 2, fiber 4, carbs 5.4, protein 5

173. Sage Rice and Veggies

Preparation time: 10 minutes
Cooking time: 12 minutes
Servings: 4

Ingredients:

- 2 cups cauliflower rice
- 2 tablespoons olive oil
- 1 avocado, peeled, pitted and cubed
- 1 green bell pepper, chopped

- 1 green chili, chopped
- 1 tomato, cubed
- 1 zucchini, cubed
- ½ cup radishes, halved
- 1 tablespoon sage, chopped
- 1 teaspoon lime juice
- A pinch of salt and black pepper

Directions:

1. Heat up a pan with the oil over medium heat, add the green chili and the cauliflower rice and sauté for 2 minutes.
2. Add the avocado, bell pepper and the other ingredients, toss, cook over medium heat for 10 minutes more, divide between plates and serve.

Nutrition: calories 202, fat 17.1, fiber 6.3, carbs 13.2, protein 3.2

174. Cauliflower Rice and Chia Mix

Preparation time: 10 minutes
Cooking time: 15 minutes
Servings: 4

Ingredients:

- 2 cups cauliflower rice
- 2 tablespoons chia seeds
- ½ cup radishes, halved
- ½ cup chives, chopped
- 2 tablespoons avocado oil
- Zest of 1 lime, grated
- 1 cup coconut cream

Directions:

1. Heat up a pan with the oil over medium heat, add the cauliflower rice, chia seeds and the other ingredients, toss, cook for 15 minutes, divide into bowls and serve.

Nutrition: calories 220, fat 19.6, fiber 6.9, carbs 10.4, protein 4.1

175. Fruity Cauliflower Rice Bowls

Preparation time: 10 minutes
Cooking time: 0 minutes
Servings: 4

Ingredients:

- ½ cup blackberries, halved
- ½ cup grapes, halved
- 2 cups cauliflower rice, steamed
- 1 cup cherry tomatoes, halved
- 1 avocado, peeled, pitted and cubed
- 2 tablespoons avocado oil
- Juice of 1 lime

Directions:

1. In a salad bowl, combine the cauliflower rice with the berries and the other ingredients, toss, divide into smaller bowls and serve.

Nutrition: calories 138, fat 10.9, fiber 5.3, carbs 11.1, protein 1.8

176. Watercress Bowls

Preparation time: 10 minutes
Cooking time: 0 minutes
Servings: 4

Ingredients:

- 1 cup watercress
- ¼ cup grapes, halved
- ½ cup cherry tomatoes, halved
- 1 tablespoon almonds, chopped
- 1 tablespoon chives, chopped
- ¼ cup baby spinach
- 2 tablespoons avocado oil
- 2 tablespoons lime juice

Directions:

1. In a bowl, combine the watercress with the grapes and the other ingredients, toss well, divide into smaller bowls and serve.

Nutrition: calories 28, fat 1.8, fiber 1, carbs 2.7, protein 1

177. Arugula Tomato Salad

Preparation Time: 20 minutes
Servings: 2Ingredients:

- 4 tablespoons olive oil
- 1 cup cherry tomatoes, halved
- 3 cups arugula, washed, drained
- 1 small red onion, chopped
- 4 tablespoons capers, canned, drained
- 2 tablespoons basil, fresh, chopped

Directions:

Add all ingredients into mixing bowl and toss. Serve fresh and enjoy!

Nutritional Values (Per Serving):

Calories: 262
Fat: 26.7 g
Carbohydrates: 6 g
Sugar: 3.1 g
Protein: 2.1 g
Cholesterol: 0 mg

178. Spicy Asian Broccoli

Preparation Time: 25 minutes
Cooking Time: 8 minutes
Servings: 4

Ingredients:

- 2 fresh limes' juice
- 2 small broccoli, cut into florets
- 2 teaspoon chili pepper, chopped
- 2 tablespoons ginger, fresh, grated
- 4 garlic cloves, chopped
- 8 tablespoons olive oil

Directions:

1. Add your broccoli florets into your steamer and steam them for 8 minutes. Meanwhile, to prepare dressing, add lime juice, garlic, chili pepper, oil, and ginger in a small mixing bowl and combine. Add steamed broccoli in a large mixing bowl and drizzle over it the dressing. Toss to blend. Serve and enjoy!

Nutritional Values (Per Servings):

Calories: 294
Fat: 26.6 g
Carbohydrates: 9.4 g
Sugar: 3.2 g
Protein: 6.3 g
Cholesterol: 0 mg

179. Tomato Cucumber Cheese Salad

Preparation Time: 15 minutes
Servings: 2

Ingredients:

- 2 cups tomatoes, sliced
- 2 cucumbers, peeled, sliced
- 2 spring onions, sliced
- 7-ounces mozzarella cheese, chopped
- 12 black olives
- 2 teaspoons basil pesto
- 2 tablespoons extra-virgin olive oil
- 2 tablespoons basil, fresh, chopped

Directions:

In a large salad bowl, add basil pesto and cheese. Mix well. Add remaining ingredients into a bowl and toss to blend. Serve fresh and enjoy!

Nutritional Values (Per Serving):

Calories: 609
Fat: 50.5 g
Carbohydrates: 13.7 g
Sugar: 7.5 g
Protein: 27.2 g
Cholesterol: 47 mg

180. Healthy Brussels Sprout Salad

Preparation Time: 15 minutes
Servings: 1

Ingredients:

- ½ teaspoon apple cider vinegar
- 6 Brussels sprouts, washed, sliced
- 1 tablespoon Parmesan cheese, fresh, grated
- 1 teaspoon extra-virgin olive oil
- ¼ teaspoon pepper
- ¼ teaspoon sea salt

Directions:

Add all your ingredients into a large salad bowl, toss to blend. Serve and enjoy!

Nutritional Values (Per Serving):

Calories: 156
Fat: 9.6 g
Carbohydrates: 10.7 g
Sugar: 2.5 g
Cholesterol: 10 mg
Protein: 10 g

181. Radish Hash Browns

Preparation Time: 10 minutes
Cooking Time: 10 minutes
Servings: 4

Ingredients:

- 2 shallots, peeled, sliced
- ¼ teaspoon thyme
- ¼ teaspoon paprika
- 1 organic egg
- 1 tablespoon coconut flour
- 2-ounces cheddar cheese
- 1 lb. radishes, shredded

- ¼ teaspoon pepper
- ¼ teaspoon sea salt

Directions:

1. Add ingredients into a mixing bowl, except for the butter and mix well. Melt the butter in a pan over medium heat. Add a scoop of mixture into the pan and fry until lightly browned on both sides. Serve and enjoy!

Nutritional Values (Per Serving):

Calories: 176
Fat: 10.4 g
Carbohydrates: 13 g
Sugar: 4 g
Cholesterol: 116 mg
Protein: 7.9 g

182. Mashed Turnips

Preparation Time: 5 minutes
Cooking Time: 20 minutes
Servings: 4

Ingredients:

- 3 cups turnip, diced
- 2 garlic cloves, minced
- ¼ cup heavy cream
- 3 tablespoons butter, melted
- Pepper and salt to taste

Directions:

1. Bring your turnip to a boil in a saucepan over medium heat. Cook for about 20 minutes, then drain turnips and mash until smooth. Add butter, garlic, heavy cream, pepper, and salt. Mix well. Serve warm and enjoy!

Nutritional Values (Per Serving):

Calories: 132
Cholesterol: 33 mg
Protein: 1.2 g
Carbohydrates: 7 g
Fat: 11.5 g

183. Creamy Coconut Curry

Preparation Time: 15 minutes
Cooking Time: 30 minutes
Servings: 4

Ingredients:

- 1 teaspoon garlic, minced
- 1 teaspoon ginger, minced
- 2 teaspoons soy sauce
- 1 tablespoon red curry paste
- 1 cup broccoli florets
- 1 handful spinach
- ¼ of an onion, sliced
- ½ cup coconut cream
- 4 tablespoons coconut oil

Directions:

1. In a saucepan over medium-high heat, heat your coconut oil. Add your onion to the pan and cook until softened. Add garlic and cook until lightly browned. Reduce heat to medium-low, adding broccoli, stir well. Cook for about 20 minutes then add the curry paste and stir. Add spinach over broccoli and cook until wilted. Add soy sauce, ginger and coconut cream, and stir. Simmer for an additional 10 minutes. Serve hot and enjoy!

Nutritional Values (Per Serving):

Calories: 235
Cholesterol: 0 mg
Sugar: 2.1 g
Carbohydrates: 8.4 g
Fat: 22.3 g
Protein: 4.1 g

184. Broccoli Omelet

Preparation Time: 10 minutes
Cooking Time: 10 minutes
Servings: 2

Ingredients:

- 1 tablespoon extra-virgin olive oil
- 1 tablespoon parsley, chopped
- 1 cup broccoli, cooked, chopped
- 4 eggs, organic
- ½ teaspoon sea salt
- ¼ teaspoon pepper

Directions:

1. In a mixing bowl beat eggs with salt and pepper. Add broccoli to egg mixture. Heat the olive oil in a pan over medium heat. Pour your broccoli and eggs mixture into the pan and cook until set. Flip and cook other side until lightly

browned. Garnish with chopped parsley. Serve and joy!

Nutritional Values (Per Serving):

Calories: 203
Fat: 15.9 g
Cholesterol: 327 mg
Protein: 12.4 g
Carbohydrates: 4 g
Sugar: 1.5 g

185. Tomato Soup

Preparation Time: 10 minutes
Cooking Time: 20 minutes
Servings: 4

Ingredients:

- 2 tablespoons tomato paste
- 1 tablespoon garlic, minced
- 1 tablespoon extra-virgin olive oil
- 4 cups vegetable broth, low-sodium
- ½ teaspoon thyme, chopped, fresh
- 1 tablespoon basil, fresh, chopped
- 1 teaspoon oregano, fresh, chopped
- 1 cup onion, chopped
- 1 cup red bell pepper, chopped
- 3 cups tomatoes, peeled, seeded, chopped
- ¼ teaspoon pepper

Directions:

1. In the saucepan heat your oil over medium heat. Add bell pepper, garlic, onion, and tomatoes, sauté for 10 minutes. Add remaining ingredients and stir to combine. Increase the heat to high and bring to a boil. Reduce heat to low and place a lid on the pan and simmer for 10 minutes. Remove from heat. Puree the soup using a blender until smooth. Serve and enjoy!

Nutritional Values (Per Serving):

Calories: 125
Cholesterol: 0 mg
Protein: 7.2 g
Sugar: 8 g
Carbohydrates: 13.7 g
Fat: 5.4 g

186. Tofu Scramble

Preparation Time: 10 minutes
Cooking Time: 10 minutes
Servings: 4

Ingredients:

- 1 garlic clove, minced
- 1 cup mushrooms, sliced
- ½ teaspoon turmeric
- ½ teaspoon pepper
- ½ teaspoon sea salt
- 1 small onion, diced
- 1 tomato, diced
- 1 bell pepper, diced
- 1 lb. tofu, firm, drained

Directions:

1. Heat a pan over medium heat, adding mushrooms, tomato, onion, garlic and bell pepper, sauté veggies for 5 minutes. Crumble the tofu into pan over the veggies. Add pepper, turmeric, sea salt and stir well. Cook tofu for 5 minutes. Serve and enjoy!

Nutritional Values (Per Serving):

Calories: 105
Cholesterol: 0mg
Sugar: 3.7 g
Fat: 5 g
Carbohydrates: 7.6 g
Protein: 10.6 g

187. Mashed Cauliflower

Preparation Time: 10 minutes
Cooking Time: 15 minutes
Servings: 6

Ingredients:

- 2 tablespoons milk
- 4 tablespoons butter
- 2 cauliflower heads, cut into florets
- ½ teaspoon onion powder
- ½ teaspoon garlic powder
- ½ teaspoon sea salt
- ½ teaspoon pepper

Directions:

1. Add your cauliflower to a saucepan filled with enough water to cover the cauliflower. Cook cauliflower over medium heat for 15 minutes. Drain your cauliflower florets and place it in a mixing

bowl. Add remaining ingredients to the bowl. Using a blender blend until smooth. Serve and enjoy!

Nutritional Values (Per Serving):

Calories: 120
Fat: 8 g
Cholesterol: 21 mg
Sugar: 5 g
Carbohydrates: 10.9 g
Protein: 4.1 g

188. Roasted Cauliflower

Preparation Time: 10 minutes
Cooking Time: 30 minutes
Servings: 4

Ingredients:

- 1 cauliflower head, cut into florets
- 2 tablespoons fresh sage, chopped
- 1 garlic clove, minced
- 1 tablespoon extra-virgin olive oil

Directions:

1. Preheat your oven to 400°Fahrenheit. Coat a baking tray with cooking spray. Spread the cauliflower florets on prepared baking tray. Bake cauliflower in the oven for 30 minutes. Meanwhile, sauté garlic in a pan with one tablespoon of olive oil. Remove from heat and set aside. Add cauliflower, garlic, and sage to a bowl and toss to mix. Serve and enjoy!

Nutritional Values (Per Serving):

Calories: 87
Cholesterol: 0 mg
Sugar: 5.1 g
Carbohydrates: 12 g
Fat: 3.8 g
Protein: 4.3 g

189. Roasted Green Beans

Preparation Time: 15 minutes
Cooking Time: 30 minutes
Servings: 4

Ingredients:

- 1 lb. green beans, frozen
- 2 tablespoons extra-virgin olive oil
- ½ teaspoon onion powder
- ½ teaspoon garlic powder
- ½ teaspoon sea salt
- ½ teaspoon pepper

Directions:

1. Preheat your oven to 425°Fahrenheit. Spray a cooking tray with cooking spray. In a bowl add all your ingredients and mix well. Spread the green beans on the prepared baking tray and bake for 30 minutes. Serve and enjoy!

Nutritional Values (Per Serving):

Calories: 98
Sugar: 1.8 g
Carbohydrates: 8.8 g
Fat: 7.2 g
Cholesterol: 0 mg
Protein: 2.2 g

190. Creamy Cauliflower Spinach Soup

Preparation Time: 10 minutes
Cooking Time: 35 minutes
Servings: 5

Ingredients:

- 5 watercress, chopped
- 8 cups vegetable broth
- 1 lb. cauliflower, chopped
- 5-ounces spinach, fresh, chopped
- ½ cup coconut milk
- Sea salt

Directions:

1. Add cauliflower along with broth to a large pot over medium heat for 15 minutes, bring to a boil. Add spinach and watercress, cook for another 10 minutes. Remove from heat and using a blender puree the soup until smooth. Add coconut milk and stir well. Season with sea salt. Serve hot and enjoy!

Nutritional Values (Per Serving):

Calories: 153
Cholesterol: 0 mg
Sugar: 4.3 g
Fat: 8.3 g
Carbohydrates: 8.7 g
Protein: 11.9 g

191. Creamy Onion Soup

Preparation Time: 15 minutes
Cooking Time: 25 minutes
Servings: 4

Ingredients:

- 1 shallot, sliced
- Sea salt
- 1 ½ tablespoons extra-virgin olive oil
- 1 leek, sliced
- 1 garlic clove, chopped
- 4 cups vegetable stock
- 1 onion, sliced

Directions:

1. Add The Olive Oil And Vegetable Stock Into A Large Saucepan Over Medium Heat, Bring To A Boil. Add The Remaining Ingredients And Stir. Cover And Simmer For 25 Minutes. Puree Your Soup Using A Blender Until Smooth. Serve Warm And Enjoy!

Nutritional Values (Per Serving):

Calories: 90
Sugar: 4.1 G
Fat: 7.4 G
Carbohydrates: 10.1 G
Cholesterol: 0 Mg
Protein: 1 G

192. Baked Zucchini Eggplant with Cheese

Preparation Time: 15 minutes
Cooking Time: 35 minutes
Servings: 6

Ingredients:

- 3-ounces Parmesan cheese, grated
- 3 medium zucchinis, sliced
- 1 tablespoon extra-virgin olive oil
- 1 medium eggplant, sliced
- 1 cup cherry tomatoes, halved
- ¼ cup parsley, chopped
- ¼ cup basil, chopped
- 4 garlic cloves, minced
- ¼ teaspoon sea salt
- ¼ teaspoon pepper

Directions:

2. Preheat your oven to 350°Fahrenheit. Spray a baking dish with cooking spray. In a mixing bowl, add eggplant, cherry tomatoes, zucchini, olive oil, cheese, basil, garlic, salt, and pepper, toss to mix. Transfer eggplant mixture to baking dish and place into preheated oven to bake for 35 minutes. Garnish with chopped parsley. Serve and enjoy!

Nutritional Values (Per Serving):

Calories: 110
Cholesterol: 10 mg
Carbohydrates: 10.4 g
Fat: 5.8 g
Sugar: 4.8 g
Protein: 7 g

193. Zucchini Hummus

Preparation Time: 10 minutes
Cooking Time: 10 minutes
Servings: 4

Ingredients:

- 3 garlic cloves
- 4 zucchinis, halved
- 3 tablespoons tahini
- 1 tablespoon extra-virgin olive oil
- 1 tablespoon lemon juice, fresh
- 1 teaspoon cumin
- ¼ cup cilantro, chopped
- Pepper and salt to taste

Directions:

1. Place your zucchini onto the grill. Season zucchini with salt and pepper. Grill for 10 minutes. Add grilled zucchini, lemon juice, cilantro, cumin, tahini, garlic, olive oil, salt, and pepper into a blender and blend until smooth. Pour the zucchini mixture into serving bowl. Sprinkle top with paprika. Serve and enjoy!

Nutritional Values (Per Serving):

Calories: 138
Cholesterol: 0 mg
Sugar: 4.9 g
Fat: 10.1 g
Carbohydrates: 11.1 g
Protein: 4.6 g

194. Artichoke Dip

Preparation Time: 5 minutes
Cooking Time: 35 minutes

Servings: 4

Ingredients:

- 15-ounces artichoke hearts, drained
- 1 cup cheddar cheese, shredded
- 3 cups arugula, chopped
- 1 teaspoon Worcestershire sauce
- ½ cup mayonnaise
- 1 tablespoon onion, minced

Directions:

2. Preheat your oven to 350°Fahrenheit. Blend all ingredients using a blender and blend until smooth. Pour artichoke mixture into a baking dish and bake in preheated oven for 30 minutes. Serve with crackers and enjoy!

Nutritional Values (Per Serving):

Calories: 284
Fat: 19.4 g
Cholesterol: 37 mg
Sugar: 3.8 g
Carbohydrates: 19 g
Protein: 11.2 g

195. Crustless Veggie Quiche

Preparation Time: 10 minutes
Cooking Time: 30 minutes
Servings: 6

Ingredients:

- 1 cup milk
- 1 cup tomatoes, chopped
- 1 cup Parmesan cheese, grated, fresh
- 1 onion, chopped
- 1 cup zucchini, chopped
- 8 eggs, organic
- ½ teaspoon pepper
- 1 teaspoon sea salt

Directions:

3. Preheat your oven to 400°Fahrenheit. In a pan placed over medium heat, melt butter, add onion and sauté until lightly brown. Add zucchini and tomatoes to pan and sauté for 5 minutes. Beat eggs with milk, cheese, pepper and salt in a bowl. Pour egg mixture over veggies and bake in preheated oven for 30 minutes. Allow dish to cool for 10 minutes, cut into slices, serve and enjoy!

Nutritional Values (Per Serving):

Calories: 257
Sugar: 4.2 g
Fat: 16.7 g
Carbohydrates: 8.1 g
Cholesterol: 257 mg
Protein: 21.4 g

196. Avocado Cilantro Dip

Preparation Time: 10 minutes
Servings: 2

Ingredients:

- 1 cup cilantro, fresh
- 1 garlic clove
- ½ cup sour cream
- ½ teaspoon onion powder
- 1 fresh lemon juice
- 2 avocados
- ¼ teaspoon sea salt

Directions:

1. Using your blender blend ingredients, and blend until smooth. Place the mixture in your fridge to combine flavors for a few hours. Serve with crackers and enjoy!

Nutritional Values (Per Serving):

Calories: 273
Cholesterol: 13 mg
Sugar: 2.1 g
Fat: 25.7 g
Carbohydrates: 11.6 g
Protein: 3 g

197. Egg Salad

Preparation Time: 15 minutes
Servings: 4

Ingredients:

- 4 eggs, organic, hard-boiled
- 1 teaspoon Dijon mustard
- ¾ cup celery, diced
- ¼ teaspoon pepper
- 1 tablespoon dill, fresh, chopped
- ¼ cup plain yogurt
- ½ teaspoon salt

Directions:

Peel your hard-boiled eggs and dice in a large mixing bowl. Add celery, yogurt, dill, pepper, and salt. Mix well. Serve and enjoy!

Nutritional Values (Per Serving):

Calories: 80
Sugar: 1.7 g
Fat: 4.7 g
Carbohydrates: 2.6 g
Cholesterol: 165 mg
Protein: 6.8 g

198. Egg Stuffed Cucumber

Preparation Time: 15 minutes
Servings: 4

Ingredients:

- 1 large cucumber
- 2 tablespoons parsley, chopped
- 2 teaspoons Dijon mustard
- 1/8 teaspoon cayenne pepper
- ¼ cup plain yogurt
- 1 celery stalk, diced
- 4 eggs, organic, hard-boiled, peeled
- 1/8 teaspoon sea salt

Directions:

1. In A Bowl Mash Your Eggs Using A Fork. Add Into Bowl Celery, Parsley, Mustard, Yogurt, Pepper And Salt And Stir Well. Slice Cucumber In Half Then Cut Each Piece In Half Lengthwise. Scoop Out Cucumber Seeds. Stuff With Egg Mixture The Four Cucumber Boats. Sprinkle Tops With Cayenne Pepper. Serve And Enjoy!

Nutritional Values (Per Serving):

Calories: 89
Sugar: 2.8 G
Fat: 4.8 G
Carbohydrates: 4.6 G
Cholesterol: 165 Mg
Protein: 7.1 G

199. Caramelized Endive with Garlic

Preparation Time: 10 minutes
Cooking Time: 22 minutes
Servings: 8

Ingredients:

- 2 tablespoons shallots, sliced
- 4 heads endive, sliced in half
- 1 teaspoon garlic, chopped
- ¼ teaspoon pepper
- ¼ cup coconut oil
- ½ teaspoon sea salt

Directions:

1. Melt the coconut oil in a pan over low heat. Once it has melted add shallots, and garlic and cook for 2 minutes. Place endive in the pan and cook for 20 minutes on low heat. Season with salt and pepper. Serve and enjoy!

Nutritional Values (Per Serving):

Calories: 105
Cholesterol: 0 mg
Sugar: 0.6 g
Fat: 7.3 g
Carbohydrates: 9.2 g
Protein: 3.3 g

200. Roasted Cauliflower and Broccoli

Preparation Time: 10 minutes
Cooking Time: 15 minutes
Servings: 12

Ingredients:

- 4 cups broccoli, florets
- 4 cups cauliflower, florets
- 6 cloves garlic, minced
- 2/3 cup Parmesan cheese, grated, divided
- 1/3 cup extra-virgin olive oil
- Pepper and salt to taste

Directions:

1. Preheat Your Oven To 450° Fahrenheit. Spray With Cooking Spray A Baking Dish, Then Set It Aside. Add Broccoli, Cauliflower, Half Of The Cheese, Garlic, And Olive Oil Into A Mixing Bowl And Toss Well To Blend. Season With Salt And Pepper. Arrange Cauliflower And Broccoli Mixture In Your Prepared Baking Dish. Bake For 15 Minutes In Preheated Oven. Just Before Serving Add Remaining Cheese On Top. Serve Hot And Enjoy!

Nutritional Values (Per Serving):

Calories: 81

Carbohydrates: 3.1 G
Fat: 6.7 G
Sugar: 1.1 G
Cholesterol: 5 Mg
Protein: 1.9 G

201. Cheesy Grits

Preparation Time: 5 minutes
Cooking Time: 8 minutes
Servings: 4

Ingredients:

- ½ cup butter, unsalted
- ½ cup vegetable broth
- ½ cup cheddar cheese, shredded
- 8 eggs, organic
- 1 teaspoon sea salt

Directions:

1. In a mixing bowl add your eggs, broth, and sea salt, mix well. Melt butter in a pan over medium heat. Place your egg mixture into the pan and cook for 8 minutes or until the mixture thickens and curds form. Add the cheese to the pan and stir well. Remove the pan from heat. Serve warm and enjoy!

Nutritional Values (Per Serving):

Calories: 388
Cholesterol: 403 mg
Sugar: 0.9 g
Fat: 36.5 g
Carbohydrates: 1.4 g
Protein: 14.8 g

202. Creamy Squash Soup

Preparation Time: 10 minutes
Cooking Time: 35 minutes
Servings: 8

Ingredients:

- 5 tablespoons extra-virgin olive oil
- 1 lb. butternut squash, peeled, diced
- 4 cups vegetable broth
- 3 garlic cloves, minced
- 2 bay leaves
- ½ cup heavy cream
- 1 teaspoon salt

Directions:

1. Heat 1 tablespoon of olive oil in a saucepan over medium heat. Add butternut squash, garlic, salt and sauté until lightly browned. About five minutes. Add the broth, bay leaves and 4 tablespoons of olive oil into a saucepan. Bring to a boil. Simmer the squash for 30 minutes or until it is completely cooked. Discard the bay leaves. Using blender puree the soup until smooth. Add heavy cream and stir well. Serve warm and enjoy!

Nutritional Values (Per Serving):

Calories: 147
Fat: 12.3 g
Cholesterol: 10 mg
Sugar: 1.6 g
Carbohydrates: 7.7 g
Protein: 3.2 g

203. Keto Caesar Salad

Preparation Time: 15 minutes
Servings: 8

Ingredients:

- 8 cups romaine lettuce, chopped
- 2 tablespoons lemon juice, fresh
- ¼ cup Parmesan cheese, grated, fresh
- ¼ teaspoon garlic powder
- 1 tablespoon mayonnaise
- ¼ cup extra-virgin olive oil
- ¼ teaspoon pepper

Directions:

1. In mixing bowl, combine olive oil, garlic powder, lemon juice and mayonnaise. Add lettuce and cheese to the bowl. Season with pepper. Cover bowl and place in the fridge for about an hour. Just before serving toss salad and enjoy!

Nutritional Values (Per Serving):

Calories: 102
Fat: 9.3 g
Sugar: 0.8 g
Cholesterol: 5 mg
Carbohydrates: 2.3 g
Protein: 3.3 g

204. Creamy Cucumber Egg Salad

Preparation Time: 15 minutes

Servings: 4

Ingredients:

- 6 eggs, organic, hard-boiled
- 1 medium cucumber, peeled, chopped
- 1 avocado, peeled, cubed
- ¼ cup mayonnaise

½ teaspoon paprika

Directions:

Peel and dice eggs. In a bowl mix ingredients well. Serve and enjoy!

Nutritional Values (Per Serving):

Calories: 176
Fat: 12.7 g
Cholesterol: 249 mg
Sugar: 2.7 g
Carbohydrates: 7.6 g
Protein: 9.2 g

205. Roasted Broccoli with Almonds

Preparation Time: 12 minutes
Cooking Time: 20 minutes
Servings: 4

Ingredients:

- 1 ½ lbs. broccoli, cut into florets
- 1 tablespoon lemon juice
- 3 tablespoons olive oil
- 2 garlic cloves, sliced
- 3 tablespoons almonds, slivered, toasted
- ¼ teaspoon pepper
- ¼ teaspoon sea salt
- ¼ cup cheese, grated

Directions:

1. Preheat your oven to 425°Fahrenheit. Spray baking dish with cooking spray. Add broccoli, garlic, oil, pepper, and salt in a mixing bowl and toss well. Spread the broccoli in the prepared baking dish and roast in preheated oven for 20 minutes. Add lemon juice, grated cheese, almonds over broccoli, toss well. Serve hot and enjoy!

Nutritional Values (Per Serving):

Calories: 206
Fat: 15.7 g
Sugar: 3.2 g
Carbohydrates: 13 g
Cholesterol: 7 mg
Protein: 7.6 g

206. Avocado Cilantro Tomato Salad

Preparation Time: 15 minutes
Servings: 4

Ingredients:

- 4 cups cherry tomatoes, halved
- 2 avocados, diced
- Juice of 1 lime, fresh
- ¼ cup cilantro, fresh, chopped
- 1 tablespoon extra-virgin olive oil
- Pepper and salt to taste

Directions:

1. In a mixing bowl add tomatoes, avocado, and cilantro. In a small bowl, combine lime juice, olive oil, pepper, and salt. Pour lime juice mixture over salad and mix well. Enjoy!

Nutritional Values (Per Serving):

Calories: 270
Fat: 23.5 g
Cholesterol: 0 mg
Sugar: 5.4 g
Carbohydrates: 16.6 g
Protein: 3.6 g

207. Mexican Vegan Mince

Preparation Time: 5 minutes
Cooking Time: 5 minutes
Serves: 4

NUTRITIONAL VALUES:

Kcal per serve: 232
Fat: 16 g.
Protein: 17 g.
Carbs: 9 g.

INGREDIENTS:

- 400 grams Seitan Mince
- 2 cloves Garlic, minced
- 2 pieces Green Chili, chopped
- 2 tbsp Nutritional Yeast
- 1 tbsp Garam Masala
- 1 tsp Cumin Powder
- ½ tsp Salt
- 1 small Red Onion, diced
- 2 Roma Tomatoes, diced

- Cilantro for garnish
- 2 tbsp Olive Oil

DIRECTIONS:

1. Heat olive oil in a non-stick pan. Add onions, garlic, and green chili. Sautee until aromatic.
2. Add mince and stir-fry for 3-5 minutes.
3. Add nutritional yeast, garam masala, and cumin powder. Stir until well combined.
4. Season with salt to taste.
5. Garnish with fresh cilantro and serve.

208. Vegan Keto Chao Fan

Preparation Time: 10 minutes
Cooking Time: 5 minutes
Serves: 4

Nutritional Values:

Kcal per serve: 234
Fat: 6 g.
Protein: 19 g.
Carbs: 8 g.

Ingredients:

- 1 cup Textured Vegetable Protein, rehydrated
- 300 grams Broccoli, riced in a food processor
- 2 tsp minced Ginger
- 1 Shallot, minced
- 4 cloves Garlic, minced
- ¼ cup Chopped Spring Onions
- 2 tbsp Peanut Oil
- 2 tbsp Tamari

DIRECTIONS:

- Heat peanut oil in a wok.
- Sautee garlic, ginger, and shallots until aromatic.
- Add hydrated TVP and stir for 2 minutes.
- Add broccoli and stir for another minute.
- Drizzle in tamari and stir until thoroughly mixed.
- Stir in chopped spring onions.
- Season with salt and pepper as needed.

209. Keto Taco Skillet

Preparation Time: 10 minutes
Cooking Time: 5 minutes
Serves: 4

Nutritional Values:

- Kcal per serve: 171
- Fat: 11 g.
- Protein: 10 g.
- Carbs: 9 g.

Ingredients:

- 1 cup Textured Vegetable Protein
- 1 packet Taco Seasoning Mix
- 2 Tomatoes, diced
- 1 Bell Pepper, sliced into strips
- 3 cups Baby Spinach
- 2 tbsp Avocado Oil

DIRECTIONS:

1. Stir together TVP and taco seasoning mix in a bowl. Pour in 2 cups of boiling water and leave for 10 minutes.
2. Heat avocado oil in a skillet.
3. Add seasoned TVP and stir for 2-3 minutes.
4. Stir in baby spinach for another minute or until slightly wilted.
5. Season to taste with salt and pepper as needed.

210. Homemade Vegan Sausages

Preparation Time: 10 minutes
Cooking Time: 15 minutes
Serves: 4

Nutritional Values:

Kcal per serve: 287
Fat: 11 g.
Protein: 38 g.
Carbs: 9 g.

Ingredients:

- 1 cup Vital Wheat Gluten
- ¼ cup Walnuts
- ¼ cup Minced Onion
- 1 tbsp Minced Garlic
- 1 tsp Cumin Powder
- 1 tsp Smoked Paprika
- ½ tsp Dried Marjoram
- ¼ tsp Dried Oregano
- ¼ tsp Salt
- ¼ tsp Pepper

- ¼ cup Water
- 2 tbsp Olive Oil

DIRECTIONS:

1. Heat olive oil in a pan. Sautee onions and garlic until soft.
2. Add onions and garlic together with the rest of the ingredients in a food processor. Pulse into a homogenous texture.
3. Shape the mixture as desired.
4. Wrap each sausage in cling film then with aluminum foil.
5. Steam for 30 minutes.
6. Sausages may be later heated up in a pan, in the oven, or on the grill.

211. Curried Cauliflower Mash

Preparation Time: 10 min
Cooking Time: 10 min
Serves: 4

Nutritional Values:

Kcal per serve: 110
Fat: 8 g.
Protein: 4 g.
Carbs: 8 g.

Ingredients:

- 400 grams Cauliflower
- 1 liter Vegetable Stock
- ½ cup Coconut Milk
- 2 tbsp Curry Powder
- 2 tbsp Tamari

DIRECTIONS:

1. Bring vegetable stock to a boil in a pot.
2. Add cauliflower and simmer until fully tender and all the stock has evaporated.
3. Stir in coconut milk, curry, and tamari.
4. Puree with an immersion blender.
5. Simmer for 1-2 minutes or until slightly thick.
6. Season with salt as needed.

212. Keto Tofu and Spinach Casserole

Preparation Time: 5 min
Cooking Time: 5 min
Serves: 4

Nutritional Values:

Kcal per serve: 222
Fat: 15 g.
Protein: 17 g.
Carbs: 7 g.

Ingredients:

- 1 block Firm Tofu, drained, pressed, and cut into cubes
- 1 Bell Pepper, diced
- ½ White Onion, minced
- 2 tbsp Olive Oil
- 100 grams Fresh Spinach
- ½ cup Diced Tomatoes
- 1 tsp Paprika
- 1 tsp Garlic Powder
- Salt and Pepper to taste

DIRECTIONS:

1. Combine all ingredients in a pot.
2. Simmer for 5 minutes

213. Low-Carb Jambalaya

Preparation Time: 10 min
Cooking Time: 10 min
Serves: 4

Nutritional Values:

Kcal per serve: 200
Fat: 15 g.
Protein: 10 g.
Carbs: 9 g.

Ingredients:

- 200 grams Seitan Sausages, chopped
- 400 grams Cauliflower, riced
- 1 cup Vegetable Broth
- 1 Red Bell Pepper, diced
- ¼ cup Frozen Peas
- 3 cloves Garlic, minced
- ½ White Onion, diced
- 3 tbsp Olive Oil
- 1 tsp Paprika
- 1 tsp Oregano
- Salt and Pepper, to taste

DIRECTIONS:

1. Heat olive oil in a pot.
2. Add seitan and sear until slightly brown.
3. Add garlic, onions, and bell pepper. Sautee until aromatic.
4. Add cauliflower, broth, oregano, paprika, salt, and pepper.

5. Simmer for 5 minutes
6. Serve hot.

214. Chili-Garlic Edamame

Preparation Time: 5 min
Cooking Time: 10 min
Serves: 4

Nutritional Values:

Kcal per serve: 126
Fat: 7 g.
Protein: 8 g.
Carbs: 8 g.

Ingredients:

- 300 grams Edamame Pods
- 1 tbsp Olive Oil
- 3 cloves Garlic, minced
- ½ tsp Red Chili Flakes
- pinch of Salt

DIRECTIONS:

1. Steam edamame for 5 minutes.
2. Heat olive oil in a pan.
3. Sautee garlic and chili until aromatic.
4. Add in steamed edamame and stir for a minute.
5. Season with salt.

215. Vegan Potstickers

Preparation Time: 25 min
Cooking Time: 5 min
Serves: 8

Nutritional Values:

Kcal per serve: 118
Fat: 9 g.
Protein: 9 g.
Carbs: 5 g.

Ingredients:

- 250 grams Firm Tofu, pressed and crumbled
- ½ cup Diced Shiitake Mushrooms
- ¼ cup Finely Chopped Carrots
- ¼ cup Finely Chopped Spring Onions
- 1 tsp Minced Ginger
- 2 tbsp Soy Sauce
- 1 tbsp Sesame Oil
- 2 tbsp Peanut Oil, plus more for pan-frying
- 1/2 tsp Salt
- ½ tsp Pepper
- 250 grams Green Cabbage

DIRECTIONS:

1. Heat peanut oil in a pan. Sautee minced ginger and spring onions until aromatic.
2. Add tofu, mushrooms, and carrots. Sautee for 2-3 minutes.
3. Take off the heat and season with soy sauce, sesame oil, salt, and pepper.
4. Blanch cabbage leaves in boiling water to soften.
5. Lay a piece cabbage leaf on your chopping board. Fill with about a tablespoon of the tofu mixture. Fold and secure with toothpicks.
6. Repeat for remaining ingredients.
7. Heat about 2 tbsp of peanut oil in a pan. Arrange dumplings in and fry for 2 minutes over medium heat.
8. Add about a quarter cup of water into the pan and cover. Steam over low heat until all water has evaporated.

216. Eggplant Pomodoro

Preparation Time: 5 min
Cooking Time: 15 min
Serves: 4

Nutritional Values:

Kcal per serve: 101
Fat: 7 g.
Protein: 1 g.
Carbs: 9 g.

Ingredients:

- 1 Medium Eggplant, diced
- 1 cup Diced Tomatoes
- ½ cup Black Olives, sliced
- 4 cloves Garlic, minced
- 2 tbsp Red Wine Vinegar
- pinch of Red Pepper Flakes
- Salt and Pepper to taste
- 2 tbsp Olive Oil
- 4 cups Shirataki Pasta
- Fresh Parsley for garnish

DIRECTIONS:

1. Heat olive oil in a pan.
2. Sautee garlic and red pepper flakes until

aromatic.

3. Add eggplants, tomatoes, olives and red wine vinegar. Stir until eggplants are soft.
4. Toss shirataki into the pan.
5. Season with salt and pepper.
6. Garnish with chopped fresh parsley for serving.

217. Vegetable Char Siu

Preparation Time: 5 min
Cooking Time: 15 min
Serves: 4

Nutritional Values:

Kcal per serve: 100
Fat: 7 g.
Protein: 1 g.
Carbs: 9 g.

Ingredients:

- 100 grams Raw Jackfruit, deseeded and rinsed
- 100 grams Cucumbers, cut into thin strips
- 50 grams Red Bell Pepper, cut into thin strips
- 2 cloves Garlic, minced
- 1 Shallot, minced
- ¼ cup Char Siu Sauce
- ¼ cup Water
- 2 tbsp Peanut Oil

DIRECTIONS:

1. Heat peanut oil in a pan.
2. Add jackfruit and stir until slightly brown.
3. Add garlic and shallots and sautee until aromatic.
4. Add water and char siu sauce. Simmer until jackfruit is tender.
5. Shred jackfruit with forks.
6. Toss in cucumbers and bell peppers.

218. Soy Chorizo

Preparation Time: 5 min
Cooking Time: 15 min
Serves: 6

Nutritional Values:

Kcal per serve: 249
Fat: 18 g.
Protein: 14 g.
Carbs: 9 g.

Ingredients:

- 500 grams Firm Tofu, pressed and drained
- ¼ cup Soy Sauce
- ¼ cup Red Wine Vinegar
- ¼ cup Tomato Paste
- 1 tsp Paprika
- 1 tsp Chili Powder
- 1 tsp Garlic Powder
- ½ tsp Onion Powder
- 1 tsp Cumin Powder
- ½ tsp Black Pepper
- ½ tsp Salt
- ¼ cup Olive Oil

DIRECTIONS:

- Crumble tofu in a bowl. Mix in all ingredients except for the olive oil.
- Heat olive oil in a non-stick pan.
- Add tofu mix and stir for 10-15 minutes.
- Serve in tacos, wraps, burritos, or rice bowls.

219. Vietnamese "Vermicelli" Salad

Preparation Time: 5 min
Cooking Time: Serves: 4

Nutritional Values:

Kcal per serve: 249
Fat: 11 g.
Protein: 5 g.
Carbs: 8 g.

Ingredients:

- 100 grams Carrot, sliced into thin strips
- 200 grams Cucumbers, spiralized
- 2 tbsp Roasted Peanuts, roughly chopped
- ¼ cup Fresh Mint, chopped
- ¼ cup Fresh Cilantro, chopped
- 1 tbsp Stevia
- 2 tbsp Fresh Lime Juice
    - tbsp Vegan Fish Sauce
- 2 cloves Garlic, minced
- 1 Green Chili, deseeded and minced
- 2 tbsp Sesame Oil

DIRECTIONS:

1. Whisk together sugar, lime juice, sesame oil, fish sauce, minced garlic, and chopped chili. Set aside.

2. In a bowl, toss together cucumbers, carrots, cucumbers, peanuts, mint, cilantro, and prepared dressing.
3. Serve chilled.

220. Enoki Mushroom and Snow Pea Soba

Preparation Time: 5 min
Cooking Time: 5 min
Serves: 2

Nutritional Values:

Kcal per serve: 167
Fat: 14 g.
Protein: 4 g.
Carbs: 8 g.

Ingredients:

- 75 grams Snow Peas
- 100 grams Shimeji Mushrooms
- 2 tsp Minced Ginger
- ¼ cup Mirin
- 3 tbsp Light Soy Sauce
- 1 tsp Erythritol
- 1 tbsp Sesame Oil
- 1 tbsp Vegetable Oil

DIRECTIONS:

1. Heat vegetable oil in a wok. Sautee ginger until aromatic.
2. Add snow peas and stir fry for 1-2 minutes.
3. Add shimeji mushrooms and stir for another minute.
4. Add mirin, soy sauce, and erythritol.
5. Turn off the heat and drizzle in sesame oil.

221. Spicy Carrot Noodles

Preparation Time: 20 minutes
Servings: 3

Ingredients:

- 5 medium carrots
- 4 tbsp red chili pepper flakes, crushed
- 2/3 cup olive oil
- 1/4 cup vinegar
- 3 garlic cloves, chopped
- 1/4 cup fresh spring onions, chopped
- 1/2 cup basil leaves
- 1 cup fresh parsley
- Salt

Directions:

1. Add red chili flakes, oil, vinegar, garlic, spring onions, basil, and parsley in a blender and blend until smooth. Pour paste into a large bowl.
2. Add water in a large saucepan with little salt and bring to boil.
3. Peel carrots and using spiralizer make noodles.
4. Add carrot noodles in boiling water and blanch for 2 minutes or until softened.
5. Add cooked noodles in large bowl and toss mix well with paste.
6. Serve immediately and enjoy.

Nutritional Value (Amount per Serving):

Calories 450
Fat 45 g
Carbohydrates 14 g
Sugar 6 g
Protein 2 g
Cholesterol 0 mg

222. Creamy Zucchini Quiche

Preparation Time: 120 minutes
Servings: 8

Ingredients:

- 2 lbs zucchini, thinly sliced
- 1 1/2 cup almond milk
- 2 large eggs
- 2 cups cheddar cheese, shredded
- Pepper
- Salt

Directions:

1. Preheat the oven to 375 F.
2. Season zucchini with pepper and salt and set aside for 30 minutes.
3. In a large bowl, beat eggs with almond milk, pepper, and salt.
4. Add shredded cheddar cheese and stir well.
5. Spray quiche pan with cooking spray and arrange zucchini slices in quiche pan.
6. Pour egg and milk mixture over zucchini

the sprinkle shredded cheese.
7. Bake in preheated oven for 60 minutes or until quiche is lightly golden brown.
8. Serve warm and enjoy.

Nutritional Value (Amount per Serving):

Calories 253
Fat 21 g
Carbohydrates 6 g
Sugar 3 g
Protein 11 g
Cholesterol 76 mg

223. Simple Garlic Cauliflower Couscous

Preparation Time: 30 minutes
Servings: 3

Ingredients:

- 1 medium cauliflower head, cut into florets
- 2 tsp parsley, dried
- 2 tsp garlic, dried
- Salt

Directions:

1. Add cauliflower florets into the food processor and process until it looks like couscous.
2. Heat large pan over medium-low heat.
3. Add cauliflower couscous, parsley, and garlic in the pan and cook until softened.
4. Stir well and season with salt.
5. Serve and enjoy.

Nutritional Value (Amount per Serving):

Calories 51
Fat 0.2 g
Carbohydrates 10 g
Sugar 4 g
Protein 3 g
Cholesterol 0 mg

224. Gluten Free Asparagus Quiche

Preparation Time: 1 hour 10 minutes
Servings: 6

Ingredients:

- 5 eggs, beaten
- 1 cup Swiss cheese, shredded
- 1/4 tsp thyme
- 1/4 tsp white pepper
- 1 cup almond milk
- 15 asparagus spears, cut woody ends and cut asparagus in half
- 1/4 tsp salt

Directions:

1. Preheat the oven to 350 F.
2. Spray a quiche dish with cooking spray and set aside.
3. In a bowl, beat together eggs, thyme, white pepper, almond milk, and salt.
4. Arrange asparagus in prepared quiche dish then pour egg mixture over asparagus.
5. Sprinkle shredded cheese all over asparagus and egg mixture.
6. Place in preheated oven and bake for 60 minutes.
7. Cut quiche into slices and serve.

Nutritional Value (Amount per Serving):

Calories 225
Fat 18 g
Carbohydrates 5 g
Sugar 3 g
Protein 11 g
Cholesterol 153 mg

225. Mini Vegetable Quiche

Preparation Time: 30 minutes
Servings: 12

Ingredients:

- 7 eggs
- 1/4 cup onion, chopped
- 1/4 cup mushroom, diced
- 1/4 cup bell pepper, diced
- 3/4 cup cheddar cheese, shredded
- 10 oz frozen spinach, chopped

Directions:

1. Line muffin cups with aluminum foil cups set aside.
2. Add all ingredients into the large bowl and beat lightly to combine.
3. Pour egg mixture into the prepared muffin tray.
4. Bake at 350 F for 20 minutes.
5. Serve warm and enjoy.

Nutritional Value (Amount per Serving):

Calories 73
Fat 5 g
Carbohydrates 1 g
Sugar 0.6 g
Protein 5 g
Cholesterol 103 mg

226. Simple Roasted Radishes

Preparation Time: 45 minutes
Servings: 2

Ingredients:

- 3 cups radish, clean and halved
- 3 tbsp olive oil
- 2 tbsp fresh rosemary, chopped
- 10 black peppercorns, crushed
- 2 tsp sea salt

Directions:

1. Preheat the oven to 425 F.
2. Add radishes, salt, peppercorns, rosemary, and 2 tablespoons of olive oil in a bowl and toss well.
3. Pour radishes mixture into the baking sheet and bake in preheated oven for 30 minutes.
4. Heat remaining olive oil in a pan over medium heat.
5. Add baked radishes in the pan and sauté for 2 minutes.
6. Serve immediately and enjoy.

Nutritional Value (Amount per Serving):

Calories 220
Fat 21 g
Carbohydrates 8 g
Sugar 3 g
Protein 1 g
Cholesterol 0 mg

227. Coconut Broccoli Cheese Loaf

Preparation Time: 35 minutes
Servings: 5

Ingredients:

- 5 eggs, lightly beaten
- 2 tsp baking powder
- 3 1/1 tbsp coconut flour
- 3/4 cup broccoli florets, chopped
- 1 cup cheddar cheese, shredded
- 1 tsp salt

Directions:

1. Preheat the oven to 350 F.
2. Spray a loaf pan with cooking spray and set aside.
3. Add all ingredients into the bowl and mix well.
4. Pour egg mixture into the prepared loaf pan and bake in preheated oven for 30 minutes.
5. Cut loaf into the slices and serve.

Nutritional Value (Amount per Serving):

Calories 209
Fat 13 g
Carbohydrates 8 g
Sugar 1 g
Protein 13 g
Cholesterol 187 mg

228. Green Parsley Broccoli Cauliflower Puree

Preparation Time: 35 minutes
Servings: 4

Ingredients:

- 1 1/3 small broccoli, cut into florets
- 4 tbsp fresh parsley
- 1 small cauliflower, cut into florets
- 2 cups vegetable broth
- 4 tbsp butter
- 1 tsp sea salt

Directions:

1. Add cauliflower and broccoli in steamer and steam for 15 minutes.
2. Add steamed cauliflower and broccoli in a blender with butter, broth, and parsley and blend until smooth.
3. Season puree with salt and serve.

Nutritional Value (Amount per Serving):

Calories 154
Fat 12 g
Carbohydrates 7 g
Sugar 2 g
Protein 5 g
Cholesterol 31 mg

229. Healthy Braised Garlic Kale

Preparation Time: 50 minutes
Servings: 4

Ingredients:

- 10 oz kale, stems removed and chopped
- 2 cups vegetable stock
- 4 tbsp coconut oil
- 1 tsp chili pepper flakes, dried
- 1 medium onion, sliced
- 4 garlic cloves, minced
- 1 tsp sea salt

Directions:

1. Heat coconut oil in a pan over medium heat.
2. Once the oil is hot then add onion, garlic and chili pepper flakes and sauté until lightly brown.
3. Pour vegetable stock and stir well.
4. Now add chopped kale and season with salt. Stir well.
5. Cover pan with lid and cook on low heat for 40 minutes.
6. Serve and enjoy.

Nutritional Value (Amount per Serving):

Calories 172
Fat 14 g
Carbohydrates 11 g
Sugar 1 g
Protein 2 g
Cholesterol 0 mg

230. Lime Basil Cucumbers

Preparation Time: 15 minutes
Servings: 4

Ingredients:

- 2 medium cucumber, remove seeds and diced
- 1 tsp basil leaves, chopped
- 1 tsp fresh lime juice
- 2 tsp turmeric powder
- 2 tbsp coconut oil
- 1/4 tsp sea salt

Directions:

1. Heat coconut oil in a pan over medium heat.
2. Once the oil is hot then, add turmeric powder and basil leaves and stir for 1 minute.
3. Now add cucumber, lime juice, and salt. Stir well.
4. Serve and enjoy.

Nutritional Value (Amount per Serving):

Calories 85
Fat 7 g
Carbohydrates 6 g
Sugar 2 g
Protein 1 g
Cholesterol 0 mg

231. Yummy Cheese Grits

Preparation Time: 10 minutes
Servings: 4

Ingredients:

- 8 large eggs
- 1/2 cup cheddar cheese, shredded
- 1/2 cup butter
- 1/2 cup vegetable broth
- 1 tsp sea salt

Directions:

1. In a bowl, whisk together eggs, salt, and broth.
2. Melt butter in a saucepan over medium heat.
3. Add egg mixture to the saucepan and cook until thickens.
4. Once the mixture is thickened and curds formed then add shredded cheese and stir well to combine.
5. Serve warm and enjoy.

Nutritional Value (Amount per Serving):

Calories 408
Fat 37 g
Carbohydrates 1 g
Sugar 1 g
Protein 17 g
Cholesterol 448 mg

232. Creamy Egg Salad

Preparation Time: 15 minutes
Servings: 4

Ingredients:

- 12 eggs, hard-boiled
- 1 scallion, sliced
- 1/2 cup celery, diced
- 1 tbsp Dijon mustard
- 3/4 cup mayonnaise
- Pepper
- Salt

Directions:

1. Separate egg yolks and egg whites.
2. Chop egg whites into the small pieces.
3. Add egg yolks, salt, mustard, and mayonnaise in a blender and blend until smooth.
4. Add chopped egg whites, scallion and celery in a large bowl then add egg yolk mixture and mix well.
5. Season with pepper and salt.
6. Serve and enjoy.

Nutritional Value (Amount per Serving):

Calories 367
Fat 28 g
Carbohydrates 12 g
Sugar 4 g
Protein 17 g
Cholesterol 503 mg

233. Simple Cheese olives Tomato Salad

Preparation Time: 15 minutes
Servings: 4

Ingredients:

- 1 cup kalamata olives, pitted
- 1 cup mozzarella cheese, chopped
- 1 cup cherry tomatoes, halved
- Pepper
- Salt

Directions:

1. Add olives, cheese, and tomatoes in a bowl and toss well.
2. Season with pepper and salt.
3. Serve and enjoy.

Nutritional Value (Amount per Serving):

Calories 67
Fat 5 g
Carbohydrates 4 g
Sugar 1 g
Protein 2 g
Cholesterol 4 mg

234.Argugula Mushroom Salad

Preparation Time: 20 minutes
Servings: 4

Ingredients:

- 10 oz mushrooms, clean and cut the steam
- 10 sun-dried tomatoes, chopped
- 4 cups arugula
- 2 tsp fresh rosemary, chopped
- 2 garlic cloves, minced
- 1 tbsp vinegar
- 6 tbsp olive oil
- 1/2 tsp sea salt

Directions:

1. In a small bowl, combine together olive oil, vinegar, salt, rosemary, and garlic.
2. Add mushroom in a bowl then pour olive oil mixture over mushrooms and set aside for 1 hour.
3. Preheat the oven to 480 F.
4. Place mushrooms on rack and grill in preheated oven for 10 minutes.
5. Place arugula on serving dish then place grilled mushrooms and chopped tomatoes.
6. Serve and enjoy.

Nutritional Value (Amount per Serving):

Calories 261
Fat 22 g
Carbohydrates 14 g
Sugar 9 g
Protein 5 g
Cholesterol 0 mg

235. Simple Grilled Mushrooms

Preparation Time: 25 minutes
Servings: 4

Ingredients:

- 40 cremini mushrooms
- 1 tsp sea salt
- 1/2 tsp black pepper
- 8 tbsp olive oil

Directions:

1. Preheat the oven to 450 F.
2. Add mushroom and olive oil in a bowl and toss well.
3. Season mushrooms with pepper and salt.
4. Place mushrooms on the rack and grilled in preheated oven for 15 minutes.
5. Serve and enjoy.

Nutritional Value (Amount per Serving):

Calories 295
Fat 28 g
Carbohydrates 8 g
Sugar 3 g
Protein 5 g
Cholesterol 0 mg

236. Healthy Green Salad with Mayonnaise

Preparation Time: 20 minutes
Servings: 2

Ingredients:

- 2 tbsp mayonnaise
- 2 cups watercress
- 2 cups iceberg lettuce, chopped
- 2 small Bok Choy, chopped
- 2 cups arugula
- Pepper

Directions:

1. Add all ingredients to the bowl and toss well.
2. Serve and enjoy.

Nutritional Value (Amount per Serving):

Calories 127
Fat 6 g
Carbohydrates 14 g
Sugar 4 g
Protein 8 g
Cholesterol 4 mg

SIDES

237. Basil Zucchinis and Eggplants

Preparation time: 10 minutes
Cooking time: 20 minutes
Servings: 4

Ingredients:

- 1 tablespoon olive oil
- 2 zucchinis, sliced
- 1 eggplant, roughly cubed
- 2 scallions, chopped
- 1 tablespoon sweet paprika
- Juice of 1 lime
- 1 teaspoon fennel seeds, crushed
- Salt and black pepper to the taste
- 1 tablespoon basil, chopped

Directions:

1. Heat up a pan with the oil over medium heat, add the scallions and fennel seeds and sauté for 5 minutes.
2. Add zucchinis, eggplant and the other ingredients, toss, cook over medium heat for 15 minutes more, divide between plates and serve as a side dish.

Nutrition: calories 97, fat 4, fiber 2, carbs 6, protein 2

238. Chard and Peppers Mix

Preparation time: 10 minutes
Cooking time: 20 minutes
Servings: 4

Ingredients:

- 2 tablespoons avocado oil
- 2 spring onions, chopped
- 2 tablespoons tomato passata
- 2 tablespoons capers, drained
- 2 green bell peppers, cut into strips
- 1 teaspoon turmeric powder
- A pinch of cayenne pepper
- Juice of 1 lime
- Salt and black pepper to the taste
- 1 bunch red chard, torn

Directions:

1. Heat up a pan with the oil over medium heat, add the spring onions, capers, turmeric and cayenne and sauté for 5 minutes.
2. Add the peppers, chard and the other ingredients, toss, cook over medium heat for 15 minutes more, divide between plates and serve.

Nutrition: calories 119, fat 7, fiber 3, carbs 7, protein 2

239. Balsamic Kale

Preparation time: 10 minutes
Cooking time: 20 minutes
Servings: 4

Ingredients:

- 1 tablespoon balsamic vinegar
- 2 tablespoons walnuts, chopped
- 1 pound kale, torn
- 1 tablespoon olive oil
- 1 teaspoon cumin, ground
- 1 teaspoon chili powder
- 3 garlic cloves, minced
- 2 tablespoons cilantro, chopped

Directions:

1. Heat up a pan with the oil over medium heat, add the garlic and the walnuts and cook for 2 minutes.
2. Add the kale, vinegar and the other ingredients, toss, cook over medium heat for 18 minutes more, divide between plates and serve as a side.

Nutrition: calories 170, fat 11, fiber 3, carbs 7, protein 7

240. Mustard Cabbage Salad

Preparation time: 10 minutes
Cooking time: 0 minutes
Servings: 4

Ingredients:

- 1 green cabbage head, shredded
- 1 red cabbage head, shredded
- 2 tablespoons avocado oil
- 2 tablespoons mustard
- 1 tablespoon balsamic vinegar

- 1 teaspoon hot paprika
- Salt and black pepper to the taste
- 1 tablespoon dill, chopped

Directions:

1. In a bowl, mix the cabbage with the oil, mustard and the other ingredients, toss, divide between plates and serve as a side salad.

Nutrition: calories 150, fat 3, fiber 2, carbs 2, protein 7

241. Cabbage and Green Beans

Preparation time: 10 minutes
Cooking time: 15 minutes
Servings: 4

Ingredients:

- 1 green cabbage head, shredded
- 2 cups green beans, trimmed and halved
- 2 tablespoons olive oil
- 1 teaspoon sweet paprika
- 1 teaspoon cumin, ground
- Salt and black pepper to the taste
- 1 tablespoon chives, chopped

Directions:

1. Heat up a pan with the oil over medium heat, add the cabbage and the paprika and sauté for 2 minutes.
2. Add the green beans and the other ingredients, toss, cook over medium heat fro 13 minutes more, divide between plates and serve.

Nutrition: calories 200, fat 4, fiber 2, carbs 3, protein 7

242. Green Beans, Avocado and Scallions

Preparation time: 10 minutes
Cooking time: 20 minutes
Servings: 4

Ingredients:

- 1 pound green beans, trimmed and halved
- 1 avocado, peeled, pitted and sliced
- 4 scallions, chopped
- 2 tablespoons olive oil
- 1 tablespoon lime juice
- Salt and black pepper to the taste
- A handful cilantro, chopped

Directions:

1. Heat up a pan with the oil over medium heat, add the scallions and sauté for 2 minutes.
2. Add the green beans, lime juice and the other ingredients, toss, cook over medium heat for 18 minutes, divide between plates and serve.

Nutrition: calories 200, fat 5, fiber 2,3, carbs 1, protein 3

243. Creamy Cajun Zucchinis

Preparation time: 10 minutes
Cooking time: 20 minutes
Servings: 4

Ingredients:

- 1 pound zucchinis, roughly cubed
- 2 tablespoons olive oil
- 4 scallions, chopped
- Salt and black pepper to the taste
- 1 teaspoon Cajun seasoning
- A pinch of cayenne pepper
- 1 cup coconut cream
- 1 tablespoon dill, chopped

Directions:

1. Heat up a pan with the oil over medium heat, add the scallions, cayenne and Cajun seasoning, stir and sauté for 5 minutes.
2. Add the zucchinis and the other ingredients, toss, cook over medium heat for 15 minutes more, divide between plates and serve.

Nutrition: calories 200, fat 2, fiber 1, carbs 5, protein 8

244. Herbed Zucchinis and Olives

Preparation time: 10 minutes
Cooking time: 20 minutes
Servings: 4

Ingredients:

- 1 cup kalamata olives, pitted
- 1 cup green olives, pitted
- 1 pound zucchinis, roughly cubed
- 1 tablespoon rosemary, chopped
- 1 tablespoon basil, chopped
- 1 tablespoon cilantro, chopped
- 2 tablespoons olive oil

- 3 garlic cloves, minced
- 1 tablespoon lemon juice
- 1 teaspoon lemon zest, grated
- 1 tablespoon sweet paprika
- A pinch of salt and black pepper

Directions:

1. Heat up a pan with the oil over medium heat, add the garlic, lemon zest and paprika and sauté for 2 minutes.
2. Add the olives, zucchinis and the other ingredients, toss, cook over medium heat for 18 minutes more, divide between plates and serve.

Nutrition: calories 200, fat 20, fiber 4, carbs 3, protein 1

245. Veggie Pan

Preparation time: 10 minutes
Cooking time: 20 minutes
Servings: 4

Ingredients:

- 1 cup green beans, trimmed and halved
- 1 cup cherry tomatoes, halved
- 1 zucchini, roughly cubed
- 1 red bell pepper, cut into strips
- 1 eggplant, cubed
- 3 scallions, chopped
- 2 tablespoons olive oil
- 2 tablespoons lime juice
- Salt and black pepper to the taste
- 1 teaspoon chili powder
- 1 tablespoon cilantro, chopped
- 3 garlic cloves, minced

Directions:

1. Heat up a pan with the oil over medium heat, add the scallions, chili powder and the garlic and sauté for 5 minutes.
2. Add the green beans, tomatoes and the other ingredients, toss, cook over medium heat for 15 minutes.
3. Divide the mix between plates and serve as a side dish.

Nutrition: calories 137, fat 7.7, fiber 7.1, carbs 18.1, protein 3.4

246. Masala Brussels Sprouts

Preparation time: 10 minutes
Cooking time: 35 minutes
Servings: 4

Ingredients:

- 1 pound Brussels sprouts, trimmed and halved
- Salt and black pepper to the taste
- 1 tablespoon garam masala
- 2 tablespoons olive oil
- 1 tablespoon caraway seeds

Directions:

- In a roasting pan, combine the sprouts with the masala and the other ingredients, toss and bake at 400 degrees F for 35 minutes.
- Divide the mix between plates and serve.

Nutrition: calories 115, fat 7.6, fiber 4.9, carbs 11.2, protein 4.2

247. Nutmeg Green Beans

Preparation time: 10 minutes
Cooking time: 30 minutes
Servings: 4

Ingredients:

- 2 tablespoons olive oil
- ½ cup coconut cream
- 1 pound green beans, trimmed and halved
- 1 teaspoon nutmeg, ground
- A pinch of salt and cayenne pepper
- ½ teaspoon onion powder
- ½ teaspoon garlic powder
- 2 tablespoons parsley, chopped

Directions:

1. Heat up a pan with the oil over medium heat, add the green beans, nutmeg and the other ingredients, toss, cook for 30 minutes, divide the mix between plates and serve.

Nutrition: calories 100, fat 13, fiber 2.3, carbs 5.1, protein 2

248. Peppers and Celery Sauté

Preparation time: 10 minutes
Cooking time: 15 minutes
Servings: 4

Ingredients:

- 1 red bell pepper, cut into medium chunks
- 1 green bell pepper, cut into medium chunks
- 1 celery stalk, chopped
- 2 scallions, chopped
- 2 tablespoons olive oil
- Salt and black pepper to the taste
- 1 tablespoons parsley, chopped
- 1 teaspoon cumin, ground
- 2 garlic cloves, minced

Directions:

2. Heat up a pan with the oil over medium heat, add the scallions, garlic and cumin and sauté for 5 minutes.
3. Add the peppers, celery and the other ingredients, toss, cook over medium heat for 10 minutes more, divide between plates and serve.

Nutrition: calories 87, fat 2.4, fiber 3, carbs 5, protein 4

249.Oregano Zucchinis and Broccoli

Preparation time: 10 minutes
Cooking time: 20 minutes
Servings: 4

Ingredients:

- 1 pound zucchinis, sliced
- 1 cup broccoli florets
- Salt and black pepper to the taste
- 2 tablespoons avocado oil
- 2 tablespoons chili powder
- ½ teaspoon oregano, dried
- 1 and ½ tablespoons coriander, chopped

Directions:

1. Heat up a pan with the oil over medium heat, add the zucchinis, broccoli and the other ingredients, toss, cook over medium heat for 20 minutes, divide between plates and serve as a side dish.

Nutrition: calories 140, fat 2, fiber 1, carbs 1, protein 6

250. Spinach Mash

Preparation time: 10 minutes
Cooking time: 15 minutes
Servings: 4

Ingredients:

- 1 pound spinach leaves
- 3 scallions, chopped
- 2 garlic cloves, minced
- ¼ cup coconut cream
- 2 tablespoons olive oil
- Salt and black pepper to the taste
- ½ tablespoon chives, chopped

Directions:

1. Heat up a pan with the oil over medium heat, add the scallions and the garlic and sauté for 2 minutes.
2. Add the spinach and the other ingredients except the chives, toss, cook over medium heat for 13 minutes, blend using an immersion blender, divide between plates, sprinkle the chives on top and serve.

Nutrition: calories 190, fat 16, fiber 7, carbs 3, protein 5

251. Jalapeno Zucchinis Mix

Preparation time: 10 minutes
Cooking time: 30 minutes
Servings: 4

Ingredients:

- 1 pound zucchinis, sliced
- ¼ cup green onions, chopped
- ½ cup cashew cheese, shredded
- 1 cup coconut cream
- 2 jalapenos, chopped
- Salt and black pepper to the taste
- 2 tablespoons chives, chopped

Directions:

1. In a baking dish, combine the zucchinis with the onions and the other ingredients, toss, bake at 390 degrees F for 30 minutes, divide between plates and serve.

Nutrition: calories 120, fat 4.2, fiber 2.3, carbs 3, protein 6

252. Coconut and Tomatoes Mix

Preparation time: 5 minutes
Cooking time: 12 minutes
Servings: 4

Ingredients:

- 1 pound tomatoes, cut into wedges

- 1 cup coconut, unsweetened and shredded
- 2 tablespoons coconut oil, melted
- 1 tablespoon chives, chopped
- 1 teaspoon coriander, ground
- 1 teaspoon fennel seeds
- Salt and black pepper to the taste

Directions:

1. Heat up a pan with the oil over medium heat, add the coriander and fennel seeds and cook for 2 minutes.
2. Add the tomatoes and the other ingredients, toss, cook over medium heat for 10 minutes, divide between plates and serve.

Nutrition: calories 152, fat 13.8, fiber 3.4, carbs 7.7, protein 1.8

253. Mushroom Rice

Preparation time: 10 minutes
Cooking time: 20 minutes
Servings: 4

Ingredients:

- 2 tablespoons olive oil
- 1 cup mushrooms, sliced
- 2 cups cauliflower rice
- 2 tablespoons lime juice
- 2 tablespoons almonds, sliced
- 1 cup veggie stock
- Salt and black pepper to the taste
- ½ teaspoon garlic powder
- 1 tablespoon parsley, chopped

Directions:

1. Heat up a pan with the oil over medium heat, add the mushrooms and the almonds and sauté for 5 minutes.
2. Add the cauliflower rice and the other ingredients, toss, cook over medium heat for 15 minutes more, divide between plates and serve.

Nutrition: calories 124, fat 2.4, fiber 1.5, carbs 2, protein 1.2

254. Cucumber and Cauliflower Mix

Preparation time: 10 minutes
Cooking time: 12 minutes
Servings: 4

Ingredients:

- 1 cucumber, cubed
- 1 pound cauliflower florets
- 1 spring onion, chopped
- 2 tablespoons avocado oil
- 1 tablespoon balsamic vinegar
- ¼ teaspoon red pepper flakes
- Salt and black pepper to the taste
- 1 tablespoon thyme, chopped

Directions:

1. Heat up a pan with the oil over medium heat, add the spring onions and the pepper flakes and sauté for 2 minutes.
2. Add the cucumber and the other ingredients, toss, cook over medium heat for 10 minutes more, divide between plates and serve.

Nutrition: calories 53, fat 1.2, fiber 3.9, carbs 9.9, protein 3

255. Mushroom and Spinach Mix

Preparation time: 10 minutes
Cooking time: 15 minutes
Servings: 4

Ingredients:

- 1 cup white mushrooms, sliced
- 3 cups baby spinach
- 2 tablespoons olive oil
- Salt and black pepper to the taste
- 2 tablespoons garlic, minced
- 2 tablespoons pine nuts, toasted
- 1 tablespoon walnuts, chopped

Directions:

1. Heat up a pan with the oil over medium heat, add the garlic, pine nuts and the walnuts and cook for 5 minutes.
2. Add the mushrooms and the other ingredients, toss, cook over medium heat for 10 minutes, divide between plates and serve.

Nutrition: calories 116, fat 11.3, fiber 1.1, carbs 3.5, protein 2.5

256. Garlic Cauliflower Rice

Preparation time: 10 minutes
Cooking time: 20 minutes
Servings: 4

Ingredients:

- 2 cups cauliflower rice
- 2 tablespoons almonds, chopped
- 1 tablespoon olive oil
- 2 green onions, chopped
- 4 garlic cloves, minced
- 3 tablespoons chives, chopped
- ½ cup vegetable stock

Directions:

1. Heat up a pan with the oil over medium heat, add the garlic and green onions and sauté for 5 minutes.
2. Add the cauliflower rice and the other ingredients, toss, cook over medium heat for 15 minutes, divide between plates and serve.

Nutrition: calories 142, fat 6.1, fiber 1.2, carbs 3, protein 1.2

257. Grapes and Tomato Salad

Preparation time: 10 minutes
Cooking time: 0 minutes
Servings: 4

Ingredients:

- 2 cups green grapes, halved
- 1 pound cherry tomatoes, halved
- 2 tablespoons olive oil
- 4 spring onions, chopped
- 1 teaspoon cumin, ground
- 1 teaspoon rosemary, dried
- 1 tablespoon balsamic vinegar
- 1 tablespoon chives, chopped

Directions:

1. In a bowl, combine the grapes with the tomatoes and the other ingredients, toss and serve as a side salad.

Nutrition: calories 140, fat 4, fiber 6, carbs 3.4, protein 4

258. Ginger Mushrooms

Preparation time: 10 minutes
Cooking time: 30 minutes
Servings: 4

Ingredients:

2. 2 tablespoons coconut oil, melted
3. 1 pound baby mushrooms
4. Salt and black pepper to the taste
5. 1 tablespoon chives, chopped
6. 2 tablespoons ginger, grated
7. 1 teaspoon garlic powder

Directions:

1. In a roasting pan, combine the mushrooms with the oil and the other ingredients, toss and bake at 390 degrees F for 30 minutes.
2. Divide the mix between plates and serve as a side dish.

Nutrition: calories 152, fat 12, fiber 5, carbs 6, protein 4

259. Tomato and Walnuts Vinaigrette

Preparation time: 10 minutes
Cooking time: 0 minutes
Serving: 4

Ingredients:

- 1 pound cherry tomatoes, halved
- 1 tablespoon walnuts, chopped
- 1 tablespoon balsamic vinegar
- 1 garlic clove, minced
- 1 teaspoon lemon juice
- 2 teaspoons smoked paprika
- ¼ teaspoon coriander, ground
- Salt and black pepper to the taste
- 1 tablespoon parsley, chopped

Directions:

In a bowl, combine the tomatoes with the walnuts and the other ingredients, toss well, and serve as a side dish.

Nutrition: calories 160, fat 12, fiber 4, carbs 6, protein 4

260. Creamy Eggplant Mix

Preparation time: 10 minutes
Cooking time: 15 minutes
Servings: 4

Ingredients:

- 1 pound eggplants, roughly cubed
- 2 scallions, chopped
- 2 tablespoon avocado oil
- 2 teaspoons garlic, minced
- ½ cup coconut cream
- 2 teaspoons chili paste

Directions:

1. Heat up a pan with the oil over medium heat, add the scallions and the garlic and sauté for 2 minutes.
2. Add the eggplants and the other ingredients, toss, cook over medium heat for 13 minutes more, divide between plates and serve as a side dish.

Nutrition: calories 142, fat 7, fiber 4, carbs 5, protein 3

261. Chives Kale and Tomato

Preparation time: 10 minutes
Cooking time: 20 minutes
Servings: 4

Ingredients:

- 1 pound kale, torn
- ½ pound tomatoes, cut into wedges
- 2 tablespoons avocado oil
- 1 teaspoon chili powder
- 1 teaspoon garam masala
- Salt and black pepper to the taste
- ¼ teaspoon coriander, ground
- A pinch of cayenne pepper
- 1 teaspoon mustard powder
- ¼ cup chives, chopped

Directions:

1. In a roasting pan, combine the kale with the tomatoes and the other ingredients, toss and bake at 380 degrees F for 20 minutes.
2. Divide the mix between plates and serve as a side dish.

Nutrition: calories 128, fat 2.3, fiber 1, carbs 3.3, protein 4

262. Cauliflower Salad

Preparation time: 10 minutes
Cooking time: 0 minutes
Servings: 4

Ingredients:

- 1 pound cauliflower florets, blanched
- 1 avocado, peeled, pitted and cubed
- 1 cup kalamata olives, pitted and halved
- Salt and black pepper to the taste
- 1 cup spring onions, chopped
- 1 tablespoon lime juice
- 1 tablespoon chives, chopped

Directions:

1. In a bowl, combine the cauliflower florets with the avocado and the other ingredients, toss and serve as a side salad.

Nutrition: calories 211, fat 20, fiber 2, carbs 3, protein 4

263. Coconut Rice

Preparation time: 10 minutes
Cooking time: 20 minutes
Servings: 4

Ingredients:

- 2 cups cauliflower rice
- 3 cups vegetable stock
- Salt and black pepper to the taste
- ¼ cup coconut milk
- 2 tablespoons coconut, unsweetened and shredded
- 1 tablespoon chives, chopped

Directions:

1. In a pot, combine the cauliflower rice with the stock, salt, pepper and the other ingredients, toss, bring to a simmer and cook over medium heat for 20 minutes.
2. Divide the rice between plates and serve as a side dish.

Nutrition: calories 51, fat 5.9, fiber 0.6, carbs 2.7, protein 0.5

264. Turmeric Carrots

Preparation time: 10 minutes
Cooking time: 40 minutes
Servings: 4

Ingredients:

- 1 pound baby carrots, peeled
- 1 tablespoon olive oil
- 2 spring onions, chopped
- 2 tablespoons balsamic vinegar
- 2 garlic cloves, minced
- 1 teaspoon turmeric powder
- 1 tablespoon chives, chopped
- ¼ teaspoon cayenne pepper
- A pinch of salt and black pepper

Directions:

1. Spread the carrots on a baking sheet lined

with parchment paper, add the oil, the spring onions and the other ingredients, toss and bake at 380 degrees F for 40 minutes.
2. Divide the carrots between plates and serve.

Nutrition: calories 79, fat 3.8, fiber 3.7, carbs 10.9, protein 1

265. Spinach Mix

Preparation time: 10 minutes
Cooking time: 12 minutes
Servings: 4

Ingredients:

- 1 pound baby spinach
- 1 yellow onion, chopped
- 1 tablespoon olive oil
- 1 tablespoon lemon juice
- 2 garlic cloves, minced
- A pinch of cayenne pepper
- ¼ teaspoon smoked paprika
- A pinch of salt and black pepper

Directions:

1. Heat up a pan with the oil over medium-high heat, add the onion and the garlic and sauté for 2 minutes.
2. Add the spinach and the other ingredients, toss, cook over medium heat for 10 minutes, divide between plates and serve as a side dish.

Nutrition: calories 71, fat 4, fiber 3.2, carbs 7.4, protein 3.7

266. Orange Carrots

Preparation time: 5 minutes
Cooking time: 25 minutes
Servings: 4

Ingredients:

- 1 pound carrots, peeled and roughly sliced
- 1 yellow onion, chopped
- 1 tablespoon olive oil
- Zest of 1 orange, grated
- Juice of 1 orange
- 1 orange, peeled and cut into segments
- 1 tablespoon rosemary, chopped
- A pinch of salt and black pepper

Directions:

1. Heat up a pan with the oil over medium-high heat, add the onion and sauté for 5 minutes.
2. Add the carrots, the orange zest and the other ingredients, toss, cook over medium heat for 20 minutes more, divide between plates and serve.

Nutrition: calories 140, fat 3.9, fiber 5, carbs 26.1, protein 2.1

267. Endive Sauté

Preparation time: 5 minutes
Cooking time: 15 minutes
Servings: 4

Ingredients:

- 3 endives, shredded
- 1 tablespoon olive oil
- 4 scallions, chopped
- ½ cup tomato sauce
- 2 garlic cloves, minced
- A pinch of sea salt and black pepper
- 1/8 teaspoon turmeric powder
- 1 tablespoon chives, chopped

Directions:

1. Heat up a pan with the oil over medium heat, add the scallions and the garlic and sauté for 5 minutes.
2. Add the endives and the other ingredients, toss, cook everything for 10 minutes more, divide between plates and serve as a side dish.

Nutrition: calories 110, fat 4.4, fiber 12.8, carbs 16.2, protein 5.6

268. Zucchini Pan

Preparation time: 5 minutes
Cooking time: 20 minutes
Servings: 4

Ingredients:

- 1 pound zucchinis, sliced
- 1 yellow onion, chopped
- 2 tablespoons olive oil
- 2 apples, peeled, cored and cubed
- 1 tomato, cubed
- 1 tablespoon rosemary, chopped
- 1 tablespoon chives, chopped

Directions:

1. Heat up a pan with the oil over medium heat, add the onion and sauté for 5 minutes.
2. Add the zucchinis and the other ingredients, toss, cook over medium heat for 15 minutes more, divide between plates and serve as a side dish.

Nutrition: calories 170, fat 5, fiber 2, carbs 11, protein 7

269. Ginger Mushrooms

Preparation time: 10 minutes
Cooking time: 20 minutes
Servings: 4

Ingredients:

- 1 pound mushrooms, sliced
- 1 yellow onion, chopped
- 1 tablespoon ginger, grated
- 1 tablespoon olive oil
- 2 tablespoons balsamic vinegar
- 2 garlic cloves, minced
- A pinch of salt and black pepper
- ¼ cup lime juice
- 2 tablespoons walnuts, chopped

Directions:

1. Heat up a pan with the oil over medium-high heat, add the onion and the ginger and sauté for 5 minutes.
2. Add the mushrooms and the other ingredients, toss, cook over medium heat for 15 minutes more, divide between plates and serve.

Nutrition: calories 120, fat 2, fiber 2, carbs 4, protein 5

270. Bell Pepper Sauté

Preparation time: 5 minutes
Cooking time: 20 minutes
Servings: 4

Ingredients:

- 1 red bell pepper, cut into strips
- 1 yellow bell pepper, cut into strips
- 1 green bell pepper, cut into strips
- 1 orange bell pepper, cut into strips
- 3 scallions, chopped
- 1 tablespoon olive oil
- 1 tablespoon coconut aminos
- A pinch of salt and black pepper
- 1 tablespoon parsley, chopped
- 1 tablespoon rosemary, chopped

Directions:

1. Heat up a pan with the oil over medium-high heat, add the scallions and sauté for 5 minutes.
2. Add the bell peppers and the other ingredients, toss, cook over medium heat for 15 minutes more, divide between plates and serve.

Nutrition: calories 120, fat 1, fiber 2, carbs 7, protein 6

271. Kale and Tomatoes

Preparation time: 5 minutes
Cooking time: 20 minutes
Servings: 4

Ingredients:

- 1 cup cherry tomatoes, halved
- 1 pound baby kale
- 1 yellow onion, chopped
- 2 tablespoons olive oil
- 1 tablespoon balsamic vinegar
- 1 tablespoon cilantro, chopped
- 2 tablespoons vegetable stock
- A pinch of salt and black pepper

Directions:

1. Heat up a pan with the oil over medium heat, add the onion and sauté for 5 minutes.
2. Add the kale, tomatoes and the other ingredients, toss, cook over medium heat for 15 minutes more, divide between plates and serve as a side dish.

Nutrition: calories 170, fat 6, fiber 6, carbs 9, protein 4

272. Chili Artichokes

Preparation time: 10 minutes
Cooking time: 25 minutes
Servings: 4

Ingredients:

- 2 artichokes, trimmed and halved
- 1 teaspoon chili powder

- 2 green chilies, mined
- 2 tablespoons olive oil
- 1 teaspoon garlic powder
- 1 teaspoon sweet paprika
- A pinch of salt and black pepper
- Juice of 1 lime

Directions:

1. In a roasting pan, combine the artichokes with the chili powder, the chilies and the other ingredients, toss and bake at 380 degrees F for 25 minutes.
2. Divide the artichokes between plates and serve.

Nutrition: calories 132, fat 2, fiber 2, carbs 4, protein 6

273. Brussels Sprouts Mix

Preparation time: 10 minutes
Cooking time: 20 minutes
Servings: 4

Ingredients:

- 2 tablespoons olive oil
- 1 pound Brussels sprouts, trimmed and halved
- 1 tablespoon ginger, grated
- 2 garlic cloves, minced
- 1 tablespoon pine nuts
- 1 tablespoon olive oil

Directions:

1. Heat up a pan with the oil over medium heat, add the garlic and the ginger and sauté for 2 minutes.
2. Add the Brussels sprouts and the other ingredients, toss, cook for 18 minutes more, divide between plates and serve.

Nutrition: calories 160, fat 2, fiber 2, carbs 4, protein 5

274. Cauliflower Mix

Preparation time: 10 minutes
Cooking time: 25 minutes
Servings: 4

Ingredients:

- 1 pound cauliflower florets
- 2 tablespoons avocado oil
- 1 teaspoon nutmeg, ground
- 1 teaspoon hot paprika
- 1 tablespoon pumpkin seeds
- 1 tablespoon chives, chopped
- A pinch of sea salt and black pepper

Directions:

1. Spread the cauliflower florets on a baking sheet lined with parchment paper, add the oil, the nutmeg and the other ingredients, toss and bake at 380 degrees F for 25 minutes.
2. Divide the cauliflower mix between plates and serve as a side dish.

Nutrition: calories 160, fat 3, fiber 2, carbs 9, protein 4

275. Baked Broccoli and Pine Nuts

Preparation time: 10 minutes
Cooking time: 30 minutes
Servings: 4

Ingredients:

- 2 tablespoons olive oil
- 1 pound broccoli florets
- 1 tablespoon garlic, minced
- 1 tablespoon pine nuts, toasted
- 1 tablespoon lemon juice
- 2 teaspoons mustard
- A pinch of salt and black pepper

Directions:

1. In a roasting pan, combine the broccoli with the oil, the garlic and the other ingredients, toss and bake at 380 degrees F for 30 minutes.
2. Divide everything between plates and serve as a side dish.

Nutrition: calories 220, fat 6, fiber 2, carbs 7, protein 6

276. Quinoa and Peas

Preparation time: 10 minutes
Cooking time: 30 minutes
Servings: 4

Ingredients:

- 1 yellow onion, chopped
- 1 tomato, cubed
- 1 cup quinoa
- 3 cups vegetable stock

- 1 tablespoon olive oil
- 1 cup peas
- 1 tablespoon cilantro, chopped
- A pinch of salt and black pepper

Directions:

1. Heat up a pot with the oil over medium heat, add the onion, stir and sauté for 5 minutes.
2. Add the quinoa, the stock and the other ingredients, toss, bring to a simmer and cook over medium heat for 25 minutes.
3. Divide everything between plates and serve as a side dish.

Nutrition: calories 202, fat 3, fiber 3, carbs 11, protein 6

277. Basil Green Beans

Preparation time: 10 minutes
Cooking time: 20 minutes
Servings: 4

Ingredients:

- 1 yellow onion, chopped
- 1 pound green beans, trimmed and halved
- 1 tablespoon avocado oil
- 2 teaspoons basil, dried
- A pinch of salt and black pepper
- 1 tablespoon tomato sauce

Directions:

1. Heat up a pan with the oil over medium-high heat, add the onion and sauté for 5 minutes.
2. Add the green beans and the other ingredients, toss, cook for 15 minutes more.
3. Divide everything between plates and serve as a side dish.

Nutrition: calories 221, fat 5, fiber 8, carbs 10, protein 8

278. Balsamic Brussels Sprouts

Preparation time: 10 minutes
Cooking time: 20 minutes
Servings: 4

Ingredients:

- 2 pounds Brussels sprouts, trimmed and halved
- 1 tablespoon avocado oil
- 2 tablespoons balsamic vinegar
- 3 garlic cloves, minced
- 1 tablespoon cilantro, chopped
- A pinch of salt and black pepper

Directions:

1. Heat up a pan with the oil over medium-high heat, add the garlic and sauté for 2 minutes.
2. Add the sprouts and the other ingredients, toss, cook over medium heat for 18 minutes more, divide between plates and serve.

Nutrition: calories 108, fat 1.2, fiber 8.7, carbs 21.7, protein 7.9

279. Beet and Cabbage

Preparation time: 10 minutes
Cooking time: 20 minutes
Servings: 4

Ingredients:

- 1 green cabbage head, shredded
- 1 yellow onion, chopped
- 1 beet, peeled and cubed
- ½ cup chicken stock
- 2 tablespoons olive oil
- A pinch of salt and black pepper
- 2 tablespoons chives, chopped

Directions:

1. Heat up a pan with the oil over medium heat, add the onion and sauté for 5 minutes.
2. Add the cabbage and the other ingredients, toss, cook over medium heat for 15 minutes more, divide between plates and serve.

Nutrition: calories 128, fat 7.3, fiber 5.6, carbs 15.6, protein 3.1

280. Chili Asparagus

Preparation time: 10 minutes
Cooking time: 15 minutes
Servings: 4

Ingredients:

- 1 yellow onion, chopped
- 2 tablespoons olive oil
- 1 bunch asparagus, trimmed and halved

- 2 garlic cloves, minced
- 1 teaspoon chili powder
- ¼ cup cilantro, chopped

Directions:

1. Heat up a pan with the oil over medium-high heat, add the onion and the garlic and sauté for 5 minutes.
2. Add the asparagus and the other ingredients, toss, cook for 10 minutes, divide between plates and serve.

Nutrition: calories 80, fat 7.2, fiber 1.4, carbs 4.4, protein 1

281. Tomato Quinoa

Preparation time: 10 minutes
Cooking time: 25 minutes
Servings: 4

Ingredients:

- 1 cup quinoa
- 3 cups chicken stock
- 1 cup tomatoes, cubed
- 1 tablespoon parsley, chopped
- 1 tablespoon basil, chopped
- 1 teaspoon turmeric powder
- A pinch of salt and black pepper

Directions:

1. In a pot, mix the quinoa with the stock, the tomatoes and the other ingredients, toss, bring to a simmer and cook over medium heat for 25 minutes.
2. Divide everything between plates and serve.

Nutrition: calories 202, fat 4, fiber 2, carbs 12, protein 10

282. Coriander Black Beans

Preparation time: 10 minutes
Cooking time: 20 minutes
Servings: 4

Ingredients:

- 1 tablespoon olive oil
- 2 cups canned black beans, drained and rinsed
- 1 green bell pepper, chopped
- 1 yellow onion, chopped
- 4 garlic cloves, minced
- 1 teaspoon cumin, ground
- ½ cup chicken stock
- 1 tablespoon coriander, chopped
- A pinch of salt and black pepper

Directions:

1. Heat up a pan with the oil over medium heat, add the onion and the garlic and sauté for 5 minutes.
2. Add the black beans and the other ingredients, toss, cook over medium heat for 15 minutes more, divide between plates and serve.

Nutrition: calories 221, fat 5, fiber 4, carbs 9, protein 11

283. Green Beans and Mango Mix

Preparation time: 10 minutes
Cooking time: 20 minutes
Servings: 4

Ingredients:

- 1 pound green beans, trimmed and halved
- 3 scallions, chopped
- 1 mango, peeled and cubed
- 2 tablespoons olive oil
- ½ cup veggie stock
- 1 tablespoon oregano, chopped
- 1 teaspoon sweet paprika
- A pinch of salt and black pepper

Directions:

1. Heat up a pan with the oil over medium heat, add the scallions and sauté for 2 minutes.
2. Add the green beans and the other ingredients, toss, cook over medium heat for 18 minutes more, divide between plates and serve.

Nutrition: calories 182, fat 4, fiber 5, carbs 6, protein 8

284. Quinoa with Olives

Preparation time: 10 minutes
Cooking time: 30 minutes
Servings: 4

Ingredients:

- 1 yellow onion, chopped
- 1 tablespoon olive oil

- 1 cup quinoa
- 3 cups vegetable stock
- ½ cup black olives, pitted and halved
- 2 green onions, chopped
- 2 tablespoons coconut aminos
- 1 teaspoon rosemary, dried

Directions:

1. Heat up a pot with the oil over medium heat, add the yellow onion and sauté for 5 minutes.
2. Add the quinoa and the other ingredients except the green onions, stir, bring to a simmer and cook over medium heat for 25 minutes.
3. Divide the mix between plates, sprinkle the green onions on top and serve.

Nutrition: calories 261, fat 6, fiber 8, carbs 10, protein 6

285. Sweet Potato Mash

Preparation time: 10 minutes
Cooking time: 25 minutes
Servings: 4

Ingredients:

- 1 cup veggie stock
- 1 pound sweet potatoes, peeled and cubed
- 1 cup coconut cream
- 2 teaspoons olive oil
- A pinch of salt and black pepper
- ½ teaspoon turmeric powder
- 1 tablespoon chives, chopped

Directions:

1. In a pot, combine the stock with the sweet potatoes and the other ingredients except the cream, the oil and the chives, stir, bring to a simmer and cook over medium heat fro 25 minutes.
2. Add the rest of the ingredients, mash the mix well, stir it, divide between plates and serve.

Nutrition: calories 200, fat 4, fiber 4, carbs 7, protein 10

286. Creamy Peas

Preparation time: 10 minutes
Cooking time: 20 minutes
Servings: 4

Ingredients:

- 1 cup coconut cream
- 1 yellow onion, chopped
- 1 tablespoon olive oil
- 2 cups green peas
- A pinch of salt and black pepper
- A pinch of salt and black pepper

Directions:

1. Heat up a pan with the oil over medium heat, add the onion and sauté for 5 minutes.
2. Add the peas and the other ingredients, toss, cook over medium heat for 15 minutes, divide between plates and serve.

Nutrition: calories 191, fat 5, fiber 4, carbs 11, protein 9

287. Mushrooms and Black Beans

Preparation time: 10 minutes
Cooking time: 25 minutes
Servings: 4

Ingredients:

- 1 pound mushrooms, sliced
- 1 yellow onion, chopped
- 1 teaspoon cumin, ground
- 1 teaspoon sweet paprika
- 1 cup canned black beans, drained and rinsed
- 2 tablespoons olive oil
- ½ cup chicken stock
- A pinch of salt and black pepper
- 2 tablespoons cilantro, chopped

Directions:

1. Heat up a pan with the oil over medium heat, add the onion and sauté for 5 minutes.
2. Add the mushrooms and sauté for 5 minutes more.
3. Add the rest of the ingredients, toss, cook over medium heat for 15 minutes more.
4. Divide everything between plates and serve as a side dish.

Nutrition: calories 189, fat 3, fiber 4, carbs 9, protein 8

288. Broccoli with Brussels Sprouts

Preparation time: 10 minutes

Cooking time: 25 minutes
Servings: 4

Ingredients:

- 1 pound broccoli florets
- ½ pound Brussels sprouts, trimmed and halved
- 2 tablespoons olive oil
- 1 tablespoon ginger, grated
- 1 tablespoon balsamic vinegar
- A pinch of salt and black pepper

Directions:

1. In a roasting pan, combine the broccoli with the sprouts and the other ingredients, toss gently and bake at 380 degrees F for 25 minutes.
2. Divide the mix between plates and serve.

Nutrition: calories 129, fat 7.6, fiber 5.3, carbs 13.7, protein 5.2

289. Glazed Cauliflower

Preparation time: 10 minutes
Cooking time: 25 minutes
Servings: 4

Ingredients:

- 1 tablespoon olive oil
- 1 pound cauliflower florets
- 1 tablespoon maple syrup
- 1 tablespoon rosemary, chopped
- A pinch of salt and black pepper
- 1 teaspoon chili powder

Directions:

1. Spread the cauliflower on a baking sheet lined with parchment paper, add the oil and the other ingredients, toss and cook in the oven at 375 degrees F for 25 minutes.
2. Divide the mix between plates and serve.

Nutrition: calories 76, fat 3.9, fiber 3.4, carbs 10.3, protein 2.4

290. Garlic Asparagus and Tomatoes

Preparation time: 10 minutes
Cooking time: 20 minutes
Servings: 4

Ingredients:

- 1 pound asparagus, trimmed and halved
- ½ pound cherry tomatoes, halved
- 2 tablespoons olive oil
- 1 teaspoon turmeric powder
- 2 tablespoons shallot, chopped
- A pinch of salt and black pepper
- 1 tablespoon chives, chopped

Directions:

1. Spread the asparagus on a baking sheet lined with parchment paper, add the tomatoes and the other ingredients, toss, cook in the oven at 375 degrees F for 20 minutes.
2. Divide everything between plates and serve as a side dish.

Nutrition: calories 132, fat 1, fiber 2, carbs 4, protein 4

291. Hot Cucumber Mix

Preparation time: 10 minutes
Cooking time: 0 minutes
Servings: 4

Ingredients:

- 1 pound cucumbers, sliced
- 1 tablespoon olive oil
- 1 teaspoon chili powder
- 1 green chili, chopped
- 1 garlic clove, minced
- 1 tablespoon dill, chopped
- 2 tablespoons lime juice
- 1 tablespoon balsamic vinegar

Directions:

In a bowl, combine the cucumbers with the garlic, the oil and the other ingredients, toss and serve as a side salad.

Nutrition: calories 132, fat 3, fiber 1, carbs 7, protein 4

292. Tomato Salad

Preparation time: 10 minutes
Cooking time: 0 minutes
Servings: 4

Ingredients:

- 1 pound cherry tomatoes, halved
- 3 scallions, chopped
- 1 tablespoon olive oil
- A pinch of salt and black pepper
- 1 tablespoon lime juice

- ¼ cup parsley, chopped

Directions:

1. In a bowl, combine the tomatoes with the scallions and the other ingredients, toss and serve as a side salad.

Nutrition: calories 180, fat 2, fiber 2, carbs 8, protein 6

293. Sage Quinoa

Preparation time: 10 minutes
Cooking time: 30 minutes
Servings: 4

Ingredients:

- 1 tablespoon olive oil
- 1 yellow onion, chopped
- 1 cup quinoa
- 2 cups chicken stock
- 1 tablespoon sage, chopped
- 2 garlic cloves, minced
- A pinch of salt and black pepper
- 1 tablespoon chives, chopped

Directions:

2. Heat up a pan with the oil over medium-high heat, add the onion and the garlic and sauté for 5 minutes.
3. Add the quinoa and the other ingredients, toss, cook over medium heat for 25 minutes more, divide between plates and serve.

Nutrition: calories 182, fat 1, fiber 1, carbs 11, protein 8

294. Beans, Carrots and Spinach Side Dish

Preparation time: 10 minutes
Cooking time: 4 hours
Servings: 6

Ingredients:

- 5 carrots, sliced
- 1 and ½ cups great northern beans, dried, soaked overnight and drained
- 2 garlic cloves, minced
- 1 yellow onion, chopped
- Salt and black pepper to the taste
- ½ teaspoon oregano, dried
- 5 ounces baby spinach
- 4 and ½ cups veggie stock
- 2 teaspoons lemon peel, grated
- 3 tablespoons lemon juice
- 1 avocado, pitted, peeled and chopped
- ¾ cup tofu, firm, pressed, drained and crumbled
- ¼ cup pistachios, chopped

Directions:

1. In your slow cooker, mix beans with onion, carrots, garlic, salt, pepper, oregano and veggie stock, stir, cover and cook on High for 4 hours.
2. Drain beans mix, return to your slow cooker and reserve ¼ cup cooking liquid.
3. Add spinach, lemon juice and lemon peel, stir and leave aside for 5 minutes.
4. Transfer beans, carrots and spinach mixture to a bowl, add pistachios, avocado, tofu and reserve cooking liquid, toss, divide between plates and serve as a side dish.
5. Enjoy!

Nutrition: calories 319, fat 8, fiber 14, carbs 43, protein 17

295. Scalloped Potatoes

Preparation time: 10 minutes
Cooking time: 4 hours
Servings: 8

Ingredients:

- Cooking spray
- 2 pounds gold potatoes, halved and sliced
- 1 yellow onion, cut into medium wedges
- 10 ounces canned vegan potato cream soup
- 8 ounces coconut milk
- 1 cup tofu, crumbled
- ½ cup veggie stock
- Salt and black pepper to the taste
- 1 tablespoons parsley, chopped

Directions:

1. Coat your slow cooker with cooking spray and arrange half of the potatoes on the bottom.
2. Layer onion wedges, half of the vegan cream soup, coconut milk, tofu, stock, salt and pepper.

3. Add the rest of the potatoes, onion wedges, cream, coconut milk, tofu and stock, cover and cook on High for 4 hours.
4. Sprinkle parsley on top, divide scalloped potatoes between plates and serve as a side dish.
5. Enjoy!

Nutrition: calories 306, fat 14, fiber 4, carbs 30, protein 12

296. Sweet Potatoes Side Dish

Preparation time: 10 minutes
Cooking time: 3 hours
Servings: 10

Ingredients:

- 4 pounds sweet potatoes, thinly sliced
- 3 tablespoons stevia
- ½ cup orange juice
- A pinch of salt and black pepper
- ½ teaspoon thyme, dried
- ½ teaspoon sage, dried
- 2 tablespoons olive oil

Directions:

1. Arrange potato slices on the bottom of your slow cooker.
2. In a bowl, mix orange juice with salt, pepper, stevia, thyme, sage and oil and whisk well.
3. Add this over potatoes, cover slow cooker and cook on High for 3 hours.
4. Divide between plates and serve as a side dish.
5. Enjoy!

Nutrition: calories 189, fat 4, fiber 4, carbs 36, protein 4

297. Cauliflower And Broccoli Side Dish

Preparation time: 10 minutes
Cooking time: 3 hours
Servings: 10

Ingredients:

- 4 cups broccoli florets
- 4 cups cauliflower florets
- 14 ounces tomato paste
- 1 yellow onion, chopped
- 1 teaspoon thyme, dried
- Salt and black pepper to the taste
- ½ cup almonds, sliced

Directions:

1. In your slow cooker, mix broccoli with cauliflower, tomato paste, onion, thyme, salt and pepper, toss, cover and cook on High for 3 hours.
2. Add almonds, toss, divide between plates and serve as a side dish.
3. Enjoy!

Nutrition: calories 177, fat 12, fiber 2, carbs 10, protein 7

298. Wild Rice Mix

Preparation time: 10 minutes
Cooking time: 6 hours
Servings: 12

Ingredients:

- 40 ounces veggie stock
- 2 and ½ cups wild rice
- 1 cup carrot, shredded
- 4 ounces mushrooms, sliced
- 2 tablespoons olive oil
- 2 teaspoons marjoram, dried and crushed
- Salt and black pepper to the taste
- 2/3 cup dried cherries
- ½ cup pecans, toasted and chopped
- 2/3 cup green onions, chopped

Directions:

1. In your slow cooker, mix stock with wild rice, carrot, mushrooms, oil, marjoram, salt, pepper, cherries, pecans and green onions, toss, cover and cook on Low for 6 hours.
2. Stir wild rice one more time, divide between plates and serve as a side dish.
3. Enjoy!

Nutrition: calories 169, fat 5, fiber 3, carbs 28, protein 5

299. Rustic Mashed Potatoes

Preparation time: 10 minutes
Cooking time: 4 hours
Servings: 6

Ingredients:

- 6 garlic cloves, peeled

- 3 pounds gold potatoes, peeled and cubed
- 1 bay leaf
- 1 cup coconut milk
- 28 ounces veggie stock
- 3 tablespoons olive oil
- Salt and black pepper to the taste

Directions:

1. In your slow cooker, mix potatoes with stock, bay leaf, garlic, salt and pepper, cover and cook on High for 4 hours.
2. Drain potatoes and garlic, return them to your slow cooker and mash using a potato masher.
3. Add oil and coconut milk, whisk well, divide between plates and serve as a side dish.
4. Enjoy!

Nutrition: calories 135, fat 5, fiber 1, carbs 20, protein 3

Glazed Carrots

Preparation time: 10 minutes
Cooking time: 4 hours
Servings: 10

Ingredients:

- 1 pound parsnips, cut into medium chunks
- 2 pounds carrots, cut into medium chunks
- 2 tablespoons orange peel, shredded
- 1 cup orange juice
- ½ cup orange marmalade
- ½ cup veggie stock
- 1 tablespoon tapioca, crushed
- A pinch of salt and black pepper
- 3 tablespoons olive oil
- ¼ cup parsley, chopped

Directions:

1. In your slow cooker, mix parsnips with carrots.
2. In a bowl, mix orange peel with orange juice, stock, orange marmalade, tapioca, salt and pepper, whisk and add over carrots.
3. Cover slow cooker and cook everything on High for 4 hours.
4. Add parsley, toss, divide between plates and serve as a side dish.
5. Enjoy!

Nutrition: calories 159, fat 4, fiber 4, carbs 30, protein 2

301. Mushroom And Peas Risotto

Preparation time: 10 minutes
Cooking time: 1 hour and 30 minutes
Servings: 8

Ingredients:

- 1 shallot, chopped
- 8 ounces white mushrooms, sliced
- 3 tablespoons olive oil
- 1 teaspoon garlic, minced
- 1 and ¾ cup white rice
- 4 cups veggie stock
- 1 cup peas
- Salt and black pepper to the taste

Directions:

1. In your slow cooker, mix oil with shallot, mushrooms, garlic, rice, stock, peas, salt and pepper, stir, cover and cook on High for 1 hour and 30 minutes.
2. Stir risotto one more time, divide between plates and serve as a side dish.
3. Enjoy!

Nutrition: calories 254, fat 7, fiber 3, carbs 27, protein 7

302. Squash And Spinach Mix

Preparation time: 10 minutes
Cooking time: 3 hours and 30 minutes
Servings: 12

Ingredients:

- 10 ounces spinach, torn
- 2 pounds butternut squash, peeled and cubed
- 1 cup barley
- 1 yellow onion, chopped
- 14 ounces veggie stock
- ½ cup water
- A pinch of salt and black pepper to the taste
- 3 garlic cloves, minced

Directions:

1. In your slow cooker, mix squash with spinach, barley, onion, stock, water, salt,

pepper and garlic, toss, cover and cook on High for 3 hours and 30 minutes.
2. Divide squash mix on plates and serve as a side dish.
3. Enjoy!

Nutrition: calories 196, fat 3, fiber 7, carbs 36, protein 7

303. Chickpeas And Veggies

Preparation time: 10 minutes
Cooking time: 8 hours
Servings: 6

Ingredients:

- 30 ounces canned chickpeas, drained
- 2 tablespoons olive oil
- 2 tablespoons rosemary, chopped
- A pinch of salt and black pepper
- 2 cups cherry tomatoes, halved
- 2 garlic cloves, minced
- 1 cup corn
- 1 pound baby potatoes, peeled and halved
- 12 small baby carrots, peeled
- 28 ounces veggie stock
- 1 yellow onion, cut into medium wedges
- 4 cups baby spinach
- 8 ounces zucchini, sliced

Directions:

1. In your slow cooker, mix chickpeas with oil, rosemary, salt, pepper, cherry tomatoes, garlic, corn, baby potatoes, baby carrots, onion, zucchini, spinach and stock, stir, cover and cook on Low for 8 hours.
2. Divide everything between plates and serve as a side dish.
3. Enjoy!

Nutrition: calories 273, fat 7, fiber 11, carbs 38, protein 12

304. Eggplant And Kale Mix

Preparation time: 10 minutes
Cooking time: 2 hours
Servings: 6

Ingredients:

- 14 ounces canned roasted tomatoes and garlic
- 4 cups eggplant, cubed
- 1 yellow bell pepper, chopped
- 1 red onion, cut into medium wedges
- 4 cups kale leaves
- 2 tablespoons olive oil
- 1 teaspoon mustard
- 3 tablespoons red vinegar
- 1 garlic clove, minced
- A pinch of salt and black pepper
- ½ cup basil, chopped

Directions:

1. In your slow cooker, mix eggplant cubes with canned tomatoes, bell pepper and onion, toss, cover and cook on High for 2 hours.
2. Add kale, toss, cover slow cooker and leave aside for now.
3. Meanwhile, in a bowl, mix oil with vinegar, mustard, garlic, salt and pepper and whisk well.
4. Add this over eggplant mix, also add basil, toss, divide between plates and serve as a side dish.
5. Enjoy!

Nutrition: calories 251, fat 9, fiber 6, carbs 34, protein 8

305. Thai Veggie Mix

Preparation time: 10 minutes
Cooking time: 3 hours
Servings: 8

Ingredients:

- 8 ounces yellow summer squash, peeled and roughly chopped
- 12 ounces zucchini, halved and sliced
- 2 cups button mushrooms, quartered
- 1 red sweet potatoes, chopped
- 2 leeks, sliced
- 2 tablespoons veggie stock
- 2 garlic cloves, minced
- 2 tablespoon Thai red curry paste
- 1 tablespoon ginger, grated
- 1/3 cup coconut milk
- ¼ cup basil, chopped

Directions:

1. In your slow cooker, mix zucchini with summer squash, mushrooms, red pepper,

leeks, garlic, stock, curry paste, ginger, coconut milk and basil, toss, cover and cook on Low for 3 hours.
2. Stir your Thai mix one more time, divide between plates and serve as a side dish.
3. Enjoy!

Nutrition: calories 69, fat 2, fiber 2, carbs 8, protein 2

306. Simple Potatoes Side Dish

Preparation time: 10 minutes
Cooking time: 3 hours
Servings: 12

Ingredients:

- 2 tablespoons olive oil
- 3 pounds new potatoes, halved
- 7 garlic cloves, minced
- 1 tablespoon rosemary, chopped
- A pinch of salt and black pepper

Directions:

1. In your slow cooker, mix oil with potatoes, garlic, rosemary, salt and pepper, toss, cover and cook on High for 3 hours.
2. Divide between plates and serve as a side dish.
3. Enjoy!

Nutrition: calories 102, fat 2, fiber 2, carbs 18, protein 2

307. Brussels Sprouts

Preparation time: 10 minutes
Cooking time: 3 hours
Servings: 12

Ingredients:

- 1 cup red onion, chopped
- 2 pounds Brussels sprouts, trimmed and halved
- A pinch of salt and black pepper
- ¼ cup apple juice
- 3 tablespoons olive oil
- ¼ cup maple syrup
- 1 tablespoon thyme, chopped

Directions:

1. In your slow cooker, mix Brussels sprouts with onion, salt, pepper and apple juice, toss, cover and cook on Low for 3 hours.
2. In a bowl, mix maple syrup with oil and thyme, whisk really well and add over Brussels sprouts.
3. Toss well, divide between plates and serve as a side dish.
4. Enjoy!

Nutrition: calories 100, fat 4, fiber 4, carbs 14, protein 3

308. Beets And Carrots

Preparation time: 10 minutes
Cooking time: 7 hours
Servings: 8

Ingredients:

- 2 tablespoons stevia
- ¾ cup pomegranate juice
- 2 teaspoons ginger, grated
- 2 and ½ pounds beets, peeled and cut into wedges
- 12 ounces carrots, cut into medium wedges

Directions:

1. In your slow cooker, mix beets with carrots, ginger, stevia and pomegranate juice, toss, cover and cook on Low for 7 hours.
2. Divide between plates and serve as a side dish.
3. Enjoy!

Nutrition: calories 125, fat 0, fiber 4, carbs 28, protein 3

309. Italian Veggie Side Dish

Preparation time: 10 minutes
Cooking time: 6 hours
Servings: 8

Ingredients:

- 38 ounces canned cannellini beans, drained
- 1 yellow onion, chopped
- ¼ cup basil pesto
- 19 ounces canned fava beans, drained
- 4 garlic cloves, minced
- 1 and ½ teaspoon Italian seasoning, dried and crushed
- 1 tomato, chopped
- 15 ounces already cooked polenta, cut into medium pieces

- 2 cups spinach
- 1 cup radicchio, torn

Directions:

1. In your slow cooker, mix cannellini beans with fava beans, basil pesto, onion, garlic, Italian seasoning, polenta, tomato, spinach and radicchio, toss, cover and cook on Low for 6 hours.
2. Divide between plates and serve as a side dish.
3. Enjoy!

Nutrition: calories 364, fat 12, fiber 10, carbs 45, protein 21

310. Acorn Squash And Great Sauce

Preparation time: 10 minutes
Cooking time: 6 hours
Servings: 4

Ingredients:

- 2 acorn squash, halved, deseeded and cut into medium wedges
- ¼ cup raisins
- 16 ounces cranberry sauce
- ¼ cup orange marmalade
- A pinch of salt and black pepper
- ¼ teaspoon cinnamon powder

Directions:

1. In your slow cooker, mix squash with raisins, cranberry sauce, orange marmalade, salt, pepper and cinnamon powder, toss, cover and cook on Low for 6 hours.
2. Stir again, divide between plates and serve as a side dish.
3. Enjoy!

Nutrition: calories 325, fat 6, fiber 3, carbs 28, protein 3

311. Pilaf

Preparation time: 10 minutes
Cooking time: 7 hours
Servings: 12

Ingredients:

- ½ cup wild rice
- ½ cup barley
- 2/3 cup wheat berries
- 27 ounces veggie stock
- 2 cups baby lima beans
- 1 red bell pepper, chopped
- 1 yellow onion, chopped
- 1 tablespoon olive oil
- A pinch of salt and black pepper
- 1 teaspoon sage, dried and crushed
- 4 garlic cloves, minced

Directions:

1. In your slow cooker, mix rice with barley, wheat berries, lima beans, bell pepper, onion, oil, salt, pepper, sage and garlic, stir, cover and cook on Low for 7 hours.
2. Stir one more time, divide between plates and serve as a side dish.
3. Enjoy!

Nutrition: calories 168, fat 5, fiber 4, carbs 25, protein 6

312. Special Potatoes Mix

Preparation time: 10 minutes
Cooking time: 7 hours
Servings: 10

Ingredients:

- 2 green apples, cored and cut into wedges
- 3 pounds sweet potatoes, peeled and cut into medium wedges
- 1 cup coconut cream
- ½ cup dried cherries
- 1 cup apple butter
- 1 and ½ teaspoon pumpkin pie spice

Directions:

1. In your slow cooker, mix sweet potatoes with green apples, cream, cherries, apple butter and spice, toss, cover and cook on Low for 7 hours.
2. Toss, divide between plates and serve as a side dish.
3. Enjoy!

Nutrition: calories 351, fat 8, fiber 5, carbs 48, protein 2

313. Creamy Corn

Preparation time: 10 minutes
Cooking time: 3 hours
Servings: 6

Ingredients:

- 50 ounces corn
- 1 cup almond milk
- 1 tablespoon stevia
- 8 ounces coconut cream
- A pinch of white pepper

Directions:

1. In your slow cooker, mix corn with almond milk, stevia, cream and white pepper, toss, cover and cook on High for 3 hours.
2. Divide between plates and serve as a side dish.
3. Enjoy!

Nutrition: calories 200, fat 5, fiber 7, carbs 12, protein 4

VEGETABLES

314. Grilled Portobello with Mashed Potatoes and Green Beans

Preparation time: 20 minutes
cooking time: 40 minutes
servings: 4

Ingredients

For the grilled portobellos

- 4 large portobello mushrooms
- 1 teaspoon olive oil
- Pinch sea salt

For the mashed potatoes

- 6 large potatoes, scrubbed or peeled, and chopped
- 3 to 4 garlic cloves, minced
- ½ teaspoon olive oil
- ½ cup non-dairy milk
- 2 tablespoons coconut oil (optional
- 2 tablespoons nutritional yeast (optional
- Pinch sea salt

For the green beans

- 2 cups green beans, cut into 1-inch pieces
- 2 to 3 teaspoons coconut oil
- Pinch sea salt
- 1 to 2 tablespoons nutritional yeast (optional

Directions

TO MAKE THE GRILLED PORTOBELLOS

1. Preheat the grill to medium, or the oven to 350°F.
2. Take the stems out of the mushrooms.
3. Wipe the caps clean with a damp paper towel, then dry them. Spray the caps with a bit of olive oil, or put some oil in your hand and rub it over the mushrooms.
4. Rub the oil onto the top and bottom of each mushroom, then sprinkle them with a bit of salt on top and bottom.
5. Put them bottom side facing up on a baking sheet in the oven, or straight on the grill. They'll take about 30 minutes in the oven, or 20 minutes on the grill. Wait until they're soft and wrinkling around the edges. If you keep them bottom up, all the delicious mushroom juice will pool in the cap. Then at the very end, you can flip them over to drain the juice. If you like it, you can drizzle it over the mashed potatoes.

TO MAKE THE MASHED POTATOES

6. Boil the chopped potatoes in lightly salted water for about 20 minutes, until soft. While they're cooking, sauté the garlic in the olive oil, or bake them whole in a 350°F oven for 10 minutes, then squeeze out the flesh. Drain the potatoes, reserving about ½ cup water to mash them. In a large bowl, mash the potatoes with a little bit of the reserved water, the cooked garlic, milk, coconut oil (if using), nutritional yeast (if using), and salt to taste. Add more water, a little at a time, if needed, to get the texture you want. If you use an immersion blender or beater to purée them, you'll have some extra-creamy potatoes.

TO MAKE THE GREEN BEAN

7. Heat a medium pot with a small amount of water to boil, then steam the green beans by either putting them directly in the pot or in a steaming basket.
8. Once they're slightly soft and vibrantly green, 7 to 8 minutes, take them off the heat and toss them with the oil, salt, and nutritional yeast (if using).

Nutrition: Calories: 263; Total fat: 7g; Carbs: 43g; Fiber: 7g; Protein: 10g

315. Tahini Broccoli Slaw

Preparation time: 15 minutes
cooking time: 0 minutes
servings: 4 to 6

Ingredients

- 1/4 cup tahini (sesame paste
- 2 tablespoons white miso
- 1 tablespoon rice vinegar
- 1 tablespoon toasted sesame oil
- 2 teaspoons soy sauce
- 1 (12-ouncebag broccoli slaw

- 2 green onions, minced
- 1/4 cup toasted sesame seeds

Directions

1. In a large bowl, whisk together the tahini, miso, vinegar, oil, and soy sauce. Add the broccoli slaw, green onions, and sesame seeds and toss to coat.
2. Set aside for 20 minutes before serving.

316. Steamed Cauliflower

Preparation time: 5 minutes
cooking time: 10 minutes
servings: 6

Ingredients

- 1 large head cauliflower
- 1 cup water
- ½ teaspoon salt
- 1 teaspoon red pepper flakes (optional

Directions

1. Remove any leaves from the cauliflower, and cut it into florets.
2. In a large saucepan, bring the water to a boil. Place a steamer basket over the water, and add the florets and salt. Cover and steam for 5 to 7 minutes, until tender. In a large bowl, toss the cauliflower with the red pepper flakes (if using). Transfer the florets to a large airtight container or 6 single-serving containers. Let cool before sealing the lids.

Nutrition: Calories: 35; Fat: 0g; Protein: 3g; Carbohydrates: 7g; Fiber: 4g; Sugar: 4g; Sodium: 236mg

317. Roasted Cauliflower Tacos

Preparation time: 10 minutes
cooking time: 30 minutes

SERVINGS: 8 TACOS

Ingredients

For the roasted cauliflower

- 1 head cauliflower, cut into bite-size pieces
- 1 tablespoon olive oil (optional
- 2 tablespoons whole-wheat flour
- 2 tablespoons nutritional yeast
- 1 to 2 teaspoons smoked paprika
- ½ to 1 teaspoon chili powder
- Pinch sea salt

For the tacos

- 2 cups shredded lettuce
- 2 cups cherry tomatoes, quartered
- 2 carrots, scrubbed or peeled, and grated
- ½ cup Fresh Mango Salsa
- ½ cup Guacamole
- 8 small whole-grain or corn tortillas
- 1 lime, cut into 8 wedges

Directions

TO MAKE THE ROASTED CAULIFLOWER

1. Preheat the oven to 350°F. Lightly grease a large rectangular baking sheet with olive oil, or line it with parchment paper. In a large bowl, toss the cauliflower pieces with oil (if using), or just rinse them so they're wet. The idea is to get the seasonings to stick. In a smaller bowl, mix together the flour, nutritional yeast, paprika, chili powder, and salt.
2. Add the seasonings to the cauliflower, and mix it around with your hands to thoroughly coat. Spread the cauliflower on the baking sheet, and roast for 20 to 30 minutes, or until softened.

TO MAKE THE TACOS.

3. Prep the veggies, salsa, and guacamole while the cauliflower is roasting. Once the cauliflower is cooked, heat the tortillas for just a few minutes in the oven or in a small skillet. Set everything out on the table, and assemble your tacos as you go. Give a squeeze of fresh lime just before eating.

Nutrition (1 taco): Calories: 198; Total fat: 6g; Carbs: 32g; Fiber: 6g; Protein: 7g

318. Cajun Sweet Potatoes

Preparation time: 5 minutes
cooking time: 30 minutes
servings: 4

Ingredients

- 2 pounds sweet potatoes
- 2 teaspoons extra-virgin olive oil
- ½ teaspoon ground cayenne pepper
- ½ teaspoon smoked paprika
- ½ teaspoon dried oregano

- ½ teaspoon dried thyme
- ½ teaspoon garlic powder
- ½ teaspoon salt (optional

Directions

1. Preheat the oven to 400°F. Line a baking sheet with parchment paper.
2. Wash the potatoes, pat dry, and cut into ¾-inch cubes. Transfer to a large bowl, and pour the olive oil over the potatoes.
3. In a small bowl, combine the cayenne, paprika, oregano, thyme, and garlic powder. Sprinkle the spices over the potatoes and combine until the potatoes are well coated. Spread the potatoes on the prepared baking sheet in a single layer. Season with the salt (if using). Roast for 30 minutes, stirring the potatoes after 15 minutes.
4. Divide the potatoes evenly among 4 single-serving containers. Let cool completely before sealing.

Nutrition: Calories: 219; Fat: 3g; Protein: 4g; Carbohydrates: 46g; Fiber: 7g; Sugar: 9g; Sodium: 125mg

319. Creamy Mint-Lime

Spaghetti Squash
Preparation time: 10 minutes
cooking time: 30 minutes
servings: 3

Ingredients

For the dressing

- 3 tablespoons tahini
- Zest and juice of 1 small lime
- 2 tablespoons fresh mint, minced
- 1 small garlic clove, pressed
- 1 tablespoon nutritional yeast
- Pinch sea salt

For the spaghetti squash

- 1 spaghetti squash
- Pinch sea salt
- 1 cup cherry tomatoes, chopped
- 1 cup chopped bell pepper, any color
- Freshly ground black pepper

Directions

TO MAKE THE DRESSING

1. Make the dressing by whisking together the tahini and lime juice until thick, stirring in water if you need it, until smooth, then add the rest of the ingredients. Or you can purée all the ingredients in a blender.

TO MAKE THE SPAGHETTI SQUASH.

2. Put a large pot of water on high and bring to a boil. Cut the squash in half and scoop out the seeds. Put the squash halves in the pot with the salt, and boil for about 30 minutes. Carefully remove the squash from the pot and let it cool until you can safely handle it. Set half the squash aside for another meal. Scoop out the squash from the skin, which stays hard like a shell, and break the strands apart. The flesh absorbs water while boiling, so set the "noodles" in a strainer for 10 minutes, tossing occasionally to drain. Transfer the cooked spaghetti squash to a large bowl and toss with the mint-lime dressing. Then top with the cherry tomatoes and bell pepper. Add an extra sprinkle of nutritional yeast and black pepper, if you wish.

Nutrition: Calories: 199; Total fat: 10g; Carbs: 27g; Fiber: 5g; Protein: 7g

320. Smoky Coleslaw

Preparation time: 10 minutes
cooking time: 0 minutes
servings: 6

Ingredients

- 1 pound shredded cabbage
- ⅓ cup vegan mayonnaise
- ¼ cup unseasoned rice vinegar
- 3 tablespoons plain vegan yogurt or plain soymilk
- 1 tablespoon vegan sugar
- ½ teaspoon salt
- ¼ teaspoon freshly ground black pepper
- ¼ teaspoon smoked paprika
- ¼ teaspoon chipotle powder

Directions

1. Put the shredded cabbage in a large bowl. In a medium bowl, whisk the mayonnaise, vinegar, yogurt, sugar, salt, pepper, paprika, and chipotle powder.

2. Pour over the cabbage, and mix with a spoon or spatula and until the cabbage shreds are coated. Divide the coleslaw evenly among 6 single-serving containers. Seal the lids.

Nutrition: Calories: 73; Fat: 4g; Protein: 1g; Carbohydrates: 8g; Fiber: 2g; Sugar: 5g; Sodium: 283mg

321. Simple Sesame Stir-Fry

Preparation time: 10 minutes
cooking time: 20 minutes
servings: 4

Ingredients

- 1 cup quinoa
- 2 cups water
- Pinch sea salt
- 1 head broccoli
- 1 to 2 teaspoons untoasted sesame oil, or olive oil
- 1 cup snow peas, or snap peas, ends trimmed and cut in half
- 1 cup frozen shelled edamame beans, or peas
- 2 cups chopped Swiss chard, or other large-leafed green
- 2 scallions, chopped
- 2 tablespoons water
- 1 teaspoon toasted sesame oil
- 1 tablespoon tamari, or soy sauce
- 2 tablespoons sesame seeds

Directions

1. Put the quinoa, water, and sea salt in a medium pot, bring it to a boil for a minute, then turn to low and simmer, covered, for 20 minutes. The quinoa is fully cooked when you see the swirl of the grains with a translucent center, and it is fluffy. Do not stir the quinoa while it is cooking.
2. Meanwhile, cut the broccoli into bite-size florets, cutting and pulling apart from the stem. Also chop the stem into bite-size pieces. Heat a large skillet to high, and sauté the broccoli in the untoasted sesame oil, with a pinch of salt to help it soften. Keep this moving continuously, so that it doesn't burn, and add an extra drizzle of oil if needed as you add the rest of the vegetables. Add the snow peas next, continuing to stir. Add the edamame until they thaw. Add the Swiss chard and scallions at the same time, tossing for only a minute to wilt. Then add 2 tablespoons of water to the hot skillet so that it sizzles and finishes the vegetables with a quick steam.
3. Dress with the toasted sesame oil and tamari, and toss one last time. Remove from the heat immediately. Serve a scoop of cooked quinoa, topped with stir-fry and sprinkled with some sesame seeds, and an extra drizzle of tamari and/or toasted sesame oil if you like.

Nutrition: Calories: 334; Total fat: 13g; Carbs: 42g; Fiber: 9g; Protein: 17g

322. Mediterranean Hummus Pizza

Preparation time: 10 minutes
cooking time: 30 minutes
servings: 2 pizzas

Ingredients

- ½ zucchini, thinly sliced
- ½ red onion, thinly sliced
- 1 cup cherry tomatoes, halved
- 2 to 4 tablespoons pitted and chopped black olives
- Pinch sea salt
- Drizzle olive oil (optional
- 2 prebaked pizza crusts
- ½ cup Classic Hummus, or Roasted Red Pepper Hummus
- 2 to 4 tablespoons Cheesy Sprinkle

Directions

1. Preheat the oven to 400°F. Place the zucchini, onion, cherry tomatoes, and olives in a large bowl, sprinkle them with the sea salt, and toss them a bit. Drizzle with a bit of olive oil (if using), to seal in the flavor and keep them from drying out in the oven.
2. Lay the two crusts out on a large baking sheet. Spread half the hummus on each crust, and top with the veggie mixture and some Cheesy Sprinkle. Pop the pizzas in

the oven for 20 to 30 minutes, or until the veggies are soft.

Nutrition (1 pizzaCalories: 500; Total fat: 25g; Carbs: 58g; Fiber: 12g; Protein: 19g

323. Baked Brussels Sprouts

Preparation time: 10 minutes
cooking time: 40 minutes
servings: 4

Ingredients

- 1 pound Brussels sprouts
- 2 teaspoons extra-virgin olive or canola oil
- 4 teaspoons minced garlic (about 4 cloves
- 1 teaspoon dried oregano
- ½ teaspoon dried rosemary
- ½ teaspoon salt
- ¼ teaspoon freshly ground black pepper
- 1 tablespoon balsamic vinegar

Directions

1. Preheat the oven to 400°F. Line a rimmed baking sheet with parchment paper. Trim and halve the Brussels sprouts. Transfer to a large bowl. Toss with the olive oil, garlic, oregano, rosemary, salt, and pepper to coat well.
2. Transfer to the prepared baking sheet. Bake for 35 to 40 minutes, shaking the pan occasionally to help with even browning, until crisp on the outside and tender on the inside. Remove from the oven and transfer to a large bowl. Stir in the balsamic vinegar, coating well.
3. Divide the Brussels sprouts evenly among 4 single-serving containers. Let cool before sealing the lids.

Nutrition: Calories: 77; Fat: 3g; Protein: 4g; Carbohydrates: 12g; Fiber: 5g; Sugar: 3g; Sodium: 320mg

324. Minted Peas

Preparation time: 5 minutes
cooking time: 5 minutes
servings: 4

Ingredients

- 1 tablespoon olive oil
- 4 cups peas, fresh or frozen (not canned
- ½ teaspoon sea salt
- freshly ground black pepper
- 3 tablespoons chopped fresh mint

Directions

1. In a large sauté pan, heat the olive oil over medium-high heat until hot. Add the peas and cook, about 5 minutes.
2. Remove the pan from heat. Stir in the salt, season with pepper, and stir in the mint.
3. Serve hot.

325. Edamame Donburi

Preparation time: 5 minutes
cooking time: 20 minutes
servings: 4

Ingredients

- 1 cup fresh or frozen shelled edamame
- 1 tablespoon canola or grapeseed oil
- 1 medium yellow onion, minced
- 5 shiitake mushroom caps, lightly rinsed, patted dry, and cut into 1/4-inch strips
- 1 teaspoon grated fresh ginger
- 3 green onions, minced
- 8 ounces firm tofu, drained and crumbled
- 2 tablespoons soy sauce
- 3 cups hot cooked white or brown rice
- 1 tablespoon toasted sesame oil
- 1 tablespoon toasted sesame seeds, for garnish

Directions

1. In a small saucepan of boiling salted water, cook the edamame until tender, about 10 minutes. Drain and set aside.
2. In a large skillet, heat the canola oil over medium heat. Add the onion, cover, and cook until softened, about 5 minutes. Add the mushrooms and cook, uncovered, 5 minutes longer. Stir in the ginger and green onions. Add the tofu and soy sauce and cook until heated through, stirring to combine well, about 5 minutes. Stir in the cooked edamame and cook until heated through, about 5 minutes.
3. Divide the hot rice among 4 bowls, top each with the edamame and tofu mixture, and drizzle on the sesame oil. Sprinkle with sesame seeds and serve immediately.

326. Sicilian Stuffed Tomatoes

Preparation time: 10 minutes
cooking time: 30 minutes
servings: 4

Ingredients

- 2 cups water
- 1 cup couscous
- Salt
- 3 green onions, minced
- 1/3 cup golden raisins
- 1 teaspoon finely grated orange zest
- 4 large ripe tomatoes
- 1/3 cup toasted pine nuts
- 1/4 cup minced fresh parsley
- Freshly ground black pepper
- 2 teaspoons olive oil

Directions

1. Preheat the oven to 375°F. Lightly oil a 9 x 13-inch baking pan and set aside. In a large saucepan, bring the water to a boil over high heat. Stir in the couscous and salt to taste and remove from the heat. Stir in the green onions, raisins, and orange zest. Cover and set aside for 5 minutes.
2. Cut a 1/2-inch-thick slice off the top of each of the tomatoes. Scoop out the pulp, keeping the tomato shells intact. Chop the pulp and place it in a large bowl. Add the couscous mixture along with the pine nuts, parsley, and salt and pepper to taste. Mix well.
3. Fill the tomatoes with the mixture and place them in the prepared pan. Drizzle the tomatoes with the oil, cover with foil, and bake until hot, about 20 minutes. Serve immediately.

327. Basic Baked Potatoes

Preparation time: 5 minutes
cooking time: 60 minutes
servings: 5

Ingredients

- 5 medium Russet potatoes or a variety of potatoes, washed and patted dry
- 1 to 2 tablespoons extra-virgin olive oil or aquafaba (see tip
- ¼ teaspoon salt
- ¼ teaspoon freshly ground black pepper

Directions

1. Preheat the oven to 400°F. Pierce each potato several times with a fork or a knife. Brush the olive oil over the potatoes, then rub each with a pinch of the salt and a pinch of the pepper.
2. Place the potatoes on a baking sheet and bake for 50 to 60 minutes, until tender. Place the potatoes on a baking rack and cool completely. Transfer to an airtight container or 5 single-serving containers. Let cool before sealing the lids.

Nutrition: Calories: 171; Fat: 3g; Protein: 4g; Carbohydrates: 34g; Fiber: 5g; Sugar: 3g; Sodium: 129mg

328. Orange-Dressed Asparagus

Preparation time: 5 minutes
cooking time: 10 minutes
servings: 4

Ingredients

- 1 medium shallot, minced
- 2 teaspoons orange zest
- 1/3 cup fresh orange juice
- 1 tablespoon fresh lemon juice
- Pinch sugar
- 2 tablespoons olive oil
- Salt and freshly ground black pepper
- 1 pound asparagus, tough ends trimmed

Directions

1. In a small bowl, combine the shallot, orange zest, orange juice, lemon juice, sugar, and oil. Add salt and pepper to taste and mix well. Set aside to allow flavors to blend, for 5 to 10 minutes.
2. Steam the asparagus until just tender, 4 to 5 minutes. If serving hot, arrange on a serving platter and drizzle the dressing over the asparagus. Serve at once.
3. If serving chilled, run the asparagus under cold water to stop the cooking process and retain the color. Drain on paper towels, then cover and refrigerate until chilled, about 1 hour. To serve, arrange the asparagus on a serving platter and drizzle with the dressing.

329. Broccoli With Almonds

Preparation time: 5 minutes
cooking time: 15 minutes
servings: 4

Ingredients

- 1 pound broccoli, cut into small florets
- 2 tablespoons olive oil
- 3 garlic cloves, minced
- 1 cup thinly sliced white mushrooms
- 1/4 cup dry white wine
- 2 tablespoons minced fresh parsley
- Salt and freshly ground black pepper
- 1/2 cup slivered toasted almonds

Directions

1. Steam the broccoli until just tender, about 5 minutes. Run under cold water and set aside.
2. In a large skillet, heat 1 tablespoon of the oil over medium heat. Add the garlic and mushrooms and cook until soft, about 5 minutes. Add the wine and cook 1 minute longer. Add the steamed broccoli and parsley and season with salt and pepper to taste. Cook until the liquid is evaporated and the broccoli is hot, about 3 minutes.
3. Transfer to a serving bowl, drizzle with the remaining 1 tablespoon oil and the almonds, and toss to coat. Serve immediately.

330. Glazed Curried Carrots

Preparation time: 5 minutes
cooking time: 15 minutes
servings: 6

Ingredients

- 1 pound carrots, peeled and thinly sliced
- 2 tablespoons olive oil
- 2 tablespoons curry powder
- 2 tablespoons pure maple syrup
- juice of ½ lemon
- sea salt
- freshly ground black pepper

Directions

1. Place the carrots in a large pot and cover with water. Cook on medium-high heat until tender, about 10 minutes. Drain the carrots and return them to the pan over medium-low heat.
2. Stir in the olive oil, curry powder, maple syrup, and lemon juice. Cook, stirring constantly, until the liquid reduces, about 5 minutes. Season with salt and pepper and serve immediately.

331. Miso Spaghetti Squash

Preparation time: 5 minutes
cooking time: 40 minutes
servings: 4

Ingredients

- 1 (3-poundspaghetti squash
- 1 tablespoon hot water
- 1 tablespoon unseasoned rice vinegar
- 1 tablespoon white miso

Directions

1. Preheat the oven to 400°F. Line a rimmed baking sheet with parchment paper. Halve the squash lengthwise and place, cut-side down, on the prepared baking sheet.
2. Bake for 35 to 40 minutes, until tender. Cool until the squash is easy to handle. With a fork, scrape out the flesh, which will be stringy, like spaghetti. Transfer to a large bowl. In a small bowl, combine the hot water, vinegar, and miso with a whisk or fork. Pour over the squash. Gently toss with tongs to coat the squash. Divide the squash evenly among 4 single-serving containers. Let cool before sealing the lids.

Nutrition: Calories: 117; Fat: 2g; Protein: 3g; Carbohydrates: 25g; Fiber: 0g; Sugar: 0g; Sodium: 218mg

332. Braised Cabbage And Apples

Preparation time: 5 minutes
cooking time: 25 minutes
servings: 6

Ingredients

- 2 tablespoons olive oil
- 1 small head red cabbage, shredded
- 1 small head savoy cabbage, shredded
- 1 Granny Smith apple
- 1 red cooking apple, such as Rome or Gala
- 2 tablespoons sugar
- 1 cup water

- 1/4 cup cider vinegar
- Salt and freshly ground black pepper

Directions

1. In a large saucepan, heat the oil over medium heat. Add the shredded red and savoy cabbage, cover, and cook until slightly wilted, 5 minutes.
2. Core the apples and cut them into 1/4-inch dice. Add the apples to the cabbage, along with the sugar, water, vinegar, and salt and pepper to taste. Reduce heat to low, cover, and simmer until the cabbage and apples are tender, stirring frequently, about 20 minutes. Serve immediately.

333. Marsala Carrots

Preparation time: 5 minutes
cooking time: 20 minutes
servings: 4

Ingredients

- 2 tablespoons vegan margarine
- 1 pound carrots, cut diagonally into 1/4-inch slices
- Salt and freshly ground black pepper
- 1/2 cup Marsala
- 1/4 cup water
- 1/4 cup chopped fresh parsley, for garnish

Directions

1. In a large skillet, melt the margarine over medium heat. Add the carrots and toss well to coat evenly with the margarine. Cover and cook, stirring occasionally, for 5 minutes.
2. Season with salt and pepper to taste, tossing to coat. Add the Marsala and water. Reduce heat to low, cover, and simmer until the carrots are tender, about 15 minutes.
3. Uncover and cook over medium-high heat until the liquid is reduced into a syrupy sauce, stirring to prevent burning.
4. Transfer to a serving bowl and sprinkle with parsley. Serve immediately.

334. Garlic And Herb Zoodles

Preparation time: 10 minutes
cooking time: 2 minutes
servings: 4

Ingredients

- 1 teaspoon extra-virgin olive oil or 2 tablespoons vegetable broth
- 1 teaspoon minced garlic (about 1 clove
- 4 medium zucchini, spiralized
- ½ teaspoon dried basil
- ½ teaspoon dried oregano
- ¼ to ½ teaspoon red pepper flakes, to taste
- ¼ teaspoon salt (optional
- ¼ teaspoon freshly ground black pepper

Directions

1. In a large skillet over medium-high heat, heat the olive oil.
2. Add the garlic, zucchini, basil, oregano, red pepper flakes, salt (if using), and black pepper. Sauté for 1 to 2 minutes, until barely tender. Divide the zoodles evenly among 4 storage containers. Let cool before sealing the lids.

Nutrition: Calories: 44; Fat: 2g; Protein: 3g; Carbohydrates: 7g; Fiber: 2g; Sugar: 3g; Sodium: 20mg

335. Ratatouille (Pressure cooker

Preparation time: 15 minutes
Servings: 4-6

Ingredients

- 1 onion, diced
- 4 garlic cloves, minced
- 1 to 2 teaspoons olive oil
- 1 cup water
- 3 or 4 tomatoes, diced
- 1 eggplant, cubed
- 1 or 2 bell peppers, any color, seeded and chopped
- 1½ tablespoons dried herbes de Provence (or any mixture of dried basil, oregano, thyme, marjoram, and rosemary
- ½ teaspoon salt
- Freshly ground black pepper

Directions

1. On your electric pressure cooker, select Sauté. Add the onion, garlic, and olive oil. Cook for 4 to 5 minutes, stirring occasionally, until the onion is softened.

Add the water, tomatoes, eggplant, bell peppers, and herbes de Provence. Cancel Sauté.

2. High pressure for 6 minutes. Close and lock the lid and ensure the pressure valve is sealed, then select High Pressure and set the time for 6 minutes.
3. Pressure Release. Once the cook time is complete, let the pressure release naturally, about 20 minutes. Once all the pressure has released, carefully unlock and remove the lid. Let cool for a few minutes, then season with salt and pepper.

Nutrition Calories: 101; Total fat: 2g; Protein: 4g; Sodium: 304mg; Fiber: 7g

336. Cardamom Carrots With Orange

Preparation time: 5 minutes
cooking time: 10 minutes
servings: 4

Ingredients

- 1 pound carrots, cut into 1⁄4-inch slices
- 2 tablespoons vegan margarine
- 1 tablespoon finely grated orange zest
- 1⁄2 teaspoon ground cardamom
- Salt
- Ground cayenne

Directions

1. Steam the carrots until tender, about 7 minutes. Set aside.
2. In a large skillet, melt the margarine over medium heat. Add the carrots, orange zest, and cardamom and season with salt and cayenne to taste. Cook, stirring occasionally, until flavors are blended, about 2 minutes. Serve immediately

337. Stuffed Baby Peppers

Preparation time: 10 minutes
Cooking time: 0 minutes
Servings: 4

Ingredients:

- 12 baby bell peppers, cut into halves lengthwise and seeds removed
- ¼ teaspoon red pepper flakes, crushed
- 1 pound shrimp, cooked, peeled and deveined
- 6 tablespoons jarred Paleo pesto
- A pinch of sea salt
- Black pepper to taste
- 1 tablespoon lemon juice
- 1 tablespoon olive oil
- A handful parsley, chopped

Directions:

1. In a bowl, mix shrimp with pepper flakes, Paleo pesto, a pinch of salt, black pepper, lemon juice, oil and parsley and whisk well.
2. Divide this into bell pepper halves, arrange on plates and serve.
3. Enjoy!

Nutritional value/serving: calories 371, fat 14, fiber 3,2, carbs 20,9, protein 30,5

338. Pork Stuffed Bell Peppers

Preparation time: 10 minutes
Cooking time: 26 minutes
Servings: 4

Ingredients:

- 1 teaspoon Cajun spice
- 1 pound pork, ground
- 1 tablespoon olive oil
- 1 tablespoon tomato paste
- 6 garlic cloves, minced
- 1 yellow onion, chopped
- 4 big bell peppers, tops cut off and seeds removed
- A pinch of sea salt
- Black pepper to taste

Directions:

1. Heat up a pan with the oil over medium-high heat, add garlic and onion, stir and cook for 4 minutes.
2. Add meat, stir and cook for 10 minutes more.
3. Add a pinch of salt, black pepper, tomato paste and Cajun seasoning, stir and cook for 3 minutes more.
4. Stuff bell peppers with this mix, place them under a preheated broiler on a medium high heat, broil for 3 minutes on each side, divide between plates and serve.
5. Enjoy!

Nutritional value/serving: calories 251, fat 7,9, fiber 2,4, carbs 13,8, protein 31,7

339. Bell Peppers Stuffed with Tuna

Preparation time: 10 minutes
Cooking time: 10 minutes
Servings: 4

Ingredients:

- 2 bell peppers, tops cut off, cut in halves and seeds removed
- 1 tablespoon capers, chopped
- 2 tablespoons tomato puree
- 4 ounces cooked salmon
- 1 scallion, chopped
- 1 tomato, chopped
- Black pepper to taste

Directions:

1. Place bell pepper halves on a lined baking sheet, place under a preheated broiler on medium-high heat, broil for 4 minutes and then leave them aside to cool down.
2. Meanwhile, in a bowl mix capers with tomato puree, salmon, tomato, black pepper and scallion and stir well.
3. Stuff bell peppers with this mix, place under preheated broiler again and cook for 5 minutes.
4. Divide between plates and serve.
5. Enjoy!

Nutritional value/serving: calories 64, fat 2, fiber 1,3, carbs 6,2, protein 6,5

340. Liver Stuffed Peppers

Preparation time: 10 minutes
Cooking time: 15 minutes
Servings: 4

Ingredients:

- 3 small shallots, peeled, chopped
- 1 white onion, chopped
- ½ pound chicken livers, chopped
- 4 garlic cloves, chopped
- 4 bell peppers, tops cut off and seeds removed
- A pinch of sea salt
- Black pepper to taste
- ½ teaspoon lemon zest, grated
- ¼ teaspoon thyme, chopped
- ¼ teaspoon dill, chopped
- A drizzle of olive oil
- A handful parsley, chopped

Directions:

1. Heat up a pan over medium heat, add chopped shallots, stir for 5 minutes.
2. Add onion and garlic, stir and cook for 2 minutes.
3. Add livers, a pinch of salt and black pepper, stir, cook for 5 minutes and take off heat.
4. Transfer this to a food processor, blend well, transfer to a bowl and aside for 10 minutes.
5. Add thyme, oil, parsley, lemon zest and dill, stir well and stuff each bell pepper with this mix.
6. Serve right away.
7. Enjoy!

Nutritional value/serving: calories 188, fat 7,6, fiber 2,5, carbs 15,6, protein 16,1

341. Baked Eggplant

Preparation time: 10 minutes
Cooking time: 30 minutes
Servings: 3

Ingredients:

- 2 eggplants, sliced
- A pinch of sea salt
- Black pepper to taste
- 1 cup almonds, ground
- 1 teaspoon garlic, minced
- 2 teaspoons olive oil

Directions:

1. Grease a baking dish with some of the oil and arrange eggplant slices on it.
2. Season them with a pinch of salt and some black pepper and leave them aside for 10 minutes.
3. In a food processor, mix almonds with the rest of the oil, garlic, a pinch of salt and black pepper and blend well.
4. Spread this over eggplant slices, place in the oven at 425 degrees F and bake for 30 minutes.
5. Divide between plates and serve.
6. Enjoy!

Nutritional value/serving: calories 303, fat 19,6, fiber 16,9, carbs 28,6, protein 10,3

342. Eggplant Mix

Preparation time: 10 minutes
Cooking time: 40 minutes
Servings: 3

Ingredients:

- 5 medium eggplants, sliced into rounds
- 1 teaspoon thyme, chopped
- 2 tablespoons balsamic vinegar
- 1 teaspoon mustard
- 2 garlic cloves, minced
- ½ cup olive oil
- Black pepper to taste
- A pinch of sea salt
- 1 teaspoon maple syrup

Directions:

1. In a bowl, mix vinegar with thyme, mustard, garlic, oil, salt, pepper and maple syrup and whisk very well.
2. Arrange eggplant round on a lined baking sheet, place in the oven at 425 degrees F and roast for 40 minutes.
3. Divide eggplants between plates and serve.
4. Enjoy!

Nutritional value/serving: calories 533, fat 35,6, fiber 32,6, carbs 56,5, protein 9,4

343. Eggplant Casserole

Preparation time: 10 minutes
Cooking time: 50 minutes
Servings: 4

Ingredients:

- 2 eggplants, sliced
- 3 tablespoons olive oil
- 1 pound beef, ground
- 1 garlic clove, minced
- ¾ cup tomato sauce
- ½ bunch basil, chopped
- A pinch of sea salt
- Black pepper to taste

Directions:

1. Heat up a pan with 1 tablespoon oil over medium-high heat, add eggplant slices, cook for 5 minutes on each side, transfer them to paper towels, drain grease and leave them aside.
2. Heat up another pan with the rest of the oil over medium-high heat, add garlic, stir and cook for 1 minute.
3. Add beef, stir and cook for 5 minutes more.
4. Add tomato sauce, stir and cook for 5 minutes more.
5. Add a pinch of sea salt and black pepper, stir, take off heat and mix with basil.
6. Place one layer of eggplant slices into a baking dish, add one layer of beef mix and repeat with the rest of the eggplant slices and beef.
7. Place in the oven at 350 degrees F and bake for 30 minutes.
8. Leave eggplant casserole to cool down, slice and serve.
9. Enjoy!

Nutritional value/serving: calories 382, fat 18,2, fiber 10,4, carbs 18,9, protein 37,8

344. Eggplant and Garlic Sauce

Preparation time: 10 minutes
Cooking time: 10 minutes
Servings: 4

Ingredients:

- 2 tablespoons avocado oil
- 2 garlic cloves, minced
- 3 eggplants, cut into halves and thinly sliced
- 1 red chili pepper, chopped
- 1 green onion stalk, chopped
- 1 tablespoon ginger, grated
- 1 tablespoon coconut aminos
- 1 tablespoon balsamic vinegar

Directions:

1. Heat up a pan with half of the oil over medium-high heat, add eggplant slices, cook for 2 minutes, flip, cook for 3 minutes more and transfer to a plate.
2. Heat up the pan with the rest of the oil over medium heat, add chili pepper, garlic, green onions and ginger, stir and cook for 1 minute.
3. Return eggplant slices to the pan, stir and cook for 1 minute.
4. Add coconut aminos and vinegar, stir,

divide between plates and serve.
5. Enjoy!

Nutritional value/serving: calories 123, fat 1,7, fiber 15,2, carbs 26,7, protein 4,4

345. Eggplant Hash

Preparation time: 20 minutes
Cooking time: 20 minutes
Servings: 4

Ingredients:

- 1 eggplant, roughly chopped
- ½ cup olive oil
- ½ pound cherry tomatoes, halved
- 1 teaspoon Tabasco sauce
- ¼ cup basil, chopped
- ¼ cup mint, chopped
- A pinch of sea salt
- Black pepper to taste

Directions:

1. Put eggplant pieces in a bowl, add a pinch of salt, toss to coat, leave aside for 20 minutes and drain using paper towels.
2. Heat up a pan with half of the oil over medium-high heat, add eggplant, cook for 3 minutes, flip, cook them for 3 minutes more and transfer to a bowl.
3. Heat up the same pan with the rest of the oil over medium-high heat, add tomatoes and cook them for 8 minutes stirring from time to time.
4. Return eggplant pieces to the pan and add a pinch of salt, black pepper, basil, mint and Tabasco sauce.
5. Stir, cook for 2 minutes more, divide between plates and serve.
6. Enjoy!

Nutritional value/serving: calories 258, fat 25,6, fiber 5,1, carbs 9,5, protein 1.9

346. Eggplant Jam

Preparation time: 10 minutes
Cooking time: 1 hour
Servings: 6

Ingredients:

- 3 eggplants, sliced lengthwise
- 2 teaspoons sweet paprika
- 2 garlic cloves, minced
- A pinch of sea salt
- A pinch of cinnamon, ground
- 1teaspoon cumin, ground
- A splash of hot sauce
- ¼ cup water
- 1 tablespoon parsley, chopped
- 2 tablespoons lemon juice

Directions:

1. Sprinkle some salt on eggplant slices and leave them aside for 10 minutes.
2. Pat dry eggplant, brush them with half of the oil, place on a lined baking sheet, place in the oven at 375 degrees F, bake for 25 minutes flipping them halfway and leave them aside to cool down.
3. In a bowl, mix paprika with garlic, cinnamon, cumin, water and hot sauce and stir well.
4. Add baked eggplant pieces and mash them with a fork.
5. Heat up a pan with the rest of the oil over medium-low heat, add eggplant mix, stir and cook for 20 minutes.
6. Add lemon juice and parsley, stir, take off heat, divide into small bowls and serve.
7. Enjoy!

Nutritional value/serving: calories 75, fat 0,7, fiber 10,1, carbs 17,2, protein 3

347. Warm Watercress Mix

Preparation time: 10 minutes
Cooking time: 10 minutes
Servings: 4

Ingredients:

- 1 pound watercress, chopped
- ¼ cup olive oil
- 1 garlic clove, cut in halves
- 1 small shallot, peeled, cooked and chopped
- ¼ cup hazelnuts, chopped
- Black pepper to taste
- ¼ cup pine nuts

Directions:

1. Heat up a pan with the oil over medium heat, add garlic clove halves, cook for 2 minutes and discard.
2. Heat up the pan with the garlic oil again

over medium heat, add hazelnuts and pine nuts, stir and cook for 6 minutes.
3. Add shallots, black pepper to taste and watercress, stir, cook for 2 minutes, divide between plates and serve right away.
4. Enjoy!

Nutritional value/serving: calories 220, fat 21,8, fiber 2,1, carbs 2,9, protein 5,3

348. Watercress Soup

Preparation time: 10 minutes
Cooking time: 20 minutes
Servings: 4

Ingredients:

- 8 ounces watercress
- 1 tablespoon lemon juice
- A pinch of nutmeg, ground
- 4 ounces coconut milk
- A pinch of sea salt
- Black pepper to taste
- 14 ounces veggie stock
- 1 celery stick, chopped
- 1 onion, chopped
- 1 tablespoon olive oil
- 12 ounces sweet potatoes, peeled and chopped

Directions:

1. Heat up a large saucepan with the oil over medium heat, add onion and celery, stir and cook for 5 minutes.
2. Add sweet potato pieces and stock, stir, bring to a simmer, cover and cook on a low heat for 10 minutes.
3. Add watercress, stir, cover saucepan again and cook for 5 minutes.
4. Blend this with an immersion blender, add a pinch of nutmeg, lemon juice, salt, pepper and coconut milk, bring to a simmer again, divide into bowls and serve.
5. Enjoy!

Nutritional value/serving: calories 224, fat 11,8, fiber 5,7, carbs 29,6, protein 4

349. Artichokes and Mushroom Mix

Preparation time: 30 minutes
Cooking time: 30 minutes
Servings: 4

Ingredients:

- 16 mushrooms, sliced
- 1/3 cup tamari sauce
- 1/3 cup olive oil
- 4 tablespoons balsamic vinegar
- 4 garlic cloves, minced
- 1 tablespoon lemon juice
- 1 teaspoon oregano, dried
- 1 teaspoon rosemary, dried
- ½ tablespoon thyme, dried
- A pinch of sea salt
- Black pepper to taste
- 1 sweet onion, chopped
- 1 jar artichoke hearts
- 4 cups spinach
- 1 tablespoon coconut oil
- 1 teaspoon garlic, minced
- 1 cauliflower head, florets separated
- ½ cup veggie stock
- 1 teaspoon garlic powder
- A pinch of nutmeg, ground

Directions:

1. In a bowl, mix vinegar with tamari sauce, lemon juice, 4 garlic cloves, olive oil, oregano, rosemary, thyme, a pinch of salt, black pepper and mushrooms, toss to coat well and leave aside for 30 minutes.
2. Transfer these to a lined baking sheet and bake them in the oven at 350 degrees F for 30 minutes.
3. In a food processor, mix cauliflower with a pinch of sea salt and black pepper and pulse until you obtain rice.
4. Heat a pan to medium-high heat, add cauliflower rice, toast for 2 minutes, add nutmeg, garlic powder, black pepper and stock, stir and cook until stock evaporated.
5. Heat a pan with the coconut oil over medium heat, add onion, artichokes, 1 teaspoon garlic and spinach, stir and cook for a few minutes.
6. Divide cauliflower rice on plates, top with artichokes and mushrooms and serve.

!Nutritional value/serving: calories 354, fat 29,9, fiber 4,3, carbs 16,5, protein 6,6

350. Artichokes with Horseradish Sauce

Preparation time: 10 minutes
Cooking time: 45 minutes
Servings: 2

Ingredients:

- 1 tablespoon horseradish, prepared
- 2 tablespoons mayonnaise
- A pinch of sea salt
- Black pepper to taste
- 1 teaspoon lemon juice
- 3 cups artichoke hearts
- 1 tablespoon lemon juice

Directions:

1. In a bowl, mix horseradish with mayo, a pinch of sea salt, black pepper and 1 teaspoon lemon juice, whisk well and leave aside for now.
2. Arrange artichoke hearts on a lined baking sheet, drizzle 2 tablespoons olive oil over them, 1 tablespoon lemon juice and sprinkle a pinch of salt and some black pepper.
3. Toss to coat well, place in the oven at 425 degrees F and roast for 45 minutes.
4. Divide artichoke hearts between plates and serve with the horseradish sauce on top.
5. Enjoy!

Nutritional value/serving: calories 107, fat 5, fiber 3,3, carbs 14,9, protein 1,7

351. Grilled Artichokes

Preparation time: 10 minutes
Cooking time: 25 minutes
Servings: 4

Ingredients:

- 2 artichokes, trimmed and halved
- Juice of 1 lemon
- 1 tablespoons lemon zest grated
- 1 rosemary spring, chopped
- 2 tablespoons olive oil
- A pinch of sea salt
- Black pepper to taste

Directions:

1. Put water in a large saucepan, add a pinch of salt and lemon juice, bring to a boil over medium-high heat, add artichokes, boil for 15 minutes, drain and leave them to cool down.
2. Drizzle olive oil over them, season with black pepper to taste, sprinkle lemon zest and rosemary, stir well and place them under a preheated grill.
3. Broil artichokes over medium-high heat for 5 minutes on each side, divide them between plates and serve.
4. Enjoy!

Nutritional value/serving: calories 98, fat 7,1, fiber 4,4, carbs 8,5, protein 2,7

352. Artichokes and Tomatoes Dip

Preparation time: 10 minutes
Cooking time: 30 minutes
Servings: 4

Ingredients:

- 2 artichokes, cut in halves and trimmed
- Juice from 3 lemons
- 4 sun-dried tomatoes, chopped
- A bunch of parsley, chopped
- A bunch of basil, chopped
- 1 garlic clove, minced
- 4 tablespoons olive oil
- Black pepper to taste

Directions:

1. In a bowl, mix artichokes with lemon juice from 1 lemon, some black pepper and toss to coat.
2. Transfer to a large saucepan, add water to cover, bring to a boil over medium-high heat, cook for 30 minutes and drain.
3. In a food processor, mix the rest of the lemon juice with tomatoes, parsley, basil, garlic, black pepper and olive oil and blend well.
4. Divide artichokes between plates and top each with the tomatoes dip.
5. Enjoy!

Nutritional value/serving: calories 193, fat 14,5, fiber 6,1, carbs 16,9, protein 4,1

352. Carrot Hash

Preparation time: 10 minutes
Cooking time: 45 minutes
Servings: 4

Ingredients:

- 1 tablespoon olive oil
- 5 small shallots, peeled, chopped
- 3 cups carrots, chopped
- ¾ pound beef, ground
- 1 yellow onion, chopped
- A pinch of sea salt
- Black pepper to taste
- 2 scallions, chopped

Directions:

1. Place carrots on a lined baking sheet, drizzle the oil, season with a pinch of salt and some black pepper, toss to coat, place in the oven at 425 degrees F and bake for 25 minutes.
2. Meanwhile, heat a pan to a medium high heat, add shallots and cook for 10 minutes.
3. Add onion and beef and some black pepper, stir and cook for 7-8 minutes more.
4. Take carrots out of the oven, add them to the beef and shallots mix, stir and cook for 10 minutes.
5. Sprinkle scallions on top, divide between plates and serve.
6. Enjoy!

Nutritional value/serving: calories 248, fat 8,9, fiber 2,8, carbs 14,2, protein 27,4

354. Carrots and Lime Mix

Preparation time: 10 minutes
Cooking time: 30 minutes
Servings: 6

Ingredients:

- 1 and ¼ pounds baby carrots
- 3 tablespoons ghee, melted
- 8 garlic cloves, minced
- A pinch of sea salt
- Black pepper to taste
- Zest of 2 limes, grated
- ½ teaspoon chili powder

Directions:

1. In a bowl, mix baby carrots with ghee, garlic, a pinch of salt, black pepper to taste, chili powder and stir well.
2. Spread carrots on a lined baking sheet, place in the oven at 400 degrees F and roast for 15 minutes.
3. Take carrots out of the oven, shake baking sheet, place in the oven again and roast for 15 minutes more.
4. Divide between plates and serve with lime on top.
5. Enjoy!

Nutritional value/serving: calories 95, fat 6,6, fiber 2,9, carbs 9,1, protein 0,9

355. Maple Glazed Carrots

Preparation time: 10 minutes
Cooking time: 15 minutes
Servings: 4

Ingredients:

- 1 pound carrots, sliced
- 1 tablespoon coconut oil
- 1 tablespoon ghee
- ½ cup pineapple juice
- 1 teaspoon ginger, grated
- ½ tablespoon maple syrup
- ½ teaspoon nutmeg
- 1 tablespoon parsley, chopped

Directions:

1. Heat a pan with the ghee and the oil over medium-high heat, add ginger, stir and cook for 2 minutes.
2. Add carrots, stir and cook for 5 minutes.
3. Add pineapple juice, maple syrup and nutmeg, stir and cook for 5 minutes more.
4. Add parsley, stir, cook for 3 minutes, divide between plates and serve.
5. Enjoy!

Nutritional value/serving: calories 130, fat 6,8, fiber 3, carbs 17,4, protein 1,1

365. Purple Carrot Mix

Preparation time: 10 minutes
Cooking time: 1 hour
Servings: 5

Ingredients:

- 6 purple carrots, peeled
- A drizzle of olive oil
- 2 tablespoons sesame seeds paste
- 6 tablespoons water
- 3 tablespoons lemon juice

- 1 garlic clove, minced
- A pinch of sea salt
- Black pepper to taste
- White sesame seeds for serving

Directions:

1. Arrange the purple carrots on a lined baking sheet, sprinkle a pinch of salt, black pepper and a drizzle of oil, place in the oven at 350 degrees F and bake for 1 hour.
2. Meanwhile, in a food processor, mix sesame seeds paste with water, lemon juice, garlic, a pinch of sea salt and black pepper and pulse well.
3. Spread over the carrots, toss gently, divide between plates and sprinkle sesame seeds on top.
4. Enjoy!

Nutritional value/serving: calories 100, fat 4,7, fiber 0,9, carbs 13,6, protein 1,2

357. Black Bean Soup

Preparation time: 10 minutes
cooking time: 15 minutes
servings: 4

Ingredients

- 2 tablespoons olive oil
- 1 onion, diced
- 1 green bell pepper, diced
- 1 carrot, peeled and diced
- 4 garlic cloves, minced
- two 15-ounce cans black beans, drained and rinsed
- 2 cups vegetable stock
- ¼ teaspoon ground cumin
- 1 teaspoon sea salt
- ¼ cup chopped cilantro, for garnish

Directions

1. In a large soup pot, heat the olive oil over medium-high heat until it shimmers.
2. Add the onion, bell pepper, and carrot and cook until the vegetables soften, about 5 -minutes. Add garlic and cook until it is fragrant, about 30 seconds. Add the black beans, vegetable stock, cumin, and salt. Cook over medium-high heat, stirring occasionally, for about 10 minutes.
3. Remove from the heat. Using a potato masher, mash the beans lightly, leaving some chunks in the soup. For a smoother soup, process in a blender or food processor. Serve hot, garnished with cilantro.

358. Creamy Garlic-Spinach Rotini Soup

Preparation time: 10 minutes
cooking time: 15 minutes
servings: 4

Ingredients

- 1 teaspoon olive oil
- 1 cup chopped mushrooms
- ¼ teaspoon plus a pinch salt
- 4 garlic cloves, minced, or 1 teaspoon garlic powder
- 2 peeled carrots or ½ red bell pepper, chopped
- 6 cups Economical Vegetable Broth or water
- Pinch freshly ground black pepper
- 1 cup rotini or gnocchi
- ¾ cup unsweetened nondairy milk
- ¼ cup nutritional yeast
- 2 cups chopped fresh spinach
- ¼ cup pitted black olives or sun-dried tomatoes, chopped
- Herbed Croutons, for topping (optional

Directions

1. Heat the olive oil in a large soup pot over medium-high heat.
2. Add the mushrooms and a pinch of salt. Sauté for about 4 minutes, until the mushrooms are softened. Add the garlic (if using freshand carrots, sauté for 1 minute more. Add the vegetable broth, remaining ¼ teaspoon of salt, and pepper (plus the garlic powder, if using). Bring to a boil and add the pasta. Cook for about 10 minutes, until the pasta is just cooked.
3. Turn off the heat and stir in the milk, nutritional yeast, spinach, and olives. Top with croutons (if using). Leftovers will keep in an airtight container for up to 1 week in the refrigerator or up to 1 month in the freezer.

Nutrition (2 cupsCalories: 207; Protein: 11g; Total fat: 5g; Saturated fat: 1g; Carbohydrates: 34g; Fiber: 7g

359. White And Wild Mushroom Barley Soup

Preparation time: 5 minutes
cooking time: 50 minutes
servings: 4 to 6

Ingredients

- 1 tablespoon olive oil
- 1 medium onion, chopped

- 1 medium carrot, chopped
- 2 celery ribs, chopped
- 12 ounces white mushrooms, lightly rinsed, patted dry, and sliced
- 8 ounces cremini, shiitake, or other wild mushrooms, lightly rinsed, patted dry, and cut into 1⁄4-inch slices
- 1 cup pearl barley
- 7 cups vegetable or mushroom broth, homemade (see Light Vegetable Broth or Mushroom Vegetable Brothor store-bought, or water
- 1 teaspoon dried dillweed
- Salt and freshly ground black pepper
- 2 tablespoons minced fresh parsley

Directions

1. In a large soup pot, heat the oil over medium heat. Add the onion, carrot, and celery. Cover and cook until soft, about 10 minutes. Uncover and stir in the mushrooms, barley, broth, dillweed, and salt and pepper to taste. Bring to a boil, then reduce heat to low and simmer, uncovered, until the barley and vegetables are tender, about 40 minutes.
2. Add the parsley, taste, adjust seasonings if necessary, and serve.

Italian Wedding Soup

Preparation time: 10 minutes
cooking time: 15 minutes
servings: 4

Ingredients

- 1 teaspoon olive oil
- 2 carrots, peeled and chopped
- ½ onion, chopped
- 3 or 4 garlic cloves, minced, or ½ teaspoon garlic powder
- Salt
- 8 cups water or Economical Vegetable Broth
- 1 cup orzo or pearl couscous
- 1 tablespoon dried herbs
- Freshly ground black pepper
- 1 recipe quinoa meatballs (from Meatball Subs recipe
- 2 cups chopped greens, such as spinach, kale, or chard

Directions

- Heat the olive oil in a large soup pot over medium-high heat.
- Add the carrots, onion, garlic (if using fresh), and a pinch of salt. Sauté for 3 to 4 minutes, until softened. Add the water, orzo, and dried herbs (plus the garlic powder, if using). Season to taste with salt and pepper, and bring the soup to a boil. Turn the heat to low and simmer until the orzo is soft, about 10 minutes. Add the meatballs and greens, and stir until the greens are wilted. Taste and season with more salt and pepper as needed. Leftovers will keep in an airtight container for up to 1 week in the refrigerator or up to 1 month in the freezer.

Nutrition (2 cupsCalories: 168; Protein: 9g; Total fat: 3g; Saturated fat: 0g; Carbohydrates: 30g; Fiber: 6g

361. Roasted Vegetable Bisque

Preparation time: 10 minutes
cooking time: 15 minutes
servings: 6

Ingredients

- 1 large onion, coarsely chopped
- 2 medium carrots, coarsely chopped
- 1 large russet potato, peeled and cut into 1⁄2-inch dice
- 1 medium zucchini, thinly sliced
- 1 large ripe tomato, quartered
- 2 garlic cloves, crushed
- 2 tablespoons olive oil
- 1⁄2 teaspoon dried savory
- 1⁄2 teaspoon dried thyme
- Salt and freshly ground black pepper
- 4 cups vegetable broth, homemade (see Light Vegetable Brothor store-bought, or water
- 1 tablespoon minced fresh parsley, for garnish

Directions

1. Preheat the oven to 400°F. In a lightly oiled 9 x 13-inch baking pan, place the onion, carrots, potato, zucchini, tomato,

and garlic. Drizzle with the oil and season with savory, thyme, and salt and pepper to taste. Cover tightly with foil and bake until softened, about 30 minutes. Uncover and bake, stirring once, until vegetables are lightly browned, about 30 minutes more.

2. Transfer the roasted vegetables to a large soup pot, add the broth, and bring to a boil. Reduce the heat to low and simmer, uncovered, for 15 minutes.
3. Puree the soup in the pot with an immersion blender or in a blender or food processor, in batches if necessary, and return to the pot. Heat over medium heat until hot. Taste, adjusting seasonings if necessary.
4. Ladle into bowls, sprinkle with parsley, and serve.

362. Spicy Gazpacho

Preparation time: 15 minutes
cooking time: 0 minutes
servings: 4

Ingredients

- 1 tablespoon olive oil
- 3 cups vegetable juice, such as v8
- 1 red onion, diced
- 3 tomatoes, chopped
- 1 red bell pepper, diced
- 2 garlic cloves, minced
- juice of 1 lemon
- 2 tablespoons chopped fresh basil
- ¼ to ½ teaspoon cayenne pepper
- sea salt
- freshly ground black pepper

Directions

1. In a blender or a food processor, combine the olive oil, vegetable juice, all but ½ cup of the onion, all but ½ cup of the tomato, all but ½ cup of the bell pepper, the garlic, lemon juice, basil, and cayenne. Season with salt and pepper and process until smooth.
2. Stir the reserved ½ cup onion, ½ cup tomatoes, and ½ cup bell pepper into the processed ingredients and refrigerate for 1 hour. Serve chilled.

363. Mushroom & Wild Rice Stew

Preparation time: 10 minutes
cooking time: 50 minutes
servings: 6

Ingredients

- 1 to 2 teaspoons olive oil
- 2 cups chopped mushrooms
- ½ to 1 teaspoon salt
- 1 onion, chopped, or 1 teaspoon onion powder
- 3 or 4 garlic cloves, minced, or ½ teaspoon garlic powder
- 1 tablespoon dried herbs
- ¾ cup brown rice
- ¼ cup wild rice or additional brown rice
- 3 cups water
- 3 cups Economical Vegetable Broth or store-bought broth
- 2 to 4 tablespoons balsamic vinegar (optional
- Freshly ground black pepper
- 1 cup frozen peas, thawed
- 1 cup unsweetened nondairy milk (optional
- 1 to 2 cups chopped greens, such as spinach, kale, or chard

Directions

1. Heat the olive oil in a large soup pot over medium-high heat.
2. Add the mushrooms and a pinch of salt, and sauté for about 4 minutes, until the mushrooms are softened. Add the onion and garlic (if using fresh), and sauté for 1 to 2 minutes more. Stir in the dried herbs (plus the onion powder and/or garlic powder, if using), white or brown rice, wild rice, water, vegetable broth, vinegar (if using), and salt and pepper to taste. Bring to a boil, turn the heat to low, and cover the pot. Simmer the soup for 15 minutes (for white riceor 45 minutes (for brown rice). Turn off the heat and stir in the peas, milk (if using), and greens. Let the greens wilt before serving.
3. Leftovers will keep in an airtight container for up to 1 week in the refrigerator or up to 1 month in the freezer.

Nutrition (2 cupsCalories: 201; Protein: 6g; Total fat: 3g; Saturated fat: 0g; Carbohydrates: 44g; Fiber: 4g

364. Almond Soup With Cardamom

Preparation time: 5 minutes
cooking time: 35 minutes total: 40minutes
servings: 4

Ingredients

- 1 tablespoon olive oil
- 1 medium onion, chopped
- 1 medium russet potato, chopped
- 1 medium red bell pepper, chopped
- 4 cups vegetable broth, homemade (see Light Vegetable Brothor store-bought, or water
- 1/2 teaspoon ground cardamom
- Salt and freshly ground black pepper
- 1/2 cup almond butter
- 1/4 cup sliced toasted almonds, for garnish

Directions

1. In a large soup pot, heat the oil over medium heat. Add the onion, potato, and bell pepper. Cover and cook until softened, about 5 minutes. Add the broth, cardamom, and salt and pepper to taste. Bring to a boil, then reduce heat to low and simmer, uncovered, until the vegetables are tender, about 30 minutes.
2. Add the almond butter and puree in the pot with an immersion blender or in a blender or food processor, in batches if necessary, and return to the pot. Reheat over medium heat until hot. Taste, adjusting seasonings if necessary, and add more broth or some soy milk if needed for desired consistency.
3. Ladle the soup into bowls, sprinkle with toasted sliced almonds, and serve.

365. Easy Corn Chowder

Preparation time: 15 minutes
cooking time: 15 minutes
servings: 4

Ingredients

- 2 tablespoons olive oil or other vegetable oil, such as coconut oil
- 1 onion, chopped
- 1 cup chopped fennel bulb or celery
- 2 carrots, peeled and chopped
- 1 red bell pepper, finely chopped
- ¼ cup all-purpose flour
- 6 cups vegetable stock
- 2 cups fresh or canned corn
- 2 cups cubed red potato
- 1 cup unsweetened almond milk or other unsweetened nut or grain milk
- ½ teaspoon sriracha sauce or chili paste (optional
- sea salt
- freshly ground black pepper

Directions

1. In a large pot, heat the olive oil over medium-high heat until it shimmers.
2. Add the onion, fennel, carrots, and bell pepper and cook, stirring occasionally, until the vegetables soften, about 3 minutes.
3. Sprinkle the flour over the vegetables and continue to cook, stirring constantly, for about 2 minutes.
4. Stir in the vegetable stock, using a spoon to scrape any bits of flour or vegetables from the bottom of the pan. Continue stirring until the liquid comes to a boil and the soup begins to thicken. Lower the heat to medium.
5. Add the corn, potatoes, almond milk, and Sriracha, if using. Simmer until the potatoes are soft, about 10 minutes. Season with salt and pepper. Serve hot.

366. Tamarind Chickpea Stew

Preparation time: 5 minutes
cooking time: 60 minutes
servings: 4

Ingredients

- 1 tablespoon olive oil
- 1 large onion, chopped
- 2 medium Yukon Gold potatoes, peeled and cut into 1/4-inch dice
- 3 cups cooked chickpeas or 2 (15.5-ouncecans chickpeas, drained and rinsed
- 1 (28-ouncecan crushed tomatoes
- 1 (4-ouncecan mild chopped green chiles,

drained

- 2 tablespoons tamarind paste
- 1/4 cup pure maple syrup
- 1 cup vegetable broth, homemade or water
- 2 tablespoons chili powder
- 1 teaspoon ground coriander
- 1/2 teaspoon ground cumin
- Salt and freshly ground black pepper
- 1 cup frozen baby peas, thawed

Directions

1. In a large saucepan, heat the oil over medium heat. Add the onion, cover, and cook until softened, about 5 minutes. Add the potatoes, chickpeas, tomatoes, and chiles and simmer, uncovered, for 5 minutes.
2. In a small bowl, combine the tamarind paste, maple syrup, and broth and blend until smooth. Stir the tamarind mixture into the vegetables, along with the chili powder, coriander, cumin, and salt and pepper to taste. Bring to a boil, then reduce the heat to medium and simmer, covered, until the potatoes are tender, about 40 minutes.
3. Taste, adjusting seasonings if necessary, and stir in the peas. Simmer, uncovered, about 10 minutes longer. Serve immediately.

367. Cream Of Artichoke Soup

Preparation time: 10 minutes
cooking time: 20 minutes
servings: 4

Ingredients

- 1 tablespoon olive oil
- 2 medium shallots, chopped
- 2 (10-ouncepackages frozen artichoke hearts, thawed
- 3 cups vegetable broth, homemade (see Light Vegetable Brothor store-bought, or water
- 1 teaspoon fresh lemon juice
- Salt
- 1/3 cup almond butter
- 1/8 teaspoon ground cayenne
- 1 cup plain unsweetened soy milk
- 1 tablespoon snipped fresh chives, for garnish
- 2 tablespoons sliced toasted almonds, for garnish

Directions

1. In a large soup pot, heat the oil over medium heat. Add the shallots, cover, and cook until softened. Uncover and stir in the artichoke hearts, broth, lemon juice, and salt to taste. Bring to a boil, then reduce heat to low and simmer, uncovered, until the artichokes are tender, about 20 minutes.
2. Add the almond butter and cayenne to the artichoke mixture. Puree in a high-speed blender or food processor, in batches if necessary, and return to the pot. Stir in the soy milk and taste, adjusting seasonings if necessary. Simmer the soup over medium heat until hot, about 5 minutes.
3. Ladle into bowls, sprinkle with chives and almonds, and serve.

368. Pomegranate-Infused Lentil And Chickpea Stew

Preparation time: 5 minutes
cooking time: 55 minutes
servings: 4

Ingredients

- ¾ cup brown lentils, picked over, rinsed, and drained
- 2 tablespoons olive oil
- 1/2 cup chopped green onions
- 2 teaspoons minced fresh ginger
- ¾ cup long-grain brown rice
- 1/2 cup dried apricots, quartered
- 1/4 cup golden raisins
- 1/4 teaspoon ground allspice
- 1/4 teaspoon ground cumin
- 1/4 teaspoon ground cayenne
- 1 teaspoon turmeric
- Salt and freshly ground black pepper
- 1/3 cup pomegranate molasses, homemade (recipe followsor store-bought
- 3 cups water
- 11/2 cups cooked or 1 (15.5-ouncecan

chickpeas, drained and rinsed
- 1/4 cup minced fresh cilantro or parsley

Directions

1. Soak the lentils in a medium bowl of hot water for 45 minutes. Drain and set aside.
2. In a large saucepan, heat the oil over medium heat. Add the green onions, ginger, soaked lentils, rice, apricots, raisins, allspice, cumin, cayenne, turmeric, and salt and pepper to taste. Cook, stirring, for 1 minute.
3. Add the pomegranate molasses and water and bring to a boil. Reduce heat to low. Cover and simmer until the lentils and rice are tender, about 40 minutes.
4. Stir in the chickpeas and cilantro. Simmer, uncovered, for 15 minutes, to heat through and allow the flavors to blend. Serve immediately.

369. Rice And Pea Soup

Preparation time: 5 minutes
cooking time: 45 minutes
servings: 4

Ingredients

- 2 tablespoons olive oil
- 1 medium onion, minced
- 2 garlic cloves minced
- 1 cup Arborio rice
- 6 cups vegetable broth, homemade (see Light Vegetable Brothor store-bought, or water
- Salt and freshly ground black pepper
- 1 (16-ouncebag frozen petite green peas
- 1/4 cup chopped fresh flat-leaf parsley

Directions

1. In a large soup pot, heat the oil over medium heat. Add the onion and garlic, cover, and cook until softened about 5 minutes.
2. Uncover and add the rice, broth, and salt and pepper to taste. Bring to a boil, then reduce heat to low. Cover and simmer until the rice begins to soften, about 30 minutes.
3. Stir in the peas and cook, uncovered, for 15 to 20 minutes longer. Stir in the parsley and serve.

370. Ethiopian Cabbage, Carrot, and Potato Stew

Preparation time: 10 minutes
cooking time: 20 minutes
servings: 6

Ingredients

- 3 russet potatoes, peeled and cut into ½-inch cubes
- 2 tablespoons olive oil
- 6 carrots, peeled, halved lengthwise, and cut into ½-inch slices
- 1 onion, chopped
- 4 garlic cloves, minced
- 1 tablespoon ground turmeric
- 1 teaspoon ground cumin
- 1 teaspoon ground ginger
- 1½ teaspoons sea salt
- 1½ cups low-sodium vegetable broth, divided
- 4 cups shredded or thinly sliced green cabbage

Directions

1. Bring a large pot of water to a boil over medium-high heat.
2. Add the potatoes and cook for 10 minutes, or until fork-tender. Drain and set aside. While the potatoes are cooking, heat the oil in a large skillet over medium-high heat. Add the carrots and onion and sauté for 5 minutes. Add the garlic, turmeric, cumin, ginger, and salt and sauté for 1 additional minute, until fragrant. Add the cooked potatoes and 1 cup of broth to the skillet, bring to a boil, and reduce to a simmer. Scatter the cabbage on top of the potatoes. Cover and simmer for 3 minutes.
3. Mix the cabbage into the potatoes, add the remaining ½ cup of broth, cover, and simmer for 5 more minutes, or until the cabbage is wilted and tender. Stir the cabbage from time to time while cooking to incorporate it with the other ingredients as it continues to wilt.

371. Thai-Inspired Coconut Soup

Preparation time: 5 minutes

cooking time: 25 minutes
servings: 4

Ingredients

- 1 tablespoon canola or grapeseed oil
- 1 medium onion, chopped
- 2 tablespoons minced fresh ginger
- 2 tablespoons soy sauce
- 1 tablespoon light brown sugar (optional
- 1 teaspoon Asian chili paste
- 21⁄2 cups light vegetable broth, homemade (see Light Vegetable Brothor store-bought, or water
- 8 ounces extra-firm tofu, drained and cut into 1⁄2-inch dice
- 2 (13.5-ouncecans unsweetened coconut milk
- 1 tablespoon fresh lime juice
- 3 tablespoons chopped fresh cilantro, for garnish

Directions

1. In a large soup pot, heat the oil over medium heat. Add the onion and ginger and cook until softened, about 5 minutes. Stir in the soy sauce, sugar, and chile paste. Add the broth and bring to a boil. Reduce heat to medium and simmer for 15 minutes.
2. Strain the broth and discard solids. Return the broth to the pot over medium heat. Add the tofu and stir in the coconut milk and lime juice. Simmer 5 minutes longer to allow flavors to blend.
3. Ladle into bowls, sprinkle with cilantro, and serve.

372. Curried Butternut And Red Lentil Soup With Chard

Preparation time: 5 minutes
cooking time: 55 minutes
servings: 4

Ingredients

- 1 tablespoon olive oil
- 1 medium onion, chopped
- 1 medium butternut squash, peeled and diced
- 1 garlic clove, minced
- 1 tablespoon minced fresh ginger
- 1 tablespoon hot or mild curry powder
- 1 (14.5-ouncecan crushed tomatoes
- 1 cup red lentils, picked over, rinsed, and drained
- 5 cups vegetable broth, homemade (see Light Vegetable Brothor store-bought, or water
- Salt and freshly ground black pepper
- 3 cups chopped stemmed Swiss chard

Directions

1. In a large soup pot, heat the oil over medium heat. Add the onion, squash, and garlic. Cover and cook until softened, about 10 minutes.
2. Stir in the ginger and curry powder, then add the tomatoes, lentils, broth, and salt and pepper to taste. Bring to boil, then reduce heat to low and simmer, uncovered, until the lentils and vegetables are tender, stirring occasionally, about 45 minutes.
3. About 15 minutes before serving, stir in the chard. Taste, adjusting seasonings if necessary, and serve.

373. Butternut Soup With A Swirl Of Cranberry

Preparation time: 10 minutes
cooking time: 30 minutes
servings: 4 to 6

Ingredients

- 2 tablespoons olive oil
- 1 medium onion, chopped
- 1 medium carrot, chopped
- 1⁄2 teaspoon ground allspice
- 1⁄4 teaspoon ground ginger
- 1 medium russet potato, peeled and chopped
- 3 pounds butternut squash, peeled, seeded, and cut into 1-inch pieces
- 4 cups vegetable broth, homemade (see Light Vegetable Brothor store-bought, or water
- Salt
- 1⁄2 cup whole berry cranberry sauce, homemade or canned
- 2 tablespoons fresh orange juice

Directions

1. In a large soup pot, heat the oil over medium heat. Add the onion and carrot, cover, and cook, stirring occasionally, until softened, about 5 minutes. Stir in the allspice, ginger, potato, squash, broth, and salt to taste. Simmer, uncovered, until the vegetables are very soft, about 30 minutes.
2. While the soup is cooking, puree the cranberry sauce and orange juice in a blender or food processor. Run the pureed cranberry sauce through a strainer and discard solids. Set aside.
3. When the soup is done cooking, puree it in the pot with an immersion blender or in a blender or food processor, in batches if necessary, and return to the pot. Reheat the soup and taste, adjusting seasonings if necessary. Ladle into bowls, swirl a tablespoon or so of the reserved cranberry puree into the center of each bowl, and serve.

374. Spinach, Walnut, And Apple Soup

Preparation time: 10 minutes
cooking time: 20 minutes
servings: 4

Ingredients

- 1 tablespoon olive oil
- 1 small onion, chopped
- 3 cups vegetable broth, homemade (see Light Vegetable Brothor store-bought, or water
- 2 Fuji or other flavorful apples
- 1 cup apple juice
- 4 cups fresh spinach
- ¾ cup ground walnuts
- 1 teaspoon minced fresh sage or 1/2 teaspoon dried
- 1/4 teaspoon ground allspice
- Salt and freshly ground black pepper
- 1 cup soy milk
- 1/4 cup toasted walnut pieces

Directions

1. In a large soup pot, heat the oil over medium heat. Add the onion, cover, and cook until softened, 5 minutes. Add about 1 cup of the vegetable broth, cover, and cook until the onion is very soft, about 5 minutes longer.
2. Peel, core, and chop one of the apples and add it to the pot with the onion and broth. Add the apple juice, spinach, ground walnuts, sage, allspice, the remaining 2 cups broth, and salt and pepper to taste. Bring to a boil, then reduce heat to low and simmer for 10 minutes.
3. Puree the soup in the pot with an immersion blender or in a blender or food processor, in batches if necessary, and return to the pot. Stir in the soy milk and reheat over medium heat until hot.
4. Chop the remaining apple. Ladle the soup into bowls, garnish each bowl with some of the chopped apple, sprinkle with the walnut pieces, and serve.

375. Squash Soup With Pecans And Ginger

Preparation time: 10 minutes
cooking time: 30 minutes
servings: 4

Ingredients

- 1/3 cup toasted pecans
- 2 tablespoons chopped crystallized ginger
- 1 tablespoon canola or grapeseed oil
- 1 medium onion, chopped
- 1 celery rib, chopped
- 1 teaspoon grated fresh ginger
- 5 cups vegetable broth, homemade (see Light Vegetable Brothor store-bought, or water
- 1 kabocha squash, peeled, seeded, and cut into 1/2-inch dice
- 1/4 cup pure maple syrup
- 2 tablespoons soy sauce
- 1/4 teaspoon ground allspice
- Salt and freshly ground black pepper
- 1 cup plain unsweetened soy milk

Directions

1. In a food processor, combine the pecans and crystallized ginger and pulse until coarsely chopped. Set aside.
2. In a large soup pot, heat the oil over medium heat. Add the onion, celery, and

fresh ginger. Cover and cook until softened, about 5 minutes. Stir in the broth and squash, cover, and bring to a boil. Reduce the heat to low and simmer, covered, stirring occasionally, until the squash is tender, about 30 minutes.

3. Stir in the maple syrup, soy sauce, allspice, and salt and pepper to taste. Puree in the pot with an immersion blender or in a blender or food processor, in batches if necessary, and return to the pot.
4. Stir in the soy milk and heat over low heat until hot. Ladle the soup into bowls and sprinkle with the pecan and ginger mixture, and serve.

376. Root Vegetable Bisque

Preparation time: 5 minutes
cooking time: 35 minutes
servings: 4 to 6

Ingredients

- 1 tablespoon olive oil
- 3 large shallots, chopped
- 2 large carrots, shredded
- 2 medium parsnips, shredded
- 1 medium potato, peeled and chopped
- 2 garlic cloves, minced
- 1/2 teaspoon dried thyme
- 1/4 teaspoon dried marjoram
- 4 cups vegetable broth, homemade (see Light Vegetable Brothor store-bought, or water
- 1 cup plain unsweetened soy milk
- Salt and freshly ground black pepper
- 1 tablespoon minced fresh parsley, garnish

Directions

1. In a large soup pot, heat the oil over medium heat. Add the shallots, carrots, parsnips, potato, and garlic. Cover and cook until softened, about 5 minutes. Add the thyme, marjoram, and broth and bring to a boil. Reduce heat to low and simmer, uncovered, until the vegetables are tender, about 30 minutes.
2. Puree the soup in the pot with an immersion blender or in a blender or food processor in batches if necessary, then return to the pot. Stir in the soy milk and taste, adjusting seasonings if necessary. Heat the soup over low heat until hot. Ladle into bowls, sprinkle with parsley, and serve.

377. Curried Pumpkin Soup

Preparation time: 5 minutes
cooking time: 22 minutes
servings: 4 to 6

Ingredients

- 1 tablespoon olive oil
- 1 medium onion, chopped
- 1 garlic clove, minced
- 1 teaspoon grated fresh ginger
- 1 tablespoon hot or mild curry powder
- 1 (16-ouncecan pumpkin puree or 2 cups cooked fresh pumpkin
- 3 cups vegetable broth, homemade (see Light Vegetable Brothor store-bought, or water
- Salt
- 1 (13.5-ouncecan unsweetened coconut milk
- 1 tablespoon minced fresh parsley, for garnish
- Mango chutney, for garnish (optional
- Chopped roasted cashews, for garnish (optional

Directions

1. In a large soup pot, heat the oil over medium heat. Add the onion and garlic and cover and cook until softened, about 7 minutes. Stir in the ginger, curry powder,and cook for 30 seconds over low heat, stirring constantly. Stir in the pumpkin, broth, and salt to taste and bring to a boil. Reduce heat to low, cover, and simmer, uncovered, until the flavors are blended, about 15 minutes.
2. Use an immersion blender to puree the soup in the pot or transfer in batches to a blender or food processor, puree, then return to the pot, and season with salt and pepper to taste. Add coconut milk and heat until hot.
3. Ladle into soup bowls, sprinkle with parsley and a spoonful of chutney sprinkled with chopped cashews, if using,

and serve.

378. Lemony Lentil And Rice Soup

Preparation time: 15 minutes
cooking time: 1hour 10 minutes
servings: 6

Ingredients

- 2 tablespoons olive oil
- 1 medium onion, chopped
- 1 medium carrot, cut into 1⁄4-inch dice
- 1 celery rib, cut into 1⁄4-inch dice
- 11⁄4 cups brown lentils, picked over, rinsed, and drained
- ¾ cup long-grain brown rice
- 1 (14.5-ouncecan crushed tomatoes
- 2 cups tomato juice
- 2 bay leaves
- 1⁄2 teaspoon ground cumin
- 6 cups water
- 1 teaspoon salt
- 1⁄4 teaspoon freshly ground black pepper
- 1 tablespoon fresh lemon juice
- 2 tablespoons minced fresh parsley

Directions

1. In a large soup pot, heat the oil over medium heat. Add the onion, carrot, and celery. Cover and cook until tender, about 10 minutes.
2. Add the lentils, rice, tomatoes, tomato juice, bay leaves, cumin, water, salt, and pepper. Bring to a boil, then reduce heat to medium low, and simmer, uncovered, until lentils and rice are tender, about 1 hour.
3. Just before serving, remove and discard the bay leaves, and stir in the lemon juice and parsley. Taste, adjusting seasonings if necessary, and serve.

379. Balsamic Lentil Stew

Preparation time: 10 minutes
cooking time: 30 minutes
servings: 5

Ingredients

- 1 teaspoon olive oil
- 4 carrots, peeled and chopped
- 1 onion, chopped
- 3 garlic cloves, minced
- 2 tablespoons balsamic vinegar
- 4 cups Economical Vegetable Broth or water
- 1 (28-ouncecan crushed tomatoes
- 1 tablespoon sugar
- 2 cups dried lentils or 2 (15-ouncecans lentils, drained and rinsed
- 1 teaspoon salt
- Freshly ground black pepper

Directions

1. Preparing the Ingredients
2. Heat the olive oil in a large soup pot over medium heat.
3. Add the carrots, onion, and garlic and sauté for about 5 minutes, until the vegetables are softened. Pour in the vinegar, and let it sizzle to deglaze the bottom of the pot. Add the vegetable broth, tomatoes, sugar, and lentils.
4. Bring to a boil, then reduce the heat to low. Simmer for about 25 minutes, until the lentils are soft. Add the salt and season to taste with pepper. Leftovers will keep in an airtight container for up to 1 week in the refrigerator or up to 1 month in the freezer.

Nutrition (2 cupsCalories: 353; Protein: 22g; Total fat: 2g; Saturated fat: 0g; Carbohydrates: 67g; Fiber: 27g

380. Tomato Orzo Soup

Preparation time: 5 minutes
cooking time: 30 minutes
servings: 4

Ingredients

- 1 tablespoon olive oil
- 1 medium onion, chopped
- 1 celery rib, minced
- 3 garlic cloves, minced
- 1 (28-ouncecan crushed tomatoes
- 3 cups chopped fresh ripe tomatoes
- 2 tablespoons tomato paste
- 3 cups vegetable broth, homemade (see Light Vegetable Brothor store-bought, or water
- 2 bay leaves

- Salt and freshly ground black pepper
- 1 cup plain unsweetened soy milk
- 11⁄2 cups cooked orzo
- 2 tablespoons chopped fresh basil, for garnish

Directions

1. In large soup pot, heat the oil over medium heat. Add the onion, celery, and garlic. Cover and cook until softened, about 5 minutes. Stir in the canned and fresh tomatoes, tomato paste, broth, sugar, and bay leaves. Season with salt and pepper to taste and bring to a boil. Reduce the heat to low, cover, and simmer, uncovered, until the vegetables are tender, about 20 minutes.
2. Remove and discard bay leaves. Puree the soup in the pot with an immersion blender or in a blender or food processor, in batches if necessary, and return to the pot. Stir in the soy milk, taste, adjusting seasonings if necessary, and heat through.
3. Spoon about 1⁄3 cup of the orzo into the bottom of each bowl, ladle the hot soup on top, and serve sprinkled with the basil.

381. Golden Potato Soup

Preparation time: 5 minutes
cooking time: 30 minutes
servings: 4 to 6

Ingredients

- 1 tablespoon olive oil3 medium shallots, chopped4 cups vegetablebroth,homemade (see Light Vegetable Brothor store-bought, or water
- 3 medium russet potatoes, peeled and diced
- 2 medium sweet potatoes, peeled and diced
- 1 cup plain unsweetened soy milk
- Salt and freshly ground black pepper
- 1 tablespoon minced chives, for garnish

Directions

1. In large saucepan, heat the oil over medium heat. Add the shallots, cover, and cook until softened, about 5 minutes. Add the broth and potatoes and bring to a boil. Reduce heat to low and simmer, uncovered, until the potatoes are soft, about 20 minutes.
2. Puree the potato mixture in the pot with an immersion blender or in a blender or food processor, in batches if necessary, and return to the pot. Stir in the soy milk and season with salt and pepper to taste. Simmer for 5 minutes to heat through and blend flavors.
3. Ladle the soup into bowls, sprinkle with chives, and serve.

382. Zucchini And Butter Bean Bisque

Preparation time: 5 minutes
cooking time: 45 minutes
servings: 4 to 6

Ingredients

- 2 tablespoons olive oil
- 1 medium onion, chopped
- 1 garlic clove, minced
- 2 cups fresh or frozen butter beans or lima beans
- 4 cups vegetable broth, homemade (see Light Vegetable Brothor store-bought, or water
- 3 medium zucchini, cut into 1⁄4-inch slices
- 1⁄2 teaspoon dried marjoram
- Salt and freshly ground black pepper
- 1⁄2 cup plain unsweetened soy milk
- 2 tablespoons minced jarred pimiento

Directions

1. In a large soup pot, heat the oil over medium heat. Add the onion and garlic, cover, and cook until softened, about 5 minutes. Add the butter beans and the broth. Cover and cook for 20 minutes. Add the zucchini, marjoram, and salt and pepper to taste. Bring to a boil, then reduce heat to low and simmer, covered, until the vegetables are soft, about 20 minutes.
2. Puree the soup in the pot with an immersion blender or in a blender or food processor, in batches if necessary, and return to the pot. Stir in the soy milk and taste, adjusting seasonings if necessary. Reheat over low heat until hot. Ladle into bowls, garnish with the pimiento, and

serve.

383. Mom's Creamy Broccoli and Rice Bake

Preparation Time: 10 Minutes
Cooking Time: 40 Minutes
Servings:7

Ingredients

- 2 cups cooked brown rice
- 1 (12-ounce) bag frozen broccoli florets, chopped, or 2 cups chopped fresh broccoli florets
- ½ cup chopped onion
- 1 celery stalk, thinly sliced
- 1 batch Easy Vegan Cheese Sauce

Directions

1. Preparing the Ingredients.
2. Preheat the oven to 425°F.
3. In a large bowl, mix together the rice, broccoli, onion, celery, and cheese sauce. Transfer to a 2-quart or 8-inch-square baking dish.
4. Bake for 40 minutes, or until the top has started to brown slightly.

384. Two-Potato Soup With Rainbow Chard

Preparation Time: 5 Minutes
Cooking Time: 45 Minutes
Servings:6

Ingredients

- 2 tablespoons olive oil
- 1 medium red onion, chopped
- 1 medium leek, white part only, well rinsed and chopped
- 2 garlic cloves, minced
- 6 cups vegetable broth, homemade (see Light Vegetable Broth) or store-bought, or water
- 1 pound red potatoes, unpeeled and cut into 1/2-inch dice
- 1 pound sweet potatoes, peeled and cut into 1/2-inch dice
- 1/4 teaspoon crushed red pepper
- Salt and freshly ground black pepper
- 1 medium bunch rainbow chard, tough stems removed and coarsely chopped

Directions

1. In large soup pot, heat the oil over medium heat. Add the onion, leek, and garlic. Cover and cook until softened, about 5 minutes. Add the broth, potatoes, and crushed red pepper and bring to a boil. Reduce heat to low, season with salt and black pepper to taste, and simmer, uncovered, for 15 minutes.
2. Stir in the chard and cook until the vegetables are tender, about 15 minutes longer and serve.

385. Hot & Sour Tofu Soup

Preparation Time: 40 Minutes
Cooking Time: 15 Minutes
Servings:3

Ingredients

- 6 to 7 ounces firm or extra-firm tofu
- 1 teaspoon olive oil
- 1 cup sliced mushrooms
- 1 cup finely chopped cabbage
- 1 garlic clove, minced
- ½-inch piece fresh ginger, peeled and minced
- Salt
- 4 cups water or Economical Vegetable Broth
- 2 tablespoons rice vinegar or apple cider vinegar
- 2 tablespoons soy sauce
- 1 teaspoon toasted sesame oil
- 1 teaspoon sugar
- Pinch red pepper flakes
- 1 scallion, white and light green parts only, chopped

Directions

1. Preparing the Ingredients.
2. Press your tofu before you start: Put it between several layers of paper towels and place a heavy pan or book (with a waterproof cover or protected with plastic wrap) on top. Let stand for 30 minutes. Discard the paper towels. Cut the tofu into ½-inch cubes.
3. In a large soup pot, heat the olive oil over medium-high heat.

4. Add the mushrooms, cabbage, garlic, ginger, and a pinch of salt. Sauté for 7 to 8 minutes, until the vegetables are softened.
5. Add the water, vinegar, soy sauce, sesame oil, sugar, red pepper flakes, and tofu.
6. Bring to a boil, then turn the heat to low. Simmer the soup for 5 to 10 minutes.
7. Serve with the scallion sprinkled on top.
8. Leftovers will keep in an airtight container for up to 1 week in the refrigerator or up to 1 month in the freezer.

Per Serving (2 cups) Calories: 161; Protein: 13g; Total fat: 9g; Saturated fat: 1g; Carbohydrates: 10g; Fiber: 3g

386. Autumn Medley Stew

Preparation Time: 5 Minutes
Cooking Time: 60 Minutes
Servings:4 To 6

Ingredients

- 2 tablespoons olive oil
- 8 ounces seitan, homemade or store-bought, cut in 1-inch cubes
- Salt and freshly ground black pepper
- 1 large yellow onion, chopped
- 2 garlic cloves, minced
- 1 large russet potato, peeled and cut into 1/2-inch dice
- 1 medium carrot, cut into 1/4-inch dice
- 1 medium parsnip, cut into 1/4-inch dice chopped
- 1 small butternut squash, peeled, halved, seeded, and cut into 1/2-inch dice
- 1 small head savoy cabbage, chopped
- 1 (14.5-ounce) can diced tomatoes, drained
- 11/2 cups cooked or 1 (15.5-ounce) can chickpeas, drained and rinsed
- 2 cups vegetable broth,
- 1/2 cup dry white wine
- 1/2 teaspoon dried marjoram
- 1/2 teaspoon dried thyme
- 1/2 cup crumbled angel hair pasta

Directions

1. In a large skillet, heat 1 tablespoon of the oil over medium-high heat. Add the seitan and cook until browned on all sides, about 5 minutes. Season with salt and pepper to taste and set aside.
2. In a large saucepan, heat the remaining 1 tablespoon oil over medium heat. Add the onion and garlic. Cover and cook for until softened, about 5 minutes. Add the potato, carrot, parsnip, and squash. Cover and cook until softened, about 10 minutes.
3. Stir in the cabbage, tomatoes, chickpeas, broth, wine, marjoram, thyme, and salt and pepper to taste. Bring to a boil, then reduce heat to low. Cover and cook, stirring occasionally, until the vegetables are tender, about 45 minutes.
4. Add the cooked seitan and the pasta and simmer until the pasta is tender and the flavors are blended, about 10 minutes longer. Serve immediately.
5. Variation: Leave out the pasta and serve with some warm crusty bread.

387. Pumpkin-Pear Soup

Preparation Time: 10 Minutes
Cooking Time: 15 Minutes
Servings:4

Ingredients

- 1 teaspoon olive oil or coconut oil
- 1 onion, diced, or 2 teaspoons onion powder
- 1-inch piece fresh ginger, peeled and diced, or 1 teaspoon ground ginger
- 1 pear, cored and chopped
- Optional spices to take the taste up a notch:
- 1 teaspoon curry powder
- ½ teaspoon pumpkin pie spice
- ½ teaspoon smoked paprika
- Pinch red pepper flakes
- 4 cups water or Economical Vegetable Broth
- 3 cups canned pumpkin purée
- 1 to 2 teaspoons salt (less if using salted broth)
- Pinch freshly ground black pepper
- ¼ to ½ cup canned coconut milk (optional)
- 2 to 4 tablespoons nutritional yeast

(optional)

Directions

1. Preparing the Ingredients.
2. Heat the olive oil in a large pot over medium heat. Add the onion, ginger, and pear and sauté for about 5 minutes, until soft. Sprinkle in any optional spices and stir to combine.
3. Add the water, pumpkin, salt, and pepper, and stir until smooth and combined. Cook until just bubbling, about 10 minutes.
4. Stir in the coconut milk (if using) and nutritional yeast (if using), and remove the soup from the heat. Leftovers will keep in an airtight container for up to 1 week in the refrigerator or up to 1 month in the freezer.

Per Serving (2 cups) Calories: 90; Protein: 2g; Total fat: 1g; Saturated fat: 0g; Carbohydrates: 17g; Fiber: 3g

388. Sweet Potato And Peanut Soup With Baby Spinach

Preparation Time: 5 Minutes
Cooking Time: 40 Minutes
Servings:4

Ingredients

- 1 tablespoon olive oil
- 1 medium onion, chopped
- 11/2 pounds sweet potatoes, peeled and cut into 1/2-inch dice
- 6 cups vegetable broth, homemade (see Light Vegetable Broth) or store-bought, or water
- 1/3 cup creamy peanut butter
- 1/4 teaspoon ground cayenne
- 1/8 teaspoon ground nutmeg
- Salt and freshly ground black pepper
- 4 cups fresh baby spinach

Directions

1. In a large soup pot, heat the oil over medium heat. Add the onion, cover, and cook until softened, about 5 minutes. Add the sweet potatoes and broth and cook, uncovered, until the potatoes are tender, about 30 minutes.
2. Ladle about a cup of hot broth into a small bowl. Add the peanut butter and stir until smooth. Stir the peanut butter mixture into the soup along with the cayenne, nutmeg, and salt and pepper to taste.
3. About 10 minutes before ready to serve, stir in the spinach, and serve.

389. Tuscan White Bean Soup

Preparation Time: 10 Minutes
Cooking Time: 15 Minutes
Servings:4

Ingredients

- 1 to 2 teaspoons olive oil
- 1 onion, chopped
- 4 garlic cloves, minced, or 1 teaspoon garlic powder
- 2 carrots, peeled and chopped
- Salt
- 1 tablespoon dried herbs
- Pinch freshly ground black pepper
- Pinch red pepper flakes
- 4 cups Economical Vegetable Broth or water
- 2 (15-ounce) cans white beans, such as cannellini, navy, or great northern, drained and rinsed
- 2 tablespoons freshly squeezed lemon juice
- 2 cups chopped greens, such as spinach, kale, arugula, or chard

Directions

1. Preparing the Ingredients.
2. Heat the olive oil in a large soup pot over medium-high heat.
3. Add the onion, garlic (if using fresh), carrots, and a pinch of salt.
4. Sauté for about 5 minutes, stirring occasionally, until the vegetables are lightly browned. Sprinkle in the dried herbs (plus the garlic powder, if using), black pepper, and red pepper flakes, and toss to combine.
5. Add the vegetable broth, beans, and another pinch of salt, and bring the soup to a low simmer to heat through. If you like, make the broth a bit creamier by puréeing 1 to 2 cups of soup in a

countertop blender and returning it to the pot. Alternatively, use a hand blender to purée about one-fourth of the beans in the pot.
6. Stir in the lemon juice and greens, and let the greens wilt into the soup before serving. Leftovers will keep in an airtight container for up to 1 week in the refrigerator or up to 1 month in the freezer.

Per Serving (2 cups) Calories: 145; Protein: 7g; Total fat: 2g; Saturated fat: 0g; Carbohydrates: 26g; Fiber: 6g

390. Mexican Fideo Soup With Pinto Beans

Preparation Time: 5 Minutes
Cooking Time: 25 Minutes
Servings:4

Ingredients

- 3 tablespoons olive oil
- 1 medium onion, chopped
- 3 garlic cloves, chopped
- 8 ounces fideo, vermicelli, or angel hair pasta, broken into 2-inch pieces
- 1 (14.5-ounce) can crushed tomatoes
- 11/2 cups cooked or 1 (15.5-ounce) can pinto beans, rinsed and drained
- 1 (4-ounce) can chopped hot or mild green chiles
- 1 teaspoon ground cumin
- 1/2 teaspoon dried oregano
- 6 cups vegetable broth, homemade (see Light Vegetable Broth) or store-bought, or water
- Salt and freshly ground black pepper
- 1/4 cup chopped fresh cilantro, for garnish

Directions

1. In a large soup pot, heat 1 tablespoon of the oil over medium heat. Add the onion, cover, and cook until soft, about 10 minutes. Stir in the garlic and cook 1 minute longer. Remove the onion mixture with a slotted spoon and set aside.
2. In the same pot, heat the remaining 2 tablespoons of oil over medium heat, add the noodles, and cook until golden, stirring frequently, 5 to 7 minutes. Be careful not to burn the noodles.
3. Stir in the tomatoes, beans, chiles, cumin, oregano, broth, and salt and pepper to taste. Stir in the onion mixture and simmer until the vegetables and noodles are tender, 10 to 15 minutes. Ladle into soup bowls, garnish with cilantro, and serve.

391. Spinach, Tomato, and Orzo Soup

Preparation Time: 10 Minutes
Cooking Time: 20 Minutes
Servings:6

Ingredients

- 1 tablespoon olive oil
- 1 onion, chopped
- 4 garlic cloves, minced
- 1 (14.5-ounce) can diced Italian tomatoes (preferably with oregano and basil)
- 4 cups low-sodium vegetable broth
- 4 cups water
- 1 teaspoon sea salt
- 1 teaspoon black pepper
- 1 pound uncooked orzo pasta
- 1 (5-ounce) package baby spinach

Directions

1. Preparing the Ingredients
2. Heat the oil in a large stockpot over medium heat. Add the onion and sauté for 3 minutes, or until soft. Add the garlic and sauté for 1 additional minute, or until fragrant. Add the tomatoes with their juice, broth, water, salt, and pepper. Cover the pot and bring to a boil. Reduce the heat to a simmer.
3. Add the orzo and cook, uncovered, for 9 minutes, or until the pasta is tender. Turn off the heat and stir in the spinach until wilted.

392. Coconut and Curry Soup

Preparation Time: 15 Minutes
Cooking Time: 15 Minutes
Servings:4

Ingredients

- 1 tablespoon coconut oil
- ½ onion, thinly sliced

- 1 carrot, peeled and julienned
- ½ cup sliced shiitake mushrooms
- 3 garlic cloves, minced
- one 14-ounce can coconut milk
- 1 cup vegetable stock
- juice from 1 lime, or 2 teaspoons lime juice
- ½ teaspoon sea salt
- 2 teaspoons curry powder

Directions

1. Preparing the Ingredients
2. In a large soup pot, heat the coconut oil over medium-high heat until it shimmers. Add the onion, carrot, and mushrooms and cook until soft, about 7 minutes. Stir in the garlic and cook until it is fragrant, about 30 seconds.
3. Add the coconut milk, vegetable stock, lime juice, salt, and curry powder and heat through. Serve immediately.

392. Black Bean Soup With A Splash

Preparation Time: 5 Minutes
Cooking Time: 45 Minutes
Servings:4 To 6

Ingredients

- 1 tablespoon olive oil
- 1 medium onion, finely chopped
- 1 celery rib, finely chopped
- 2 medium carrots, finely chopped
- 1 small green bell pepper, finely chopped
- 2 garlic cloves, minced
- 4 cups vegetable broth, homemade (see Light Vegetable Broth) or store-bought, or water
- 41/2 cups cooked or 3 (15.5-ounce) cans black beans, drained and rinsed
- 1 teaspoon dried thyme
- 1 teaspoon salt
- 1/4 teaspoon ground cayenne
- 2 tablespoons minced fresh parsley, for garnish
- 1/3 cup dry sherry

Directions

1. In a large soup pot, heat the oil over medium heat. Add the onion, celery, carrots, bell pepper, and garlic. Cover and cook until tender, stirring occasionally, about 10 minutes. Add the broth, beans, thyme, salt, and cayenne. Bring to a boil, then reduce the heat to low and simmer, uncovered, until the soup has thickened, about 45 minutes.
2. Puree the soup in the pot with an immersion blender or in a blender or food processor, in batches if necessary, and return to the pot. Reheat if necessary.
3. Ladle the soup into bowls and garnish with parsley. Serve accompanied by the sherry.

394. Cream of Tomato Soup

Preparation Time: 5 Minutes
Cooking Time: 5 Minutes
Servings:2

Ingredients

- 1 (28-ounce) can crushed, diced, or whole peeled tomatoes, undrained
- 1 to 2 teaspoons dried herbs
- 2 to 3 teaspoons onion powder (optional)
- ¾ to 1 cup unsweetened nondairy milk
- ½ teaspoon salt, or to taste
- Freshly ground black pepper

Directions

1. Preparing the Ingredients.
2. Pour the tomatoes and their juices into a large pot and bring them to near-boiling over medium heat.
3. Add the dried herbs, onion powder (if using), milk, salt, and pepper to taste. Stir to combine. If you used diced or whole tomatoes, use a hand blender to purée the soup until smooth. (Alternatively, let the soup cool for a few minutes, then transfer to a countertop blender.) Leftovers will keep in an airtight container for up to 1 week in the refrigerator or up to 1 month in the freezer (though if you want leftovers for this soup, you might want to double the recipe).

Per Serving (2 cups) Calories: 90; Protein: 4g; Total fat: 3g; Saturated fat: 0g; Carbohydrates: 16g; Fiber: 4g

395. Southern Succotash Stew

Preparation Time: 5 Minutes
Cooking Time: 60 Minutes
Servings:4

Ingredients

- 8 ounces tempeh
- 2 tablespoons olive oil
- 1 large sweet yellow onion, finely chopped
- 2 medium russet potatoes, peeled and cut into 1/2-inch dice
- 2 carrots, cut into 1/4-inch slices
- 1 (14.5-ounce) can diced tomatoes, drained
- 1 (16-ounce) package frozen succotash
- 2 cups vegetable broth or water
- 2 tablespoons soy sauce
- 1 teaspoon dry mustard
- 1/2 teaspoon dried thyme
- 1/2 teaspoon ground allspice
- 1/4 teaspoon ground cayenne
- Salt and freshly ground black pepper
- 1/2 teaspoon liquid smoke

Directions

1. In a medium saucepan of simmering water, cook the tempeh for 30 minutes. Drain, pat dry, and cut into 1-inch dice.
2. In a large skillet, heat 1 tablespoon of the oil over medium heat. Add the tempeh and cook until browned on both sides, about 10 minutes. Set aside.
3. In a large saucepan, heat the remaining 1 tablespoon oil over medium heat. Add the onion and cook until softened, 5 minutes. Add the potatoes, carrots, tomatoes, succotash, broth, soy sauce, mustard, sugar, thyme, allspice, and cayenne. Season with salt and pepper to taste. Bring to a boil, then reduce heat to low and add the tempeh. Simmer, covered, until the vegetables are tender, stirring occasionally, about 45 minutes.
4. About 10 minutes before the stew is finished cooking, stir in the liquid smoke. Taste, adjusting seasonings if necessary. Serve immediately.

396. Quick Thai Coconut Mushroom Soup

Preparation Time: 5 Minutes
Cooking Time: 10 Minutes
Servings:4

Ingredients

- 1½ cups low-sodium vegetable broth, divided
- 2 garlic cloves, minced
- 1 tablespoon minced fresh ginger
- 1 (8-ounce) package baby bella or white button mushrooms, stemmed and sliced
- 1 (13.5-ounce) can full-fat coconut milk
- Juice of ½ lemon
- Juice of ½ lime
- 2 tablespoons chopped fresh Thai basil
- 1 tablespoon chopped fresh cilantro
- Fresh cilantro leaves, for garnish (optional)
- Lime wedges, for garnish (optional)

Directions

1. Preparing the Ingredients.
2. Heat ½ cup of broth in a large saucepot over medium-high heat. Sauté the garlic and ginger in the broth for 1 minute, or until fragrant.
3. Add the mushrooms and slowly pour in the remaining 1 cup of broth. Bring to a boil and reduce the heat to a simmer. Add the coconut milk, lemon juice, lime juice, basil, and chopped cilantro.
4. Let simmer for 5 minutes, or until heated through. Garnish with whole cilantro leaves and lime wedges, if desired.

397. Chilled Avocado-Tomato Soup

Preparation Time: 15 Minutes
Cooking Time: 0 Minutes
Servings:4

Ingredients

- 2 garlic cloves, crushed
- Salt
- 2 ripe Hass avocados
- 2 teaspoons lemon juice
- 2 pounds ripe plum tomatoes, coarsely chopped
- 1 (14.5-ounce) can crushed tomatoes
- 1 cup tomato juice

- Freshly ground black pepper
- 8 fresh basil leaves, for garnish

Directions

1. In a blender or food processor, combine the garlic and 1/2 teaspoon of salt and process to a paste. Pit and peel one of the avocados and add it to the food processor along with the lemon juice. Process until smooth. Add the fresh and canned tomatoes, tomato juice, and salt and pepper to taste. Process until smooth.
2. Transfer the soup to a large container, cover, and refrigerate until chilled, 2 to 3 hours.
3. Taste, adjusting seasonings if necessary. Pit and peel the remaining avocado and cut it into a small dice. Slice the basil leaves into thin strips. Ladle the soup into bowls, add the diced avocado, garnish with basil, and serve.

398. Spicy Black Bean Orzo Soup

Preparation Time: 5 Minutes
Cooking Time: 50 Minutes
Servings:4 To 6

Ingredients

- 2 tablespoons olive oil
- 3 garlic cloves, minced
- 1 tablespoon chili powder
- 1 teaspoon dried oregano
- 41/2 cups cooked or 3 (15.5-ounce) cans black beans, drained and rinsed
- 1 small jalapeño, seeded and finely chopped (optional)
- 1/4 cup minced oil-packed sun-dried tomatoes
- 4 cups vegetable broth, homemade (see Light Vegetable Broth) or store-bought, or water
- 1 cup water
- Salt and freshly ground black pepper
- 1/2 cup orzo
- 2 tablespoons chopped fresh cilantro, for garnish

Directions

1. In a large soup pot, heat the oil over medium heat. Add the garlic and cook until fragrant, about 1 minute. Stir in the chili powder, oregano, beans, jalapeño, if using, tomatoes, broth, water, and salt and pepper to taste. Simmer for 30 minutes to blend flavors.
2. Puree the soup in the pot with an immersion blender or in a blender or food processor, in batches if necessary, and return to the pot. Cook the soup 15 minutes longer over medium heat. Taste, adjusting seasonings, and add more water if necessary.
3. While the soup is simmering, cook the orzo in a pot of boiling salted water, stirring occasionally, until al dente, about 5 minutes. Drain the orzo and divide it among the soup bowls. Ladle the soup into the bowls, garnish with cilantro, and serve.

399. Root Vegetable Soup

Preparation Time: 15 Minutes
Cooking Time: 15 Minutes
Servings:4

Ingredients

- 2 tablespoons olive oil
- 1 onion, diced
- 3 garlic cloves, minced
- 1 carrot, julienned or grated
- 1 rutabaga, julienned or grated
- 1 parsnip, julienned or grated
- 1 red potato, julienned or grated
- 5 cups vegetable stock
- 2 teaspoons dried thyme
- sea salt
- freshly ground black pepper

Directions

1. In a large soup pot, heat the olive oil over medium-high heat until it shimmers.
2. Add the onion and cook until it softens, about 5 minutes. Add the garlic and cook until it is fragrant, about 30 seconds. Add the carrot, rutabaga, parsnip, potato, vegetable stock, and thyme. Cover and boil until vegetables soften, about 10 minutes.
3. Remove from the heat. Using a food processor or blender, purée the soup in

batches. Season with salt and pepper. Serve immediately.

400. Minestrone

Preparation Time: 15 Minutes
Cooking Time: 15 Minutes
Servings:4

Ingredients

- 2 tablespoons olive oil
- ½ onion, diced
- 1 carrot, peeled and diced
- 1 stalk celery, diced
- 4 garlic cloves, minced
- 5 cups vegetable stock
- 1 zucchini, diced
- one 15-ounce can kidney beans, drained and rinsed
- one 15-ounce can chopped tomatoes with liquid, or 2 fresh tomatoes, peeled and chopped
- 2 teaspoons italian seasoning
- sea salt
- freshly ground pepper

Directions

1. In a large soup pot, heat the olive oil over medium-high heat until it shimmers.
2. Add the onion, carrot, and celery and cook until vegetables soften, about 5 minutes. Add the garlic and cook until it is fragrant, about 30 seconds. Add the vegetable stock, zucchini, kidney beans, tomatoes, and Italian seasoning. Simmer the soup until the vegetables are soft, about 10 minutes. Season with salt and pepper and serve immediately.

401. Black Bean And Corn Soup

Preparation Time: 5 Minutes
Cooking Time: 50 Minutes
Servings:4

Ingredients

- 2 tablespoons olive oil
- 1 medium red onion, chopped
- 1 medium red or yellow bell pepper, chopped
- 1 medium carrot, minced
- 4 garlic cloves, minced
- 1 teaspoon ground cumin
- 1 teaspoon dried oregano
- 1 (14.5-ounce) can diced tomatoes, drained
- 4 1/2 cups cooked or 3 (15.5-ounce) cans black beans, rinsed and drained
- 6 cups vegetable broth, homemade (see Light Vegetable Broth) or store-bought, or water
- 2 cups fresh, frozen, or canned corn kernels
- 1 teaspoon fresh lemon juice
- Salt and freshly ground black pepper
- Tabasco sauce, to serve

Directions

1. In a large soup pot, heat the oil over medium heat. Add the onion, bell pepper, carrot, and garlic, cover, and cook until soft, about 10 minutes. Uncover and stir in the cumin and oregano, tomatoes, beans, and broth. Bring to a boil, then reduce heat to low and simmer, uncovered, for 30 minutes, stirring occasionally.
2. Puree about one-third of the soup in the pot with an immersion blender, or in a blender or food processor, then return to the pot. Add the corn, and simmer uncovered, for 10 minutes to heat through and blend flavors.
3. Just before serving, stir in the lemon juice and season with salt and pepper to taste. Ladle into bowls and serve with hot sauce on the side.

402. Chickpea, Tomato, And Eggplant Stew

Preparation Time: 5 Minutes
Cooking Time: 55 Minutes
Servings:4

Ingredients

- 1 tablespoon olive oil
- 1 large onion, chopped
- 1 medium eggplant, peeled and cut into 1/2-inch dice
- 2 medium carrots, cut into 1/4-inch slices
- 1 large Yukon Gold potato, peeled and cut

into 1/2-inch dice
- 1 medium red bell pepper, cut into 1-inch dice
- 3 garlic cloves, minced
- 2 cups cooked or 1 (15.5-ounce) cans chickpeas, drained and rinsed if canned
- 1 (28-ounce) can diced tomatoes, undrained
- 1 tablespoon minced fresh parsley
- 1/2 teaspoon dried oregano
- 1/2 teaspoon dried basil
- 1 tablespoon soy sauce
- 1/2 cup vegetable broth, or water
- Salt and freshly ground black pepper

Directions

1. In a large saucepan, heat the oil over medium heat. Add the onion, eggplant, and carrots, cover, and cook until vegetables begin to soften, about 5 minutes.
2. Reduce heat to low. Add the potato, bell pepper, and garlic and cook, stirring, uncovered, for 5 minutes. Stir in the chickpeas, tomatoes, parsley, oregano, basil, soy sauce, and broth. Season with salt and black pepper to taste. Cover and cook until vegetables are tender, about 45 minutes. Serve immediately.

403. Tomato Cream Pasta (Pressure Cooker)

Preparation Time: 10 Minutes • Pressure: 4 Minutes • Pressure Level: High • Release: Natural
Servings:4

Ingredients

- 1 (28-ounce) can crushed tomatoes
- 1 tablespoon dried basil
- ½ teaspoon garlic powder
- 10 ounces whole-grain pasta
- ½ teaspoon salt, plus more as needed
- 1½ cups water or unsalted vegetable broth
- 1 cup unsweetened nondairy milk or creamer
- 2 cups chopped fresh spinach (optional)
- Freshly ground black pepper

Directions

1. Preparing the Ingredients. In your electric pressure cooker's cooking pot, combine the tomatoes, basil, garlic powder, pasta, salt, and water.
2. High pressure for 4 minutes. Close and lock the lid and ensure the pressure valve is sealed, then select High Pressure and set the time for 4 minutes.
3. Pressure Release. Once the cook time is complete, let the pressure release naturally for 5 minutes, then quick release any remaining pressure, being careful not to get your fingers or face near the steam release. Once all the pressure has released, carefully unlock and remove the lid.
4. Stir in the milk and spinach (if using). Taste and season with more salt, if needed, and pepper. On your pressure cooker, select Sauté or Simmer. Let cook for 4 to 5 minutes, until the sauce thickens and the greens wilt.

Per Serving Calories: 321; Protein: 14g; Total fat: 3g; Saturated fat: 0g; Carbohydrates: 16g; Fiber: 9g

404. Senegalese Soup

Preparation Time: 5 Minutes
Cooking Time: 40 Minutes
Servings:4

Ingredients

- 1 tablespoon canola or grapeseed oil
- 1 medium onion, chopped
- 1 medium carrot, chopped
- 1 garlic clove, minced
- 3 Granny Smith apples, peeled, cored, and chopped
- 2 tablespoons hot or mild curry powder
- 2 teaspoons tomato paste
- 3 cups light vegetable broth, homemade (see Light Vegetable Broth) or store-bought, or water
- Salt
- 1 cup plain unsweetened soy milk
- 4 teaspoons mango chutney, homemade or store-bought, for garnish

Directions

1. In a large soup pot, heat the oil over medium heat. Add the onion, carrot, and

garlic. Cover and cook until softened, about 10 minutes. Add the apples and continue to cook, uncovered, stirring occasionally, until the apples begin to soften, about 5 minutes. Add the curry powder and cook, stirring, 1 minute. Stir in the tomato paste, broth, and salt to taste. Simmer, uncovered, for 30 minutes.
2. Puree the soup in the pot with an immersion blender or in a blender or food processor, in batches if necessary. Pour the soup into a large container, stir in the soy milk, cover, and refrigerate until chilled, about 3 hours.
3. Ladle the soup into bowls, garnish each with a teaspoonful of chutney, and serve.

405. Three Bean Soup

Preparation Time: 5 Minutes
Cooking Time: 52 Minutes
Servings:4 To 6

Ingredients

- 2 tablespoons olive oil
- 1 medium onion, chopped
- 1 medium carrot, chopped
- 1 cup chopped celery
- 2 garlic cloves, minced
- 1 (14.5-ounce) can diced tomatoes, drained
- 11⁄2 cups cooked or 1 (15.5-ounce) can dark red kidney beans, drained and rinsed
- 11⁄2 cups cooked or 1 (15.5-ounce) can black beans, drained and rinsed
- 11⁄2 cups cooked or 1 (15.5-ounce) can navy or other white beans, drained and rinsed
- 4 cups vegetable broth, homemade (see Light Vegetable Broth) or store-bought, or water
- 1 tablespoon soy sauce
- 1 teaspoon dried thyme
- 1 bay leaf
- Salt and freshly ground black pepper
- 2 tablespoons chopped fresh parsley

Directions

1. In a large soup pot, heat the oil over medium heat. Add the onion, carrot, celery, and garlic. Cover and cook until softened, about 7 minutes. Uncover, and stir in the tomatoes, all the beans, and the broth. Add the soy sauce, thyme, and bay leaf and season with salt and pepper to taste. Bring to a boil, then reduce heat to low and simmer until the vegetables are tender, about 45 minutes.
2. Remove the bay leaf and discard before serving. Add the parsley and serve.

406. Creamy Potato-Cauliflower Soup

Preparation Time: 10 Minutes
Cooking Time: 25 Minutes
Servings:6

Ingredients

- 1 teaspoon olive oil
- 1 onion, chopped
- 3 cups chopped cauliflower
- 2 potatoes, scrubbed or peeled and chopped
- 6 cups water or Economical Vegetable Broth
- 2 tablespoons dried herbs
- Salt
- Freshly ground black pepper
- 1 or 2 scallions, white and light green parts only, sliced

Directions

1. Heat the olive oil in a large soup pot over medium-high heat.
2. Add the onion and cauliflower, and sauté for about 5 minutes, until the vegetables are slightly softened. Add the potatoes, water, and dried herbs, and season to taste with salt and pepper. Bring the soup to a boil, reduce the heat to low, and cover the pot. Simmer for 15 to 20 minutes, until the potatoes are soft.
3. Using a hand blender, purée the soup until smooth. (Alternatively, let it cool slightly, then transfer to a countertop blender.) Stir in the scallions and serve. Leftovers will keep in an airtight container for up to 1 week in the refrigerator or up to 1 month in the freezer.

Per Serving (2 cups) Calories: 80; Protein: 2g; Total fat: 1g; Saturated fat: 0g; Carbohydrates:

17g; Fiber: 3g

407. Spicy Pinto Bean Soup

Preparation Time: 5 Minutes
Cooking Time: 25 Minutes
Servings:4

Ingredients

- 41/2 cups cooked or 3 (15.5-ounce) cans pinto beans, drained and rinsed
- 1 (14.5-ounce) can crushed tomatoes
- 1 teaspoon chipotle chile in adobo
- 2 tablespoons olive oil
- 1 medium onion, chopped
- 1/4 cup chopped celery
- 2 garlic cloves, minced
- 1/2 teaspoon ground cumin
- 1/2 teaspoon dried oregano
- 4 cups vegetable broth, homemade (see Light Vegetable Broth) or store-bought, or water
- Salt and freshly ground black pepper
- 2 tablespoons chopped fresh cilantro, for garnish

Directions

1. In a food processor, puree 11/2 cups of the pinto beans with the tomatoes and chipotle. Set aside.
2. In a large soup pot, heat the oil over medium heat. Add the onion, celery, and garlic. Cover and cook until soft, stirring occasionally, about 10 minutes. Stir in the cumin, oregano, broth, pureed bean mixture, and the remaining 3 cups beans. Season with salt and pepper to taste.
3. Bring to a boil and reduce heat to low and simmer, uncovered, stirring occasionally, until the flavors are incorporated and the soup is hot, about 15 minutes. Ladle into bowls, garnish with cilantro, and serve.

408. Black And Gold Gazpacho

Preparation Time: 15 Minutes
Cooking Time: 0 Minutes
Servings:4

Ingredients

- 11/2 pounds ripe yellow tomatoes, chopped
- 1 large cucumber, peeled, seeded, and chopped
- 1 large yellow bell pepper, seeded, and chopped
- 4 green onions, white part only
- 2 garlic cloves, minced
- 2 tablespoons olive oil
- 2 tablespoons white wine vinegar
- Salt
- Ground cayenne
- 11/2 cups cooked or 1 (15.5-ounce) can black beans, drained and rinsed
- 2 tablespoons minced fresh parsley
- 1 cup toasted croutons (optional)

Directions

1. In a blender or food processor, combine half the tomatoes with the cucumber, bell pepper, green onions, and garlic. Process until smooth. Add the oil and vinegar, season with salt and cayenne to taste, and process until blended.
2. Transfer the soup to a large nonmetallic bowl and stir in the black beans and remaining tomatoes. Cover the bowl and refrigerate for 1 to 2 hours. Taste, adjusting seasonings if necessary.
3. Ladle the soup into bowls, garnish with parsley and croutons, if using, and serve.

409. Black-Eyed Pea & Sweet Potato Soup

Preparation Time: 10 Minutes
Cooking Time: 25 Minutes
Servings:4

Ingredients

- 1 teaspoon olive oil
- 2 to 3 cups peeled, cubed sweet potato, squash, or pumpkin
- ½ onion, chopped
- 1 garlic clove, minced
- Salt
- 2 cups water
- 1 (15-ounce) can black-eyed peas, drained and rinsed
- 2 tablespoons freshly squeezed lime juice
- 1 tablespoon sugar

- 1 teaspoon smoked or regular paprika
- Pinch red pepper flakes or cayenne pepper
- 3 cups shredded cabbage
- 1 cup corn kernels, thawed if frozen, drained if canned

Directions

1. Heat the olive oil in a large soup pot over medium-high heat.
2. Add the sweet potato, onion, garlic, and a pinch of salt. Sauté for 3 to 4 minutes, until the onion and garlic are softened. Add the water, black-eyed peas, lime juice, sugar, paprika, red pepper flakes, and salt to taste. Bring to a boil and cook for 15 minutes. Add the cabbage and corn to the pot, stirring to combine, and cook for 5 minutes more, or until the sweet potato is tender.
3. Turn off the heat, let cool for a few minutes, and serve. Leftovers will keep in an airtight container for up to 1 week in the refrigerator or up to 1 month in the freezer.

Per Serving (2 cups) Calories: 224; Protein: 9g; Total fat: 2g; Saturated fat: 0g; Carbohydrates: 46g; Fiber: 10g

410. Soba And Green Lentil Soup

Preparation Time: 5 Minutes
Cooking Time: 55 Minutes
Servings:4 To 6

Ingredients

- 2 tablespoons olive oil
- 1 medium onion, minced
- 1 medium carrot, halved lengthwise and sliced diagonally
- 2 garlic cloves, minced
- 1 (28-ounce) can crushed tomatoes
- 1 cup green (French) lentils, picked over, rinsed, and drained
- 1 teaspoon dried thyme
- 6 cups vegetable broth, homemade (see Light Vegetable Broth) or store-bought, or water
- Salt and freshly ground black pepper
- 4 ounces soba noodles, broken into thirds

Directions

1. In a large soup pot over medium heat, heat the oil. Add the onion, carrot, and garlic. Cover and cook until softened, about 7 minutes. Uncover and stir in the tomatoes, lentils, thyme, and broth and bring to a boil. Reduce heat to medium, season with salt and pepper to taste, and cover and simmer until the lentils are just tender, about 45 minutes.
2. Stir in the noodles and cook until tender, about 10 minutes longer, and serve.

411. Brown Rice and Lentil Pilaf

Preparation time: 15 minutes
cooking time: 50 minutes
servings: 4 to 6

Ingredients

- 1 tablespoon olive oil
- 1 large yellow onion, minced
- 1 medium carrot, chopped
- 2 garlic cloves, minced
- 1 cup long-grain brown rice
- 11⁄2 teaspoons ground coriander
- 1⁄2 teaspoon ground cumin
- 3 cups water
- Salt
- 3 tablespoons minced fresh cilantro
- Freshly ground black pepper

Directions

1. Bring a saucepan of salted water to a boil over high heat. Add the lentils, return to a boil, then reduce heat to medium and cook for 15 minutes. Drain and set aside. In a large saucepan, heat the oil over medium heat. Add the onion, carrot, and garlic, cover, and cook until tender, 10 minutes.
2. Add the lentils to the vegetable mixture. Add the rice, coriander, and cumin. Stir in the water and bring to a boil. Reduce heat to low, salt the water, and cook, covered, until the lentils and rice are tender, about 30 minutes. Remove from heat and set aside for 10 minutes.
3. Transfer to a large bowl, fluff with a fork, and sprinkle with the cilantro and freshly ground black pepper. Serve immediately.

412. Savory Beans And Rice

Preparation time: 5 minutes
cooking time: 40 minutes
servings: 4

Ingredients

- 1 tablespoon olive oil
- 3 green onions, chopped
- 1 teaspoon grated fresh ginger
- 1 cup brown basmati rice
- 2 cups water
- 1 tablespoon soy sauce
- Salt
- 11⁄2 cups cooked or 1 (15.5-ouncecan Great Northern white beans, drained and rinsed
- 1 tablespoon nutritional yeast
- 1 tablespoon minced fresh savory or 11⁄2 teaspoons dried

Directions

1. In a large saucepan, heat the oil over medium heat. Add the green onions and ginger and cook until fragrant, about 1 minute. Add the rice, water, soy sauce, and salt to taste. Cover and bring to a boil.
2. Reduce heat to low and simmer, covered, until the rice is tender, about 30 minutes. Stir in the beans, nutritional yeast, and savory. Cook, uncovered, stirring, until heated through and the liquid is absorbed, about 10 minutes. Serve immediately.

413. Mexican Green Rice And Beans

Preparation time: 10 minutes
cooking time: 40 minutes
servings: 4

Ingredients

- 1 large green bell pepper
- 2 or 3 small fresh jalapeño or other hot green chiles
- 21⁄2 cups vegetable broth
- 1⁄2 cup coarsely chopped fresh parsley
- 1 small yellow onion, chopped
- 2 garlic cloves, chopped
- 1⁄4 teaspoon freshly ground black pepper
- 1 teaspoon sugar
- 1⁄2 teaspoon dried oregano
- 1⁄4 teaspoon ground cumin
- 3 tablespoons canola or grapeseed oil
- 1 cup long-grain white rice
- Salt

- 11⁄2 cups cooked or 1 (15.5-ouncecan dark red kidney beans, drained and rinsed
- 2 tablespoons minced fresh cilantro, garnish

Directions

1. Roast the bell pepper and chiles over a gas flame or under a broiler until the skin blisters, turning on all sides. Place in a paper bag for 5 minutes. Use a damp towel to rub off scorched bits of skin. Stem, seed, and chop the bell pepper and chiles and place them in a food processor. Add 1 cup of the broth, parsley, onion, garlic, pepper, sugar, oregano, and cumin and process until smooth. Set aside.
2. In a large skillet, heat the oil over medium heat. Add the rice and stir constantly for a few minutes to coat the rice with the oil. Add the pureed vegetables and simmer, stirring occasionally, for 5 minutes. Add the remaining 11⁄2 cups broth and bring to a boil. Reduce the heat to medium, add salt to taste, cover, and cook until the liquid is absorbed, about 30 minutes. About 10 minutes before ready to serve, stir in the kidney beans. Garnish with cilantro and serve immediately.

414. Balsamic Black Beans

Preparation time: 5 minutes
cooking time: 20 minutes
servings: 5

Ingredients

- 1 teaspoon extra-virgin olive oil or vegetable broth
- ½ cup diced sweet onion
- 1 teaspoon ground cumin
- 1 teaspoon ground cardamom (optional
- 2 (14.5-ouncecans black beans, rinsed and drained
- ¼ to ½ cup vegetable broth
- 2 tablespoons balsamic vinegar

Directions

1. In a large pot over medium-high heat, heat the olive oil.
2. Add the onion, cumin, and cardamom (if usingand sauté for 3 to 5 minutes, until the onion is translucent. Add the beans and ¼ cup broth, and bring to a boil. Add up to ½ cup more of broth for "soupier" beans.
3. Cover, reduce the heat, and simmer for 10 minutes. Add the balsamic vinegar, increase the heat to medium-high, and cook for 3 more minutes uncovered. Transfer to a large storage container, or divide the beans evenly among 5 single-serving storage containers. Let cool before sealing the lids.
4. Place the airtight containers in the refrigerator for up to 5 days or freeze for up to 2 months. To thaw, refrigerate overnight. Reheat in the microwave for 1½ to 3 minutes.

Nutrition: Calories: 200; Fat: 2g; Protein: 13g; Carbohydrates: 34g; Fiber: 12g; Sugar: 1g; Sodium: 41mg

415. Pesto & White Bean Pasta

Preparation time: 15 minutes
cooking time: 10 minutes
servings: 4

Ingredients

- 8 ounces rotini pasta, cooked according to the package directions, drained, and rinsed with cold water to cool
- 1½ cups canned cannellini beans or navy beans, drained and rinsed
- ½ cup Spinach Pesto
- 1 cup chopped tomato or red bell pepper
- ¼ red onion, finely diced
- ½ cup chopped pitted black olives

Directions

1. In a large bowl, combine the pasta, beans, and pesto. Toss to combine.
2. Add the tomato, red onion, and olives, tossing thoroughly. Store leftovers in an airtight container in the refrigerator for up to 1 week.

Nutrition Calories: 544; Protein: 23g; Total fat: 17g; Saturated fat: 3g; Carbohydrates: 83g; Fiber: 13g

416. Dilly White Beans

Preparation time: 5 minutes
cooking time: 20 minutes

servings: 6

Ingredients

- 1 teaspoon extra-virgin olive oil or ¼ cup vegetable broth
- 1 small sweet onion, cut into half-moon slices
- 2 (14.5-ouncecans great northern beans, rinsed and drained
- ½ cup vegetable broth
- 2 teaspoons dried dill
- ½ teaspoon salt (optional
- ¼ teaspoon freshly ground black pepper

Directions

1. In a large skillet or wok over medium-high heat, heat the olive oil. Sauté the onion slices for 3 to 5 minutes, until the onion is translucent.
2. Add the beans, broth, dill, salt (if using), and pepper. Bring to a boil. Reduce the heat to low and simmer, uncovered, for 10 minutes.
3. Transfer to a large storage container, or scoop ½ cup of beans into each of 6 storage containers. Let cool before sealing the lids.

Nutrition: Calories: 155; Fat: 1g; Protein: 10g; Carbohydrates: 26g; Fiber: 9g; Sugar: 1g; Sodium: 67mg

417. Quinoa Pilaf

Preparation time: 10 minutes
cooking time: 15 minutes
servings: 4

Ingredients

- 1 cup quinoa
- 2 cups vegetable stock
- ¼ cup pine nuts
- 2 tablespoons olive oil
- ½ onion, chopped
- ⅓ cup chopped fresh parsley
- sea salt
- freshly ground black pepper

Directions

1. In a medium pot, bring the quinoa and vegetable stock to a boil over medium-high heat, stirring occasionally. Reduce to a simmer.
2. Cover and cook until the quinoa is soft, about 15 minutes. Meanwhile, heat a large sauté pan over medium-high heat. Add the pine nuts to the dry hot pan and toast, stirring frequently, until the nuts are fragrant, 2 to 3 minutes. Remove the pine nuts from the pan and set aside. Add the olive oil to the same pan and heat until it shimmers. Add the onion and cook until soft, about 5 minutes. When the quinoa is soft and all the liquid is absorbed, remove it from the heat and fluff it with a fork. Stir in the pine nuts, onion, and parsley. Season with salt and pepper. Serve hot.

418. Five-Spice Farro

Preparation time: 3 minutes
cooking time: 35 minutes
servings: 4

Ingredients

- 1 cup dried farro, rinsed and drained
- 1 teaspoon five-spice powder

Directions

1. In a medium pot, combine the farro, five-spice powder, and enough water to cover.
2. Bring to a boil; reduce the heat to medium-low, and simmer for 30 minutes. Drain off any excess water.
3. Transfer to a large storage container, or scoop 1 cup farro into each of 4 storage containers. Let cool before sealing the lids.
4. Place the airtight containers in the refrigerator for 1 week or freeze for up to 3 months. To thaw, refrigerate overnight. Reheat in the microwave for 1½ to 3 minutes.

Nutrition: Calories: 73; Fat: 0g; Protein: 3g; Carbohydrates: 15g; Fiber: 1g; Sugar: 0g; Sodium: 0mg

419. Italian Rice With Seitan And Mushrooms

Preparation time: 15 minutes
cooking time: 0 minutes
servings: 4

Ingredients

- 2 cups water

- 1 cup long-grain brown or white rice
- 2 tablespoons olive oil
- 1 medium yellow onion, chopped
- 2 garlic cloves, minced
- 8 ounces seitan, homemade or store-bought, chopped
- 8 ounces white mushrooms, chopped
- 1 teaspoon dried basil
- 1/2 teaspoon ground fennel seed
- 1/4 teaspoon crushed red pepper
- Salt and freshly ground black pepper

Directions

1. In a large saucepan, bring the water to boil over high heat. Add the rice, reduce the heat to low, cover, and cook until tender, about 30 minutes.
2. In a large skillet, heat the oil over medium heat. Add the onion, cover, and cook until softened, about 5 minutes. Add the seitan and cook uncovered until browned. Stir in the mushrooms and cook until tender, about 5 minutes longer. Stir in the basil, fennel, crushed red pepper, and salt and black pepper to taste.
3. Transfer the cooked rice to large serving bowl. Stir in the seitan mixture and mix thoroughly. Add a generous amount of black pepper and serve immediately.

420. Spanish Rice And Beans

Preparation time: 10 minutes
cooking time: 40 minutes
servings: 4

Ingredients

- 1 tablespoon olive oil
- 1 medium yellow onion, chopped
- 1 medium green bell pepper, chopped
- 2 garlic cloves, minced
- 1 (14.5-ouncecan diced tomatoes, undrained
- 1 tablespoon capers, chopped if large
- 1/4 teaspoon crushed red pepper
- 11/2 cups long-grain brown rice
- 3 cups vegetable broth
- Salt
- 11/2 cups cooked or 1 (15.5-ouncecan dark red kidney beans, drained and rinsed
- 1/4 cup sliced pitted kalamata olives
- 2 tablespoons minced fresh parsley

Directions

- In a large saucepan, heat the oil over medium heat. Add the onion, bell pepper, and garlic. Cover and cook until softened, about 5 minutes. Add the tomatoes and their juice, the capers, and the crushed red pepper. Stir to combine and simmer for 5 minutes to blend the flavors.
- Add the rice and broth and bring to a boil, then reduce heat to low. Add salt to taste. Cover and cook until the rice is tender and the liquid is evaporated, 30 to 40 minutes. Remove from heat and stir in the beans, olives, and parsley. Cover and set aside for 10 minutes before serving. Serve immediately.

421. GGB Bowl

Preparation time: 10 minutes
cooking time: 5 minutes
servings: 2

Ingredients

- 2 teaspoons olive oil
- 1 cup cooked brown rice, quinoa, or your grain of choice
- 1 (15-ouncecan chickpeas or your beans of choice, rinsed and drained
- 1 bunch spinach or kale, stemmed and roughly chopped
- 1 tablespoon soy sauce or gluten-free tamari
- Sea salt
- Black pepper

Directions

1. In a large skillet, heat the oil over medium heat.
2. Add the rice, beans, and greens and stir continuously until the greens have wilted and everything is heated through, 3 to 5 minutes. Drizzle in the soy sauce, mix to combine, and season with salt and pepper.

422. Brown Rice With Artichokes, Chickpeas, And Tomatoes

Preparation time: 5 minutes

cooking time: 30 minutes
servings: 4

Ingredients

- 2 tablespoons olive oil
- 3 garlic cloves, minced
- 1 cup frozen artichokes hearts, thawed and chopped
- 1 teaspoon dried basil
- 1/2 teaspoon dried marjoram
- 11/2 cups cooked or 1 (15.5-ouncecan chickpeas, drained and rinsed
- 11/2 cups long-grain brown rice
- 3 cups vegetable broth
- Salt and freshly ground black pepper
- 1 cup ripe grape tomatoes, quartered
- 2 tablespoons minced fresh parsley

Directions

1. In a large saucepan, heat the oil over medium heat. Add the garlic and cook until softened, about 1 minute. Add the artichokes, basil, marjoram, and chickpeas. Stir in the rice and broth. Season with salt and pepper to taste.
2. Cover tightly and reduce heat to low. Simmer until the rice is cooked, about 30 minutes. Transfer to a serving bowl, add the tomatoes and parsley, taste, adjusting seasonings if necessary, and fluff with a fork. Serve immediately.

423. Fried Rice

Preparation time: 10 minutes
cooking time: 15 minutes
servings: 6

Ingredients

- 2 tablespoons sesame oil
- 1 onion, diced
- 1 carrot, diced
- 1 cup sugar snap peas
- 1 cup sliced shiitake mushrooms
- 2 garlic cloves, minced
- 1 tablespoon grated fresh ginger
- ¼ cup soy sauce
- 2 cups prepared rice (brown or white
- 3 green onions (white and green parts), chopped

Directions

1. In a large sauté pan or wok, heat the sesame oil until it shimmers. Add the onion and carrot. Cook until the vegetables soften, about 3 minutes. Add the peas and mushrooms and cook, stirring frequently, until they soften, 5 to 7 minutes. Add the garlic and ginger and cook until they are fragrant, about 30 seconds.
2. Add the soy sauce and rice. Cook, stirring, until heated through. Stir in the green onions and serve immediately.

424. Baked Wild Rice

Preparation time: 5 minutes
cooking time: 1 hour 10 minutes total: 1 hour 15minutes
servings: 4

Ingredients

- 1 tablespoon vegan butter or extra-virgin olive oil or 2 tablespoons water
- 1 cup chopped white or yellow onion
- ½ cup chopped carrot
- ½ cup chopped celery
- 1 cup chopped mushrooms
- 1½ cups wild rice
- 4 cups vegetable broth
- 1 cup chopped dried cranberries or cherries
- ½ cup chopped pistachios

Directions

1. Preheat the oven to 375°F.
2. In a Dutch oven with a lid or in a large, oven-safe skillet over medium-high heat, heat the vegan butter. Add the onion, carrot, and celery and sauté for 5 minutes. Add the mushrooms and sauté for 3 more minutes. Stir in the rice and broth, mixing well.
3. Cover with a lid or aluminum foil and bake for 30 minutes Remove the pan from the oven, uncover, and stir in the dried cranberries. Return to the oven uncovered and bake for 20 to 30 minutes longer, until the liquid is absorbed and the rice is tender. Remove from the oven and stir in the pistachios.

4. Divide the rice evenly among 4 storage containers. Let cool before sealing the lids.

Nutrition: Calories: 355; Fat: 8g; Protein: 11g; Carbohydrates: 63g; Fiber: 7g; Sugar: 14g; Sodium: 496mg

425. Stovetop Thanksgiving Rice Stuffing

Preparation time: 10 minutes
cooking time: 15 minutes
servings: 8

Ingredients

- ¼ cup vegan butter
- 1 onion, chopped
- 2 celery stalks, thinly sliced
- 1 (8-ouncepackage baby bella or white button mushrooms, stemmed and sliced
- 3 garlic cloves, minced
- ½ cup low-sodium vegetable broth
- ½ cup dried cranberries or cherries
- ½ cup chopped walnuts, toasted
- 2 cups cooked wild-rice blend or brown rice
- 1 teaspoon poultry seasoning
- 1 teaspoon sea salt
- Chopped fresh parsley, for garnish

Directions

1. Melt the butter in a large skillet over medium heat.
2. Add the onion, celery, and mushrooms and sauté for 5 minutes, or until soft. Add the garlic and sauté for 1 additional minute, or until fragrant. Add the broth, cranberries, and walnuts. Bring to a boil, cover, reduce the heat, and simmer for 5 minutes, or until fragrant. Add the rice, poultry seasoning, and salt and mix well to combine. Continue to cook, uncovered, for 4 minutes, stirring occasionally, or until heated through and all the liquid evaporates. Transfer to a serving dish and garnish with parsley.

426. Easy Kitchari

Preparation time: 20 minutes
cooking time: 20 minutes
servings: 5

Ingredients

- ½ cup yellow mung beans or split peas
- ½ cup basmati rice
- 1 small red onion, diced
- 1 (14.5-ouncecan diced tomatoes
- 5 teaspoons minced garlic (about 5 cloves
- 1 jalapeño, seeded
- ½ teaspoon ground ginger or 2 tablespoons minced fresh ginger
- 1 teaspoon ground turmeric
- 2 tablespoons to ¼ cup water
- 1 teaspoon extra-virgin olive oil or 1 to 2 tablespoons vegetable broth
- 1¼ teaspoons ground cumin
- 1¼ teaspoons ground coriander
- 1 teaspoon fennel seeds
- 4 cups chopped vegetables (mix of carrot, cauliflower, summer or winter squash, broccoli, and/or potatoes
- 3 cups water
- Juice of 1 large lemon
- 1 to 2 teaspoons salt, to taste
- ½ teaspoon freshly ground black pepper

Directions

1. Rinse and drain the beans and rice. Transfer to a small bowl and soak in water for 15 minutes.
2. In a food processor or blender, purée the onion, tomatoes with their juices, garlic, jalapeño, ginger, turmeric, and 2 tablespoons of water, adding water as necessary, until you reach a sauce consistency that pours easily and is not chunky.
3. In a large pot over medium-high heat, heat the olive oil. Add the cumin, coriander, and fennel seeds and sauté, stirring constantly, just until fragrant.
4. Transfer the purée to the pot. Drain and rinse the soaked rice and beans, and add them to the pot. Add the chopped vegetables and water and combine well.
5. Bring to a boil. Cover, reduce the heat to low, and simmer for 15 to 20 minutes, until the beans and rice are soft but not mushy. Add the lemon juice, and taste before adding the salt and pepper. Into each of 5 single-serving storage

containers, spoon 2 cups.

6. Let cool before sealing.

Nutrition: Calories: 234; Fat: 3g; Protein: 7g; Carbohydrates: 47g; Fiber: 13g; Sugar: 5g; Sodium: 862mg

427. Chickpea And Artichoke Curry

Preparation time: 10 minutes
cooking time: 15 minutes
servings: 4

Ingredients

- 1 teaspoon extra-virgin olive oil or 2 teaspoons vegetable broth
- 1 small onion, diced
- 2 teaspoons minced garlic (2 cloves
- 1 (14.5-ouncecan chickpeas, rinsed and drained
- 1 (14.5-ouncecan artichoke hearts, drained and quartered
- 2 teaspoons curry powder
- ½ teaspoon ground coriander
- ½ teaspoon ground cumin
- 1 (5.4-ouncecan unsweetened coconut milk

Directions

1. In a large skillet or pot over medium-high heat, heat the olive oil. Add the onion and garlic and sauté for about 5 minutes. Add the chickpeas, artichoke hearts, curry powder, coriander, and cumin. Stir to combine well.
2. Pour the coconut milk into the pot, mix well, and bring to a boil. Cover, reduce the heat to low, and simmer for 10 minutes.
3. Divide the curry evenly among 4 wide-mouth glass jars or single-compartment containers. Let cool before sealing the lids.

Nutrition: Calories: 267; Fat: 12g; Protein: 9g; Carbohydrates: 36g; Fiber: 11g; Sugar: 3g; Sodium: 373mg

428. Curried Lentils (Pressure cooker)

Preparation time: 6 minutes
Servings: 6-8

Ingredients

- 1 tablespoon coconut oil
- 2 tablespoons mild curry powder
- 1 teaspoon ground ginger
- ½ teaspoon ground turmeric (optional
- 1 cup dried green lentils or brown lentils
- 3 cups water
- 1 teaspoon freshly squeezed lime juice (optional
- ½ teaspoon salt
- Freshly ground black pepper (optional

Directions

1. On your electric pressure cooker, select Sauté. Add the coconut oil, curry powder, ginger, and turmeric (if usingand toss to toast for 1 minute. Add the lentils and toss with the spices. Add the water. Cancel Sauté.
2. High pressure for 20 minutes. Close and lock the lid and ensure the pressure valve is sealed, then select High Pressure and set the time for 20 minutes.
3. Pressure Release. Once the cook time is complete, let the pressure release naturally, about 30 minutes.
4. Once all the pressure has released, carefully unlock and remove the lid. Stir in the lime juice (if using). Season with the salt and pepper, if you like.

NUTRITION Calories: 212; Total fat: 5g; Protein: 13g; Sodium: 2mg; Fiber: 16g

429. Pest Pearled Barley

Preparation time: 1 minute
cooking time: 50 minutes
servings: 4

Ingredients

- 1 cup dried barley
- 2½ cups vegetable broth
- ½ cup Parm-y Kale Pesto

Directions

1. In a medium saucepan, combine the barley and broth and bring to a boil.
2. Cover, reduce the heat to low, and simmer for about 45 minutes, until tender.
3. Remove from the stove and let stand for 5 minutes. Fluff the barley, then gently fold in the pesto.
4. Scoop about ¾ cup into each of 4 single-compartment storage containers. Let cool

before sealing the lids.

Nutrition: Calories: 237; Fat: 6g; Protein: 9g; Carbohydrates: 40g; Fiber: 11g; Sugar: 2g; Sodium: 365mg

430. Spicy Picnic Beans

Preparation time: 15 minutes
cooking time: 15 minutes
servings: 6

Ingredients

- 1 jalapeño, cut into strips
- 1 red bell pepper, cut into strips
- 1 green bell pepper, cut into strips
- 1 onion, chopped
- 5 garlic cloves, minced
- two 15-ounce cans pinto beans, drained and rinsed
- one 15-ounce can kidney beans, drained and rinsed
- one 15-ounce can chickpeas, drained and rinsed
- one 18-ounce bottle barbecue sauce
- ½ teaspoon chipotle powder
- sea salt
- freshly ground black pepper

Directions

1. In the bowl of a food processor, combine the jalapeño, bell peppers, onion, and garlic and blend for ten 1-second pulses, stopping halfway through to scrape down the sides of the bowl. In a large pot, combine the processed mixture with the beans, barbecue sauce, and chipotle powder.
2. Simmer over medium-high heat, stirring frequently to blend the flavors, about 15 minutes. Season with salt and pepper. Serve hot. You can make this ahead of time and store it in a tightly sealed container for up to 3 days in the refrigerator. The flavors will blend and deepen as the beans rest.

431. Chipotle Chickpeas (Pressure Cooker

Preparation time: 8 minutes
Servings: 4-6

Ingredients

- 1 cup dried chickpeas, soaked in water overnight
- 2 cups water
- ¼ cup sun-dried tomatoes, chopped
- 1 to 2 tablespoons olive oil
- 2 teaspoons ground chipotle pepper
- 1½ teaspoons ground cumin
- 1½ teaspoons onion powder
- 1 teaspoon dried oregano
- ¾ teaspoon garlic powder
- ½ teaspoon smoked paprika
- ¼ to ½ teaspoon salt

Directions

1. Drain and rinse the chickpeas, drain again, and put them in your electric pressure cooker's cooking pot. Add the water, sun-dried tomatoes, olive oil, chipotle pepper, cumin, onion powder, oregano, garlic powder, and paprika.
2. High pressure for 20 minutes. Close and lock the lid and ensure the pressure valve is sealed, then select High Pressure and set the time for 20 minutes.
3. Pressure Release. Once the cook time is complete, let the pressure release naturally, about 15 minutes. Once all the pressure has released, carefully unlock and remove the lid. Taste and season with salt and more oil or seasonings if you like.

NUTRITION Calories: 280; Total fat: 7g; Protein: 13g; Sodium: 168mg; Fiber: 12g

432. Cinnamon Chickpeas (Pressure Cooker

Preparation time: 12 minutes
Servings: 4-6

Ingredients

- 1 cup dried chickpeas, soaked in water overnight
- 2 cups water
- 2 teaspoons ground cinnamon, plus more as needed
- ½ teaspoon ground nutmeg (optional
- 1 tablespoon coconut oil
- 2 to 4 tablespoons unrefined sugar or

brown sugar, plus more as needed

Directions

1. Drain and rinse the chickpeas, then put them in your electric pressure cooker's cooking pot. Add the water, cinnamon, and nutmeg (if using).
2. High pressure for 30 minutes. Close and lock the lid and ensure the pressure valve is sealed, then select High Pressure and set the time for 30 minutes.
3. Pressure Release. Once the cook time is complete, let the pressure release naturally, about 15 minutes. Once all the pressure has released, carefully unlock and remove the lid. Drain any excess water from the chickpeas and add them back to the pot. Stir in the coconut oil and sugar. Taste and add more cinnamon, if desired.
4. Select Sauté and cook for about 5 minutes, stirring the chickpeas occasionally, until there's no liquid left and the sugar has melted onto the chickpeas. Transfer to a bowl and toss with additional sugar if you want to add a crunchy texture.

NUTRITION Calories: 253; Total fat: 7g; Protein: 11g; Sodium: 9mg; Fiber: 10g

433. Lentil Spinach Curry

Preparation time: 5 minutes
cooking time: 30 minutes
servings: 4

Ingredients

- 1 teaspoon olive oil
- 1 onion, chopped
- ½-inch piece fresh ginger, peeled and minced
- 1 to 2 tablespoons mild curry powder
- 1½ cups dried green or brown lentils
- 2½ cups water or Economical Vegetable Broth
- 1 cup canned diced tomatoes
- 2 to 4 cups finely chopped raw spinach
- ½ cup nondairy milk
- 2 tablespoons soy sauce (optional
- 1 tablespoon apple cider vinegar or rice vinegar
- 1 teaspoon salt (or 2 teaspoons if omitting soy sauce

Directions

1. Heat the olive oil in a large pot over medium heat. Add the onion, and sauté for about 3 minutes, until soft.
2. Add the ginger, and cook for 1 minute more. Stir in the curry powder, lentils, and water. Bring to a boil, turn the heat to low, and cover the pot. Simmer for 15 to 20 minutes, until the lentils are soft. Stir in the tomatoes, spinach, milk, soy sauce (if using), vinegar, and salt. Simmer for about 3 minutes, until heated through. If you prefer, use an immersion blender to half-blend this in the pot for a creamier texture and to hide the spinach. Store in an airtight container for 4 to 5 days in the refrigerator or up to 1 month in the freezer.

Nutrition Calories: 313; Protein: 21g; Total fat: 3g; Saturated fat: 0g; Carbohydrates: 52g; Fiber: 24g

434. Peas and Pesto Rice

Preparation time: 5 minutes
cooking time: 5 minutes
servings: 3

Ingredients

- 1 cup Pistachio Pesto or store bought vegan pesto
- 1 cup frozen peas, thawed
- 2 cups cooked brown rice

Directions

1. In a large skillet, warm the pesto sauce and peas over low heat for 3 to 5 minutes, until heated through. Add the rice and mix until everything is coated.

435. White Bean Burgers

Preparation time: 10 minutes
cooking time: 10 minutes
servings: 4

Ingredients

- 1 tablespoon olive oil, plus more for coating the baking sheet
- ¼ cup couscous
- ¼ cup boiling water
- 1 (15-ouncecan white beans, drained and rinsed

- 2 tablespoons balsamic vinegar
- 2 tablespoons chopped sun-dried tomatoes or olives
- ½ teaspoon garlic powder or 1 garlic clove, finely minced
- ½ teaspoon salt
- 4 burger buns
- Lettuce leaves, for serving
- Tomato slices, for serving
- Condiments of choice, such as ketchup, olive tapenade, Creamy Tahini Dressing, and/or Spinach Pesto

Directions

1. If baking, preheat the oven to 350°F.
2. Coat a rimmed baking sheet with olive oil or line it with parchment paper or a silicone mat. In a medium heat-proof bowl, combine the couscous and boiling water.
3. Cover and set aside for about 5 minutes. Once the couscous is soft and the water is absorbed, fluff it with a fork. Add the beans, and mash them to a chunky texture. Add the vinegar, olive oil, sun-dried tomatoes, garlic powder, and salt; stir until combined but still a bit chunky. Divide the mixture into 4 portions, and shape each into a patty. Put the patties on the prepared baking sheet, and bake for 25 to 30 minutes, until slightly crispy on the edges. Alternatively, heat some olive oil in a large skillet over medium heat, then add the patties, making sure each has oil under it.
4. Fry for about 5 minutes, until the bottoms are browned. Flip, adding more oil as needed, and fry for about 5 minutes more. Serve the burgers on buns with lettuce, tomato, and your choice of condiments.

436. Chickpeas with Lemon and Spinach

Preparation time: 10 minutes
cooking time: 10 minutes
servings: 4

Ingredients

- 3 tablespoons olive oil
- one 15-ounce can chickpeas, drained and rinsed
- 10 ounces baby spinach
- ½ teaspoon sea salt
- juice and zest of 1 lemon
- freshly ground black pepper

Directions

1. In a large sauté pan, heat the olive oil over medium-high heat until it shimmers. Add the chickpeas and cook until they are heated through, about 5 minutes.
2. Add the spinach and stir just until it wilts, about 5 minutes. Add the salt, lemon juice, lemon zest, and pepper and stir to combine. Serve immediately.

437. Brown Rice and Lentils

Preparation time: 10 minutes
cooking time: 15 minutes
servings: 4

Ingredients

- 2 tablespoons olive oil
- 1 onion, diced
- 1 carrot, diced
- 1 celery stalk, diced
- two 15-ounce cans lentils, drained and rinsed
- one 15-ounce can diced tomatoes with juice
- 1 tablespoon dried rosemary
- 1 tablespoon garlic powder
- 2 cups prepared brown rice
- sea salt
- freshly ground black pepper

Directions

1. In a large pot, heat the olive oil over medium-high heat until it shimmers.
2. Add the onion, carrot, and celery and cook until the vegetables soften, about 5 minutes. Add the lentils, tomatoes, rosemary, and garlic powder. Lower the heat to -medium-low and simmer to blend the flavors, 5 to 7 minutes. Stir the rice into lentils and heat through, 2 to 3 minutes. Season with salt and -pepper and serve immediately.

438. Baked Beans

Preparation Time: 10 minutes

Cooking time: 55 minutes
Servings: 4

Ingredients:

- 1 cup white beans
- 5 cups of water
- 2 tablespoons tomato paste
- 1 teaspoon salt
- 1 teaspoon dried dill
- 1 teaspoon sugar
- ½ cup barbecue sauce
- ½ cup vegetable broth
- 1 carrot, chopped
- ½ teaspoon ground black pepper

Directions:

1. Place white bean and water in the instant pot.
2. Close and seal the lid and cook on High for 30 minutes.
3. Then use quick pressure release.
4. Drain water from beans.
5. In the instant pot, add tomato paste, salt, dried dill, barbecue sauce, vegetable broth, chopped carrot, and ground black pepper.
6. Mix up the beans mixture until homogenous.
7. Close the lid and set Saute mode.
8. Cook beans for 25 minutes more.

Nutrition: calories 238, fat 0.8, fiber 8.7, carbs 46.2, protein 13

439. Mexican Pinto Beans

Preparation Time: 10 minutes
Cooking time: 50 minutes
Servings: 5

Ingredients:

- 2 cups pinto beans
- 6 cups of water
- 1 teaspoon salt
- 1 teaspoon ground black pepper
- ½ cup fresh cilantro, chopped
- 1 jalapeno pepper, chopped
- 1 teaspoon onion powder
- 1 teaspoon garlic powder
- 1 tablespoon almond butter
- 3 tablespoon coconut yogurt
- 1 tablespoon tomato paste

Directions:

1. Put all the ingredients in the instant pot bowl.
2. Mix up the mixture well until it gets the red color.
3. Then close and seal the lid. Set Manual mode (High pressure).
4. Cook pinto beans for 50 minutes.
5. After this, use quick pressure release.
6. Mix up the cooked beans carefully before serving.

Nutrition: calories 300, fat 3, fiber 12.7, carbs 51.3, protein 17.8

440. Vegan Black Beans

Preparation Time: 10 minutes
Cooking time: 45 minutes
Servings: 4

Ingredients:

- 1 ½ cup black beans
- 3 cups of water
- 1 teaspoon salt
- ¼ teaspoon peppercorn
- 1 tablespoon chives, chopped
- 1 tablespoon coconut oil
- 1 teaspoon chili flakes

Directions:

1. Place black beans, salt, peppercorn, and water in the instant pot.
2. Close and seal the lid. Set Manual mode and cook beans on High for 30 minutes.
3. Then make quick pressure release and open the lid.
4. Add chopped chives, chili flakes, coconut oil, and mix up well.
5. Close the lid and saute black beans for 15 minutes more on Saute mode.
6. The cooked beans should be served warm.

Nutrition: calories 278, fat 4.4, fiber 11.1, carbs 45.5, protein 15.8

441. Lentil Radish Salad

Preparation Time: 10 minutes
Cooking time: 10 minutes
Servings: 2

Ingredients:

- 1 cup radish

- 1 cup lettuce, chopped
- ½ cup lentils
- ½ cup vegetable broth
- 1 teaspoon garam masala
- 1 teaspoon coconut yogurt
- 1 teaspoon olive oil
- ½ teaspoon minced garlic

Directions:

1. Place lentils and vegetable broth in the instant pot.
2. Add garam masala and close the lid.
3. Set Manual mode and cook lentils for 10 minutes.
4. Then make quick pressure release.
5. Meanwhile, slice radish and place in the salad bowl.
6. Add chopped lettuce.
7. In the separated small bowl whisk together coconut yogurt, olive oil, and minced garlic.
8. Add lentils in radish mixture and stir gently.
9. Pour the salad with garlic mixture and stir only before serving.

Nutrition: calories 214, fat 3.3, fiber 15.8, carbs 32.2, protein 14.2

442. Lebanese Lemon and Beans Salad

Preparation Time: 5 minutes
Cooking time: 6 minutes
Servings: 4

Ingredients:

- 2 cups green beans
- 1 teaspoon chili pepper
- ½ lemon, sliced
- 1 cup tomatoes, chopped
- 1 white onion, chopped
- 2 tablespoons tomato sauce
- ½ teaspoon salt
- 1 teaspoon ground coriander
- ½ teaspoon cayenne pepper
- ½ cup of coconut milk

Directions:

1. Chop the green beans roughly and place them in the instant pot.
2. Add chili pepper, chopped tomatoes, onion, tomato sauce, salt, ground coriander, cayenne pepper, and coconut milk.
3. Mix up all the ingredients very carefully and top with the sliced lemon.
4. Close the lid and set Manual mode (High pressure). Cook salad for 6 minutes.
5. Then use quick pressure release.
6. Open the lid and discard sliced lemon. Transfer the cooked salad into the serving bowls.

Nutrition: calories 110, fat 7.4, fiber 4.1, carbs 11.3, protein 2.6

443. Lentil Tacos

Preparation Time: 10 minutes
Cooking time: 10 minutes
Servings: 6

Ingredients:

- 1 cup lentils
- 1 teaspoon salt
- 1 cup vegetable broth
- 2 cups salsa
- 1 teaspoon garlic powder
- ½ teaspoon onion powder
- 6 tablespoons coconut yogurt
- 6 corn tortillas

Directions:

1. Place lentil, salt, salsa, and vegetable broth in the instant pot bowl.
2. Add garlic powder and onion powder. Close the lid.
3. Cook the lentils on Manual for 10 minutes. Then make quick pressure release.
4. When the lentils are cooked, open the lid and chill them at least till the room temperature.
5. Fill corn tortillas with the lentils mixture and sprinkle with coconut yogurt.

Nutrition: calories 200, fat 1.4, fiber 12.9, carbs 37.2, protein 11.3

444. Red Kidney Beans Burrito

Preparation Time: 10 minutes
Cooking time: 15 minutes
Servings: 2

Ingredients:

- ½ avocado, sliced
- 1 bell pepper, sliced
- ½ onion, peeled
- 1 tablespoon olive oil
- 1 teaspoon tomato paste
- ½ teaspoon chili flakes
- ½ cup red kidney beans, canned
- ½ teaspoon ground cumin
- ½ teaspoon ground coriander
- ½ cup fresh cilantro, chopped
- 2 burritos

Directions:

1. Preheat instant pot on Saute mode for 3 minutes.
2. Pour olive oil and add sliced bell pepper. Start to saute vegetable, stir it from time to time.
3. Meanwhile cut the onion into the petals and add in the instant pot too.
4. Add chili flakes, ground cumin, coriander, and tomato paste. Stir it and add red kidney beans. Mix it up.
5. Close the lid and saute the mixture for 10 minutes.
6. Then switch off the instant pot and open the lid.
7. Fill the burritos with the bean mixture, add cilantro, avocado, and roll.

Nutrition: calories 352, fat 17.6, fiber 11.9, carbs 40.3, protein 12.4

445. Lentil Meatballs

Preparation Time: 10 minutes
Cooking time: 20 minute
Servings: 4

Ingredients:

- 1 ½ cup lentils
- 3 cups of water
- 1 teaspoon salt
- 1 tablespoon olive oil
- 1 teaspoon turmeric
- 1 teaspoon dried oregano
- 1 teaspoon dried dill
- 1 carrot, grated
- 2 tablespoons oatmeal flour
- 1 onion, diced

Directions:

1. Pour water in the instant pot.
2. Add lentils and salt and close the lid. Cook it on Manual mode for 7 minutes. Then use quick pressure release.
3. Meanwhile, mix up together grated carrot and diced onion.
4. Transfer the cooked lentils in the mixing bowl.
5. Pour olive oil in the instant pot and add carrot mixture.
6. Close the lid and saute it for 10 minutes. Open the lid and stir it from time to time.
7. When the carrot mixture is cooked, transfer it in the lentils.
8. Add turmeric, dried oregano, and dill. Then add oatmeal flour and mix up until smooth and homogenous.
9. Make the medium size meatballs from the lentil mixture and transfer in the instant pot.
10. Set Saute mode, close the lid and cook the meal for 3 minutes.

Nutrition: calories 313, fat 4.5, fiber 23.5, carbs 49.4, protein 19.5

446. Black Beans Chili

Preparation Time: 10 minutes
Cooking time: 15 minutes
Servings: 4

Ingredients:

- 1 cup black beans, canned
- 1 cup vegetable broth
- 1 cup tomato sauce
- 1 cup fresh cilantro, chopped
- 1 teaspoon chili flakes
- 1 teaspoon ground coriander
- 1 teaspoon dried rosemary
- 1 chipotle pepper, chopped
- 2 sweet green pepper, chopped
- 1 garlic clove, diced
- 3 tomatoes, chopped
- 1 red onion, roughly chopped
- 1 tablespoon almond butter
- 1 teaspoon garlic powder

Directions:

1. Melt the almond butter in the instant pot

on Saute mode.
2. Add diced garlic onion, garlic powder, green pepper, chipotle, rosemary, coriander, chili flakes, vegetable broth, and stir well.
3. Saute the ingredients for 10 minutes.
4. After this, add black beans and tomato sauce. Mix up the chili very carefully.
5. Add tomatoes, close and seal the lid.
6. Set Manual mode and cook chili for 3 minutes, use quick pressure release.
7. Open the lid and mix up chili well.
8. Transfer the cooked meal in the serving bowls and sprinkle with chopped cilantro.

Nutrition: calories 264, fat 3.8, fiber 11.9, carbs 45.6, protein 15.5

447. Burrito Bowl

Preparation Time: 10 minutes
Cooking time: 7 minutes
Servings: 2

Ingredients:

- 1 cup of water
- 1 cup quinoa
- 1 teaspoon salt
- 1 teaspoon ground cumin
- ½ cup red beans, cooked
- 1 bell pepper, chopped
- ½ avocado, sliced
- ¼ cup of coconut milk

Directions:

1. Transfer quinoa and water in the instant pot. Add salt, bell pepper, and close the lid.
2. Seal and set Manual mode.
3. Cook the ingredients for 7 minutes. Then use quick pressure release.
4. Transfer the cooked quinoa mixture in the bowl. Add red beans and ground cumin. Mix up well.
5. Add avocado slices and sprinkle the meal with the coconut milk.

Nutrition: calories 662, fat 23, fiber 17.9, carbs 93.7, protein 24.8

448. Cowboy Caviar

Preparation Time: 10 minutes
Cooking time: 6 minutes
Servings: 4

Ingredients:

- ½ black-eyed peas
- 1 cup of water
- 4 tomatoes, chopped
- 1 tablespoon apple cider vinegar
- 1 tablespoon lemon juice
- 1 jalapeno pepper, chopped
- ½ cup fresh parsley, chopped
- 2 tablespoons olive oil
- ½ teaspoon salt

Directions:

1. In the instant pot combine together black-eyed peas and water. Close the lid.
2. Set manual mode and cook on Pressure for 6 minutes. Then make quick pressure release.
3. In the mixing bowl mix up together chopped tomatoes, jalapeno pepper, parsley, and apple cider vinegar.
4. When the black-eyed peas are chilled, add them in the tomato mixture.
5. Add olive oil, salt, and lemon juice.
6. Mix up the caviar carefully before serving.

Nutrition: calories 99, fat 7.5, fiber 2.4, carbs 7.6, protein 2.1

449. Chipotle Chili with Hot Sauce

Preparation Time: 10 minutes
Cooking time: 15 minutes
Servings: 4

Ingredients:

- 1 tablespoon almond butter
- ½ cup mushrooms, chopped
- 1 teaspoon chipotle powder
- 1 cup black beans, canned
- ¼ cup hot sauce
- 1 cup tomato sauce
- ½ cup of water
- 2 garlic cloves, diced
- 1 tomato, chopped
- 1 red bell pepper, chopped

Directions:

1. Melt almond butter in the instant pot on Saute mode.
2. Add mushrooms, diced garlic, tomato, and

bell pepper. Saute the vegetables for 10 minutes.
3. Then sprinkle the mixture with chipotle powder.
4. Add hot sauce, tomato sauce, water, and black beans.
5. Mix up carefully. Close the lid.
6. Set Manual mode and cook chili for 5 minutes more. Then make quick pressure release.
7. Chill the cooked chili for 5-10 minutes before serving.

Nutrition: calories 223, fat 3.3, fiber 9.4, carbs 38.2, protein 13

450. Vaquero Beans Chili with Tempeh

Preparation Time: 15 minutes
Cooking time: 35 minutes
Servings: 4

Ingredients:

- 7 oz tempeh, chopped
- 1 tablespoon olive oil
- 1 teaspoon salt
- ¼ cup onion, diced
- 2 cups vaquero beans, canned
- ½ cup of water
- ½ cup tomato juice
- 1 teaspoon paprika
- 1 teaspoon turmeric
- 1 teaspoon ground black pepper
- ½ cup tomatoes, canned

Directions:

1. Saute onion with olive oil in the instant pot for 5 minutes.
2. Then add chopped tempeh, salt, vaquero beans, water, tomato juice, paprika, turmeric, and ground black pepper.
3. Add canned tomatoes and mix up mixture gently. Close the lid.
4. Cook chili on Saute mode for 30 minutes.
5. When the time is over, open the lid and chill chili for 10 minutes.

Nutrition: calories 160, fat 9.2, fiber 2.9, carbs 12.4, protein 10.9

451. Creamy Kidney Beans

Preparation Time: 10 minutes
Cooking time: 25 minutes
Servings: 4

Ingredients:

- 2 cups kidney beans
- 2 cups of water
- 2 cups almond milk
- 1 tablespoon coconut oil
- 1 teaspoon salt
- 1 tablespoon tomato paste
- 1 garlic clove, peeled
- 1 tablespoon Taco seasoning

Place kidney beans, water, almond milk, coconut oil, salt, tomato paste, garlic clove, and Taco seasoning in the instant pot.
Mix up the ingredients until homogenous.
Close and seal the lid. Set manual mode and cook meal for 25 minutes. Then use quick pressure release.
Mix up the kidneys gently before serving.

Nutrition: calories 620, fat 33, fiber 16.8, carbs 64.1, protein 23.7

452. Spicy Tacos with Beans

Preparation Time: 10 minutes
Cooking time: 15 minutes
Servings: 2

Ingredients:

- 4 oz red cabbage, shredded
- 1 tablespoon tomato paste
- ¼ onion, diced
- 1 teaspoon olive oil
- 1 jalapeno pepper, chopped
- 1/3 cup black beans, canned
- ½ cup of water
- ½ teaspoon salt
- 1 tablespoon vegan mayonnaise
- 2 taco shells

Directions:

1. Mix up together tomato paste, salt, water, black beans, jalapeno pepper, and diced onion in the instant pot.
2. Add olive oil and close the lid. Saute the ingredients for 15 minutes on Saute mode.
3. Then chill bean mixture till the room temperature.
4. Fill the tacos shells with bean mixture and red cabbage.

5. Sprinkle the tacos with mayonnaise before serving.

Nutrition: calories 276, fat 9.1, fiber 8.1, carbs 40.3, protein 9.8

453. Edamame Dip

Preparation Time: 10 minutes
Cooking time: 6 minutes
Servings: 4

Ingredients:

- 1 cup edamame beans
- 1 cup of water
- 1 tablespoon miso paste
- 4 tablespoons vegetable broth
- ½ teaspoon minced garlic
- ¼ teaspoon minced ginger
- 1 teaspoon onion powder
- 1/3 cup fresh dill, chopped
- ½ cup of coconut milk

Directions:

1. In the instant pot, combine together edamame beans and water.
2. Close and seal the lid. Set manual mode and cook beans for 6 minutes. Then use quick pressure release.
3. Transfer all the remaining ingredients in the food processor.
4. Drain water from the cooked beans and chill them.
5. Add edamame beans into the food processor too.
6. Blend the mixture until smooth and soft.
7. Transfer the cooked dip in the bowl.

Nutrition: calories 114, fat 8.4, fiber 2.3, carbs 7.5, protein 4.1

454. Zoodles with Lentils

Preparation Time: 10 minutes
Cooking time: 8 minutes
Servings: 4

Ingredients:

- 1 cup lentils
- 1 cup of water
- 1 zucchini
- 1 teaspoon chili flakes
- 1 tablespoon cashew milk

Directions:

1. Place lentils and water in the instant pot bowl.
2. Close the lid and cook on Manual for 5 minutes. Then use quick pressure release.
3. After this, spiralize the zucchini with the help of the spiralizer.
4. Sprinkle zoodles with chili flakes and transfer in the lentils.
5. Add cashew milk and mix up it well.
6. Close the lid and saute the meal for 3 minutes on Saute mode.

Nutrition: calories 178, fat 0.6, fiber 15.2, carbs 30.5, protein 13

455. Buffalo Chickpea

Preparation Time: 5 minutes
Cooking time: 5 minutes
Servings: 4

Ingredients:

- 2 cups chickpea, cooked
- 3 tablespoons Buffalo hot sauce
- 1 tablespoon olive oil
- 1 teaspoon dried dill

Directions:

1. Place chickpeas and Buffalo hot sauce in the instant pot.
2. Add olive oil and dried dill. Mix up the ingredients and close the lid.
3. Set Saute mode and cook meal for 5 minutes. Stir it from time to time.

Nutrition: calories 417, fat 9.6, fiber 17.4, carbs 66, protein 19.4

456. Mung Beans Croquettes

Preparation Time: 10 minutes
Cooking time: 10 minutes
Servings: 6

Ingredients:

- 1 cup mung beans, soaked
- 1 green bell pepper, chopped
- ½ chipotle pepper, chopped
- ½ teaspoon minced garlic
- 1 tablespoon sesame oil

Directions:

1. Place mung beans in the food processor and blend well.
2. Add bell pepper, chipotle, and minced

garlic.
3. Blend the mixture until smooth.
4. Then transfer it in the mixing bowl.
5. Wet your hands and make the small croquettes.
6. Set saute mode and preheat instant pot.
7. Add sesame oil and croquettes.
8. Cook them for 2 minutes from each side or until light brown.

Nutrition: calories 148, fat 2.7, fiber 6, carbs 23.5, protein 8.5

457. Pinto Beans Quinoa Salad

Preparation Time: 10 minutes
Cooking time: 2 minutes
Servings: 2

Ingredients:

- ½ cup quinoa
- 1 cup of water
- ½ cup pinto beans, canned
- 1 cup fresh cilantro, chopped
- 1 sweet red pepper, chopped
- 1 tablespoon olive oil
- 1 teaspoon salt

Directions:

1. In the instant pot combine together quinoa and water. Close and seal the lid.
2. Cook it on Manula mode for 2 minutes. Use quick pressure release.
3. Then open the lid and chill quinoa till the room temperature.
4. Transfer it in the salad bowl.
5. Add fresh cilantro, pinto beans, salt, and olive oil.
6. Mix up the salad carefully.

Nutrition: calories 405, fat 10.4, fiber 11.5, carbs 62.2, protein 17.1

458. Beanballs

Preparation Time: 20 minutes
Cooking time: 25 minutes
Servings: 2

Ingredients:

- 1 cup red kidney beans, soaked
- 4 cups of water
- 1 teaspoon salt
- 1 teaspoon onion powder
- 1 teaspoon garlic powder
- 1 teaspoon paprika
- ½ teaspoon chili flakes

Directions:

1. In the instant pot put red kidney beans and water. Close and seal the lid.
2. Cook beans on Manual mode (high pressure) for 25 minutes. Then allow natural pressure release for 15 minutes.
3. Drain water and transfer beans in the food processor.
4. Add onion powder, garlic powder, paprika, chili flakes, and salt.
5. Blend the mixture until it has puree texture.
6. Then make the beanballs. Store them in the fridge before serving.

Nutrition: calories 322, fat 1.1, fiber 14.6, carbs 59, protein 21.3

459. Lentil Stew with Spinach

Preparation Time: 10 minutes
Cooking time: 10 minutes
Servings: 2

Ingredients:

- 1 cup green lentils
- 1 cup of water
- 1 cup tomatoes, canned
- 1 teaspoon ground black pepper
- 2 cups spinach, chopped
- 1 teaspoon paprika
- 1 teaspoon turmeric
- 1 teaspoon olive oil
- 1 carrot, chopped

Directions:

- Place lentils, water, tomatoes, ground black pepper, paprika, turmeric, and carrot in the instant pot.
- Add olive oil and close the lid.
- Seal it and set High-pressure mode. Cook the ingredients for 6 minutes.
- After this, use quick pressure release. Then open the lid.
- Add chopped spinach and mix up it well.
- Close the lid and set Saute mode.
- Cook stew for 4 minutes more.

Nutrition: calories 404, fat 3.9, fiber 32.7, carbs 67.3, protein 27

460. Bean Loaf

Preparation Time: 10 minutes
Cooking time: 4 minutes
Servings: 4

Ingredients:

- 1 cup red beans, canned
- 1 tablespoon oatmeal
- 1 tablespoon wheat flour
- 1 teaspoon salt
- 1 teaspoon tahini paste
- 1 potato, peeled, boiled
- 1 tablespoon tomato sauce
- 1 teaspoon olive oil

Directions:

1. Mash red beans and potato until you get soft puree mixture.
2. Add oatmeal, wheat flour, salt, tahini paste, and tomato sauce.
3. Mix up the mixture until smooth.
4. Then take instant pot loaf pan and line it with parchment.
5. Place mixture into the loaf pan and make the shape of the loaf.
6. Brush it with the olive oil.
7. Pour water in the instant pot and insert rack.
8. Place loaf pan on the rack and close the lid.
9. Then seal it and set High-pressure mode.
10. Cook the bean loaf for 4 minutes. Then use quick pressure release.
11. Chill the bean loaf well and them a slice.

Nutrition: calories 218, fat 2.5, fiber 8.3, carbs 38.4, protein 11.9

461. Bean Enchiladas

Preparation Time: 15 minutes
Cooking time: 15 minutes
Servings: 6

Ingredients:

- 6 corn tortillas
- ½ cup corn kernels
- 3 tablespoon Enchilada sauce
- 2 sweet potatoes, chopped
- 1 yellow onion, chopped
- 1 cup kidney beans, cooked
- 2 red sweet peppers, chopped
- 1 teaspoon paprika
- 1 teaspoon ground cumin
- ½ teaspoon ground black pepper
- 1 teaspoon salt
- 7 oz vegan Parmesan, grated
- 1 tablespoon olive oil
- 1 jalapeno, sliced

Directions:

1. Preheat instant pot on Saute mode, when it shows "hot" add olive oil.
2. Then add sweet peppers and yellow onion.
3. Cook the vegetables for 5 minutes.
4. After this, add corn sweet potato, Enchilada sauce, corn kernels, paprika, ground cumin, ground black pepper, salt, and sliced jalapeno.
5. Mix the ingredients up.
6. Close and seal the lid. Set Manual mode and cook the meal for 6 minutes.
7. When the time is over, make quick pressure release.
8. Chop the corn tortillas.
9. Open the lid and place tortillas over the mixture.
10. Then make the cheese layer. Close the lid and cook meal for 3 minutes more on Saute mode.
11. Switch off the instant pot and let the cooked meal rest for 10 minutes before serving.

Nutrition: calories 319, fat 3.9, fiber 8.5, carbs 46, protein 23.3

462. Rice and Beans Bowl

Preparation Time: 10 minutes
Cooking time: 30 minutes
Servings: 4

Ingredients:

- 1 cup black beans, soaked
- 1 cup of rice
- 1 teaspoon salt
- 4 cups of water
- 1 cup of salsa
- 1cup fresh parsley, chopped

- 1 tablespoon almond butter

Directions:

1. Place black beans, rice, water, salsa, salt, and almond butter in the instant pot.
2. Close and seal the lid.
3. Set Manual mode (high pressure) and cook a meal for 30 minutes.
4. Then use quick pressure release.
5. After this, open the lid and mix up the meal well.
6. Add parsley and mix it up one more time.
7. Transfer the cooked meal into the serving bowls.

Nutrition: calories 382, fat 3.5, fiber 9.9, carbs 73, protein 16.1

463. Frijoles Negros

Preparation Time: 10 minutes
Cooking time: 60 minutes
Servings: 4

Ingredients:

- 1 cup black beans
- 1 tablespoon BBQ seasoning
- 1 teaspoon salt
- 1 teaspoon garlic powder
- 1 teaspoon onion powder
- 3 cups vegetable broth
- 1 teaspoon dried cilantro

Directions:

1. Place black beans in the instant pot.
2. Sprinkle them with BBQ seasoning, salt, garlic powder, onion powder, and dried cilantro. Add vegetable broth and stir gently.
3. Close and seal the lid. Set Manual mode and cook meal for 40 minutes.
4. When the time is over, allow natural pressure release for 20 minutes more.

Nutrition: calories 201, fat 1.7, fiber 7.5, carbs 32.2, protein 14.3

464. Bean Casserole

Preparation Time: 10 minutes
Cooking time: 50 minutes
Servings: 6

Ingredients:

- 2 golden potatoes, peeled, sliced
- 6 oz vegan Parmesan, grated
- ½ cup mushrooms, sliced
- 1 cup green beans, roughly chopped
- 4 tablespoons bread crumbs
- 1 yellow onion, sliced
- 1 teaspoon coconut oil
- ½ cup of coconut yogurt
- 1 teaspoon salt
- 1 teaspoon ground black pepper
- 1 teaspoon paprika

Directions:

1. Mix up together paprika, ground black pepper, and salt.
2. Then grease instant pot pan with coconut oil.
3. Place the layer of sliced potato inside and sprinkle it with the small amount of paprika mixture.
4. Then add a layer of mushrooms and sliced onion.
5. Sprinkle the layers with the remaining paprika mixture and add green beans.
6. Sprinkle the green beans with bread crumbs. Pour coconut yogurt over the mixture.
7. Cover the casserole with the foil and secure the edges.
8. Transfer it in the instant pot. Close the lid.
9. Set Saute mode and cook meal for 50 minutes.

Nutrition: calories 179, fat 1.5, fiber 2.3, carbs 23.9, protein 14.5

465. Spaghetti Squash Bean Bowl

Preparation Time: 15 minutes
Cooking time: 8 minutes
Servings: 4

Ingredients:

- 1 cup red kidney beans, canned
- 1-pound spaghetti squash, seeded, cut into halves
- ¼ cup fresh parsley, chopped
- 1 teaspoon minced garlic
- 1 tablespoon tomato sauce
- ½ teaspoon white pepper
- 3 oz vegan Cheddar, grated
- 1 cup water, for cooking

Directions:

1. Pour water in the instant pot and insert steamer rack.
2. Put spaghetti squash on the rack, close and seal the lid.
3. Set Manual mode and cook it for 8 minutes.
4. When the time is over, use quick pressure release.
5. Remove the squash from the instant pot and shred spaghetti squash flesh. Do it carefully yo get spaghetti squash cups from the squash skin.
6. Mix up together shredded squash with kidney beans, fresh parsley, minced garlic, tomato sauce, white pepper, and fill the spaghetti squash bowls.
7. Sprinkle the meal with grated Cheddar cheese.

Nutrition: calories 262, fat 7.2, fiber 8, carbs 42.1, protein 12.1

466. Red Beans Cauliflower Rice

Preparation Time: 15 minutes
Cooking time: 60 minutes
Servings: 2

Ingredients:

- ½ cup cauliflower, shredded
- ½ teaspoon turmeric
- ½ teaspoon salt
- 1 cup black beans, soaked
- 3 cups of water
- 1 teaspoon ground black pepper
- ½ cup of coconut milk
- 1 teaspoon Italian seasoning
- ½ cup water, for cooking

Directions:

1. Place black beans and 3 cups of water in the instant pot. Close and seal the lid.
2. Cook it for 40 minutes on Manual mode. Then allow natural pressure release for 20 minutes
3. Transfer the beans in the bowl and clean the instant pot.
4. After this, pour ½ cup of water in the instant pot and insert rack.
5. Take a pan and place shredded cauliflower inside.
6. Add salt, turmeric, ground black pepper, and mix it up.
7. Insert the pan on the rack and close the lid.
8. Set Manual mode or High pressure and cook cauliflower for 1 minute. Then use quick pressure release.
9. Transfer the cauliflower over the beans and mix up.
10. Whisk together Italian seasoning and coconut milk.
11. Pour liquid over the cauliflower-beans mixture.

Nutrition: calories 487, fat 16.5, fiber 17.1, carbs 66.4, protein 23

467. Stuffed Sweet Potato with Beans

Preparation Time: 10 minutes
Cooking time: 10 minutes
Servings: 4

Ingredients:

- 2 sweet potatoes
- 1 tablespoon chives, chopped
- 1 cup red kidney beans, canned
- 1 tablespoon lemon juice
- 1 teaspoon salt
- 1 teaspoon cayenne pepper
- 1 tablespoon fresh parsley
- 1 cup water, for cooking

Directions:

1. Pour water in the instant pot and insert steamer rack.
2. Cut sweet potatoes into halves and place on the steamer rack.
3. Close the lid and cook on Manual for 7 minutes. Then allow natural pressure release for 3 minutes.
4. Meanwhile, mix up together chives, red kidney beans, lemon juice, salt, cayenne pepper, and parsley.
5. Shred the flesh of cooked sweet potatoes and mix it up with the beans mixture.

Fill the sweet potato skins with this mixture and transfer on the serving plates.

Nutrition: calories 159, fat 0.6, fiber 7.2, carbs 28.8, protein 10.5

468. Curry White Beans

Preparation Time: 5 minutes
Cooking time: 2 hours
Servings: 6

Ingredients:

- 1 cup of brown rice
- 2 cups white beans
- 1 tablespoon curry paste
- 1 teaspoon ground cumin
- 1 teaspoon salt
- 7 cups of water
- 1 tablespoon dried dill
- 1 teaspoon tomato paste
- 1 garlic clove, peeled

Directions:

1. Place all the ingredients in the instant pot and mix them up until you get a homogenous liquid mixture.
2. Then close the lid.
3. Set Saute mode and cook the meal for 2 hours.
4. When the time is over, open the instant pot lid and mix it up.

Nutrition: calories 360, fat 3, fiber 11.5, carbs 66.2, protein 18.5

469. Kidney Beans Koftas with Mushrooms

Preparation Time: 15 minutes
Cooking time: 10 minutes
Servings: 4

Ingredients:

- 1 cup red kidney beans, canned
- ½ cup mushrooms
- 1 tablespoon tomato paste
- ½ cup of water
- 1 teaspoon salt
- ½ onion, diced
- 1 teaspoon ground black pepper
- 1 teaspoon dried dill
- 1 tablespoon wheat flour
- 1 tablespoon bread crumbs
- 1 teaspoon chili flakes

Directions:

1. Put red kidney beans and mushrooms in the food processor.
2. Blend the mixture until smooth and transfer in the mixing bowl.
3. Add diced onion, dried dill, wheat flour, bread crumbs, and chili flakes.
4. Mix it up until smooth.
5. After this, pour water in the instant pot.
6. Add tomato paste, salt, and ground black pepper.
7. Stir it until homogenous. Start to preheat the liquid on Saute mode for 5 minutes.
8. Meanwhile, make medium size bowls (koftas) from the bean mixture.
9. Put them in the preheated tomato mixture and close instant pot lid.
10. Set Manual mode and cook the meal for 4 minutes. Then allow quick pressure release.
11. Chill the cooked koftas for 10 minutes before serving.

Nutrition: calories 182, fat 0.7, fiber 7.8, carbs 33.7, protein 11.5

470. Stuffed Peppers with Kidney Beans

Preparation Time: 15 minutes
Cooking time: 4 minutes
Servings: 2

Ingredients:

- 2 big sweet peppers
- 1 cup kale, chopped
- ¼ cup red kidney beans, canned
- 3 oz vegan Parmesan, grated
- 1 tablespoon coconut cream
- ½ teaspoon cayenne pepper

Directions:

1. Chop kale into the tiny pieces.
2. Mash red kidney beans.
3. In the mixing bowl mix up together kale, mashed beans, coconut cream, and cayenne pepper.
4. Cut the sweet peppers into halves and remove seeds.
5. Then fill peppers with beans mixture and sprinkle with grated cheese.
6. Wrap the stuffed peppers in the foil and place in the instant pot.
7. Close and seal the lid.
8. Cook the meal on Manual for 4 minutes. Then use quick pressure release.

Nutrition: calories 281, fat 2.4, fiber 5.9, carbs 35.9, protein 25

471. Chickpea Shakshuka

Preparation Time: 10 minutes
Cooking time: 15 minutes
Servings: 2

Ingredients:

- ½ cup tomato puree
- 1 shallot, diced
- 1 bell pepper, chopped
- ½ cup chickpeas, cooked
- ¼ teaspoon ground cinnamon
- 1 tablespoon coconut oil
- 1 teaspoon tomato puree
- 1 tablespoon chives, chopped
- 1 tablespoon fresh dill, chopped
- 2 oz mushrooms, sliced
- ¼ cup of water

Directions:

1. Set instant pot on Saute mode.
2. Add coconut oil and melt it.
3. Then add diced shallot and mushrooms. Mix the ingredients up and saute for 5 minutes.
4. Then add chopped pepper, tomato puree, and tomato paste. Mix it up.
5. Add chickpeas, water, dill, chives, and ground cinnamon.
6. Mix the meal up and close the lid.
7. Saute it for 10 minutes.
8. When the time is over, mix up the cooked shakshuka one more time.

Nutrition: calories 296, fat 10.3, fiber 11.4, carbs 42.8, protein 12.6

472. Buddha Bowl

Preparation Time: 10 minutes
Cooking time: 10 minutes
Servings: 4

Ingredients:

- 2 yams, chopped
- 2 tablespoons almond butter
- 1 cup chickpeas, cooked
- 1 teaspoon harissa
- ½ cup of water
- 1 cup spinach, chopped
- 1 tablespoon lemon juice
- 1 teaspoon garlic powder

Directions:

1. Place almond butter in the instant pot and melt it on Saute mode.
2. Then add chopped yams, sprinkle them with harissa and close the lid.
3. Saute the vegetables for 7 minutes.
4. After this, open the lid, stir the yams gently, add chickpeas, spinach, and water.
5. Sprinkle the ingredients with harissa, lemon juice, and garlic powder. Mix it up.
6. Close and seal the lid.
7. Set Manual mode (high pressure) and cook a meal for 3 minutes. Then use quick pressure release.
8. Open the lid and transfer the meal into the bowls.

Nutrition: calories 266, fat 7.9, fiber 10.7, carbs 39.1, protein 12.4

473. Chickpea Curry

Preparation Time: 10 minutes
Cooking time: 60 minutes
Servings: 4

Ingredients:

- 1 ½ cup chickpeas, soaked
- 1 cup tomatoes, chopped
- 1 tablespoon curry powder
- ½ cup fresh cilantro, chopped
- 5 cups of water
- 1 teaspoon salt
- 1 teaspoon ground coriander
- ½ teaspoon ground cumin
- ½ teaspoon ground nutmeg
- ½ teaspoon minced garlic
- 1 white onion, diced
- ½ cup of coconut milk

Directions:

1. Place all the ingredients in the instant pot and mix up carefully until homogenous and gets a light yellow color.
2. Then close and seal the lid.
3. Set Manual (pressure cook) mode and cook the meal for 40 minutes.
4. When the time is over, allow natural pressure release for 20 minutes.

5. Then open the lid and mix up cooked curry well. Transfer it into the serving bowls.

Nutrition: calories 370, fat 12.2, fiber 15.5, carbs 52.8, protein 16.2

474. Chickpea Salad

Preparation Time: 20 minutes
Cooking time: 25 minutes
Servings: 5

Ingredients:

- 1 cup chickpea
- 1 red onion, sliced
- ½ cup fresh parsley, chopped
- 1 tablespoon olive oil
- 1 teaspoon salt
- 3 cups vegetable broth
- 1 teaspoon garam masala

Directions:

Place chickpeas and vegetable broth in the instant pot. Add garam masala.

1. Close and seal the lid. Set High-pressure mode and cook chickpeas for 25 minutes.
2. After this, allow naturally pressure release for 10 minutes.
3. In the salad bowl combine together cooked chickpeas, chopped parsley, sliced onion, salt, and olive oil.
4. Mix up the salad carefully before serving.

Nutrition: calories 184, fat 5.3, fiber 7.8, carbs 27.3, protein 8.2

475. Buffalo Chickpea

Preparation Time: 20 minutes
Cooking time: 45 minutes
Servings: 4

Ingredients:

- ¼ cup Buffalo sauce
- ½ cup tomato puree
- 1 cup chickpeas, soaked
- 3 cups of water
- ½ teaspoon chili powder

Directions:

1. In the instant pot combine together Buffalo sauce, tomato puree, and water.
2. Add chili powder and stir it carefully with the help of the spoon until you get homogenous liquid.
3. Then add chickpeas and close the lid.
4. Set High-pressure cook mode, close and seal the lid.
5. Cook chickpeas for 45 minutes. Allow natural pressure release for 15 minutes.
6. Open the lid and mix up the meal.

Nutrition: calories 196, fat 3.2, fiber 9.5, carbs 33.5, protein 10.2

476. Edamame Toast

Preparation Time: 15 minutes
Cooking time: 10 minutes
Servings: 4

Ingredients:

- 4 bread slices, toasted
- 1 avocado, peeled
- ½ cup edamame beans
- 2 cups of water
- 1 teaspoon salt
- 1 teaspoon chili flakes
- 1 teaspoon ground black pepper
- 1 tablespoon cashew milk

Directions:

1. Pour water in the instant pot.
2. Add edamame beans and salt. Close the lid and set Manual mode.
3. Cook the beans for 10 minutes. Then allow natural pressure release for 10 minutes more.
4. Meanwhile, in the food processor blend together avocado, chili flakes, ground black pepper, and cashew milk.
5. When the mixture is smooth, transfer it into the bowl.
6. Chill the cooked edamame beans till the room temperature and blend in the food processor until smooth.
7. Mix up together edamame beans and avocado mixture. You will get the paste.
8. Spread the bread toasts with the paste.

Nutrition: calories 164, fat 12, fiber 5.1, carbs 10.2, protein 5.2

477. Lentils Shepherd's Pie

Preparation Time: 25 minutes
Cooking time: 10 minutes
Servings: 6

Ingredients:

- 1 cup lentils
- 2 cups of water
- 1 teaspoon salt
- 1 teaspoon chili flakes
- 1 teaspoon ground black pepper
- 1 teaspoon dried dill
- 1 teaspoon dried oregano
- 2 carrots, chopped
- 1 onion, diced
- ½ cup almond milk
- 1 teaspoon cayenne pepper
- 1-pound cauliflower

Directions:

1. Place lentils, carrots, and onion in the instant pot. Add water, almond milk, and stir the mixture.
2. Insert steamer rack and put cauliflower on it. Close and seal the lid.
3. Set Manual mode and cook ingredients for 7 minutes.
4. Then allow natural pressure release for 10 minutes.
5. Open the lid and transfer the cauliflower in the food processor. Add salt and blend it until smooth.
6. Add chili flakes, ground black pepper, dried dill and oregano, cayenne pepper in the lentils mixture and mix it up. Transfer it in the serving bowls.
7. Place smooth cauliflower puree over lentils.

Nutrition: calories 197, fat 5.3, fiber 13.3, carbs 28.7, protein 10.7

478. Lentil Bolognese

Preparation Time: 7 minutes
Cooking time: 7 minutes
Servings: 2

Ingredients:

- ½ cup green lentils
- 1 cup of water
- 1 oz celery stalk, chopped
- 1 tablespoon fresh parsley, chopped
- 1 tablespoon fresh dill, chopped
- 1 teaspoon salt
- ½ cup tomato puree
- 1 teaspoon paprika
- 1 tablespoon fresh basil, chopped
- 1 bell pepper, chopped

Directions:

1. Place all the ingredients in the instant pot and mix up gently.
2. Close and seal the lid. Set Manual (High pressure) mode. Cook the meal for 7 minutes.
3. Then make quick pressure release and open the lid.
4. Mix up lentil bolognese carefully before serving.

Nutrition: calories 222, fat 1.1, fiber 17.5, carbs 41, protein 14.7

479. Lentil Loaf

Preparation Time: 10 minutes
Cooking time: 20 minutes
Servings: 6

Ingredients:

- 2 cups lentils
- 6 cups of water
- 1 teaspoon salt
- 1 teaspoon ground black pepper
- 1 onion, diced
- ½ cup mushrooms, chopped
- 1 tablespoon olive oil
- 2 tablespoons tomato paste
- 2 tablespoons wheat flour
- 1 tablespoon flax meal
- 1 tablespoon dried oregano
- 1 tablespoon dried cilantro
- 1 tablespoon coconut oil

Directions:

1. Cook lentils: Place lentils, water, and salt in the instant pot. Set manual mode and cook the mixture for 7 minutes. Then make quick pressure release.
2. After this, open the lid and transfer lentils in the mixing bowl.
3. Clean the instant pot and pour olive oil inside.
4. Add diced onion and mushrooms. Cook the vegetables on Saute mode for 10

minutes or until tender. Stir them from time to time.
5. Then transfer the cooked vegetables in the lentils.
6. Add wheat flour, flax meal, dried oregano, cilantro, and mix it up until smooth.
7. Grease the instant pot bowl with coconut oil and place lentil mixture inside.
8. Flatten it well and spread with tomato paste.
9. Close and seal the lid.
10. Cook the lentil loaf on Manual mode for 3 minutes. Use quick pressure release.
11. Chill the cooked meal for 1-2 hours before slicing.

Nutrition: calories 296, fat 5.9, fiber 21, carbs 44.4, protein 17.8

480. Lentil Chili

Preparation Time: 15 minutes
Cooking time: 6 minutes
Servings: 4

Ingredients:

- ½ cup tomatoes, canned
- 1 jalapeno pepper, chopped
- 1 onion, chopped
- 1 cup green lentils
- 2 cups of water
- 1 teaspoon chili flakes
- 1 teaspoon salt
- 1 teaspoon paprika
- 1 teaspoon oregano
- ½ teaspoon minced garlic
- 4 oz vegan Cheddar, grated

Directions:

1. Put the canned tomatoes, jalapeno pepper, onion, green lentils, and water in the instant pot.
2. Add chili flakes, salt, paprika, oregano, and minced garlic.
3. Close and seal the lid.
4. Cook chili for 6 minutes on Manual mode (high pressure).
5. Then allow natural pressure release for 5 minutes and open the lid.
6. Stir the cooked lentil chili well and transfer in the serving bowls.
7. Sprinkle the grated cheese over the chili before serving.

Nutrition: calories 279, fat 8.7, fiber 17, carbs 40.2, protein 14.1

481. Sloppy Lentils

Preparation Time: 10 minutes
Cooking time: 7 minutes
Servings: 4

Ingredients:

- 1 cup lentils
- 1 white onion, sliced
- 2 carrots, diced
- 2 cups of water
- 1 teaspoon salt
- 1 teaspoon paprika
- 1 teaspoon ground black pepper
- ¼ teaspoon ground nutmeg
- ½ teaspoon minced garlic
- 1 tablespoon mustard
- 1 tablespoon tomato sauce
- 3 tablespoons ketchup

4 burger buns

Directions:

1. Place lentils, water, carrot, salt, paprika, ground black pepper, ground nutmeg, minced garlic, mustard, tomato sauce, and ketchup in the instant pot. Stir it gently.
2. Close the lid and cook on High-pressure mode for 7 minutes. Then make quick pressure release.
3. Open the lid and stir the mixture well.
4. Fill the burger buns with the lentils mixture and sliced onion and serve.

Nutrition: calories 222, fat 1.5, fiber 18.9, carbs 78.3, protein 21.2

482. Masala Lentils

Preparation Time: 15 minutes
Cooking time: 5 minutes
Servings: 2

Ingredients:

- 1 teaspoon ginger powder
- 1 teaspoon turmeric
- 1 tablespoon garam masala
- 1 cup almond milk
- ½ cup lentils

- 1 teaspoon minced garlic
- 1 tablespoon fresh parsley, chopped
- 1 teaspoon salt

Directions:

1. Put lentils and all spices in the instant pot.
2. Add minced garlic and almond milk and close the lid.
3. Set Manual mode and cook the meal for 5 minutes. Then allow natural pressure release for 10 minutes.
4. Mix up the cooked lentils well and transfer into the bowls. Garnish the meal with fresh parsley.

Nutrition: calories 455, fat 29.3, fiber 17.7, carbs 37.4, protein 15.5

483. Lentil Ragout

Preparation Time: 15 minutes
Cooking time: 15 minutes
Servings: 4

Ingredients:

- 1 tomato, roughly chopped
- 2 oz celery, chopped
- 1 carrot, chopped
- 1 cup lentils
- 1 ½ cup vegetable broth
- 1 teaspoon salt
- 1 teaspoon oregano
- 1 teaspoon chili flakes
- 2 teaspoons olive oil
- 1 teaspoon tomato paste

Directions:

1. Pour olive oil in the instant pot and set Saute mode.
2. Add chopped celery, carrot, and mix up the ingredients. Saute them for 5 minutes,
3. Then add tomato and lentils. Stir and cook for 3 minutes more.
4. After this, sprinkle the mixture with salt, oregano, and chili flakes.
5. Add tomato paste and vegetable broth. Stir it until homogenous.
6. Close and seal the lid. Set Manual or High-pressure mode and cook ragout for 5 minutes.
7. Then allow natural pressure release for 10 minutes.
8. Open the lid and transfer cooked ragout into the bowls. Do not stir it anymore.

Nutrition: calories 209, fat 2.9, fiber 16, carbs 33, protein 12.9

484. Lentil Mash

Preparation Time: 10 minutes
Cooking time: 8 minutes
Servings: 4

Ingredients:

- 2 cup lentils
- 3 cups of water
- ½ cup tomato sauce
- ½ cup kale, chopped

Directions:

1. Place all the ingredients in the instant pot. Close and seal the lid.
2. Set High-pressure mode and cook the mass for 8 minutes.
3. After this, use quick pressure release and open the lid.
4. Use the hand blender to blend the mixture until you get mash.
5. Transfer the mash into the serving bowls. It is recommended to eat the meal until it is warm.

Nutrition: calories 350, fat 1.1, fiber 29.9, carbs 60.2, protein 25.4

485. Red Lentil Dal

Preparation Time: 15 minutes
Cooking time: 10 minutes
Servings: 3

Ingredients:

- 1 cup red lentils
- 2 cups of water
- 1 tablespoon coconut oil
- ½ teaspoon cumin
- 1 tablespoon garlic, diced
- ½ chipotle pepper, chopped
- 1 tomato, chopped
- 1 teaspoon ground coriander
- ¾ teaspoon ground nutmeg
- 1 teaspoon salt
- ½ teaspoon chili powder

Directions:

1. Preheat instant pot on Saute mode and add coconut oil. Melt it.
2. Add tomato, chipotle pepper, and diced garlic. Stir it and saute for 3 minutes.
3. After this, add cumin, ground coriander, nutmeg, salt, and chili powder. Mit it up and cook for 2 minutes more.
4. Then add red lentils and water.
5. Close and seal the lid. Cook lentil dal for 5 minutes on Manual mode.
6. Then allow natural pressure release for 10 minutes.
7. Open the lid and stir the meal. Season it with salt or any other spices if needed.

Nutrition: calories 281, fat 5.6, fiber 20.2, carbs 41.6, protein 17.2

486. Lentil Tomato Salad

Preparation Time: 10 minutes
Cooking time: 7 minutes
Servings: 5

Ingredients:

- 2 cups baby spinach
- 1 cup lentils
- 2 cups of water
- 1 teaspoon salt
- 1 teaspoon ground black pepper
- 3 tomatoes, chopped
- 1 red onion, sliced
- 2 tablespoons olive oil
- 1 tablespoon lemon juice

Directions:

1. Cook lentils: mix up lentils, water, and salt. Transfer the mixture in the instant pot.
2. Close and seal the lid and cook on Manual for 7 minutes. Then use quick pressure release.
3. Meanwhile, make all the remaining preparations: combine together baby spinach with tomatoes, and red onion in the salad bowl.
4. Sprinkle with lemon juice, olive oil, and ground black pepper. Don't stir the salad.
5. Chill the cooked lentils till the room temperature and add in the salad bowl.
6. Mix up the cooked meal carefully and serve it warm.

Nutrition: calories 210, fat 6.3, fiber 13.5, carbs 28.8, protein 11.2

487. Cabbage Rolls with Lentils

Preparation Time: 15 minutes
Cooking time: 21 minutes
Servings: 4

Ingredients:

- 9 oz cabbage, petals
- ½ cup lentils
- 1 onion, diced
- 1 carrot, diced
- 1 cup of water
- 1 teaspoon salt
- 1 teaspoon ground black pepper
- ½ cup tomato juice
- ¼ cup almond milk
- ½ teaspoon cayenne pepper

Directions:

1. Put lentils and water in the instant pot.
2. Add diced onion and carrot. Close and seal the lid. Cook the ingredients for 6 minutes on High-pressure mode.
3. Then open the lid and transfer lentil mixture in the bowl.
4. Add salt, ground black pepper, and mix it up.
5. Fill the cabbage petals with the mixture and roll them.
6. Place the cabbage rolls in the instant pot. Add tomato juice and almond milk.
7. Sprinkle the meal with cayenne pepper and close the lid.
8. Cook it on Saute mode for 15 minutes.
9. Chill the meal for 10-15 minutes before serving.

Nutrition: calories 160, fat 4, fiber 10.5, carbs 24.8, protein 8.1

Salads

488. Black Bean Taco Salad Bowl

Preparation time: 15 minutes
cooking time: 5 minutes
servings: 3

Ingredients

For the black bean salad

- 1 (14-ouncecan black beans, drained and rinsed, or 1½ cups cooked
- 1 cup corn kernels, fresh and blanched, or frozen and thawed
- ¼ cup fresh cilantro, or parsley, chopped
- Zest and juice of 1 lime
- 1 to 2 teaspoons chili powder
- Pinch sea salt
- 1½ cups cherry tomatoes, halved
- 1 red bell pepper, seeded and chopped
- 2 scallions, chopped
- For 1 serving of tortilla chips
- 1 large whole-grain tortilla or wrap
- 1 teaspoon olive oil
- Pinch sea salt
- Pinch freshly ground black pepper
- Pinch dried oregano

Pinch chili powder

- For 1 bowl
- 1 cup fresh greens (lettuce, spinach, or whatever you like
- ¾ cup cooked quinoa, or brown rice, millet, or other whole grain
- ¼ cup chopped avocado, or Guacamole
- ¼ cup Fresh Mango Salsa

Directions

1. To Make The Black Bean Salad
2. Toss All The Ingredients Together In A Large Bowl.
3. To Make The Tortilla Chips
4. Brush The Tortilla With Olive Oil, Then Sprinkle With Salt, Pepper, Oregano, Chili Powder, And Any Other Seasonings You Like. Slice It Into Eighths Like A Pizza.
5. Transfer The Tortilla Pieces To A Small Baking Sheet Lined With Parchment Paper And Put In The Oven Or Toaster Oven To Toast Or Broil For 3 To 5 Minutes, Until Browned. Keep An Eye On Them, As They Can Go From Just Barely Done To Burned Very Quickly.
6. To Make The Bowl
7. Lay The Greens In The Bowl, Top With The Cooked Quinoa, ⅓ Of The Black Bean Salad, The Avocado, And Salsa.

Nutrition: Calories: 589; Total fat: 14g; Carbs: 101g; Fiber: 20g; Protein: 21g

489. Romaine And Grape Tomato Salad With Avocado And Baby Peas

Preparation time: 15 minutes
cooking time: 0 minutes
servings: 4

Ingredients

- 1 garlic clove, chopped
- 1 tablespoon chopped shallot
- 1/2 teaspoon dried basil
- 1/2 teaspoon salt
- 1/8 teaspoon freshly ground black pepper
- 1/4 teaspoon brown sugar (optional
- 3 tablespoons white wine vinegar
- 1/3 cup olive oil
- 1 medium head romaine lettuce, cut into 1/4-inch strips
- 12 ripe grape tomatoes, halved
- 1/2 cup frozen baby peas, thawed
- 8 kalamata olives, pitted
- 1 ripe Hass avocado

Directions

1. In a blender or food processor, combine the garlic, shallot, basil, salt, pepper, sugar, and vinegar until smooth. Add the oil and blend until emulsified. Set aside.
2. In a large bowl, combine the lettuce, tomatoes, peas, and olives. Pit and peel the avocado and cut into 1/2-inch dice. Add to the bowl, along with enough dressing to lightly coat. Toss gently to combine and serve.

490. Warm Vegetable "Salad"

Preparation time: 10 minutes
cooking time: 15 minutes
servings: 4
Ingredients

- Salt for salting water, plus ½ teaspoon (optional
- 4 red potatoes, quartered
- 1 pound carrots, sliced into ¼-inch-thick rounds
- 1 tablespoon extra-virgin olive oil (optional
- 2 tablespoons lime juice
- 2 teaspoons dried dill
- ¼ teaspoon freshly ground black pepper
- 1 cup Cashew Cream or Parm-y Kale Pesto

Directions

1. In a large pot, bring salted water to a boil. Add the potatoes and cook for 8 minutes. Add the carrots and continue to boil for another 8 minutes, until both the potatoes and carrots are crisp tender. Drain and return to the pot. Add the olive oil (if using), lime juice, dill, remaining ½ teaspoon of salt (if using), and pepper, and stir to coat well.
2. Divide the vegetables evenly among 4 single-compartment storage containers or wide-mouth pint glass jars, and spoon ¼ cup of cream or pesto over the vegetables in each. Let cool before sealing the lids.

Nutrition: Calories: 393; Fat: 15g; Protein: 10g; Carbohydrates: 52g; Fiber: 9g; Sugar: 8g; Sodium: 343mg

491. Puttanesca Seitan And Spinach Salad

Preparation time: 5 minutes
cooking time: 6 minutes
servings: 4

Ingredients

- 4 tablespoons olive oil
- 8 ounces seitan, homemade or store-bought, cut into 1/2-inch strips
- 3 garlic cloves, minced
- 1/2 cup kalamata olives, pitted and halved
- 1/2 cup green olives, pitted and halved
- 2 tablespoons capers
- 3 cups fresh baby spinach, cut into strips
- 11/2 cups ripe cherry tomatoes, halved
- 2 tablespoons balsamic vinegar
- 1/4 teaspoon salt (optional
- 1/4 teaspoon freshly ground black pepper
- 2 tablespoons torn fresh basil leaves
- 2 tablespoons minced fresh parsley

Directions

1. In a large skillet, heat 1 tablespoon of the oil over medium heat. Add the seitan and cook until browned on both sides, about 5 minutes. Add the garlic and cook until fragrant, about 30 seconds. Transfer to a large bowl and set aside to cool, about 15 minutes.
2. When the seitan has cooled to room temperature, add the kalamata and green olives, capers, spinach, and tomatoes. Set aside.
3. In a small bowl, combine the remaining 3 tablespoons oil with the vinegar, salt, and pepper. Whisk until blended, then pour the dressing over the salad. Add the basil and parsley, toss gently to combine, and serve.

492. Rice Salad With Cashews And Dried Papaya

Preparation time: 15 minutes
cooking time: 0 minutes
servings: 4

Ingredients

- 31/2 cups cooked brown rice
- 1/2 cup chopped roasted cashews
- 1/2 cup thinly sliced dried papaya
- 4 green onions, chopped
- 3 tablespoons fresh lime juice
- 2 teaspoons agave nectar
- 1 teaspoon grated fresh ginger
- 1/3 cup grapeseed oil
- Salt and freshly ground black pepper

Directions

1. In a large bowl, combine the rice, cashews, papaya, and green onions. Set aside.
2. In a small bowl, combine the lime juice,

agave nectar, and ginger. Whisk in the oil and season with the salt and pepper to taste. Pour the dressing over the rice mixture, mix well, and serve.

493. Spinach Salad With Orange-Dijon Dressing

Preparation time: 10 minutes
cooking time: 0 minutes
servings: 4

Ingredients

- 2 tablespoons Dijon mustard
- 2 tablespoons olive oil
- 1⁄4 cup fresh orange juice
- 1 teaspoon agave nectar
- 1⁄2 teaspoon salt
- 1⁄4 teaspoon freshly ground black pepper
- 2 tablespoons minced fresh parsley
- 1 tablespoon minced green onions
- 5 cups fresh baby spinach, torn into bite-size pieces
- 1 navel orange, peeled and segmented
- 1⁄2 small red onion, sliced paper thin

Directions

1. In a blender or food processor combine the mustard, oil, orange juice, agave nectar, salt, pepper, parsley, and green onions. Blend well and set aside.
2. In a large bowl, combine the spinach, orange, and onion. Add the dressing, toss gently to combine, and serve.

494. Caramelized Onion And Beet Salad

Preparation time: 10 minutes
cooking time: 40 minutes
servings: 4

Ingredients

- 3 medium golden beets
- 2 cups sliced sweet or Vidalia onions
- 1 teaspoon extra-virgin olive oil or no-beef broth
- Pinch baking soda
- ¼ to ½ teaspoon salt, to taste
- 2 tablespoons unseasoned rice vinegar, white wine vinegar, or balsamic vinegar

Directions

1. Cut the greens off the beets, and scrub the beets.
2. In a large pot, place a steamer basket and fill the pot with 2 inches of water.
3. Add the beets, bring to a boil, then reduce the heat to medium, cover, and steam for about 35 minutes, until you can easily pierce the middle of the beets with a knife.
4. Meanwhile, in a large, dry skillet over medium heat, sauté the onions for 5 minutes, stirring frequently.
5. Add the olive oil and baking soda, and continuing cooking for 5 more minutes, stirring frequently. Stir in the salt to taste before removing from the heat. Transfer to a large bowl and set aside.
6. When the beets have cooked through, drain and cool until easy to handle. Rub the beets in a paper towel to easily remove the skins. Cut into wedges, and transfer to the bowl with the onions. Drizzle the vinegar over everything and toss well.
7. Divide the beets evenly among 4 wide-mouth jars or storage containers. Let cool before sealing the lids.

Nutrition: Calories: 104; Fat: 2g; Protein: 3g; Carbohydrates: 20g; Fiber: 4g; Sugar: 14g; Sodium: 303mg

495. Treasure Barley Salad

Preparation time: 10 minutes
cooking time: 30 minutes
servings: 4 to 6

Ingredients

- 1 cup pearl barley
- 11⁄2 cups cooked or 1 (15.5-ouncecan navy beans, drained and rinsed
- 1 celery rib, finely chopped
- 1 medium carrot, shredded
- 3 green onions, minced
- 1⁄2 cup chopped pitted kalamata olives
- 1⁄2 cup dried cherries or sweetened dried cranberries
- 1⁄2 cup toasted pecans pieces, coarsely chopped
- 1⁄2 cup minced fresh parsley
- 1 garlic clove, pressed
- 3 tablespoons sherry vinegar

- Salt and freshly ground black pepper
- 1/4 cup grapeseed oil

Directions

1. In a large saucepan, bring 21/2 cups salted water to boil over high heat. Add the barley and return to a boil. Reduce heat to low, cover, and simmer until the barley is tender, about 30 minutes. Transfer to a serving bowl.
2. Add the beans, celery, carrot, green onions, olives, cherries, pecans, and parsley. Set aside.
3. In a small bowl, combine the garlic, vinegar, and salt and pepper to taste. Whisk in the oil until well blended. Pour the dressing over the salad, toss to combine, and serve.

496. Golden Couscous Salad

Preparation time: 5 minutes
cooking time: 12 minutes
servings: 4

Ingredients

- 1/4 cup olive oil
- 1 medium shallot, minced
- 1/2 teaspoon ground coriander
- 1/2 teaspoon turmeric
- 1/4 teaspoon ground cayenne
- 1 cup couscous
- 2 cups vegetable broth, homemade or store-bought, or water
- Salt
- 1 medium yellow bell pepper, chopped
- 1 medium carrot, shredded
- 1/2 cup chopped dried apricots
- 1/4 cup golden raisins
- 1/4 cup chopped unsalted roasted cashews
- 11/2 cups cooked or 1 (15.5-ouncecan chickpeas, drained and rinsed
- 2 tablespoons minced fresh cilantro leaves
- 2 tablespoons fresh lemon juice

Directions

1. In a large saucepan, heat 1 tablespoon of the oil over medium heat. Add the shallot, coriander, turmeric, cayenne, and couscous and stir until fragrant, about 2 minutes, being careful not to burn. Stir in the broth and salt to taste. Bring to a boil, then remove from the heat, cover, and let stand for 10 minutes.
2. Transfer the cooked couscous to a large bowl. Add the bell pepper, carrot, apricots, raisins, cashews, chickpeas, and cilantro. Toss gently to combine and set aside.
3. In a small bowl, combine the remaining 3 tablespoons of oil with the lemon juice, stirring to blend. Pour the dressing over the salad, toss gently to combine, and serve.

497. Chopped Salad

Preparation time: 15 minutes
cooking time: 0 minutes
servings: 4

Ingredients

- ¾ cup olive oil
- 1/4 cup white wine vinegar
- 2 teaspoons Dijon mustard
- 1 garlic clove
- 1 tablespoon minced green onions
- 1/2 teaspoon salt (optional
- 1/4 teaspoon ground black pepper
- 1/2 small head romaine lettuce, chopped
- 1/2 small head iceberg lettuce, chopped
- 11/2 cups cooked or 1 (15.5-ouncecan chickpeas, drained and rinsed
- 2 ripe tomatoes, cut into 1/2-inch dice
- 1 medium English cucumber, peeled, halved lengthwise, and chopped
- 2 celery ribs, chopped celery
- 1 medium carrot, chopped
- 1/2 cup halved pitted kalamata olives
- 3 small red radishes, chopped
- 2 tablespoons chopped fresh parsley
- 1 ripe Hass avocado, pitted, peeled, and cut into 1/2-inch dice

Directions

1. In a blender or food processor, combine the oil, vinegar, mustard, garlic, green onions, salt, and pepper. Blend well and set aside.
2. In a large bowl, combine the romaine and iceberg lettuces. Add the chickpeas,

tomatoes, cucumber, celery, carrot, olives, radishes, parsley, and avocado. Add enough dressing to lightly coat. Toss gently to combine and serve.

498. Warm Lentil Salad with Red Wine Vinaigrette

Preparation time: 10 minutes
cooking time: 50 minutes
servings: 4

Ingredients

- 1 teaspoon olive oil plus ¼ cup, divided, or 1 tablespoon vegetable broth or water
- 1 small onion, diced
- 1 garlic clove, minced
- 1 carrot, diced
- 1 cup lentils
- 1 tablespoon dried basil
- 1 tablespoon dried oregano
- 1 tablespoon red wine or balsamic vinegar (optional
- 2 cups water
- ¼ cup red wine vinegar or balsamic vinegar
- 1 teaspoon sea salt
- 2 cups chopped Swiss chard
- 2 cups torn red leaf lettuce
- 4 tablespoons Cheesy Sprinkle

Directions

1. Heat 1 teaspoon of the oil in a large pot on medium heat, then sauté the onion and garlic until they are translucent, about 5 minutes.
2. Add the carrot and sauté until it is slightly cooked, about 3 minutes. Stir in the lentils, basil, and oregano, then add the wine or balsamic vinegar (if using).
3. Pour the water into the pot and turn the heat up to high to bring to a boil.
4. Turn the heat down to a simmer and let the lentils cook, uncovered, 20 to 30 minutes, until they are soft but not falling apart.
5. While the lentils are cooking, whisk together the red wine vinegar, olive oil, and salt in a small bowl and set aside. Once the lentils have cooked, drain any excess liquid and stir in most of the red wine vinegar dressing. Set a little bit of dressing aside. Add the Swiss chard to the pot and stir it into the lentils. Leave the heat on low and cook, stirring, for at least 10 minutes. Toss the lettuce with the remaining dressing. Place some lettuce on a plate, and top with the lentil mixture. Finish the plate off with a little Cheesy Sprinkle and enjoy.

Nutrition Calories: 387; Total fat: 17g; Carbs: 42g; Fiber: 19g; Protein: 18g

499. Carrot And Orange Salad With Cashews And Cilantro

Preparation time: 15 minutes
cooking time: 0 minutes
servings: 4

Ingredients

- 1 pound carrots, shredded
- 2 oranges, peeled, segmented, and chopped
- 1/2 cup unsalted roasted cashews
- 1/4 cup chopped fresh cilantro
- 2 tablespoons fresh orange juice
- 2 tablespoons fresh lime juice
- 2 teaspoons brown sugar (optional
- Salt (optional) and freshly ground black pepper
- 1/3 cup olive oil

Directions

1. In a large bowl, combine the carrots, oranges, cashews, and cilantro and set aside.
2. In a small bowl, combine the orange juice, lime juice, sugar, and salt and pepper to taste. Whisk in the oil until blended. Pour the dressing over the carrot mixture, stirring to lightly coat. Taste, adjusting seasonings if necessary. Toss gently to combine and serve.

500. Not-Tuna Salad

Preparation time: 5 minutes
cooking time: 0 minutes
servings: 4

Ingredients

- 1 (15.5-ouncecan chickpeas, drained and rinsed
- 1 (14-ouncecan hearts of palm, drained and chopped
- ½ cup chopped yellow or white onion
- ½ cup diced celery
- ¼ cup vegan mayonnaise, plus more if needed
- ½ teaspoon salt
- ¼ teaspoon freshly ground black pepper

Directions

1. In a medium bowl, use a potato masher or fork to roughly mash the chickpeas until chunky and "shredded." Add the hearts of palm, onion, celery, vegan mayonnaise, salt, and pepper.
2. Combine and add more mayonnaise, if necessary, for a creamy texture. Into each of 4 single-serving containers, place ¾ cup of salad. Seal the lids.

Nutrition: Calories: 214; Fat: 6g; Protein: 9g; Carbohydrates: 35g; Fiber: 8g; Sugar: 1g; Sodium: 765mg

501. Dazzling Vegetable Salad

Preparation time: 15 minutes
cooking time: 0 minutes
servings: 4

Ingredients

- 1 medium carrot, shredded
- 1 cup finely shredded red cabbage
- 1 cup ripe grape or cherry tomatoes, halved
- 1 medium yellow bell pepper, cut into matchsticks
- 11/2 cups cooked or 1 (15.5-ouncecan chickpeas, rinsed and drained
- 1/4 cup halved pitted kalamata olives
- 1 ripe Hass avocado, pitted, peeled, and cut into 1/2-inch dice
- 1/4 cup olive oil
- 11/2 tablespoons fresh lemon juice
- 1/2 teaspoon salt
- 1/8 teaspoon freshly ground black pepper
- Pinch sugar (optional

Directions

1. In a large bowl, combine the watercress, carrot, cabbage, tomatoes, bell pepper, chickpeas, olives, and avocado and set aside.
2. In a small bowl, combine the oil, lemon juice, salt, black pepper, and sugar. Blend well and add to the salad. Toss gently to combine and serve.

502. Red Bean and Corn Salad

Preparation time: 15 minutes
cooking time: 0 minutes
servings: 4

Ingredients

- ¼ cup Cashew Cream or other salad dressing
- 1 teaspoon chili powder
- 2 (14.5-ouncecans kidney beans, rinsed and drained
- 2 cups frozen corn, thawed, or 2 cups canned corn, drained
- 1 cup cooked farro, barley, or rice (optional
- 8 cups chopped romaine lettuce

Directions

1. Line up 4 wide-mouth glass quart jars.
2. In a small bowl, whisk the cream and chili powder. Pour 1 tablespoon of cream into each jar. In each jar, add ¾ cup kidney beans, ½ cup corn, ¼ cup cooked farro (if using), and 2 cups romaine, punching it down to fit it into the jar. Close the lids tightly.

Nutrition: Calories: 303; Fat: 9g; Protein: 14g; Carbohydrates: 45g; Fiber: 15g; Sugar: 6g; Sodium: 654mg

503. Mango And Snow Pea Salad

Preparation time: 15 minutes
cooking time: 0 minutes
servings: 4

Ingredients

- 1/2 teaspoon minced garlic
- 1/2 teaspoon grated fresh ginger
- 1/4 cup creamy peanut butter
- 1 tablespoon plus 1 teaspoon light brown sugar

- 1/4 teaspoon crushed red pepper
- 3 tablespoons rice vinegar
- 3 tablespoons water
- 1 tablespoon soy sauce
- 2 cups snow peas, trimmed and lightly blanched
- 2 ripe mangos, peeled, pitted, cut into 1/2-inch dice
- 1 large carrot, shredded
- 1 medium cucumber, peeled, halved lengthwise, and seeded
- 3 cups shredded romaine lettuce
- 1/2 cup chopped unsalted roasted peanuts, for garnish

Directions

1. In a small bowl, combine the garlic, ginger, peanut butter, sugar, and crushed red pepper. Stir in the vinegar, water, and soy sauce. Taste, adjusting seasonings, if necessary, and set aside.
2. Cut the snow peas diagonally into a thin matchsticks and place in a large bowl. Add the mangos and carrot. Cut the cucumber into 1/4-inch slices and add to the bowl.
3. Pour the dressing onto the salad and toss gently to combine. Spoon the salad onto a bed of shredded lettuce, sprinkle with peanuts, and serve.

504. Cucumber-Radish Salad With Tarragon Vinaigrette

Preparation time: 15 minutes
cooking time: 0 minutes
servings: 4

Ingredients

- 2 medium English cucumbers, peeled, halved, seeded, cut into 1/4-inch slices
- 6 small red radishes, cut into 1/8-inch slices
- 21/2 tablespoons tarragon vinegar
- 1/2 teaspoon dried tarragon
- 1/4 teaspoon sugar
- Salt and freshly ground black pepper
- 1/4 cup olive oil

Directions

1. In a large bowl, combine the cucumbers and the radishes and set aside.
2. In a small bowl, combine the vinegar, tarragon, sugar, and salt and pepper to taste. Whisk in the oil until well blended, then add the dressing to the salad. Toss gently to combine and serve.

505. Italian-Style Pasta Salad

Preparation time: 5 minutes
cooking time: 10 minutes
servings: 4 to 6

Ingredients

- 8 ounces penne, rotini, or other small pasta
- 11/2 cups cooked or 1 (15.5-ouncecan chickpeas, drained and rinsed
- 1/2 cup pitted kalamata olives
- 1/2 cup minced oil-packed sun-dried tomatoes
- 1 (6-ouncejar marinated artichoke hearts, drained
- 2 jarred roasted red peppers, chopped
- 1/2 cup frozen peas, thawed
- 1 tablespoon capers
- 2 teaspoons dried chives
- 1/2 cup olive oil
- 1/4 cup white wine vinegar
- 1/2 teaspoon dried basil
- 1 garlic clove, minced
- Salt and freshly ground black pepper

Directions

1. In a pot of boiling salted water, cook the pasta, stirring occasionally, until al dente, about 10 minutes. Drain well and transfer to a large bowl. Add the chickpeas, olives, tomatoes, artichoke hearts, roasted peppers, peas, capers, and chives. Toss gently and set aside.
2. In a small bowl, combine the oil, vinegar, basil, garlic, sugar, and salt and black pepper to taste. Pour the dressing onto the pasta salad and toss to combine. Serve chilled or at room temperature.

506. Tabbouleh Salad

Preparation time: 15 minutes
cooking time: 10 minutes
servings: 4

Ingredients

- 1 cup whole-wheat couscous
- 1 cup boiling water
- Zest and juice of 1 lemon
- 1 garlic clove, pressed
- Pinch sea salt
- 1 tablespoon olive oil, or flaxseed oil (optional
- ½ cucumber, diced small
- 1 tomato, diced small
- 1 cup fresh parsley, chopped
- ¼ cup fresh mint, finely chopped
- 2 scallions, finely chopped
- 4 tablespoons sunflower seeds (optional

Directions

1. Put the couscous in a medium bowl, and cover with boiling water until all the grains are submerged. Cover the bowl with a plate or wrap. Set aside.
2. Put the lemon zest and juice in a large salad bowl, then stir in the garlic, salt, and the olive oil (if using).
3. Put the cucumber, tomato, parsley, mint, and scallions in the bowl, and toss them to coat with the dressing. Take the plate off the couscous and fluff with a fork.
4. Add the cooked couscous to the vegetables, and toss to combine.
5. Serve topped with the sunflower seeds (if using).

Nutrition Calories: 304; Total fat: 11g; Carbs: 44g; Fiber: 6g; Protein: 10g

507. Tuscan White Bean Salad

Preparation time: 10 minutes • marinating time: 30 minutes •
servings: 2

Ingredients

For the dressing

- 1 tablespoon olive oil
- 2 tablespoons balsamic vinegar
- 1 teaspoon minced fresh chives, or scallions
- 1 garlic clove, pressed or minced
- 1 tablespoon fresh rosemary, chopped, or 1 teaspoon dried
- 1 tablespoon fresh oregano, chopped, or 1 teaspoon dried
- Pinch sea salt

For the salad

- 1 (14-ouncecan cannellini beans, drained and rinsed, or 1½ cups cooked
- 6 mushrooms, thinly sliced
- 1 zucchini, diced
- 2 carrots, diced
- 2 tablespoons fresh basil, chopped

Directions

- Make the dressing by whisking all the dressing ingredients together in a large bowl.
- Toss all the salad ingredients with the dressing. For the best flavor, put the salad in a sealed container, shake it vigorously, and leave to marinate 15 to 30 minutes.

Nutrition Calories: 360; Total fat: 8g; Carbs: 68g; Fiber: 15g; Protein: 18g

508. Indonesian Green BeanSalad With Cabbage And Carrots

Preparation time: 15 minutes
cooking time: 0 minutes
servings: 4

Ingredients

- 2 cups green beans, trimmed and cut into 1-inch pieces
- 2 medium carrots, cut into 1/4-inch slices
- 2 cups finely shredded cabbage
- 1/3 cup golden raisins
- 1/4 cup unsalted roasted peanuts
- 1 garlic clove, minced
- 1 medium shallot, chopped
- 11/2 teaspoons grated fresh ginger
- 1/3 cup creamy peanut butter
- 2 tablespoons soy sauce
- 2 tablespoons fresh lemon juice
- 1 teaspoon sugar(optional
- 1/4 teaspoon salt(optional
- 1/8 teaspoon ground cayenne
- ¾ cup unsweetened coconut milk

Directions

1. Lightly steam the green beans, carrots, and

2. (continued) cabbage for about 5 minutes, then place them in a large bowl. Add the raisins and peanuts and set aside to cool.
2. In a food processor or blender, puree the garlic, shallot, and ginger. Add the peanut butter, soy sauce, lemon juice, sugar, salt, and cayenne, and process until blended. Add the coconut milk and blend until smooth. Pour the dressing over the salad, toss gently to combine, and serve.

509. Cucumber And Onion Quinoa Salad

Preparation time: 15 minutes
cooking time: 20 minutes
servings: 4

Ingredients

- 1½ cups dry quinoa, rinsed and drained
- 2¼ cups water
- ⅓ cup white wine vinegar
- 2 tablespoons extra-virgin olive oil
- 1 tablespoon chopped fresh dill
- 1½ teaspoons vegan sugar
- 2 pinches salt
- ¼ teaspoon freshly ground black pepper
- 2 cups sliced sweet onions
- 2 cups diced cucumber
- 4 cups shredded lettuce

Directions

1. In a medium pot, combine the quinoa and water. Bring to a boil.
2. Cover, reduce the heat to medium-low, and simmer for 15 to 20 minutes, until the water is absorbed. Remove from the stove and let stand for 5 minutes. Fluff with a fork and set aside.
3. Meanwhile, in a small bowl, mix the vinegar, olive oil, dill, sugar, salt, and pepper. Set aside. Into each of 4 wide-mouth jars, add 2 tablespoons of dressing, ½ cup of onions, ½ cup of cucumber, 1 cup of cooked quinoa, and 1 cup of shredded lettuce. Seal the lids tightly.

Nutrition: Calories: 369; Fat: 11g; Protein: 10g; Carbohydrates: 58g; Fiber: 6g; Sugar: 12g; Sodium: 88mg

510. Moroccan Aubergine Salad

Preparation time: 30 minutes
cooking time: 15 minutes
servings: 2

Ingredients

- 1 teaspoon olive oil
- 1 eggplant, diced
- ½ teaspoon ground cumin
- ½ teaspoon ground ginger
- ¼ teaspoon turmeric
- ¼ teaspoon ground nutmeg
- Pinch sea salt
- 1 lemon, half zested and juiced, half cut into wedges
- 2 tablespoons capers
- 1 tablespoon chopped green olives
- 1 garlic clove, pressed
- Handful fresh mint, finely chopped
- 2 cups spinach, chopped

Directions

1. Heat the oil in a large skillet on medium heat, then sauté the eggplant. Once it has softened slightly, about 5 minutes, stir in the cumin, ginger, turmeric, nutmeg, and salt. Cook until the eggplant is very soft, about 10 minutes.
2. Add the lemon zest and juice, capers, olives, garlic, and mint. Sauté for another minute or two, to blend the flavors. Put a handful of spinach on each plate, and spoon the eggplant mixture on top.
3. Serve with a wedge of lemon, to squeeze the fresh juice over the greens.
4. To tenderize the eggplant and reduce some of its naturally occurring bitter taste, you can sweat the eggplant by salting it. After dicing the eggplant, sprinkle it with salt and let it sit in a colander for about 30 minutes. Rinse the eggplant to remove the salt, then continue with the recipe as written.

Nutrition Calories: 97; Total fat: 4g; Carbs: 16g; Fiber: 8g; Protein: 4g

511. Potato Salad With Artichoke Hearts

Preparation time: 15 minutes
cooking time: 15 minutes
servings: 4 to 6

Ingredients

- 11/2 pounds Yukon Gold potatoes, peeled and cut into 1-inch dice
- 1 (10-ouncepackage frozen artichoke hearts, cooked
- 2 cups halved ripe grape tomatoes
- 1/2 cup frozen peas, thawed
- 3 green onions, minced
- 1 tablespoon minced fresh parsley
- 1/3 cup olive oil
- 2 tablespoons fresh lemon juice
- 1 garlic clove, minced
- Salt and freshly ground black pepper

Directions

1. In a large pot of boiling salted water, cook the potatoes until just tender but still firm, about 15 minutes. Drain well and transfer to a large bowl.
2. Quarter the artichokes and add them to the potatoes. Add the tomatoes, peas, green onions, and parsley and set aside.
3. In a small bowl, combine the oil, lemon juice, garlic, and salt and pepper to taste. Mix well, pour the dressing over potato salad, and toss gently to combine. Set aside at room temperature to allow flavors to blend, about 20 minutes. Taste, adjusting seasonings if necessary, and serve.

512. Giardiniera

Preparation time: 15 minutes
cooking time: 0 minutes
servings: 6

Ingredients

- 1 medium carrot, cut into 1/4-inch rounds
- 1 medium red bell pepper, cut into 1/2-inch dice
- 1 cup small cauliflower florets
- 2 celery ribs, finely chopped
- 1/2 cup chopped onion
- 2 tablespoons salt (optional
- 1/4 cup sliced pimiento-stuffed green olives
- 1 garlic clove, minced
- 1/2 teaspoon sugar (optional
- 1/2 teaspoon crushed red pepper
- 1/4 teaspoon freshly ground black pepper
- 3 tablespoons white wine vinegar
- 1/3 cup olive oil

Directions

1. In a large bowl, combine the carrot, bell pepper, cauliflower, celery, and onion. Stir in the salt and add enough cold water to cover. Tightly cover the bowl and refrigerate for 4 to 6 hours.
2. Drain and rinse the vegetables and place them in a large bowl. Add the olives and set aside.
3. In a small bowl, combine the garlic, sugar, crushed red pepper, black pepper, vinegar, and oil, and mix well. Pour the dressing over the vegetables and toss gently to combine. Cover and refrigerate overnight before serving.

513. Creamy Avocado-Dressed Kale Salad

Preparation time: 10 minutes
cooking time: 20 minutes
servings: 4

Ingredients

For The Dressing

- 1 avocado, peeled and pitted
- 1 tablespoon fresh lemon juice, or 1 teaspoon lemon juice concentrate and 2 teaspoons water
- 1 tablespoon fresh or dried dill1 small garlic clove, pressed
- 1 scallion, chopped
- Pinch sea salt
- ¼ cup water

For The Salad

- 8 large kale leaves
- ½ cup chopped green beans, raw or lightly steamed
- 1 cup cherry tomatoes, halved
- 1 bell pepper, chopped
- 2 scallions, chopped
- 2 cups cooked millet, or other cooked whole grain, such as quinoa or brown rice
- Hummus (optional

Directions

1. TO MAKE THE DRESSING
2. Put all the ingredients in a blender or food processor. Purée until smooth, then add

water as necessary to get the consistency you're looking for in your dressing. Taste for seasoning, and add more salt if you need to.

3. TO MAKE THE SALAD
4. Chop the kale, removing the stems if you want your salad less bitter, and then massage the leaves with your fingers until it wilts and gets a bit moist, about 2 minutes. You can use a pinch salt if you like to help it soften. Toss the kale with the green beans, cherry tomatoes, bell pepper, scallions, millet, and the dressing. Pile the salad onto plates, and top them off with a spoonful of hummus (if using).

Nutrition Calories: 225; Total fat: 7g; Carbs: 37g; Fiber: 7g; Protein: 7g

514. Indonesian-Style Potato Salad

Preparation time: 10 minutes
cooking time: 30 minutes
servings: 4 to 6

Ingredients

- 11/2 pounds small white potatoes, unpeeled
- 1 cup frozen peas, thawed
- 1/2 cup shredded carrot
- 4 green onions, chopped
- 1 tablespoon grapeseed oil
- 1 garlic clove, minced
- 1/3 cup creamy peanut butter
- 1/2 teaspoon Asian chili paste
- 2 tablespoons soy sauce
- 1 tablespoon rice vinegar
- ¾ cup unsweetened coconut milk
- 3 tablespoons chopped unsalted roasted peanuts, for garnish

Directions

1. In a large pot of boiling salted water, cook the potatoes until tender, 20 to 30 minutes. Drain well and set aside to cool.
2. When cool enough to handle, cut the potatoes into 1-inch chunks and transfer to a large bowl. Add the peas, carrot, and green onions, and set aside.
3. In a small saucepan, heat the oil over medium heat. Add the garlic and cook until fragrant, about 30 seconds. Stir in the peanut butter, chili paste, soy sauce, vinegar, and about half of the coconut milk. Simmer over medium heat for 5 minutes, stirring frequently to make a smooth sauce. Add as much of the remaining coconut milk as needed for a creamy consistency. Pour the dressing over the salad and toss well to combine. Garnish with peanuts and serve.

515. Roasted Beet and Avocado Salad

Preparation time: 10 minutes
cooking time: 30minutes
servings: 2

Ingredients

- 2 beets, peeled and thinly sliced
- 1 teaspoon olive oil
- Pinch sea salt
- 1 avocado
- 2 cups mixed greens
- 3 to 4 tablespoons Creamy Balsamic Dressing
- 2 tablespoons chopped almonds, pumpkin seeds, or sunflower seeds (raw or toasted

Directions

- Preheat the oven to 400°F.
- Put the beets, oil, and salt in a large bowl, and toss the beets with your hands to coat. Lay them in a single layer in a large baking dish, and roast them in the oven 20 to 30 minutes, or until they're softened and slightly browned around the edges.
- While the beets are roasting, cut the avocado in half and take the pit out. Scoop the flesh out, as intact as possible, and slice it into crescents.
- Once the beets are cooked, lay slices out on two plates and top each beet slice with a similar-size avocado slice.
- Top with a handful of mixed greens. Drizzle the dressing over everything, and sprinkle on a few chopped almonds.

Nutrition Calories: 167; Total fat: 13g; Carbs: 15g; Fiber: 5g; Protein: 4g

516. Creamy Coleslaw

Preparation time: 10 minutes
cooking time: 0 minutes

servings: 4

Ingredients

- 1 small head green cabbage, finely shredded
- 1 large carrot, shredded
- ¾ cup vegan mayonnaise, homemade or store-bought
- 1/4 cup soy milk
- 2 tablespoons cider vinegar
- 1/2 teaspoon dry mustard
- 1/4 teaspoon celery seeds
- 1/2 teaspoon salt (optional
- Freshly ground black pepper

Directions

1. In a large bowl, combine the cabbage and carrot and set aside.
2. In a small bowl, combine the mayonnaise, soy milk, vinegar, mustard, celery seeds, salt, and pepper to taste. Mix until smooth and well blended. Add the dressing to the slaw and mix well to combine. Taste, adjusting seasonings if necessary, and serve.

517. Sesame Cucumber Salad

Preparation time: 15 minutes
cooking time: 0 minutes
servings: 4 to 6

Ingredients

- 2 medium English cucumbers, peeled and cut into 1/4-inch slices
- 2 tablespoons chopped fresh parsley
- 3 tablespoons toasted sesame oil
- 2 tablespoons soy sauce
- 1 tablespoon mirin
- 2 teaspoons rice vinegar
- 1 teaspoon brown sugar (optional
- 2 tablespoons toasted sesame seeds

Directions

1. In a small bowl, combine the cucumbers and parsley and set aside.
2. In a separate small bowl, combine the oil, soy sauce, mirin, vinegar, and sugar, stirring to blend. Pour the dressing over the cucumbers. Set aside for at least 10 minutes.
3. Spoon the cucumber salad into small bowls, sprinkle with sesame seeds, and serve.

518. Basil Mango Jicama Salad

Preparation Time: 15 Minutes • Chill Time: 60 Minutes •
Servings:6

Ingredients

- 1 jicama, peeled and grated
- 1 mango, peeled and sliced
- ¼ cup non-dairy milk
- 2 tablespoons fresh basil, chopped
- 1 large scallion, chopped
- ⅛ teaspoon sea salt
- 1½ tablespoons tahini (optional)
- Fresh greens (for serving)
- Chopped cashews (optional, for serving)
- Cheesy Sprinkle (optional, for serving)

Directions

1. Put the jicama in a large bowl.
2. Purée the mango in a food processor or blender, with just enough non-dairy milk to make a thick sauce.
3. Add the basil, scallions, and salt. Stir in the tahini if you want to make a thicker, creamier, and more filling sauce.
4. Pour the dressing over the jicama and marinate, covered in the fridge, for 1 hour or more to break down some of the starch. Serve over a bed of greens, topped with chopped cashews and/or Cheesy Sprinkle (if using).

Per Serving Calories: 76; Total fat: 2g; Carbs: 14g; Fiber: 5g; Protein: 1g

519. Red Cabbage Slaw With Black-Vinegar Dressing

Preparation Time: 15 Minutes
Cooking Time: 0 Minutes
Servings:6

Ingredients

- 4 cups shredded red cabbage
- 2 cups thinly sliced napa cabbage
- 1 cup shredded daikon radish
- 1/4 cup fresh orange juice
- 2 tablespoons Chinese black vinegar

- 1 tablespoon soy sauce
- 1 tablespoon grapeseed oil
- 1 tablespoon toasted sesame oil
- 1 teaspoon grated fresh ginger
- 1⁄2 teaspoon ground Szechuan peppercorns
- 1 tablespoon black sesame seeds, for garnish

Directions

1. In a large bowl, combine the red cabbage, napa, and daikon and set aside.
2. In a small bowl, combine the orange juice, vinegar, soy sauce, grapeseed oil, sesame oil, ginger, and peppercorns. Blend well. Pour the dressing onto the slaw, stirring to coat. Taste, adjusting seasonings if necessary. Cover and refrigerate to allow flavors to blend, about 2 hours. Sprinkle with sesame seeds and serve.

520.Corn And Red Bean Salad

Preparation Time: 10 Minutes
Cooking Time: 0 Minutes
Servings:4

Ingredients

- 1 (10-ounce) package frozen corn kernels, cooked
- 11⁄2 cups cooked or 1 (15.5-ounce) can dark red kidney beans, drained and rinsed
- 1 celery rib, cut into 1⁄4-inch slices
- 2 green onions, minced
- 2 tablespoons chopped fresh cilantro or parsley
- 1⁄4 cup olive oil
- 2 tablespoons white wine vinegar
- 1⁄2 teaspoon ground cumin
- 1⁄4 teaspoon sugar (optional)
- 1⁄2 teaspoon salt (optional)
- 1⁄8 teaspoon freshly ground black pepper

Directions

1. In a large bowl, combine the corn, beans, celery, green onions, and cilantro, and set aside.
2. In a small bowl, combine the oil, vinegar, cumin, sugar, salt, and pepper. Mix well and pour the dressing over the vegetables. Toss gently to combine and serve.

521. Greek Potato Salad

Preparation Time: 10 Minutes
Cooking Time: 20 Minutes
Servings:4

Ingredients

- 6 potatoes, scrubbed or peeled and chopped
- Salt
- ¼ cup olive oil
- 2 tablespoons apple cider vinegar
- 2 tablespoons freshly squeezed lemon juice
- 1 teaspoon dried herbs
- ½ cucumber, chopped
- ¼ red onion, diced
- ¼ cup chopped pitted black olives
- Freshly ground black pepper

Directions

1. Put the potatoes in a large pot, add a pinch of salt, and pour in enough water to cover. Bring the water to a boil over high heat. Cook the potatoes for 15 to 20 minutes, until soft. Drain and set aside to cool. (Alternatively, put the potatoes in a large microwave-safe dish with a bit of water. Cover and heat on high power for 10 minutes.)
2. In a large bowl, whisk together the olive oil, vinegar, lemon juice, and dried herbs. Toss the cucumber, red onion, and olives with the dressing. Add the cooked, cooled potatoes, and toss to combine. Taste and season with salt and pepper as needed. Store leftovers in an airtight container in the refrigerator for up to 1 week.

Per Serving Calories: 358; Protein: 5g; Total fat: 16g; Saturated fat: 2g; Carbohydrates: 52g; Fiber: 5g

522. Rainbow Quinoa Salad

Preparation Time: 51 Minutes
Cooking Time: 0 Minutes
Servings:6-8

Ingredients

- 3 tablespoons olive oil
- Juice of 1½ lemons

- 1 teaspoon garlic powder
- ½ teaspoon dried oregano
- 1 bunch curly kale, stemmed and roughly chopped
- 2 cups cooked tricolor quinoa
- 1 cup canned mandarin oranges in juice, drained
- 1 cup diced yellow summer squash
- 1 red bell pepper, seeded and diced
- ½ red onion, thinly sliced
- ½ cup dried cranberries or cherries
- ½ cup slivered almonds

Directions

1. In a small bowl, whisk together the oil, lemon juice, garlic powder, and oregano.
2. In a large bowl, toss the kale with the oil-lemon mixture until well coated. Add the quinoa, oranges, squash, bell pepper, and red onion and toss until all the ingredients are well combined. Divide among bowls or transfer to a large serving platter. Top with the cranberries and almonds.

523. Yellow Mung Bean Salad With Broccoli And Mango

Preparation Time: 5 Minutes
Cooking Time: 20 Minutes
Servings:4

Ingredients

- 1/2 cup yellow mung beans, picked over, rinsed, and drained
- 3 cups small broccoli florets, blanched
- 1 ripe mango, peeled, pitted, and chopped
- 1 small red bell pepper, chopped
- 1 jalapeño or other hot green chile, seeded and minced
- 2 tablespoons chopped fresh cilantro
- 1 teaspoon grated fresh ginger
- 2 tablespoons fresh lemon juice
- 3 tablespoons grapeseed oil
- 1/3 cup unsalted roasted cashews, for garnish

Directions

1. In a saucepan of boiling salted water, cook the mung beans until just tender, 18 to 20 minutes. Drain and run under cold water to cool. Transfer the beans to a large bowl. Add the broccoli, mango, bell pepper, chile, and cilantro. Set aside.
2. In a small bowl, combine the ginger, lemon juice, oil. Stir to mix well, then pour the dressing over the vegetables and toss to combine. Sprinkle with cashews and serve.

524. Asian Slaw

Preparation Time: 15 Minutes
Cooking Time: 0 Minutes
Servings:4

Ingredients

- 8 ounces napa cabbage, cut crosswise into 1/4-inch strips
- 1 cup grated carrot
- 1 cup grated daikon radish
- 2 green onions, minced
- 2 tablespoons chopped fresh parsley
- 2 tablespoons rice vinegar
- 1 tablespoon grapeseed oil
- 2 teaspoons toasted sesame oil
- 1 tablespoon soy sauce
- 1 teaspoon grated fresh ginger
- 1/2 teaspoon dry mustard
- Salt and freshly ground black pepper
- 2 tablespoons chopped unsalted roasted peanuts, for garnish (optional)

Directions

1. In a large bowl, combine the napa cabbage, carrot, daikon, green onions, and parsley. Set aside.
2. In a small bowl, combine the vinegar, grapeseed oil, sesame oil, soy sauce, ginger, mustard, and salt and pepper to taste. Stir until well blended. Pour the dressing over the vegetables and toss gently to coat. Taste, adjusting seasonings if necessary. Cover and refrigerate to allow flavors to blend, about 2 hours. Sprinkle with peanuts, if using, and serve.

525. The Great Green Salad

Preparation Time: 10 Minutes
Cooking Time: 0 Minutes
Servings:

Ingredients

1. 1 head Boston or Bibb lettuce
2. 8 asparagus spears, trimmed and cut into 2-inch pieces
3. 2 mini seedless cucumbers, sliced
4. 1 small zucchini, cut into ribbons with potato peeler
5. 1 avocado, peeled, pitted, and sliced
6. ½ cup Green Goddess Dressing or store-bought vegan green goddess dressing
7. 2 scallions, thinly sliced

Directions

1. Divide the lettuce leaves among 4 plates. Top each with some of the asparagus, cucumber, zucchini, and avocado. Drizzle each bowl with 2 tablespoons of dressing and sprinkle with scallions.

526. Summer Berries With Fresh Mint

Preparation Time: 15 Minutes
Cooking Time: 0 Minutes
Servings:4 To 6

Ingredients

- 2 tablespoons fresh orange or pineapple juice
- 1 tablespoon fresh lime juice
- 1 tablespoon agave nectar
- 2 teaspoons minced fresh mint
- 2 cups pitted fresh cherries
- 1 cup fresh blueberries
- 1 cup fresh strawberries, hulled and halved
- 1/2 cup fresh blackberries or raspberries

Directions

1. In a small bowl, combine the orange juice, lime juice, agave nectar, and mint. Set aside.
2. In a large bowl, combine the cherries, blueberries, strawberries, and blackberries. Add the dressing and toss gently to combine. Serve immediately.

527. Curried Fruit Salad

Preparation Time: 15 Minutes
Cooking Time: 0 Minutes
Servings:4 To 6

Ingredients

- ¾ cup vegan vanilla yogurt
- 1/4 cup finely chopped mango chutney
- 1 tablespoon fresh lime juice
- 1 teaspoon mild curry powder
- 1 Fuji or Gala apple, cored and cut into 1/2-inch dice
- 2 ripe peaches, halved, pitted, and cut into 1/2-inch dice
- 4 ripe black plums, halved and cut into 1/4-inch slices
- 1 ripe mango, peeled, pitted, and cut into 1/2-inch dice
- 1 cup red seedless grapes, halved
- 1/4 cup unsweetened toasted shredded coconut
- 1/4 cup toasted slivered almonds

Directions

1. In a small bowl, combine the yogurt, chutney, lime juice, and curry powder and stir until well blended. Set aside.
2. In a large bowl, combine the apple, peaches, plums, mango, grapes, coconut, and almonds. Add the dressing, toss gently to coat, and serve.

528. Stuffed Avocado

Preparation Time: 10 Minutes
Cooking Time: 0 Minutes
Servings:4

Ingredients

- 2 avocados, halved and pitted
- 1 (15-ounce) can black beans, rinsed and drained
- 1 cup frozen (and thawed) or fresh corn kernels
- ½ cup seeded and diced tomato
- Juice of ½ lime
- 1 tablespoon maple syrup
- 1 teaspoon olive oil
- 2 pinches sea salt
- 2 pinches black pepper
- 1 tablespoon chopped fresh cilantro

Directions

1. Scoop some avocado flesh from each half with a spoon, leaving a ¼- to ½-inch wall of avocado in the shell.
2. In a large bowl, mix together the scooped-

out avocado, beans, corn, tomato, lime juice, maple syrup, oil, salt, pepper, and cilantro until well incorporated.
3. Spoon the filling into the avocado shells and enjoy.

529. Cranberry-Carrot Salad

Preparation Time: 15 Minutes
Cooking Time: 0 Minutes
Servings:4

Ingredients

- 1 pound carrots, shredded
- 1 cup sweetened dried cranberries
- 1/2 cup toasted walnut pieces
- 2 tablespoons fresh lemon juice
- 3 tablespoons toasted walnut oil
- 1/8 teaspoon freshly ground black pepper

Directions

1. In a large bowl, combine the carrots, cranberries, and walnuts. Set aside.
2. In a small bowl, whisk together the lemon juice, walnut oil and pepper. Pour the dressing over the salad, toss gently to combine and serve.

530. Almond Crunch Chopped Kale Salad

Preparation Time: 10 Minutes
Cooking Time: 10 Minutes
Servings:4

Ingredients

For The Dressing

- ¼ cup tahini
- 2 tablespoons Dijon mustard
- 2 tablespoons maple syrup
- 1 tablespoon lemon juice
- ¼ teaspoon salt

For The Almond Crunch

- ½ cup finely chopped raw almonds
- 2 teaspoons soy sauce or gluten-free tamari
- 1 teaspoon maple syrup
- ¼ teaspoon sea salt

For The Salad

- 1 bunch lacinato kale, stemmed and roughly chopped
- 1 green apple, cored and thinly sliced

Directions

1. Preheat the oven to 325°F. Line a baking sheet with parchment paper.
2. To make the dressing: Whisk together all the dressing ingredients in a small bowl and set aside.
3. To make the almond crunch: Mix together all the almond crunch ingredients in a medium bowl and spread out evenly on the prepared baking sheet. Bake for 5 to 7 minutes, until slightly darker in color and crunchy. Let cool for 3 minutes.
4. To make the salad: In a large bowl, mix together the kale and apples. Toss with the dressing and top with the almond crunch.

531. Apple-Sunflower Spinach Salad

Preparation Time: 5 Minutes
Cooking Time: 0 Minutes
Servings:1

Ingredients

- 1 cup baby spinach
- ½ apple, cored and chopped
- ¼ red onion, thinly sliced (optional)
- 2 tablespoons sunflower seeds or Cinnamon-Lime Sunflower Seeds
- 2 tablespoons dried cranberries
- 2 tablespoons Raspberry Vinaigrette

Directions

1. Arrange the spinach on a plate. Top with the apple, red onion (if using), sunflower seeds, and cranberries, and drizzle with the vinaigrette.

Per Serving Calories: 444; Protein: 7g; Total fat: 28g; Saturated fat: 3g; Carbohydrates: 53g; Fiber: 8g

532. Ruby Grapefruit and Radicchio Salad

Preparation Time: 10 Minutes
Cooking Time: 0 Minutes
Servings:4

Ingredients

For The Salad

- 1 large ruby grapefruit
- 1 small head radicchio, torn into bite-size pieces
- 2 cups green leaf lettuce, torn into bite-size pieces
- 2 cups baby spinach

- 1 bunch watercress
- 4 to 6 radishes, sliced paper-thin

For The Dressing

- juice of 1 lemon
- 2 teaspoons agave
- 1 teaspoon white wine vinegar
- ½ teaspoon sea salt
- ½ teaspoon freshly ground black pepper
- ¼ cup extra-virgin olive oil

Directions

1. To make the salad: Cut both ends off of the grapefruit, stand it on a cutting board on one of the flat sides, and, using a sharp knife, cut away the peel and all of the white pith. Remove the individual segments by slicing between the membrane and fruit on each side of each segment, dropping the fruit into a large salad bowl as you go. Add the radicchio, lettuce, spinach, watercress, and radishes to the bowl and toss well.
2. To make the dressing: Whisk together the lemon juice, agave, vinegar, salt, and pepper. Slowly whisk in the olive oil until the mixture is well combined and -emulsified. Toss the salad with the dressing and serve immediately.

533. Darn Good Caesar Salad

Preparation Time: 10 Minutes
Cooking Time: 0 Minutes
Servings:4

Ingredients

For The Dressing

- ½ cup walnuts
- ½ cup water
- 3 tablespoons olive oil
- Juice of ½ lime
- 1 tablespoon white miso paste
- 1 teaspoon soy sauce or gluten-free tamari
- 1 teaspoon Dijon mustard
- 1 teaspoon garlic powder
- ¼ teaspoon sea salt
- ½ teaspoon black pepper

For The Salad

- 2 heads romaine lettuce, chopped
- 1 cup cherry tomatoes, halved
- Walnut Parmesan or store-bought vegan Parmesan, for garnish
- Vegan croutons, for garnish (optional)

Directions

1. To make the dressing: In a blender, combine all the dressing ingredients and blend until almost smooth, about 2 minutes. It's okay if this dressing is slightly chunky, which is more like a classic Caesar dressing texture.
2. To make the salad: In a large bowl, toss the lettuce with half of the dressing. Add more as desired. Divide among serving plates and top with the tomatoes and Parmesan. Finish the salad off with croutons, if desired.

534. Potato Salad Redux

Preparation Time: 5 Minutes
Cooking Time: 30 Minutes
Servings:4 To 6

Ingredients

- 11⁄2 pounds small white potatoes, unpeeled
- 2 celery ribs, cut into 1⁄4-inch slices
- 1⁄4 cup sweet pickle relish
- 3 tablespoons minced green onions
- 1⁄2 to ¾ cup vegan mayonnaise, homemade or store-bought
- 1 tablespoon soy milk
- 1 tablespoon tarragon vinegar
- 1 teaspoon Dijon mustard
- 1⁄2 teaspoon salt (optional)
- Freshly ground black pepper

Directions

1. In a large pot of salted boiling water, cook the potatoes until just tender, about 30 minutes. Drain and set aside to cool. When cool enough to handle, peel the potatoes and cut them into 1-inch dice. Transfer the potatoes to a large bowl and add the celery, pickle relish, and green onions. Set aside.
2. In a small bowl, combine the mayonnaise, soy milk, vinegar, mustard, salt, and pepper to taste. Mix until well blended. Pour the dressing onto the potato mixture, toss gently to combine, and serve.

535. Apple and Ginger Slaw

Preparation Time: 10 Minutes
Cooking Time: 0 Minutes
Servings:4

Ingredients

- 2 tablespoons olive oil
- juice of 1 lemon, or 2 tablespoons prepared lemon juice
- 1 teaspoon grated fresh ginger
- pinch of sea salt
- 2 apples, peeled and julienned
- 4 cups shredded red cabbage

Directions

1. In a small bowl, whisk together the olive oil, lemon juice, ginger, and salt and set aside.
2. In a large bowl, combine the apples and cabbage.
3. Toss with the vinaigrette and serve immediately. Store leftovers in an airtight container in the refrigerator for up to 3 days.

536. Sunshine Fiesta Salad

Preparation Time: 15 Minutes
Cooking Time: 0 Minutes
Servings:4

Ingredients

For The Vinaigrette

- Juice of 2 limes
- 1 tablespoon olive oil
- 1 tablespoon maple syrup or agave
- ¼ teaspoon sea salt

For The Salad

- 2 cups cooked quinoa
- 1 tablespoon Taco Seasoning or store-bought taco seasoning
- 2 heads romaine lettuce, roughly chopped
- 1 (15-ounce) can black beans, rinsed and drained
- 1 cup cherry tomatoes, halved
- 1 cup frozen (and thawed) or fresh corn kernels
- 1 avocado, peeled, pitted, and diced
- 4 scallions, thinly sliced
- 12 tortilla chips, crushed

Directions

1. To make the vinaigrette: In a small bowl, whisk together all the vinaigrette ingredients.
2. To make the salad: In a medium bowl, mix together the quinoa and taco seasoning. In a large bowl, toss the romaine with the vinaigrette. Divide among 4 bowls. Top each bowl with equal amounts quinoa, beans, tomatoes, corn, avocado, scallions, and crushed tortillas chips.

537. French-Style Potato Salad

Preparation Time: 5 Minutes
Cooking Time: 30 Minutes
Servings:4 To 6

Ingredients

- 11/2 pounds small white potatoes, unpeeled
- 2 tablespoons minced fresh parsley
- 1 tablespoon minced fresh chives
- 1 teaspoon minced fresh tarragon or 1/2 teaspoon dried
- 1/3 cup olive oil
- 2 tablespoons white wine or tarragon vinegar
- 1/8 teaspoon freshly ground black pepper

Directions

1. In a large pot of boiling salted water, cook the potatoes until tender but still firm, about 30 minutes. Drain and cut into 1/4-inch slices. Transfer to a large bowl and add the parsley, chives, and tarragon. Set aside.
2. In a small bowl, combine the oil, vinegar, pepper. Pour the dressing onto the potato mixture and toss gently to combine.
3. Taste, adjusting seasonings if necessary. Chill for 1 to 2 hours before serving.

538. Roasted Carrot Salad

Preparation Time: 10 Minutes
Cooking Time: 30 Minutes
Servings:3

Ingredients

- 4 carrots, peeled and sliced
- 1 to 2 teaspoons olive oil or coconut oil

- ½ teaspoon ground cinnamon or pumpkin pie spice
- Salt
- 1 (15-ounce) can cannellini beans or navy beans, drained and rinsed
- 3 cups chopped hearty greens, such as spinach, kale, chard, or collards
- ⅓ cup dried cranberries or pomegranate seeds
- ⅓ cup slivered almonds or Cinnamon-Lime Sunflower Seeds
- ¼ cup Raspberry Vinaigrette or Cilantro-Lime Dressing, or 2 tablespoons freshly squeezed orange or lemon juice whisked with 2 tablespoons olive oil and a pinch of salt

Directions

1. Preheat the oven or toaster oven to 400°F.
2. In a medium bowl, toss the carrots with the olive oil and cinnamon and season to taste with salt. Transfer to a small tray, and roast for 15 minutes or until browned around the edges. Toss the carrots, add the beans, and roast for 15 minutes more. Let cool while you prep the salad. Divide the greens among three plates or containers, top with the cranberries and almonds, and add the roasted carrots and beans.
3. Drizzle with the dressing of your choice. Store leftovers in an airtight container in the refrigerator for up to 1 week.
4. Roasted Potato Salad

539. With Chickpeas And Tomatoes

Preparation Time: 5 Minutes
Cooking Time: 20 Minutes
Servings:4 To 6

Ingredients

- 11⁄2 pounds Yukon Gold potatoes, cut into 1⁄2-inch dice
- 1 medium shallot, halved lengthwise and cut into 1⁄4-inch slices
- 1⁄4 cup olive oil
- Salt and freshly ground black pepper
- 3 tablespoons white wine vinegar
- 11⁄2 cups cooked or 1 (15.5-ounce) can chickpeas, drained and rinsed
- 1⁄3 cup chopped drained oil-packed sun-dried tomatoes
- 1⁄4 cup green olives, pitted and halved
- 1⁄4 cup chopped fresh parsley

Directions

1. Preheat the oven to 425°F. In a large bowl, combine the potatoes, shallot, and 1 tablespoon of the oil. Season with salt and pepper to taste and toss to coat. Transfer the potatoes and shallot to a baking sheet and roast, turning once, until tender and golden brown, about 20 minutes. Transfer to a large bowl and set aside to cool.
2. In a small bowl, combine the remaining 3 tablespoons oil with the vinegar and pepper to taste. Add the chickpeas, tomatoes, olives, and parsley to the cooked potatoes and shallots. Drizzle with the dressing and toss gently to combine. Taste, adjusting seasonings if necessary. Serve warm or at room temperature.

540. Spinach and Pomegranate Salad

Preparation Time: 10 Minutes
Cooking Time: 0 Minutes
Servings:4

Ingredients

- 10 ounces baby spinach
- seeds from 1 pomegranate
- 1 cup fresh blackberries
- ¼ red onion, thinly sliced
- ½ cup chopped pecans
- ¼ cup balsamic vinegar
- ¾ cup olive oil
- ½ teaspoon sea salt
- ½ teaspoon freshly ground black pepper

Directions

1. In a large bowl, combine the spinach, pomegranate seeds, blackberries, red onion, and pecans.
2. In a small bowl, whisk together the vinegar, olive oil, salt, and pepper. Toss with the salad and serve immediately.

541. Cobb Salad with Portobello Bacon

Preparation Time: 15 Minutes
Cooking Time: 0 Minutes

Servings:4

Ingredients

- 2 heads romaine lettuce, finely chopped
- 1 pint cherry tomatoes, halved
- 1 avocado, peeled, pitted, and diced
- 1 cup frozen (and thawed) or fresh corn kernels
- 1 large cucumber, peeled and diced
- Portobello Bacon or store-bought vegan bacon
- 4 scallions, thinly sliced
- Unhidden Valley Ranch Dressing or store-bought vegan ranch dressing

Directions

1. Scatter a layer of romaine in the bottom of each of 4 salad bowls. With the following ingredients, create lines that cross the top of the romaine, in this order: tomatoes, avocado, corn, cucumber, and portobello bacon.
2. Sprinkle with the scallions and drizzle with ranch dressing.

542. German-Style Potato Salad

Preparation Time: 15 Minutes
Cooking Time: 0 Minutes
Servings:4 To 6

Ingredients

- 11⁄2 pounds white potatoes, unpeeled
- 1⁄2 cup olive oil
- 4 slices tempeh bacon, homemade or store-bought
- 1 medium bunch green onions, chopped
- 1 tablespoon whole-wheat flour
- 2 tablespoons sugar
- 1⁄3 cup white wine vinegar
- 1⁄4 cup water
- 1⁄2 teaspoon salt
- 1⁄8 teaspoon freshly ground black pepper

Directions

1. In a large pot of boiling salted water, cook the potatoes until just tender, about 30 minutes. Drain well and set aside to cool.
2. In a large skillet, heat the oil over medium heat. Add the tempeh bacon and cook until browned on both sides, about 5 minutes total. Remove from skillet, and set aside to cool.
3. Cut the cooled potatoes into 1-inch chunks and place in a large bowl. Crumble or chop the cooked tempeh bacon and add to the potatoes.
4. Reheat the skillet over medium heat. Add the green onions and cook for 1 minute to soften. Stir in the flour, sugar, vinegar, water, salt, and pepper, and bring to a boil, stirring until smooth. Pour the hot dressing onto the potatoes. Stir gently to combine and serve.

543. Sweet Pearl Couscous Salad with Pear & Cranberries

Preparation Time: 5 Minutes
Cooking Time: 10 Minutes
Servings:4

Ingredients

- 1 cup pearl couscous
- 1½ cups water
- Salt
- ¼ cup olive oil
- ¼ cup freshly squeezed orange juice
- 1 tablespoon sugar, maple syrup, or Simple Syrup
- 1 pear, cored and diced
- ½ cucumber, diced
- ¼ cup dried cranberries or raisins

Directions

1. In a small pot, combine the couscous, water, and a pinch of salt. Bring to a boil over high heat, turn the heat to low, and cover the pot. Simmer for about 10 minutes, until the couscous is al dente.
2. Meanwhile, in a large bowl, whisk together the olive oil, orange juice, and sugar. Season to taste with salt and whisk again to combine.
3. Add the pear, cucumber, cranberries, and cooked couscous. Toss to combine. Store leftovers in an airtight container in the refrigerator for up to 1 week.

Per Serving Calories: 365; Protein: 6g; Total fat: 14g; Saturated fat: 2g; Carbohydrates: 55g; Fiber: 4g

544. Pear and Arugula Salad

Preparation Time: 10 Minutes
Cooking Time: 8 Minutes
Servings:4

Ingredients

- ¼ cup chopped pecans
- 10 ounces arugula
- 2 pears, thinly sliced
- 1 tablespoon finely minced shallot
- 2 tablespoons champagne vinegar
- 2 tablespoons olive oil
- ¼ teaspoon sea salt
- ¼ teaspoon freshly ground black pepper
- ¼ teaspoon dijon mustard

Directions

1. Preheat the oven to 350°F.
2. Spread the pecans in a single layer on a baking sheet. Toast in the preheated oven until fragrant, about 6 minutes. Remove from the oven and let cool. In a large bowl, toss the pecans, arugula, and pears. In a small bowl, whisk together the shallot, vinegar, olive oil, salt, pepper, and -mustard. Toss with the salad and serve immediately.

545. Quinoa Salad With Black Beans And Tomatoes

Preparation Time: 5 Minutes
Cooking Time: 20 Minutes
Servings:4

Ingredients

- 3 cups water
- 11/2 cups quinoa, well rinsed
- Salt
- 11/2 cups cooked or 1 (15.5-ounce) can black beans, drained and rinsed
- 4 ripe plum tomatoes, cut into 1/4-inch dice
- 1/3 cup minced red onion
- 1/4 cup chopped fresh parsley
- 1/4 cup olive oil
- 2 tablespoons sherry vinegar
- 1/4 teaspoon freshly ground black pepper

Directions

- In a large saucepan, bring the water to boil over high heat. Add the quinoa, salt the water, and return to a boil. Reduce heat to low, cover, and simmer until the water is absorbed, about 20 minutes.
- Transfer the cooked quinoa to a large bowl. Add the black beans, tomatoes, onion, and parsley.
- In a small bowl, combine the olive oil, vinegar, salt to taste, and pepper. Pour the dressing over the salad and toss well to combine. Cover and set aside for 20 minutes before serving.

546. Mediterranean Quinoa Salad

Preparation Time: 5 Minutes
Cooking Time: 20 Minutes
Servings:4

Ingredients

- 2 cups water
- 1 cup quinoa, well rinsed
- Salt
- 11/2 cups cooked or 1 (15.5-ounce) can chickpeas, drained and rinsed
- 1 cup ripe grape or cherry tomatoes, halved
- 2 green onions, minced
- 1/2 medium English cucumber, peeled and chopped
- 1/4 cup pitted brine-cured black olives
- 2 tablespoons toasted pine nuts
- 1/4 cup small fresh basil leaves
- 1 medium shallot, chopped
- 1 garlic clove, chopped
- 1 teaspoon Dijon mustard
- 2 tablespoons white wine vinegar
- 1/4 cup olive oil
- Freshly ground black pepper

Directions

1. In a large saucepan, bring the water to boil over high heat. Add the quinoa, salt the water, and return to a boil. Reduce heat to low, cover, and simmer until water is absorbed, about 20 minutes.
2. Transfer the cooked quinoa to a large bowl. Add the chickpeas, tomatoes, green onions, cucumber, olives, pine nuts, and

basil. Set aside.

3. In a blender or food processor, combine the shallot, garlic, mustard, vinegar, oil, and salt and pepper to taste. Process until well blended. Pour the dressing over the salad, toss gently to combine, and serve.

547. Apple, Pecan, and Arugula Salad

Preparation Time: 10 Minutes
Cooking Time: 0 Minutes
Servings:4

Ingredients

- Juice of 1 lemon
- 2 tablespoons olive oil
- 1 tablespoon maple syrup
- 2 pinches sea salt
- 1 (5-ounce) package arugula
- 1 cup frozen (and thawed) or fresh corn kernels
- ½ red onion, thinly sliced
- 2 apples (preferably Gala or Fuji), cored and sliced
- ½ cup chopped pecans
- ¼ cup dried cranberries

Directions

1. In a small bowl, whisk together the lemon juice, oil, maple syrup, and salt. In a large bowl, combine the arugula, corn, red onion, and apples. Add the lemon-juice mixture and toss to combine.
2. Divide evenly among 4 plates and top with the pecans and cranberries.

548. Caesar Salad

Preparation Time: 10 Minutes
Cooking Time: 0 Minutes
Servings:1

Ingredients

For The Caesar Salad

2 cups chopped romaine lettuce

- 2 tablespoons Caesar Dressing
- 1 serving Herbed Croutons or store-bought croutons
- Vegan cheese, grated (optional)

Make It A Meal

- ½ cup cooked pasta
- ½ cup canned chickpeas, drained and rinsed
- 2 additional tablespoons Caesar Dressing

Directions

1. To Make The Caesar Salad. In a large bowl, toss together the lettuce, dressing, croutons, and cheese (if using).
2. To Make It A Meal. Add the pasta, chickpeas, and additional dressing. Toss to coat.
3. Per Serving (in a meal) Calories: 415; Protein: 19g; Total fat: 8g; Saturated fat: 1g; Carbohydrates: 72g; Fiber: 13g

548. Classic Potato Salad

Preparation Time: 10 Minutes
Cooking Time: 15 Minutes
Servings:4

Ingredients

- 6 potatoes, scrubbed or peeled and chopped
- Pinch salt
- ½ cup Creamy Tahini Dressing or vegan mayo
- 1 teaspoon dried dill (optional)
- 1 teaspoon Dijon mustard (optional)
- 4 celery stalks, chopped
- 2 scallions, white and light green parts only, chopped

Directions

1. Put the potatoes in a large pot, add the salt, and pour in enough water to cover. Bring the water to a boil over high heat. Cook the potatoes for 15 to 20 minutes, until soft. Drain and set aside to cool. (Alternatively, put the potatoes in a large microwave-safe dish with a bit of water. Cover and heat on high power for 10 minutes.)
2. In a large bowl, whisk together the dressing, dill (if using), and mustard (if using). Toss the celery and scallions with the dressing. Add the cooked, cooled potatoes and toss to combine. Store leftovers in an airtight container in the refrigerator for up to 1 week.

Per Serving Calories: 269; Protein: 6g; Total fat: 5g; Saturated fat: 1g; Carbohydrates: 51g; Fiber: 6g

550. Brown Rice and Pepper Salad

Preparation Time: 15 Minutes
Cooking Time: 0 Minutes
Servings:4

Ingredients

- 2 cups prepared brown rice
- ½ red onion, diced
- 1 red bell pepper, diced
- 1 orange bell pepper, diced
- 1 carrot, diced
- ¼ cup olive oil
- 2 tablespoons unseasoned rice vinegar
- 1 tablespoon soy sauce
- 1 garlic clove, minced
- 1 tablespoon grated fresh ginger
- ¼ teaspoon sea salt
- ¼ teaspoon freshly ground black pepper

Directions

1. In a large bowl, combine the rice, onion, bell peppers, and carrot. In a small bowl, whisk together the olive oil, rice vinegar, soy sauce, garlic, ginger, salt, and pepper. Toss with the rice mixture and serve immediately.

551. Mediterranean Orzo & Chickpea Salad

Preparation Time: 15 Minutes
Cooking Time: 8 Minutes
Servings:4

Ingredients

- ¼ cup olive oil
- 2 tablespoons freshly squeezed lemon juice
- Pinch salt
- 1½ cups canned chickpeas, drained and rinsed
- 2 cups orzo or other small pasta shape, cooked according to the package directions, drained, and rinsed with cold water to cool
- 2 cups raw spinach, finely chopped
- 1 cup chopped cucumber
- ¼ red onion, finely diced

Directions

1. In a large bowl, whisk together the olive oil, lemon juice, and salt. Add the chickpeas and cooked orzo, and toss to coat.
2. Stir in the spinach, cucumber, and red onion. Store leftovers in an airtight container in the refrigerator for up to 5 days.

Per Serving Calories: 233; Protein: 6g; Total fat: 15g; Saturated fat: 2g; Carbohydrates: 20g; Fiber: 5g

552. Nori Snack Rolls

Preparation time: 5 minutes
cooking time: 10 minutes
servings: 4 rolls

Ingredients

- 2 tablespoons almond, cashew, peanut, or other nut butter
- 2 tablespoons tamari, or soy sauce
- 4 standard nori sheets
- 1 mushroom, sliced
- 1 tablespoon pickled ginger
- ½ cup grated carrots

Directions

1. Preheat the oven to 350°F.
2. Mix together the nut butter and tamari until smooth and very thick. Lay out a nori sheet, rough side up, the long way.
3. Spread a thin line of the tamari mixture on the far end of the nori sheet, from side to side. Lay the mushroom slices, ginger, and carrots in a line at the other end (the end closest to you).
4. Fold the vegetables inside the nori, rolling toward the tahini mixture, which will seal the roll. Repeat to make 4 rolls.
5. Put on a baking sheet and bake for 8 to 10 minutes, or until the rolls are slightly browned and crispy at the ends. Let the rolls cool for a few minutes, then slice each roll into 3 smaller pieces.

Nutrition (1 rollCalories: 79; Total fat: 5g; Carbs: 6g; Fiber: 2g; Protein: 4g

553. Risotto Bites

Preparation time: 15 minutes
cooking time: 20 minutes
servings: 12 bites

Ingredients

- ½ cup panko bread crumbs
- 1 teaspoon paprika
- 1 teaspoon chipotle powder or ground cayenne pepper
- 1½ cups cold Green Pea Risotto
- Nonstick cooking spray

Directions

1. Preheat the oven to 425°F.
2. Line a baking sheet with parchment paper.
3. On a large plate, combine the panko, paprika, and chipotle powder. Set aside.
4. Roll 2 tablespoons of the risotto into a ball.
5. Gently roll in the bread crumbs, and place on the prepared baking sheet. Repeat to make a total of 12 balls.
6. Spritz the tops of the risotto bites with nonstick cooking spray and bake for 15 to 20 minutes, until they begin to brown. Cool completely before storing in a large airtight container in a single layer (add a piece of parchment paper for a second layeror in a plastic freezer bag.

Nutrition (6 bites): Calories: 100; Fat: 2g; Protein: 6g; Carbohydrates: 17g; Fiber: 5g; Sugar: 2g; Sodium: 165mg

554. Jicama and Guacamole

Preparation time: 15 minutes
cooking time: 0 minutes
servings: 4

Ingredients

- juice of 1 lime, or 1 tablespoon prepared lime juice
- 2 hass avocados, peeled, pits removed, and cut into cubes
- ½ teaspoon sea salt
- ½ red onion, minced
- 1 garlic clove, minced
- ¼ cup chopped cilantro (optional
- 1 jicama bulb, peeled and cut into matchsticks

Directions

1. In a medium bowl, squeeze the lime juice over the top of the avocado and sprinkle with salt.
2. Lightly mash the avocado with a fork. Stir in the onion, garlic, and cilantro, if using.

3. Serve with slices of jicama to dip in guacamole.
4. To store, place plastic wrap over the bowl of guacamole and refrigerate. The guacamole will keep for about 2 days.

555. Curried Tofu "Egg Salad" Pitas

Preparation time: 15 minutes
cooking time: 0 minutes
servings: 4 sandwiches

Ingredients

- 1 pound extra-firm tofu, drained and patted dry
- 1⁄2 cup vegan mayonnaise, homemade or store-bought
- 1⁄4 cup chopped mango chutney, homemade or store-bought
- 2 teaspoons Dijon mustard
- 1 tablespoon hot or mild curry powder
- 1 teaspoon salt
- 1⁄8 teaspoon ground cayenne
- ¾ cup shredded carrots
- 2 celery ribs, minced
- 1⁄4 cup minced red onion
- 8 small Boston or other soft lettuce leaves
- 4 (7-inchwhole wheat pita breads, halved

Directions

1. Crumble the tofu and place it in a large bowl. Add the mayonnaise, chutney, mustard, curry powder, salt, and cayenne, and stir well until thoroughly mixed.
2. Add the carrots, celery, and onion and stir to combine. Refrigerate for 30 minutes to allow the flavors to blend.
3. Tuck a lettuce leaf inside each pita pocket, spoon some tofu mixture on top of the lettuce, and serve.

556. Garden Patch Sandwiches On Multigrain Bread

Preparation time: 15 minutes
cooking time: 0 minutes
servings: 4 sandwiches

Ingredients

- 1pound extra-firm tofu, drained and patted dry
- 1 medium red bell pepper, finely chopped
- 1 celery rib, finely chopped
- 3 green onions, minced
- 1⁄4 cup shelled sunflower seeds
- 1⁄2 cup vegan mayonnaise, homemade or store-bought
- 1⁄2 teaspoon salt
- 1⁄2 teaspoon celery salt
- 1⁄4 teaspoon freshly ground black pepper
- 8 slices whole grain bread
- 4 (1⁄4-inchslices ripe tomato
- 4 lettuce leaves

Directions

1. Crumble the tofu and place it in a large bowl. Add the bell pepper, celery, green onions, and sunflower seeds. Stir in the mayonnaise, salt, celery salt, and pepper and mix until well combined.
2. Toast the bread, if desired. Spread the mixture evenly onto 4 slices of the bread. Top each with a tomato slice, lettuce leaf, and the remaining bread. Cut the sandwiches diagonally in half and serve.

557. Garden Salad Wraps

Preparation time: 15 minutes
cooking time: 10 minutes
servings: 4 wraps

Ingredients

- 6 tablespoons olive oil
- 1 pound extra-firm tofu, drained, patted dry, and cut into 1⁄2-inch strips
- 1 tablespoon soy sauce
- 1⁄4 cup apple cider vinegar
- 1 teaspoon yellow or spicy brown mustard
- 1⁄2 teaspoon salt
- 1⁄4 teaspoon freshly ground black pepper
- 3 cups shredded romaine lettuce
- 3 ripe Roma tomatoes, finely chopped
- 1 large carrot, shredded
- 1 medium English cucumber, peeled and chopped
- 1⁄3 cup minced red onion
- 1⁄4 cup sliced pitted green olives
- 4 (10-inchwhole-grain flour tortillas or lavash flatbread

Directions

1. In a large skillet, heat 2 tablespoons of the oil over medium heat. Add the tofu and cook until golden brown, about 10 minutes. Sprinkle with soy sauce and set aside to cool.
2. In a small bowl, combine the vinegar, mustard, salt, and pepper with the remaining 4 tablespoons oil, stirring to blend well. Set aside.
3. In a large bowl, combine the lettuce, tomatoes, carrot, cucumber, onion, and olives. Pour on the dressing and toss to coat.
4. To assemble wraps, place 1 tortilla on a work surface and spread with about one-quarter of the salad. Place a few strips of tofu on the tortilla and roll up tightly. Slice in half

558. Black Sesame Wonton Chips

Preparation time: 5 minutes
cooking time: 5 minutes
servings: 24 chips

Ingredients

- 12 Vegan Wonton Wrappers
- Toasted sesame oil
- 1/3 cup black sesame seeds
- Salt

Directions

1. Preheat the oven to 450°F. Lightly oil a baking sheet and set aside. Cut the wonton wrappers in half crosswise, brush them with sesame oil, and arrange them in a single layer on the prepared baking sheet.
2. Sprinkle wonton wrappers with the sesame seeds and salt to taste, and bake until crisp and golden brown, 5 to 7 minutes. Cool completely before serving. These are best eaten on the day they are made but, once cooled, they can be covered and stored at room temperature for 1 to 2 days.

Marinated Mushroom Wraps

Preparation time: 15 minutes
cooking time: 0 minutes
servings: 2 wraps

Ingredients

- 3 tablespoons soy sauce
- 3 tablespoons fresh lemon juice
- 11/2 tablespoons toasted sesame oil
- 2 portobello mushroom caps, cut into 1/4-inch strips
- 1 ripe Hass avocado, pitted and peeled
- 2 (10-inchwhole-grain flour tortillas
- 2 cups fresh baby spinach leaves
- 1 medium red bell pepper, cut into 1/4-inch strips
- 1 ripe tomato, chopped
- Salt and freshly ground black pepper

Directions

1. In a medium bowl, combine the soy sauce, 2 tablespoons of the lemon juice, and the oil. Add the portobello strips, toss to combine, and marinate for 1 hour or overnight. Drain the mushrooms and set aside.
2. Mash the avocado with the remaining 1 tablespoon of lemon juice.
3. To assemble wraps, place 1 tortilla on a work surface and spread with some of the mashed avocado. Top with a layer of baby spinach leaves. In the lower third of each tortilla, arrange strips of the soaked mushrooms and some of the bell pepper strips. Sprinkle with the tomato and salt and black pepper to taste. Roll up tightly and cut in half diagonally. Repeat with the remaining Ingredients and serve.

559. Tamari Toasted Almonds

Preparation time: 2 minutes
cooking time: 8 minutes
servings: ½ cup

Ingredients

- ½ cup raw almonds, or sunflower seeds
- 2 tablespoons tamari, or soy sauce
- 1 teaspoon toasted sesame oil

Directions

1. Heat a dry skillet to medium-high heat, then add the almonds, stirring very frequently to keep them from burning. Once the almonds are toasted, 7 to 8 minutes for almonds, or 3 to 4 minutes for sunflower seeds, pour the tamari and

sesame oil into the hot skillet and stir to coat.
2. You can turn off the heat, and as the almonds cool the tamari mixture will stick to and dry on the nuts.

Nutrition (1 tablespoonCalories: 89; Total fat: 8g; Carbs: 3g; Fiber: 2g; Protein: 4g

560. Avocado And Tempeh Bacon Wraps

Preparation time: 10 minutes
cooking time: 8 minutes
servings: 4 wraps

Ingredients

- 2 tablespoons olive oil
- 8 ounces tempeh bacon, homemade or store-bought
- 4 (10-inchsoft flour tortillas or lavash flat bread
- 1/4 cup vegan mayonnaise, homemade or store-bought
- 4 large lettuce leaves
- 2 ripe Hass avocados, pitted, peeled, and cut into 1/4-inch slices
- 1 large ripe tomato, cut into 1/4-inch slices

Directions

1. In a large skillet, heat the oil over medium heat. Add the tempeh bacon and cook until browned on both sides, about 8 minutes. Remove from the heat and set aside.
2. Place 1 tortilla on a work surface. Spread with some of the mayonnaise and one-fourth of the lettuce and tomatoes.
3. Pit, peel, and thinly slice the avocado and place the slices on top of the tomato. Add the reserved tempeh bacon and roll up tightly. Repeat with remaining Ingredients and serve.

561. Kale Chips

Preparation time: 5 minutes
cooking time: 25 minutes
servings: 2

Ingredients

- 1 large bunch kale
- 1 tablespoon extra-virgin olive oil
- ½ teaspoon chipotle powder
- ½ teaspoon smoked paprika
- ¼ teaspoon salt

Directions

1. Preheat the oven to 275°F.
2. Line a large baking sheet with parchment paper. In a large bowl, stem the kale and tear it into bite-size pieces. Add the olive oil, chipotle powder, smoked paprika, and salt.
3. Toss the kale with tongs or your hands, coating each piece well.
4. Spread the kale over the parchment paper in a single layer.
5. Bake for 25 minutes, turning halfway through, until crisp.
6. Cool for 10 to 15 minutes before dividing and storing in 2 airtight containers.

Nutrition: Calories: 144; Fat: 7g; Protein: 5g; Carbohydrates: 18g; Fiber: 3g; Sugar: 0g; Sodium: 363mg

562. Tempeh-Pimiento Cheeze Ball

Preparation time: 5 minutes
cooking time: 30 minutes
servings: 8

Ingredients

- 8 ounces tempeh, cut into 1/2-inch pieces
- 1 (2-ouncejar chopped pimientos, drained
- 1/4 cup nutritional yeast
- 1/4 cup vegan mayonnaise, homemade or store-bought
- 2 tablespoons soy sauce
- ¾ cup chopped pecans

Directions

1. In a medium saucepan of simmering water, cook the tempeh for 30 minutes. Set aside to cool. In a food processor, combine the cooled tempeh, pimientos, nutritional yeast, mayo, and soy sauce. Process until smooth.
2. Transfer the tempeh mixture to a bowl and refrigerate until firm and chilled, at least 2 hours or overnight.
3. In a dry skillet, toast the pecans over medium heat until lightly toasted, about 5 minutes. Set aside to cool.
4. Shape the tempeh mixture into a ball, and roll it in the pecans, pressing the nuts

slightly into the tempeh mixture so they stick. Refrigerate for at least 1 hour before serving. If not using right away, cover and keep refrigerated until needed. Properly stored, it will keep for 2 to 3 days.

563. Peppers and Hummus

Preparation time: 15 minutes
cooking time: 0 minutes
servings: 4

Ingredients

- one 15-ounce can chickpeas, drained and rinsed
- juice of 1 lemon, or 1 tablespoon prepared lemon juice
- ¼ cup tahini
- 3 tablespoons olive oil
- ½ teaspoon ground cumin
- 1 tablespoon water
- ¼ teaspoon paprika
- 1 red bell pepper, sliced
- 1 green bell pepper, sliced
- 1 orange bell pepper, sliced

Directions

1. In a food processor, combine chickpeas, lemon juice, tahini, 2 tablespoons of the olive oil, the cumin, and water.
2. Process on high speed until blended, about 30 seconds. Scoop the hummus into a bowl and drizzle with the remaining tablespoon of olive oil. Sprinkle with paprika and serve with sliced bell peppers.

564. Deconstructed Hummus Pitas

Preparation time: 15 minutes
cooking time: 0 minutes
servings: 4 pitas

Ingredients

- 1 garlic clove, crushed
- ¾ cup tahini (sesame paste
- 2 tablespoons fresh lemon juice
- 1 teaspoon salt
- 1/8 teaspoon ground cayenne
- 1/4 cup water
- 11/2 cups cooked or 1 (15.5-ouncecan chickpeas, rinsed and drained
- 2 medium carrots, grated (about 1 cup
- 4 (7-inchpita breads, preferably whole wheat, halved
- 1 large ripe tomato, cut into 1/4-inch slices
- 2 cups fresh baby spinach

Directions

1. In a blender or food processor, mince the garlic. Add the tahini, lemon juice, salt, cayenne, and water. Process until smooth.
2. Place the chickpeas in a bowl and crush slightly with a fork. Add the carrots and the reserved tahini sauce and toss to combine. Set aside.
3. Spoon 2 or 3 tablespoons of the chickpea mixture into each pita half. Tuck a tomato slice and a few spinach leaves into each pocket and serve.

565. Savory Roasted Chickpeas

Preparation time: 5 minutes
cooking time: 25 minutes
servings: 1 cup

Ingredients

- 1 (14-ouncecan chickpeas, rinsed and drained, or 1½ cups cooked
- 2 tablespoons tamari, or soy sauce
- 1 tablespoon nutritional yeast
- 1 teaspoon smoked paprika, or regular paprika
- 1 teaspoon onion powder
- ½ teaspoon garlic powder

Directions

1. Preheat the oven to 400°F.
2. Toss the chickpeas with all the other ingredients, and spread them out on a baking sheet. Bake for 20 to 25 minutes, tossing halfway through.
3. Bake these at a lower temperature, until fully dried and crispy, if you want to keep them longer.
4. You can easily double the batch, and if you dry them out they will keep about a week in an airtight container.

Nutrition (¼ cupCalories: 121; Total fat: 2g; Carbs: 20g; Fiber: 6g; Protein: 8g

566. Savory Seed Crackers

Preparation time: 5 minutes
cooking time: 50 minutes

servings: 20 crackers

Ingredients

- ¾ cup pumpkin seeds (pepitas
- ½ cup sunflower seeds
- ½ cup sesame seeds
- ¼ cup chia seeds
- 1 teaspoon minced garlic (about 1 clove
- 1 teaspoon tamari or soy sauce
- 1 teaspoon vegan Worcestershire sauce
- ½ teaspoon ground cayenne pepper
- ½ teaspoon dried oregano
- ½ cup water

Directions

1. Preheat the oven to 325°F.
2. Line a rimmed baking sheet with parchment paper.
3. In a large bowl, combine the pumpkin seeds, sunflower seeds, sesame seeds, chia seeds, garlic, tamari, Worcestershire sauce, cayenne, oregano, and water.
4. Transfer to the prepared baking sheet, spreading out to all sides.
5. Bake for 25 minutes. Remove the pan from the oven, and flip the seed "dough" over so the wet side is up. Bake for another 20 to 25 minutes, until the sides are browned.
6. Cool completely before breaking up into 20 pieces. Divide evenly among 4 glass jars and close tightly with lids.

Nutrition (5 crackers): Calories: 339; Fat: 29g; Protein: 14g; Carbohydrates: 17g; Fiber: 8g; Sugar: 1g; Sodium: 96mg

567. Tomato and Basil Bruschetta

Preparation time: 10 minutes
cooking time: 6 minutes
servings: 12 bruschetta

Ingredients

- 3 tomatoes, chopped
- ¼ cup chopped fresh basil
- 1 tablespoon olive oil
- pinch of sea salt
- 1 baguette, cut into 12 slices
- 1 garlic clove, sliced in half

Directions

1. In a small bowl, combine the tomatoes, basil, olive oil, and salt and stir to mix. Set aside. Preheat the oven to 425°F.
2. Place the baguette slices in a single layer on a baking sheet and toast in the oven until brown, about 6 minutes.
3. Flip the bread slices over once during cooking. Remove from the oven and rub the bread on both sides with the sliced clove of -garlic.
4. Top with the tomato-basil mixture and serve immediately.

568. Refried Bean And Salsa Quesadillas

Preparation time: 5 minutes
cooking time: 6 minutes
servings: 4 quesadillas

Ingredients

- 1 tablespoon canola oil, plus more for frying
- 11⁄2 cups cooked or 1 (15.5-ouncecan pinto beans, drained and mashed
- 1 teaspoon chili powder
- 4 (10-inchwhole-wheat flour tortillas
- 1 cup tomato salsa, homemade or store-bought
- 1⁄2 cup minced red onion (optional

Directions

1. In a medium saucepan, heat the oil over medium heat. Add the mashed beans and chili powder and cook, stirring, until hot, about 5 minutes. Set aside.
2. To assemble, place 1 tortilla on a work surface and spoon about 1⁄4 cup of the beans across the bottom half. Top the beans with the salsa and onion, if using. Fold top half of the tortilla over the filling and press slightly.
3. In large skillet heat a thin layer of oil over medium heat. Place folded quesadillas, 1 or 2 at a time, into the hot skillet and heat until hot, turning once, about 1 minute per side.
4. Cut quesadillas into 3 or 4 wedges and arrange on plates. Serve immediately.
5. Tempeh Tantrum Burgers

569. Preparation time: 15 minutes

cooking time: 0 minutes

servings: 4 burgers

Ingredients

- 8 ounces tempeh, cut into 1/2-inch dice
- ¾ cup chopped onion
- 2 garlic cloves, chopped
- ¾ cup chopped walnuts
- 1/2 cup old-fashioned or quick-cooking oats
- 1 tablespoon minced fresh parsley
- 1/2 teaspoon dried oregano
- 1/2 teaspoon dried thyme
- 1/2 teaspoon salt
- 1/4 teaspoon freshly ground black pepper
- 3 tablespoons olive oil
- Dijon mustard
- 4 whole grain burger rolls
- Sliced red onion, tomato, lettuce, and avocado

Directions

1. In a medium saucepan of simmering water, cook the tempeh for 30 minutes. Drain and set aside to cool.
2. In a food processor, combine the onion and garlic and process until minced. Add the cooled tempeh, the walnuts, oats, parsley, oregano, thyme, salt, and pepper. Process until well blended. Shape the mixture into 4 equal patties.
3. In a large skillet, heat the oil over medium heat. Add the burgers and cook until cooked thoroughly and browned on both sides, about 7 minutes per side.
4. Spread desired amount of mustard onto each half of the rolls and layer each roll with lettuce, tomato, red onion, and avocado, as desired. Serve immediately.

570. Sesame- Wonton Crisps

Preparation time: 10 minutes
cooking time: 10 minutes
servings: 12 crisps

Ingredients

- 12 Vegan Wonton Wrappers
- 2 tablespoons toasted sesame oil
- 12 shiitake mushrooms, lightly rinsed, patted dry, stemmed, and cut into 1/4-inch slices
- 4 snow peas, trimmed and cut crosswise into thin slivers
- 1 teaspoon soy sauce
- 1 tablespoon fresh lime juice
- 1/2 teaspoon brown sugar
- 1 medium carrot, shredded
- Toasted sesame seeds or black sesame seeds, if available

Directions

1. Preheat the oven to 350°F. Lightly oil a baking sheet and set aside. Brush the wonton wrappers with 1 tablespoon of the sesame oil and arrange on the baking sheet. Bake until golden brown and crisp, about 5 minutes. Set aside to cool. (Alternately, you can tuck the wonton wrappers into mini-muffin tins to create cups for the filling. Brush with sesame oil and bake them until crisp.
2. In a large skillet, heat the extra olive oil over medium heat. Add the mushrooms and cook until softened, 3 to 5 minutes. Stir in the snow peas and the soy sauce and cook 30 seconds. Set aside to cool.
3. In a large bowl, combine the lime juice, sugar, and remaining 1 tablespoon sesame oil. Stir in the carrot and cooled shiitake mixture. Top each wonton crisp with a spoonful of the shiitake mixture. Sprinkle with sesame seeds and arrange on a platter to serve.

571. Macadamia-Cashew Patties

Preparation time: 10 minutes
cooking time: 10 minutes
servings: 4 patties

Ingredients

- ¾ cup chopped macadamia nuts
- ¾ cup chopped cashews
- 1 medium carrot, grated
- 1 small onion, chopped
- 1 garlic clove, minced
- 1 jalapeño or other green chile, seeded and minced
- ¾ cup old-fashioned oats
- ¾ cup dry unseasoned bread crumbs
- 2 tablespoons minced fresh cilantro

- 1/2 teaspoon ground coriander
- Salt and freshly ground black pepper
- 2 teaspoons fresh lime juice
- Canola or grapeseed oil, for frying
- 4 sandwich rolls
- Lettuce leaves and condiment of choice

Directions

1. In a food processor, combine the macadamia nuts, cashews, carrot, onion, garlic, chile, oats, bread crumbs, cilantro, coriander, and salt and pepper to taste. Process until well mixed. Add the lime juice and process until well blended. Taste, adjusting seasonings if necessary. Shape the mixture into 4 equal patties.
2. In a large skillet, heat a thin layer of oil over medium heat. Add the patties and cook until golden brown on both sides, turning once, about 10 minutes total. Serve on sandwich rolls with lettuce and condiments of choice.

572. Garlic Tahini Spread

Preparation time: 10 minutes
Cooking time: 15 minutes
Servings: 4

Ingredients:

- 1 cup coconut cream
- 2 tablespoons tahini paste
- 4 garlic cloves, minced
- Juice of 1 lime
- ¼ teaspoon turmeric powder
- A pinch of salt and black pepper
- 1 teaspoon sweet paprika
- 1 tablespoon olive oil

Directions:

1. Heat up a pan with the oil over medium heat, add the garlic, turmeric and paprika and cook for 5 minutes.
2. Add the rest of the ingredients, stir, cook over medium heat for 10 minutes more, blend using an immersion blender, divide into bowls and serve.

Nutrition: calories 170, fat 7.3, fiber 4, carbs 1, protein 5

573. Balsamic Pearl Onions Bowls

Preparation time: 5 minutes
Cooking time: 15 minutes
Servings: 4

Ingredients:

- 1 pound pearl onions, peeled
- A pinch of salt and black pepper
- 2 tablespoons avocado oil
- 4 tablespoons balsamic vinegar
- 1 tablespoon chives, chopped

Directions:

1. Heat up a pan with the oil over medium heat, add the pearl onions, salt, pepper and the other ingredients, cook for 15 minutes, divide into bowls and serve as a snack.

Nutrition: calories 120, fat 2, fiber 1, carbs 2, protein 2

574. Basil Rice Bowls

Preparation time: 10 minutes
Cooking time: 20 minutes
Servings: 4

Ingredients:

- 2 cups cauliflower rice
- 1 cup veggie stock
- A pinch of salt and black pepper
- 1 teaspoon turmeric powder
- 1 teaspoon cumin, ground
- 1 teaspoon fennel seeds, crushed
- 2 tablespoons olive oil
- 2 tomatoes, cubed
- 1 cup black olives, pitted and sliced
- 1 bunch basil, chopped

Directions:

1. Heat up a pan with the oil over medium heat, add the cauliflower rice, stock, salt, pepper and the other ingredients, stir, cook for 20 minutes, divide into small bowls and serve as an appetizer.

Nutrition: calories 118, fat 11.5, fiber 2.2, carbs 5.9, protein 4

575. Turmeric Peppers Platter

Preparation time: 10 minutes
Cooking time: 20 minutes
Servings: 4

Ingredients:

- 2 green bell peppers, cut into wedges
- 2 red bell peppers, cut into wedges
- 2 yellow bell peppers, cut into wedges
- 2 tablespoons avocado oil
- 2 garlic cloves, minced
- 1 bunch basil, chopped
- A pinch of salt and black pepper
- 2 tablespoons balsamic vinegar

Directions:

1. Heat up a pan with the oil over medium heat, add the garlic and the vinegar and cook for 2 minutes.
2. Add the peppers and the other ingredients, toss, cook over medium heat for 18 minutes, arrange them on a platter and serve as an appetizer.

Nutrition: calories 120, fat 8.2, fiber 2, carbs 4, protein 2.3

576. Capers Dip

Preparation time: 10 minutes
Cooking time: 20 minutes
Servings: 4

Ingredients:

- 2 tablespoons olive oil
- 4 scallions, chopped
- 1 teaspoon rosemary, dried
- 2 tablespoons capers, drained
- 1 cup coconut cream
- 2 tablespoons pine nuts
- 1 bunch basil, chopped

Directions:

1. Heat up a pan with the oil over medium heat, add the scallions and the capers and sauté for 5 minutes.
2. Add the cream and the other ingredients, stir, cook over medium heat for 15 minutes more, blend using an immersion blender, divide into bowls and serve.

Nutrition: calories 127, fat 3, fiber 3, carbs 6, protein 7

577. Radish and Walnuts Dip

Preparation time: 10 minutes
Cooking time: 20 minutes
Servings: 4

Ingredients:

- 2 tablespoons walnuts, chopped
- 1 cup coconut cream
- 2 cups radishes, chopped
- 4 scallions, chopped
- 2 tablespoons olive oil
- 1 teaspoon chili powder
- A pinch of salt and black pepper
- 2 teaspoons mustard powder
- 2 teaspoons garlic powder
- 2 teaspoons cumin, ground

Directions:

1. Heat up a pan with the oil over medium heat, add the scallions, mustard powder, garlic powder and cumin, stir and sauté for 5 minutes.
2. Add the walnuts, and the other ingredients, stir, cook over medium heat for 15 minutes, blend well using an immersion blender, divide into bowls and serve.

Nutrition: calories 192, fat 5, fiber 7, carbs 12, protein 5

578. Mushroom Cakes

Preparation time: 10 minutes
Cooking time: 12 minutes
Servings: 6

Ingredients:

- 1 cup shallots, chopped
- 2 tablespoons olive oil
- 3 garlic cloves, minced
- 1 pound mushrooms, minced
- 2 tablespoons almond flour
- ¼ cup coconut cream
- 1 tablespoon flaxseed mixed with 2 tablespoons water
- ¼ cup parsley, chopped

Directions:

1. In a bowl, combine the shallots with the garlic, the mushrooms and the other ingredients except the oil, stir well and shape medium cakes out of this mix.
2. Heat up a pan with the oil over medium heat, add the mushroom cakes, cook for 6 minutes on each side, arrange them on a

platter and serve as an appetizer.

Nutrition: calories 222, fat 4, fiber 3, carbs 8, protein 10

579. Cabbage Sticks

Preparation time: 10 minutes
Cooking time: 30 minutes
Servings: 4

Ingredients:

- 1 pound cabbage, leaves separated and cut into thick strips
- 1 tablespoon olive oil
- 1 tablespoon balsamic vinegar
- 1 teaspoon ginger, grated
- 1 teaspoon hot paprika
- A pinch of salt and black pepper

Directions:

1. Spread the cabbage strips on a baking sheet lined with parchment paper, add the oil, the vinegar and the other ingredients, toss and cook at 400 degrees F for 30 minutes.
2. Divide the cabbage strips into bowls and serve as a snack.

Nutrition: calories 300, fat 4, fiber 7, carbs 18, protein 6

580. Crispy Brussels Sprouts

Preparation time: 10 minutes
Cooking time: 30 minutes
Servings: 4

Ingredients:

- 2 pounds Brussels sprouts, trimmed and halved
- 1 teaspoon red pepper flakes
- 1 tablespoon smoked paprika
- 2 tablespoons avocado oil
- 1 tablespoon balsamic vinegar
- A pinch of salt and black pepper

Directions:

1. In a roasting pan, combine the sprouts with the pepper flakes, paprika and the other ingredients, toss and cook at 400 degrees F for 30 minutes.
2. Divide the Brussels sprouts into bowls and serve as a snack.

Nutrition: calories 162, fat 4, fiber 3, carbs 7, protein 8

581. Arugula Dip

Preparation time: 10 minutes
Cooking time: 0 minutes
Servings: 4

Ingredients:

- ½ cup coconut cream
- 2 cups baby arugula
- Juice of 1 lime
- 2 tablespoons walnuts, chopped
- 2 tablespoons olive oil
- A pinch of salt and black pepper
- 2 garlic cloves minced
- ¼ teaspoon red pepper flakes, crushed

Directions:

1. In a blender, combine the arugula with the cream, lime juice and the other ingredients, pulse well, divide into bowls and serve as a party dip.

Nutrition: calories 100, fat 0, fiber 1, carbs 1, protein 3

582. Coconut Bites

Preparation time: 10 minutes
Cooking time: 25 minutes
Servings: 6

Ingredients:

- 1 cup coconut milk
- 1 and ½ cup coconut flesh, unsweetened and shredded
- A pinch of salt
- ¼ cup chives, chopped
- 2 teaspoons rosemary, dried
- Cooking spray

Directions:

2. In a pan, combine the coconut with the coconut milk and the other ingredients except the cooking sp ray, whisk and cook over medium heat for 10 minutes.
3. Take spoonfuls of this mix, shape medium balls, arrange them all on a baking sheet lined with parchment paper, grease them with the cooking spray, and cook at 450 degrees F for 15 minutes.
4. Serve the coconut bites cold.

Nutrition: calories 112, fat 3, fiber 3, carbs 3, protein 8

583. Basil Eggplant Tapenade

Preparation time: 10 minutes
Cooking time: 15 minutes
Servings: 4

Ingredients:

- 1 cup cherry tomatoes, cubed
- 2 eggplants, cubed
- 2 tablespoons kalamata olives, pitted and cubed
- 1 avocado, peeled, pitted and cubed
- 2 tablespoons olive oil
- 3 garlic cloves, minced
- 2 teaspoons balsamic vinegar
- 1 tablespoon basil, chopped
- A pinch of salt and black pepper

Directions:

1. Heat up a pan with the oil over medium heat, add the garlic, salt and pepper and sauté for 2 minutes.
2. Add the tomatoes, eggplants and the other ingredients, toss, cook over medium heat for 13 minutes, divide into small bowls and serve as an appetizer.

Nutrition: calories 121, fat 3, fiber 1, carbs 8, protein 12

584. Hot Eggplant and Broccoli Spread

Preparation time: 10 minutes
Cooking time: 25 minutes
Servings: 8

Ingredients:

- ½ cup walnuts, chopped
- 2 eggplants, cubed
- 1 cup broccoli florets
- 1 cup coconut cream
- 1 teaspoon hot paprika
- ½ teaspoon chili powder
- A pinch of salt and black pepper
- ½ teaspoon garlic powder
- 1 teaspoon cumin, ground
- ½ teaspoon rosemary, dried

Directions:

1. Heat up a pan with the cream over medium heat, add the walnuts, eggplants, broccoli and the other ingredients, stir, cook for 25 minutes and transfer to a blender.
2. Pulse well, divide into bowls and serve as a party spread.

Nutrition: calories 192, fat 5, fiber 7, carbs 9, protein 8

585. Almond and Pine Nuts Spread

Preparation time: 10 minutes
Cooking time: 15 minutes
Servings: 8

Ingredients:

- 1 cup coconut cream
- ½ cup almonds, chopped
- 2 tablespoons pine nuts, toasted
- 1 tablespoon olive oil
- 1 teaspoon sage, ground
- 1 teaspoon chili powder
- A pinch of salt and black pepper

Directions:

1. In a pot, combine the almonds with the pine nuts, cream and the other ingredients, stir, cook over medium heat for 15 minutes and transfer to a blender.
2. Pulse well, divide into bowls and serve as a party spread.

Nutrition: calories 112, fat 5, fiber 2, carbs 8, protein 10

586. Coconut Cashew Dip

Preparation time: 10 minutes
Cooking time: 30 minutes
Servings: 4

Ingredients:

- ½ cup coconut cream
- 1 cup cashews, chopped
- 2 tablespoons cashew cheese, shredded
- 1 teaspoon balsamic vinegar
- 1 tablespoon chives, chopped
- A pinch of salt and black pepper

Directions:

1. In a pot, combine the cream with the cashew, cashew cheese and the other ingredients, stir, cook over medium heat for 30 minutes and transfer to a blender.

2. Pulse well, divide into bowls and serve.

Nutrition: calories 100, fat 2, fiber 1, carbs 6, protein 6

587. Green Beans Dip

Preparation time: 10 minutes
Cooking time: 25 minutes
Servings: 4

Ingredients:

- 1 pound green beans, trimmed and halved
- 4 scallions, chopped
- 1 teaspoon turmeric powder
- 3 garlic cloves, minced
- 1 teaspoon rosemary, dried
- 1 and ½ cups coconut cream
- A pinch of salt and black pepper
- 1 tablespoon chives, chopped

Directions:

1. In a pan, combine the green beans with the scallions, turmeric and the other ingredients, stir, cook over medium heat for 25 minutes and transfer to a bowl.
2. Blend the mix well, divide into bowls and serve as a party dip.

Nutrition: calories 172, fat 6, fiber 3, carbs 6, protein 8

588. Coriander Mint Chutney

Preparation time: 10 minutes
Cooking time: 12 minutes
Servings: 4

Ingredients:

- 1 and ½ teaspoons cumin seeds
- 1 and ½ teaspoons garam masala
- ½ teaspoon mustard seeds
- 2 tablespoons avocado oil
- 2 garlic cloves, minced
- ¼ cup veggie stock
- 1 cup mint
- 1 tablespoon ginger, grated
- 2 teaspoons lime juice
- A pinch of salt and black pepper

Directions:

1. Heat up a pan with the oil over medium heat, add the cumin, garam masala, mustard seeds, garlic and ginger and cook for 5 minutes.
2. Add the mint and the other ingredients, stir, cook over medium heat for 7 minutes more, divide into bowls and serve as a snack.

Nutrition: calories 241, fat 4, fiber 7, carbs 10, protein 6

589. Spiced Okra Bites

Preparation time: 10 minutes
Cooking time: 15 minutes
Servings: 4

Ingredients:

- 2 cups okra, sliced
- 2 tablespoons avocado oil
- ¼ teaspoon chili powder
- ¼ teaspoon mustard powder
- ¼ teaspoon garlic powder
- ¼ teaspoon onion powder
- A pinch of salt and black pepper

Directions:

1. Spread the okra on a baking sheet lined with parchment paper, add the oil and the other ingredients, toss and roast at 400 degrees F for 15 minutes.
2. Divide the okra into bowls and serve as a snack.

Nutrition: calories 200, fat 2, fiber 2, carbs 6, protein 7

590. Rosemary Chard Dip

Preparation time: 10 minutes
Cooking time: 20 minutes
Servings: 4

Ingredients:

- 4 cups chard, chopped
- 2 cups coconut cream
- ½ cup cashews, chopped
- A pinch of salt and black pepper
- 1 teaspoon smoked paprika
- ½ teaspoon chili powder
- ¼ teaspoon mustard powder
- ½ cup cilantro, chopped

Directions:

1. In a pan, combine the chard with the cream, cashews and the other ingredients,

stir, cook over medium heat for 20 minutes and transfer to a blender.

2. Pulse well, divide into bowls and serve as a party dip.

Nutrition: calories 200, fat 4, fiber 3, carbs 6, protein 7

591. Spinach and Chard Hummus

Preparation time: 10 minutes
Cooking time: 10 minutes
Servings: 4

Ingredients:

- 2 garlic cloves, minced
- 2 cup chard leaves
- 2 cups baby spinach
- ½ cup coconut cream
- ¼ cup sesame paste
- A pinch of salt and black pepper
- 2 tablespoons olive oil
- Juice of ½ lemon

Directions:

1. Put the cream in a pan, heat it up over medium heat, add the chard, garlic and the other ingredients, stir, cook for 10 minutes, blend using an immersion blender, divide into bowls and serve.

Nutrition: calories 172, fat 4, fiber 3, carbs 7, protein 8

592. Veggie Spread

Preparation time: 10 minutes
Cooking time: 20 minutes
Servings: 4

Ingredients:

- 2 tablespoons olive oil
- 1 cup shallots, chopped
- 2 garlic cloves, minced
- ½ cup eggplant, chopped
- ½ cup red bell pepper, chopped
- ¼ cup tomatoes, cubed
- 2 tablespoons coconut cream
- ¼ cup veggie stock
- Salt and black pepper to the taste

Directions:

2. Heat up a pan with the oil over medium heat, add the shallots and the garlic and sauté for 5 minutes.
3. Add the eggplant, tomatoes and the other ingredients, stir and cook for 15 minutes more.
4. Blend the mix a bit with an immersion blender, divide into bowls and serve cold as a party spread.

Nutrition: calories 163, fat 4, fiber 3, carbs 7, protein 8

593. Pomegranate Dip

Preparation time: 10 minutes
Cooking time: 0 minutes
Servings: 6

Ingredients:

- 2 cups coconut cream
- 2 tablespoons walnuts, chopped
- ½ cup pomegranate seeds
- A pinch of salt and white pepper
- 2 tablespoons mint, chopped
- 2 tablespoons olive oil

Directions:

1. In a blender, combine the cream with the pomegranate seeds and the other ingredients, pulse well, divide into bowls and serve cold.

Nutrition: calories 294, fat 18, fiber 1, carbs 21, protein 10

594. Tomato and Watermelon Bites

Preparation time: 10 minutes
Cooking time: 0 minutes
Servings: 6

Ingredients:

- 1/3 cup basil, chopped
- 1 pound cherry tomatoes, halved
- 2 cups watermelon, peeled and roughly cubed
- 1 teaspoon avocado oil
- 1 tablespoon balsamic vinegar

Directions:

2. In a bowl, combine the cherry tomatoes with the watermelon cubes and the other ingredients, toss, arrange on a platter and serve as an appetizer.

Nutrition: calories 162, fat 4 fiber 7, carbs 29, protein 4

595. Artichoke and Spinach Salad

Preparation time: 5 minutes
Cooking time: 0 minutes
Servings: 4

Ingredients:

- 2 tablespoons avocado oil
- 2 garlic cloves, minced
- 2 tablespoons cilantro, chopped
- 14 ounces canned artichokes, drained and halved
- 2 cups baby spinach, chopped
- ½ cup cucumber, roughly cubed
- ½ teaspoon basil, dried
- Salt and black pepper to the taste

Directions:

1. In a bowl, combine the artichokes with the garlic, the oil and the other ingredients, toss, divide into smaller bowls and serve as an appetizer.

Nutrition: calories 223, fat 11.2, fiber 5.34, carbs 15.5, protein 7.4

596. Red Pepper and Cheese Dip

Preparation time: 10 minutes
Cooking time: 10 minutes
Servings: 4

Ingredients:

- 7 ounces roasted red peppers, chopped
- ½ cup cashew cheese, grated
- 2 tablespoons parsley, chopped
- 2 tablespoons olive oil
- ¼ cup capers, drained
- 1 tablespoon lemon juice

Directions:

1. Heat up a pan with the oil over medium heat, add the peppers and the other ingredients, stir, cook for 10 minutes and take off the heat.
2. Blend using an immersion blender, divide the mix into bowls and serve.

Nutrition: calories 95, fat 8.6, fiber 1.2, carbs 4.7, protein 1.4

597. Mushroom Falafel

Preparation time: 10 minutes
Cooking time: 12 minutes
Servings: 6

Ingredients:

- 1 cup mushrooms, chopped
- 1 bunch parsley leaves
- 4 scallions, hopped
- 5 garlic cloves, minced
- 1 teaspoon coriander, ground
- A pinch of salt and black pepper
- ¼ teaspoon baking soda
- 1 teaspoon lemon juice
- 3 tablespoons almond flour
- 2 tablespoons avocado oil

Directions:

1. In your food processor, combine the mushrooms with the parsley and the other ingredients except the flour and the oil and pulse well.
2. Transfer the mix to a bowl, add the flour, stir well, shape medium balls out of this mix and flatten them a bit.
3. Heat up a pan with the over medium-high heat, add the falafels, cook them for 6 minutes on each side, drain excess grease using paper towels, arrange them on a platter and serve as an appetizer.

Nutrition: calories 55, fat 3.5, fiber 1.5, carbs 4.5, protein 2.3

598. Maple-Walnut Oatmeal Cookies

Preparation time: 5 minutes
cooking time: 10 minutes
servings: about 2 dozen cookies

Ingredients

- 11⁄2 cups whole-grain flour
- 1 teaspoon baking powder
- 1⁄8 teaspoon salt
- 1 teaspoon ground cinnamon
- 1⁄4 teaspoon ground nutmeg
- 11⁄2 cups old-fashioned oats
- 1 cup chopped walnuts
- 1⁄2 cup vegan margarine, melted
- 1⁄2 cup pure maple syrup
- 1⁄4 cup light brown sugar
- 2 teaspoons pure vanilla extract

Directions

1. Preheat the oven to 375°F. In a large bowl, sift together the flour, baking powder, salt, cinnamon, and nutmeg. Stir in the oats and walnuts.
2. In a medium bowl, combine the margarine, maple syrup, sugar, and vanilla and mix well.
3. Add the wet Ingredients to the dry Ingredients, stirring to mix well.
4. Drop the cookie dough by the tablespoonful onto an ungreased baking sheet and press down slightly with a fork. Bake until browned, 10 to 12 minutes. Cool the cookies slightly before transferring to a wire rack to cool completely. Store in an airtight container.

599. Banana-Nut Bread Bars

Preparation time: 5 minutes
cooking time: 30 minutes
servings: 9 bars

Ingredients

- Nonstick cooking spray (optional
- 2 large ripe bananas
- 1 tablespoon maple syrup
- ½ teaspoon vanilla extract
- 2 cups old-fashioned rolled oats
- ½ teaspoons salt
- ¼ cup chopped walnuts

Directions

1. Preheat the oven to 350ºF. Lightly coat a 9-by-9-inch baking pan with nonstick cooking spray (if usingor line with parchment paper for oil-free baking.
2. In a medium bowl, mash the bananas with a fork. Add the maple syrup and vanilla extract and mix well. Add the oats, salt, and walnuts, mixing well.
3. Transfer the batter to the baking pan and bake for 25 to 30 minutes, until the top is crispy. Cool completely before slicing into 9 bars. Transfer to an airtight storage container or a large plastic bag.

Nutrition (1 bar): Calories: 73; Fat: 1g; Protein: 2g; Carbohydrates: 15g; Fiber: 2g; Sugar: 5g; Sodium: 129mg

600. Apple Crumble

Preparation time: 20 minutes
cooking time: 25 minutes
servings: 6

Ingredients

For the filling

- 4 to 5 apples, cored and chopped (about 6 cups
- ½ cup unsweetened applesauce, or ¼ cup water
- 2 to 3 tablespoons unrefined sugar (coconut, date, sucanat, maple syrup
- 1 teaspoon ground cinnamon
- Pinch sea salt
- For the crumble
- 2 tablespoons almond butter, or cashew or sunflower seed butter
- 2 tablespoons maple syrup
- 1½ cups rolled oats
- ½ cup walnuts, finely chopped
- ½ teaspoon ground cinnamon
- 2 to 3 tablespoons unrefined granular sugar (coconut, date, sucanat

Directions

1. Preheat the oven to 350°F. Put the apples and applesauce in an 8-inch-square baking dish, and sprinkle with the sugar, cinnamon, and salt. Toss to combine.
2. In a medium bowl, mix together the nut butter and maple syrup until smooth and creamy. Add the oats, walnuts, cinnamon, and sugar and stir to coat, using your hands if necessary. (If you have a small food processor, pulse the oats and walnuts together before adding them to the mix.
3. Sprinkle the topping over the apples, and put the dish in the oven.
4. Bake for 20 to 25 minutes, or until the fruit is soft and the topping is lightly browned.

Nutrition Calories: 356; Total fat: 17g; Carbs: 49g; Fiber: 7g; Protein: 7g

601. Chocolate-Cranberry Oatmeal Cookies

Preparation time: 5 minutes
cooking time: 15 minutes
servings: about 2 dozen cookies

Ingredients

- 1/2 cup vegan margarine
- 1 cup sugar
- 1/4 cup apple juice
- 1 cup whole-grain flour
- 1 teaspoon baking powder
- 1/2 teaspoon salt
- 1 teaspoon pure vanilla extract
- 1 cup old-fashioned oats
- 1/2 cup vegan semisweet chocolate chips
- 1/2 cup sweetened dried cranberries

Directions

1. Preheat the oven to 375°F. In a large bowl, cream together the margarine and the sugar until light and fluffy. Blend in the juice.
2. Add the flour, baking powder, salt, and vanilla, blending well. Stir in the oats, chocolate chips, and cranberries and mix well.
3. Drop the dough from a teaspoon onto an ungreased baking sheet. Bake until nicely browned, about 15 minutes. Cool the cookies slightly before transferring to a wire rack to cool completely. Store in an airtight container.

602. Cashew-Chocolate Truffles

Preparation time: 15 minutes
cooking time: 0 minutes • plus 1 hour to set
servings: 12 truffles

Ingredients

- 1 cup raw cashews, soaked in water overnight
- ¾ cup pitted dates
- 2 tablespoons coconut oil
- 1 cup unsweetened shredded coconut, divided
- 1 to 2 tablespoons cocoa powder, to taste

Directions

1. In a food processor, combine the cashews, dates, coconut oil, ½ cup of shredded coconut, and cocoa powder. Pulse until fully incorporated; it will resemble chunky cookie dough. Spread the remaining ½ cup of shredded coconut on a plate.
2. Form the mixture into tablespoon-size balls and roll on the plate to cover with the shredded coconut. Transfer to a parchment paper–lined plate or baking sheet. Repeat to make 12 truffles.
3. Place the truffles in the refrigerator for 1 hour to set. Transfer the truffles to a storage container or freezer-safe bag and seal.

Nutrition (1 truffle): Calories 238: Fat: 18g; Protein: 3g; Carbohydrates: 16g; Fiber: 4g; Sugar: 9g; Sodium: 9mg

603. Banana Chocolate Cupcakes

Preparation time: 20 minutes
cooking time: 20 minutes
servings: 12 cupcakes

Ingredients

- 3 medium bananas
- 1 cup non-dairy milk
- 2 tablespoons almond butter
- 1 teaspoon apple cider vinegar
- 1 teaspoon pure vanilla extract

- 1¼ cups whole-wheat flour
- ½ cup rolled oats
- ¼ cup coconut sugar (optional
- 1 teaspoon baking powder
- ½ teaspoon baking soda
- ½ cup unsweetened cocoa powder
- ¼ cup chia seeds, or sesame seeds
- Pinch sea salt
- ¼ cup dark chocolate chips, dried cranberries, or raisins (optional

Directions

1. Preheat the oven to 350°F. Lightly grease the cups of two 6-cup muffin tins or line with paper muffin cups.
2. Put the bananas, milk, almond butter, vinegar, and vanilla in a blender and purée until smooth. Or stir together in a large bowl until smooth and creamy.
3. Put the flour, oats, sugar (if using), baking powder, baking soda, cocoa powder, chia seeds, salt, and chocolate chips in another large bowl, and stir to combine. Mix together the wet and dry ingredients, stirring as little as possible. Spoon into muffin cups, and bake for 20 to 25 minutes. Take the cupcakes out of the oven and let them cool fully before taking out of the muffin tins, since they'll be very moist.

Nutrition (1 cupcakeCalories: 215; Total fat: 6g; Carbs: 39g; Fiber: 9g; Protein: 6g

604. Minty Fruit Salad

Preparation time: 15 minutes
cooking time: 5 minutes
servings: 4

Ingredients

- ¼ cup lemon juice (about 2 small lemons
- 4 teaspoons maple syrup or agave syrup
- 2 cups chopped pineapple
- 2 cups chopped strawberries
- 2 cups raspberries
- 1 cup blueberries
- 8 fresh mint leaves

Directions

1. Beginning with 1 mason jar, add the ingredients in this order:
2. 1 tablespoon of lemon juice, 1 teaspoon of maple syrup, ½ cup of pineapple, ½ cup of strawberries, ½ cup of raspberries, ¼ cup of blueberries, and 2 mint leaves.
3. Repeat to fill 3 more jars. Close the jars tightly with lids.
4. Place the airtight jars in the refrigerator for up to 3 days.

Nutrition: Calories: 138; Fat: 1g; Protein: 2g; Carbohydrates: 34g; Fiber: 8g; Sugar: 22g; Sodium: 6mg

605. Sesame Cookies

Preparation time: 15 minutes
cooking time: 0 minutes
servings: 3 dozen cookies

Ingredients

- ¾ cup vegan margarine, softened
- 1/2 cup light brown sugar
- 1 teaspoon pure vanilla extract
- 2 tablespoons pure maple syrup
- 1/4 teaspoon salt
- 2 cups whole-grain flour
- ¾ cup sesame seeds, lightly toasted

Directions

1. In a large bowl, cream together the margarine and sugar until light and fluffy. Blend in the vanilla, maple syrup, and salt. Stir in the flour and sesame seeds and mix well.
2. Roll the dough into a cylinder about 2 inches in diameter. Wrap it in plastic wrap and refrigerate for 1 hour or longer. Preheat the oven to 325°F.
3. Slice the cookie dough into 1/8-inch-thick rounds and arrange on an ungreased baking sheet about 2 inches apart. Bake until light brown, about 12 minutes. When completely cool, store in an airtight container.

606. Mango Coconut Cream Pie

Preparation time: 20 minutes • chill time: 30 minutes
servings: 8

Ingredients

For the crust

- ½ cup rolled oats

- 1 cup cashews
- 1 cup soft pitted dates
- For the filling
- 1 cup canned coconut milk
- ½ cup water
- 2 large mangos, peeled and chopped, or about 2 cups frozen chunks
- ½ cup unsweetened shredded coconut

Directions

1. Put all the crust ingredients in a food processor and pulse until it holds together. If you don't have a food processor, chop everything as finely as possible and use ½ cup cashew or almond butter in place of half the cashews. Press the mixture down firmly into an 8-inch pie or springform pan.
2. Put the all filling ingredients in a blender and purée until smooth (about 1 minute). It should be very thick, so you may have to stop and stir until it's smooth.
3. Pour the filling into the crust, use a rubber spatula to smooth the top, and put the pie in the freezer until set, about 30 minutes. Once frozen, it should be set out for about 15 minutes to soften before serving.
4. Top with a batch of Coconut Whipped Cream scooped on top of the pie once it's set. Finish it off with a sprinkling of toasted shredded coconut.

Nutrition (1 sliceCalories: 427; Total fat: 28g; Carbs: 45g; Fiber: 6g; Protein: 8g

607. Cherry-Vanilla Rice Pudding (Pressure cooker

Preparation time: 5 minutes
Servings: 4-6

Ingredients

- 1 cup short-grain brown rice
- 1¾ cups nondairy milk, plus more as needed
- 1½ cups water
- 4 tablespoons unrefined sugar or pure maple syrup (use 2 tablespoons if you use a sweetened milk), plus more as needed
- 1 teaspoon vanilla extract (use ½ teaspoon if you use vanilla milk
- Pinch salt
- ¼ cup dried cherries or ½ cup fresh or frozen pitted cherries

Directions

1. In your electric pressure cooker's cooking pot, combine the rice, milk, water, sugar, vanilla, and salt.
2. High pressure for 30 minutes. Close and lock the lid and ensure the pressure valve is sealed, then select High Pressure and set the time for 30 minutes.
3. Pressure Release. Once the cook time is complete, let the pressure release naturally, about 20 minutes. Once all the pressure has released, carefully unlock and remove the lid. Stir in the cherries and put the lid back on loosely for about 10 minutes. Serve, adding more milk or sugar, as desired.

Nutrition Calories: 177; Total fat: 1g; Protein: 3g; Sodium: 27mg; Fiber: 2g

608. Chocolate Coconut Brownies

Preparation time: 5 minutes
cooking time: 35 minutes
servings: 12 brownies

Ingredients

- 1 cup whole-grain flour
- 1/2 cup unsweetened cocoa powder
- 1 teaspoon baking powder
- 1/2 teaspoon salt
- 1 cup light brown sugar
- 1/2 cup canola oil
- ¾ cup unsweetened coconut milk
- 1 teaspoon pure vanilla extract
- 1 teaspoon coconut extract
- 1/2 cup vegan semisweet chocolate chips
- 1/2 cup sweetened shredded coconut

Directions

1. Preheat the oven to 350°F. Grease an 8-inch square baking pan and set aside. In a large bowl, combine the flour, cocoa, baking powder, and salt. Set aside.
2. In a medium bowl, mix together the sugar and oil until blended. Stir in the coconut milk
3. and the extracts and blend until smooth.

Add the wet Ingredients to the dry Ingredients, stirring to blend. Fold in the chocolate chips and coconut.

4. Scrape the batter into the prepared baking pan and bake until the center is set and a toothpick inserted in the center comes out clean, 35 to 40 minutes. Let the brownies cool 30 minutes before serving. Store in an airtight container.

609. Lime in the Coconut Chia Pudding

Preparation time: 10 minutes • chill time: 20 minutes
servings: 4

Ingredients

- Zest and juice of 1 lime
- 1 (14-ouncecan coconut milk
- 1 to 2 dates, or 1 tablespoon coconut or other unrefined sugar, or 1 tablespoon maple syrup, or 10 to 15 drops pure liquid stevia
- 2 tablespoons chia seeds, whole or ground
- 2 teaspoons matcha green tea powder (optional

Directions

1. Blend all the ingredients in a blender until smooth. Chill in the fridge for about 20 minutes, then serve topped with one or more of the topping ideas.
2. Try blueberries, blackberries, sliced strawberries, Coconut Whipped Cream, or toasted unsweetened coconut.

Nutrition Calories: 226; Total fat: 20g; Carbs: 13g; Fiber: 5g; Protein: 3g

610. Strawberry Parfaits With Cashew Crème

Preparation time: 10 minutes • chill time: 50 minutes •
servings: 4

Ingredients

- 1/2 cup unsalted raw cashews
- 4 tablespoons light brown sugar
- 1/2 cup plain or vanilla soy milk
- ¾ cup firm silken tofu, drained
- 1 teaspoon pure vanilla extract
- 2 cups sliced strawberries
- 1 teaspoon fresh lemon juice
- Fresh mint leaves, for garnish

Directions

1. In a blender, grind the cashews and 3 tablespoons of the sugar to a fine powder. Add the soy milk and blend until smooth. Add the tofu and vanilla and continue to blend until smooth and creamy. Scrape the cashew mixture into a medium bowl, cover, and refrigerate for 30 minutes.
2. In a large bowl, combine the strawberries, lemon juice, and remaining 1 tablespoon sugar. Stir gently to combine and set aside at room temperature for 20 minutes.
3. Spoon alternating layers of the strawberries and cashew crème into parfait glasses or wineglasses, ending with a dollop of the cashew crème. Garnish with mint leaves and serve.

611. Mint Chocolate Chip Sorbet

Preparation time: 5 minutes
cooking time: 0 minutes
servings: 1

Ingredients

- 1 frozen banana
- 1 tablespoon almond butter, or peanut butter, or other nut or seed butter
- 2 tablespoons fresh mint, minced
- ¼ cup or less non-dairy milk (only if needed
- 2 to 3 tablespoons non-dairy chocolate chips, or cocoa nibs
- 2 to 3 tablespoons goji berries (optional

Directions

1. Put the banana, almond butter, and mint in a food processor or blender and purée until smooth.
2. Add the non-dairy milk if needed to keep blending (but only if needed, as this will make the texture less solid). Pulse the chocolate chips and goji berries (if usinginto the mix so they're roughly chopped up.

Nutrition Calories: 212; Total fat: 10g; Carbs: 31g; Fiber: 4g; Protein: 3g

612. Peach-Mango Crumble (Pressure

cooker

Preparation time: 10 minutes
Servings: 4-6

Ingredients

- 3 cups chopped fresh or frozen peaches
- 3 cups chopped fresh or frozen mangos
- 4 tablespoons unrefined sugar or pure maple syrup, divided
- 1 cup gluten-free rolled oats
- ½ cup shredded coconut, sweetened or unsweetened
- 2 tablespoons coconut oil or vegan margarine

Directions

1. In a 6- to 7-inch round baking dish, toss together the peaches, mangos, and 2 tablespoons of sugar. In a food processor, combine the oats, coconut, coconut oil, and remaining 2 tablespoons of sugar. Pulse until combined. (If you use maple syrup, you'll need less coconut oil. Start with just the syrup and add oil if the mixture isn't sticking together.Sprinkle the oat mixture over the fruit mixture.
2. Cover the dish with aluminum foil. Put a trivet in the bottom of your electric pressure cooker's cooking pot and pour in a cup or two of water. Using a foil sling or silicone helper handles, lower the pan onto the trivet.
3. High pressure for 6 minutes. Close and lock the lid and ensure the pressure valve is sealed, then select High Pressure and set the time for 6 minutes.
4. Pressure Release. Once the cook time is complete, quick release the pressure, being careful not to get your fingers or face near the steam release. Once all the pressure has released, carefully unlock and remove the lid.
5. Let cool for a few minutes before carefully lifting out the dish with oven mitts or tongs. Scoop out portions to serve.

NUTRITION Calories: 321; Total fat: 18g; Protein: 4g; Sodium: 2mg; Fiber: 7g

613. Ginger-Spice Brownies

Preparation time: 5 minutes
cooking time: 35 minutes
servings: 12 brownies

Ingredients

- 1¾ cups whole-grain flour
- 1 teaspoon baking powder
- 1 teaspoon baking soda
- 1/2 teaspoon salt
- 1 tablespoon ground ginger
- 1/2 teaspoon ground cinnamon
- 1/2 teaspoon ground allspice
- 3 tablespoons unsweetened cocoa powder
- 1/2 cup vegan semisweet chocolate chips
- 1/2 cup chopped walnuts
- 1/4 cup canola oil
- 1/2 cup dark molasses
- 1/2 cup water
- 1/3 cup light brown sugar
- 2 teaspoons grated fresh ginger

Directions

1. Preheat the oven to 350°F. Grease an 8-inch square baking pan and set aside. In a large bowl, combine the flour, baking powder, baking soda, salt, ground ginger, cinnamon, allspice, and cocoa. Stir in the chocolate chips and walnuts and set aside.
2. In medium bowl, combine the oil, molasses, water, sugar, and fresh ginger and mix well.
3. Pour the wet Ingredients into the dry Ingredients and mix well.
4. Scrape the dough into the prepared baking pan. The dough will be sticky, so wet your hands to press it evenly into the pan. Bake until a toothpick inserted in the center comes out clean, 30 to 35 minutes. Cool on a wire rack 30 minutes before cutting. Store in an airtight container.

614. Zesty Orange-Cranberry Energy Bites

Preparation time: 10 minutes • chill time: 15 minutes
servings: 12 bites

Ingredients

- 2 tablespoons almond butter, or cashew or sunflower seed butter

- 2 tablespoons maple syrup, or brown rice syrup
- ¾ cup cooked quinoa
- ¼ cup sesame seeds, toasted
- 1 tablespoon chia seeds
- ½ teaspoon almond extract, or vanilla extract
- Zest of 1 orange
- 1 tablespoon dried cranberries
- ¼ cup ground almonds

Directions

1. In a medium bowl, mix together the nut or seed butter and syrup until smooth and creamy. Stir in the rest of the ingredients, and mix to make sure the consistency is holding together in a ball. Form the mix into 12 balls.
2. Place them on a baking sheet lined with parchment or waxed paper and put in the fridge to set for about 15 minutes.
3. If your balls aren't holding together, it's likely because of the moisture content of your cooked quinoa. Add more nut or seed butter mixed with syrup until it all sticks together.

Nutrition (1 biteCalories: 109; Total fat: 7g; Carbs: 11g; Fiber: 3g; Protein: 3g

615. Chocolate And Walnut Farfalle

Preparation time: 10 minutes
cooking time: 0 minutes
servings: 4

Ingredients

- 1/2 cup chopped toasted walnuts
- 1/4 cup vegan semisweet chocolate pieces
- 8 ounces farfalle
- 3 tablespoons vegan margarine
- 1/4 cup ight brown sugar

Directions

1. In a food processor or blender, grind the walnuts and chocolate pieces until crumbly. Do not overprocess. Set aside.
2. In a pot of boiling salted water, cook the farfalle, stirring occasionally, until al dente, about 8 minutes. Drain well and return to the pot.
3. Add the margarine and sugar and toss to combine and melt the margarine.
4. Transfer the noodle mixture to a serving

Almond-Date Energy Bites

Preparation time: 5 minutes • chill time: 15 minutes
servings: 24 bites

Ingredients

- 1 cup dates, pitted
- 1 cup unsweetened shredded coconut
- ¼ cup chia seeds
- ¾ cup ground almonds
- ¼ cup cocoa nibs, or non-dairy chocolate chips

Directions

1. Purée everything in a food processor until crumbly and sticking together, pushing down the sides whenever necessary to keep it blending. If you don't have a food processor, you can mash soft Medjool dates. But if you're using harder baking dates, you'll have to soak them and then try to purée them in a blender.
2. Form the mix into 24 balls and place them on a baking sheet lined with parchment or waxed paper. Put in the fridge to set for about 15 minutes. Use the softest dates you can find. Medjool dates are the best for this purpose. The hard dates you see in the baking aisle of your supermarket are going to take a long time to blend up. If you use those, try soaking them in water for at least an hour before you start, and then draining.

Nutrition (1 biteCalories: 152; Total fat: 11g; Carbs: 13g; Fiber: 5g; Protein: 3g

616. Pumpkin Pie Cups (Pressure cooker

Preparation time: 5 minutes
Servings: 4-6

Ingredients

- 1 cup canned pumpkin purée
- 1 cup nondairy milk
- 6 tablespoons unrefined sugar or pure maple syrup (less if using sweetened milk), plus more for sprinkling
- ¼ cup spelt flour or all-purpose flour
- ½ teaspoon pumpkin pie spice

- Pinch salt

Directions

1. In a medium bowl, stir together the pumpkin, milk, sugar, flour, pumpkin pie spice, and salt. Pour the mixture into 4 heat-proof ramekins. Sprinkle a bit more sugar on the top of each, if you like. Put a trivet in the bottom of your electric pressure cooker's cooking pot and pour in a cup or two of water. Place the ramekins onto the trivet, stacking them if needed (3 on the bottom, 1 on top).
2. High pressure for 6 minutes. Close and lock the lid and ensure the pressure valve is sealed, then select High Pressure and set the time for 6 minutes.
3. Pressure Release. Once the cook time is complete, quick release the pressure, being careful not to get your fingers or face near the steam release. Once all the pressure has released, carefully unlock and remove the lid. Let cool for a few minutes before carefully lifting out the ramekins with oven mitts or tongs. Let cool for at least 10 minutes before serving.

Nutrition Calories: 129; Total fat: 1g; Protein: 3g; Sodium: 39mg; Fiber: 3g

617. Coconut and Almond Truffles

Preparation time: 15 minutes
cooking time: 0 minutes
servings: 8 truffles

Ingredients

- 1 cup pitted dates
- 1 cup almonds
- ½ cup sweetened cocoa powder, plus extra for coating
- ½ cup unsweetened shredded coconut
- ¼ cup pure maple syrup
- 1 teaspoon vanilla extract
- 1 teaspoon almond extract
- ¼ teaspoon sea salt

Directions

1. In the bowl of a food processor, combine all the ingredients and process until smooth. Chill the mixture for about 1 hour.
2. Roll the mixture into balls and then roll the balls in cocoa powder to coat.
3. Serve immediately or keep chilled until ready to serve.

618. Pecan and Date-Stuffed Roasted Pears

Preparation time: 10 minutes
cooking time: 30 minutes
servings: 4

Ingredients

- 4 firm ripe pears, cored
- 1 tablespoon fresh lemon juice
- 1/2 cup finely chopped pecans
- 4 dates, pitted and chopped
- 1 tablespoon vegan margarine
- 1 tablespoon pure maple syrup
- 1/4 teaspoon ground cinnamon
- 1/8 teaspoon ground ginger
- 1/2 cup pear, white grape, or apple juice

Directions

1. Preheat the oven to 350°F. Grease a shallow baking dish and set aside. Halve the pears lengthwise and use a melon baller to scoop out the cores. Rub the exposed part of the pears with the lemon juice to avoid discoloration.
2. In a medium bowl, combine the pecans, dates, margarine, maple syrup, cinnamon, and ginger and mix well.
3. Stuff the mixture into the centers of the pear halves and arrange them in the prepared baking pan. Pour the juice over the pears. Bake until tender, 30 to 40 minutes. Serve warm.

619. Almond Balls

Preparation time: 10 minutes
Cooking time: 0 minutes
Servings: 6

Ingredients:

- ½ cup coconut oil, melted
- 5 tablespoons almonds, chopped
- 1 tablespoon stevia
- ¼ cup coconut flesh, unsweetened and shredded

Directions:

1. In a bowl, combine the coconut oil with

the almonds and the other ingredients, stir well and spoon into round moulds.
2. Serve them cold.

Nutrition: calories 194, fat 21.2, fiber 0.7, carbs 1, protein 1.4

620. Grapefruit Cream

Preparation time: 10 minutes
Cooking time: 0 minutes
Servings: 4

Ingredients:

- 2 cups coconut cream
- 1 cup grapefruit, peeled, and chopped
- 2 tablespoons stevia
- 1 teaspoon vanilla extract

Directions:

1. In a blender, combine the coconut cream with the grapefruit and the other ingredients, pulse well, divide into bowls and serve cold.

Nutrition: calories 346, fat 35.5, fiber 0, carbs 3.4, protein 4.6

621. Tangerine Stew

Preparation time: 10 minutes
Cooking time: 10 minutes
Servings: 4

Ingredients:

- 1 cup coconut water
- 2 cups tangerines, peeled and cut into segments
- 1 tablespoon lime juice
- 1 tablespoon stevia
- ½ teaspoon vanilla extract

Directions:

1. In a pan, combine the coconut water with the tangerines and the other ingredients, toss, bring to a simmer and cook over medium heat for 10 minutes.
2. Divide into bowls and serve cold.

Nutrition: calories 289, fat 26.1, fiber 3.9, carbs 10.3, protein 5.7

622. Creamy Pineapple Mix

Preparation time: 10 minutes
Cooking time: 10 minutes
Servings: 4

Ingredients:

- 1 teaspoon nutmeg, ground
- 1 cup pineapple, peeled and cubed
- 1 cup coconut cream
- ½ cup stevia
- 1 teaspoon vanilla extract

Directions:

1. In a pan, combine the pineapple with the nutmeg and the other ingredients, toss, cook over medium heat for 10 minutes, divide into bowls and serve.

Nutrition: calories 329, fat 32.7, fiber 0, carbs 2.5, protein 5.7

623. Avocado and Pineapple Bowls

Preparation time: 10 minutes
Cooking time: 0 minutes
Servings: 4

Ingredients:

- 2 tablespoons avocado oil
- 1 cup pineapple, peeled and cubed
- 2 avocados, peeled, pitted and cubed
- 2 tablespoons stevia
- Juice of 1 lime

Directions:

1. In a bowl, combine the pineapple with the avocados and the other ingredients, toss, and serve cold.

Nutrition: calories 312, fat 29.5, fiber 3.3, carbs 16.7, protein 5

624. Pineapple and Melon Stew

Preparation time: 10 minutes
Cooking time: 15 minutes
Servings: 4

Ingredients:

- 2 tablespoons stevia
- 1 cup pineapple, peeled and cubed
- 1 cup melon, peeled and cubed
- 2 cups water
- 1 teaspoon vanilla extract

Directions:

1. In a pan, combine the pineapple with the melon and the other ingredients, toss gently, cook over medium-low heat for 15 minutes, divide into bowls and serve cold.

Nutrition: calories 40, fat 4.3, fiber 2.3, carbs 3.4, protein 0.8

625. Cocoa Muffins

Preparation time: 10 minutes
Cooking time: 25 minutes
Servings: 6

Ingredients:

- ½ cup coconut oil, melted
- 3 tablespoons stevia
- 1 cup almond flour
- ¼ cup cocoa powder
- 3 tablespoons flaxseed mixed with 4 tablespoons water
- ¼ teaspoon vanilla extract
- 1 teaspoon baking powder
- Cooking spray

Directions:

1. In bowl, combine the coconut oil with the stevia, the flour and the other ingredients except the cooking spray and whisk well.
2. Grease a muffin pan with the cooking spray, divide the muffin mix in each mould, bake at 370 degrees F for 25 minutes, cool down and serve.

Nutrition: calories 344, fat 35.1, fiber 3.4, carbs 8.3, protein 4.5

626. Melon Coconut Mousse

Preparation time: 10 minutes
Cooking time: 0 minutes
Servings: 6

Ingredients:

- 2 cups coconut cream
- 1 teaspoon vanilla extract
- 1 tablespoon stevia
- 1 cup melon, peeled and chopped

Directions:

1. In a blender, combine the melon with the cream and the other ingredients, pulse well, divide into bowls and serve cold.

Nutrition: calories 219, fat 21.1, fiber 0.9, carbs 7, protein 1.4

627. Chia and Strawberries Mix

Preparation time: 10 minutes
Cooking time: 0 minutes
Servings: 4

Ingredients:

- 1 cup strawberries, halved
- 2 tablespoons chia seeds
- ¼ cup coconut milk
- 1 tablespoon stevia

Directions:

1. In a bowl, combine the berries with the chia seeds, the milk and stevia and whisk well.
2. Divide the mix into bowls and serve cold.

Nutrition: calories 265, fat 6.3, fiber 2, carbs 4, protein 6

628. Watermelon Mousse

Preparation time: 10 minutes
Cooking time: 0 minutes
Servings: 4

Ingredients:

- 1 cup coconut cream
- 1 tablespoon lemon juice
- 1 tablespoon stevia
- 2 cups watermelon, peeled and cubed

Directions:

1. In a blender, combine the watermelon with the cream, the lemon juice and stevia, pulse well, divide into bowls and serve cold.

Nutrition: calories 332, fat 31.4, fiber 0.5, carbs 9.2, protein 5.5

629. Fruit Salad

Preparation time: 2 hours
Cooking time: 0 minutes
Servings: 4

Ingredients:

- 2 avocados, peeled, pitted and cubed
- ½ cup blackberries
- ½ cup strawberries, halved
- ½ cup pineapple, peeled and cubed
- ¼ teaspoon vanilla extract
- 2 tablespoons stevia
- Juice of 1 lime

Directions:

1. In a bowl, combine the avocados with the

berries and the other ingredients, toss and keep in the fridge for 2 hours before serving.

Nutrition: calories 243, fat 22, fiber 0, carbs 6.2, protein 4

630. Chia Bars

Preparation time: 10 minutes
Cooking time: 20 minutes
Servings: 6

Ingredients:

- 1 cup coconut oil, melted
- ½ teaspoon baking soda
- 3 tablespoons chia seeds
- 2 tablespoons stevia
- 1 cup coconut cream
- 3 tablespoons flaxseed mixed with 4 tablespoons water

Directions:

1. In a bowl, combine the coconut oil with the cream, the chia seeds and the other ingredients, whisk well, pour everything into a square baking dish, introduce in the oven at 370 degrees F and bake for 20 minutes.
2. Cool down, slice into squares and serve.

Nutrition: calories 220, fat 2, fiber 0.5, carbs 2, protein 4

631. Fruits Stew

Preparation time: 10 minutes
Cooking time: 10 minutes
Servings: 4

Ingredients:

- 1 avocado, peeled, pitted and sliced
- 1 cup plums, stoned and halved
- 2 cups water
- 2 teaspoons vanilla extract
- 1 tablespoon lemon juice
- 2 tablespoons stevia

Directions:

1. In a pan, combine the avocado with the plums, water and the other ingredients, bring to a simmer and cook over medium heat for 10 minutes.
2. Divide the mix into bowls and serve cold.

Nutrition: calories 178, fat 4.4, fiber 2, carbs 3, protein 5

632. Avocado and Rhubarb Salad

Preparation time: 10 minutes
Cooking time: 0 minutes
Servings: 4

Ingredients:

- 1 tablespoon stevia
- 1 cup rhubarb, sliced and boiled
- 2 avocados, peeled, pitted and sliced
- 1 teaspoon vanilla extract
- Juice of 1 lime

Directions:

1. In a bowl, combine the rhubarb with the avocado and the other ingredients, toss and serve.

Nutrition: calories 140, fat 2, fiber 2, carbs 4, protein 4

633. Plums and Nuts Bowls

Preparation time: 5 minutes
Cooking time: 0 minutes
Servings: 2

Ingredients:

- 2 tablespoons stevia
- 1 cup walnuts, chopped
- 1 cup plums, pitted and halved
- 1 teaspoon vanilla extract

Directions:

1. In a bowl, mix the plums with the walnuts and the other ingredients, toss, divide into 2 bowls and serve cold.

Nutrition: calories 400, fat 23, fiber 4, carbs 6, protein 7

634. Avocado and Strawberries Salad

Preparation time: 5 minutes
Cooking time: 0 minutes
Servings: 4

Ingredients:

- 2 avocados, pitted, peeled and cubed
- 1 cup strawberries, halved
- Juice of 1 lime
- 1 teaspoon almond extract
- 2 tablespoons almonds, chopped
- 1 tablespoon stevia

Directions:

In a bowl, combine the avocados with the strawberries, and the other ingredients, toss and serve.

Nutrition: calories 150, fat 3, fiber 3, carbs 5, protein 6

635. Chocolate Watermelon Cups

Preparation time: 2 hours
Cooking time: 0 minutes
Servings: 4

Ingredients:

- 2 cups watermelon, peeled and cubed
- 1 tablespoon stevia
- 1 cup coconut cream
- 1 tablespoon cocoa powder
- 1 tablespoon mint, chopped

Directions:

1. In a blender, combine the watermelon with the stevia and the other ingredients, pulse well, divide into cups and keep in the fridge for 2 hours before serving.

Nutrition: calories 164, fat 14.6, fiber 2.1, carbs 9.9, protein 2.1

636. Vanilla Raspberries Mix

Preparation time: 10 minutes
Cooking time: 10 minutes
Servings: 4

Ingredients:

- 1 cup water
- 1 cup raspberries
- 3 tablespoons stevia
- 1 teaspoon nutmeg, ground
- ½ teaspoon vanilla extract

Directions:

1. In a pan, combine the raspberries with the water and the other ingredients, toss, cook over medium heat for 10 minutes, divide into bowls and serve.

Nutrition: calories 20, fat 0.4, fiber 2.1, carbs 4, protein 0.4

637. Ginger Cream

Preparation time: 10 minutes
Cooking time: 10 minutes
Servings: 4

Ingredients:

- 2 tablespoons stevia
- 2 cups coconut cream
- 1 teaspoon vanilla extract
- 1 tablespoon cinnamon powder
- ¼ tablespoon ginger, grated

Directions:

1. In a pan, combine the cream with the stevia and other ingredients, stir, cook over medium heat for 10 minutes, divide into bowls and serve cold.

Nutrition: calories 280, fat 28.6, fiber 2.7, carbs 7, protein 2.8

638. Chocolate Ginger Cookies

Preparation time: 10 minutes
Cooking time: 20 minutes
Servings: 6

Ingredients:

- 2 cups almonds, chopped
- 2 tablespoons flaxseed mixed with 3 tablespoons water
- ¼ cup avocado oil
- 2 tablespoons stevia
- ¼ cup cocoa powder
- 1 teaspoon baking soda

Directions:

1. In your food processor, combine the almonds with the flaxseed mix and the other ingredients, pulse well, scoop tablespoons out of this mix, arrange them on a lined baking sheet, flatten them a bit and cook at 360 degrees F for 20 minutes.
2. Serve the cookies cold.

Nutrition: calories 252, fat 41.6, fiber 6.5, carbs 11.7, protein 3

639. Coconut Salad

Preparation time: 10 minutes
Cooking time: 0 minutes
Servings: 6

Ingredients:

- 2 cups coconut flesh, unsweetened and shredded
- ½ cup walnuts, chopped
- 1 cup blackberries

- 1 tablespoon stevia
- 1 tablespoon coconut oil, melted

Directions:

In a bowl, combine the coconut with the walnuts and the other ingredients, toss and serve.

Nutrition: calories 250, fat 23.8, fiber 5.8, carbs 8.9, protein 4.5

640. Mint Cookies

Preparation time: 10 minutes
Cooking time: 20 minutes
Servings: 6

Ingredients:

- 2 cups coconut flour
- 3 tablespoons flaxseed mixed with 4 tablespoons water
- ½ cup coconut cream
- ½ cup coconut oil, melted
- 3 tablespoons stevia
- 2 teaspoons mint, dried
- 2 teaspoons baking soda

Directions:

1. In a bowl, mix the coconut flour with the flaxseed, coconut cream and the other ingredients, and whisk really well.
2. Shape balls out of this mix, place them on a lined baking sheet, flatten them, introduce in the oven at 370 degrees F and bake for 20 minutes.
3. Serve the cookies cold.

Nutrition: calories 190, fat 7.32, fiber 2.2, carbs 4, protein 3

641. Mint Avocado Bars

Preparation time: 10 minutes
Cooking time: 25 minutes
Servings: 6

Ingredients:

- 1 teaspoon almond extract
- ½ cup coconut oil, melted
- 2 tablespoons stevia
- 1 avocado, peeled, pitted and mashed
- 2 cups coconut flour
- 1 tablespoon cocoa powder

Directions:

1. In a bowl, combine the coconut oil with the almond extract, stevia and the other ingredients and whisk well.
2. Transfer this to baking pan, spread evenly, introduce in the oven and cook at 370 degrees F and bake for 25 minutes.
3. Cool down, cut into bars and serve.

Nutrition: calories 230, fat 12.2, fiber 4.2, carbs 15.4, protein 5.8

642. Coconut Chocolate Cake

Preparation time: 10 minutes
Cooking time: 30 minutes
Servings: 12

Ingredients:

- 4 tablespoons flaxseed mixed with 5 tablespoons water
- 1 cup coconut flesh, unsweetened and shredded
- 1 teaspoon vanilla extract
- 2 tablespoons cocoa powder
- 1 teaspoon baking soda
- 2 cups almond flour
- 4 tablespoons stevia
- 2 tablespoons lime zest
- 2 cups coconut cream

Directions:

1. In a bowl, combine the flaxmeal with the coconut, the vanilla and the other ingredients, whisk well and transfer to a cake pan.
2. Cook the cake at 360 degree F for 30 minutes, cool down and serve.

Nutrition: calories 268, fat 23.9, fiber 5.1, carbs 9.4, protein 6.1

643. Mint Chocolate Cream

Preparation time: 10 minutes
Cooking time: 0 minutes
Servings: 6

Ingredients:

- 1 cup coconut oil, melted
- 4 tablespoons cocoa powder
- 1 teaspoon vanilla extract
- 1 cup mint, chopped
- 2 cups coconut cream
- 4 tablespoons stevia

Directions:

1. In your food processor, combine the coconut oil with the cocoa powder, the cream and the other ingredients, pulse well, divide into bowls and serve really cold.

Nutrition: calories 514, fat 56, fiber 3.9, carbs 7.8, protein 3

644. Cranberries Cake

Preparation time: 10 minutes
Cooking time: 30 minutes
Servings: 6

Ingredients:

- 2 cups coconut flour
- 2 tablespoon coconut oil, melted
- 3 tablespoons stevia
- 1 tablespoon cocoa powder, unsweetened
- 2 tablespoons flaxseed mixed with 3 tablespoons water
- 1 cup cranberries
- 1 cup coconut cream
- ¼ teaspoon vanilla extract
- ½ teaspoon baking powder

Directions:

1. In a bowl, combine the coconut flour with the coconut oil, the stevia and the other ingredients, and whisk well.
2. Pour this into a cake pan lined with parchment paper, introduce in the oven and cook at 360 degrees F for 30 minutes.
3. Cool down, slice and serve.

Nutrition: calories 244, fat 16.7, fiber 11.8, carbs 21.3, protein 4.4

645. Sweet Zucchini Buns

Preparation time: 10 minutes
Cooking time: 30 minutes
Servings: 8

Ingredients:

- 1 cup almond flour
- 1/3 cup coconut flesh, unsweetened and shredded
- 1 cup zucchinis, grated
- 2 tablespoons stevia
- 1 teaspoon baking soda
- ½ teaspoon cinnamon powder
- 3 tablespoons flaxseed mixed with 4 tablespoons water
- 1 cup coconut cream

Directions:

1. In a bowl, mix the almond flour with the coconut flesh, the zucchinis and the other ingredients, stir well until you obtain a dough, shape 8 buns and arrange them on a baking sheet lined with parchment paper.
2. Introduce in the oven at 350 degrees and bake for 30 minutes.
3. Serve these sweet buns warm.

Nutrition: calories 169, fat 15.3, fiber 3.9, carbs 6.4, protein 3.2

646. Lime Custard

Preparation time: 10 minutes
Cooking time: 20 minutes
Servings: 6

Ingredients:

- 1 pint almond milk
- 4 tablespoons lime zest, grated
- 3 tablespoons lime juice
- 3 tablespoons flaxseed mixed with 4 tablespoons water
- tablespoons stevia
- 2 teaspoons vanilla extract

Directions:

1. In a bowl, combine the almond milk with the lime zest, lime juice and the other ingredients, whisk well and divide into 4 ramekins.
2. Bake in the oven at 360 degrees F for 30 minutes.
3. Cool the custard down and serve.

Nutrition: calories 234, fat 21.6, fiber 4.3, carbs 9, protein 3.5

647. Warm Rum Butter Spiced Cider

Preparation Time: 15 Minutes
Servings: 4

Ingredients:

- 3/4 cup rum
- 4 cups apple cider
- 2 cinnamon sticks
- 4 cardamom pods
- 1/4 teaspoon ground allspice

- 4 whole cloves
- 1 teaspoon lime juice
- 4 teaspoons nondairy butter

Directions:

1. Combine all the ingredients in the instant pot. Seal the lid and cook on high 5 minutes. Let the pressure release naturally.

648. Peppermint Patty Cocoa

Preparation Time: 15 Minutes
Servings: 4

Ingredients:

- 4 cups almond milk
- 3 ounces semisweet chocolate chips
- 1 teaspoon cocoa powder
- 1 teaspoon vanilla extract
- 1/4 cup sugar
- 1 tablespoon agave nectar
- 1 teaspoon peppermint extract

Directions:

1. Combine all the ingredients in the instant pot. Seal the lid and cook on high 4 minutes, then let the pressure release naturally.
2. Serve garnished with a sprig of mint or topped with vegan marshmallows!

649. Apple & Walnut Cake.

Preparation Time: 20 Minutes
Servings: 6

Ingredients:

- 1¾ cups unbleached all-purpose flour
- 1 cup unsweetened applesauce
- ⅔ cup packed light brown sugar
- ½ cup chopped walnuts
- ¼ cup vegetable oil
- 1 tablespoon freshly squeezed lemon juice
- 1 teaspoon pure vanilla extract
- 1½ teaspoons ground cinnamon
- 1 teaspoon baking powder
- ½ teaspoon baking soda
- ½ teaspoon salt
- ¼ teaspoon ground allspice
- ¼ teaspoon ground nutmeg
- ⅛ teaspoon ground cloves

Directions:

1. Lightly oil a baking tray that will fit in the steamer basket of your Instant Pot.
2. In a bowl, combine the flour, baking powder, baking soda, sugar, cinnamon, allspice, nutmeg, cloves, and salt.
3. In another bowl combine the applesauce, oil, vanilla, and lemon juice.
4. Stir the wet mixture into the dry mixture slowly until they form a smooth mix.
5. Fold in the walnuts.
6. Pour the batter into your baking tray and put the tray in your steamer basket.
7. Pour the minimum amount of water into the base of your Instant Pot and lower the steamer basket.
8. Seal and cook on Steam for 12 minutes.
9. Release the pressure quickly and set to one side to cool a little.

650. Fat Free Apple Cake.

Preparation Time: 20 Minutes
Servings: 8

Ingredients:

- 2 granny smith apples, peeled, cored, and diced
- 1¾ cups unbleached all-purpose flour
- ⅔ cup packed light brown sugar
- ½ cup applesauce
- 1 tablespoon freshly squeezed lemon juice
- 1½ teaspoons ground cinnamon
- 1 teaspoon pure vanilla extract
- 1 teaspoon baking powder
- ½ teaspoon baking soda
- ½ teaspoon salt
- ¼ teaspoon ground allspice
- ¼ teaspoon ground nutmeg
- ⅛ teaspoon ground cloves

Directions:

1. Lightly oil a baking tray that will fit in the steamer basket of your Instant Pot.
2. In a bowl, combine the flour, baking powder, baking soda, sugar, cinnamon, allspice, nutmeg, cloves, and salt.
3. In another bowl combine the applesauce, vanilla, and lemon juice.
4. Fold in the diced apples.

5. Stir the wet mixture into the dry mixture slowly until they form a smooth mix.
6. Pour the batter into your baking tray and put the tray in your steamer basket.
7. Pour the minimum amount of water into the base of your Instant Pot and lower the steamer basket.
8. Seal and cook on Steam for 12 minutes.
9. Release the pressure quickly and set to one side to cool a little.

651. Pina-Colada Cake.

Preparation Time: 20 Minutes
Servings: 6

Ingredients:

- 2 cups unbleached all-purpose flour
- 1 cup cream of coconut
- 1 cup confectioners' sugar
- ¾ cup canned pineapple, well drained, juice reserved
- ⅓ cup packed light brown sugar or granulated natural sugar
- ¼ cup unsweetened shredded coconut
- 3 tablespoons vegan butter, softened, or vegetable oil
- 1 tablespoon dark rum or 1 teaspoon rum extract
- 1½ teaspoons baking powder
- 1 teaspoon apple cider vinegar
- ½ teaspoon salt
- ½ teaspoon baking soda
- ½ teaspoon coconut extract

Directions:

1. Lightly oil a baking tray that will fit in the steamer basket of your Instant Pot.
2. In a bowl combine the flour, sugar, shredded coconut, baking soda, baking powder, and salt.
3. In another bowl combine the cream of coconut, pineapple juice and flesh, rum, vinegar, and coconut extract.
4. Combine the wet and dry mixes and stir well to ensure they are evenly combined.
5. Pour the batter into your baking tray and put the tray in your steamer basket.
6. Pour the minimum amount of water into the base of your Instant Pot and lower the steamer basket.
7. Seal and cook on Steam for 12 minutes.
8. Release the pressure quickly and set to one side to cool a little.
9. When the cake is cool glaze with a light mix of confectioners' sugar and water.

652. Pumpkin Spice Cake.

Preparation Time: 28 Minutes
Servings: 6

Ingredients:

- 1¾ cups unbleached all-purpose flour
- 1 cup canned solid-pack pumpkin
- ¾ cup packed light brown sugar or granulated natural sugar
- ½ cup chopped pecans
- ¼ cup unsweetened almond milk
- ¼ cup vegetable oil
- 1½ teaspoons baking powder
- 1 teaspoon ground cinnamon
- 1 teaspoon pure vanilla extract
- ½ teaspoon salt
- ½ teaspoon ground nutmeg
- ½ teaspoon ground allspice
- ¼ teaspoon ground cloves

Directions:

1. Lightly oil a baking tray that will fit in the steamer basket of your Instant Pot.
2. In a bowl combine the flour, baking powder, cinnamon, nutmeg, allspice, cloves, sugar, and salt.
3. In another bowl combine the pumpkin, oil, almond milk, and vanilla.
4. Mix the wet and dry mixtures together until the mix is evenly smooth.
5. Fold in the pecans.
6. Pour the batter into your baking tray and put the tray in your steamer basket.
7. Pour the minimum amount of water into the base of your Instant Pot and lower the steamer basket.
8. Seal and cook on Steam for 12 minutes.
9. Release the pressure quickly and set to one side to cool a little.

653. Fudgy Chocolate Cake.

Preparation Time: 20 Minutes
Servings: 8

Ingredients:

Cake:

- 1½ cups unbleached all-purpose flour
- 1 cup non-dairy milk
- 2/3 cup granulated natural sugar
- ¼ cup unsweetened cocoa powder
- 3 tablespoons vegan butter, softened
- 1½ teaspoons baking powder
- 1 teaspoon pure vanilla extract
- ½ teaspoon cider vinegar
- ¼ teaspoon salt
- ¼ teaspoon baking soda

Frosting:

- 1½ cups confectioners' sugar, plus more if needed
- ¼ cup unsweetened cocoa powder
- 2 tablespoons vegan butter, melted
- 3 tablespoons non-dairy milk, plus more if needed
- 1 teaspoon pure vanilla extract

Directions:

1. Lightly oil a baking tray that will fit in the steamer basket of your Instant Pot.
2. In a bowl combine the flour, cocoa powder, baking soda, baking powder, and salt.
3. Whisk the vegan butter and granulated sugar until they form a creamy blend.
4. Add the milk, vinegar, and vanilla.
5. Add the flour mixture and stir until evenly mixed.
6. Pour the batter into your baking tray and put the tray in your steamer basket.
7. Pour the minimum amount of water into the base of your Instant Pot and lower the steamer basket.
8. Seal and cook on Steam for 12 minutes.
9. Release the pressure quickly and set to one side to cool a little.
10. For the frosting, stir the cocoa into the melted butter until smoothly blended.
11. Add the milk and vanilla and mix well again.
12. Stir in the sugar until you have an almost pourable frosting.
13. Refrigerate until it's time to frost your cake.

654. Carrot & Pineapple Cake.

Preparation Time: 20 Minutes
Servings: 6

Ingredients:

- 1½ cups unbleached all-purpose flour
- 2 carrots, peeled and finely shredded (1 cup packed
- ¾ cup packed light brown sugar or granulated natural sugar
- ½ cup pineapple juice from the chopped pineapple
- ½ cup chopped macadamia nuts
- ⅓ cup canned pineapple, well drained, juice reserved
- ¼ cup vegetable oil
- 1½ teaspoons baking powder
- 1 teaspoon ground cinnamon
- ½ teaspoon salt
- ¼ teaspoon ground nutmeg

Directions:

1. Lightly oil a baking tray that will fit in the steamer basket of your Instant Pot.
2. In a bowl combine the flour, sugar, baking powder, cinnamon, nutmeg, and salt.
3. In another bowl combine the carrot, pineapple, pineapple juice, and oil.
4. Combine the wet and dry mix until a batter forms.
5. Fold in the macadamias.
6. Pour the batter into your baking tray and put the tray in your steamer basket.
7. Pour the minimum amount of water into the base of your Instant Pot and lower the steamer basket.
8. Seal and cook on Steam for 12 minutes.
9. Release the pressure quickly and set to one side to cool a little.

655. Cream Cheese Frosting.

Preparation Time: 5 Minutes
Servings: 2.5 cups

Ingredients:

- 1½ cups confectioners' sugar
- 1 cup vegan cream cheese at room temperature
- ½ cup vegan butter, at room temperature
- 1 teaspoon pure vanilla extract

Directions:

1. Combine all the ingredients until smoothly blended.

656. Orange Polenta Cake.

Preparation Time: 30 Minutes
Servings: 6

Ingredients:

- 1¼ cups all-purpose flour
- 1 cup unsweetened almond milk
- 2/3 cup plus 1 tablespoon natural sugar
- ⅓ cup fine-ground cornmeal
- ⅓ cup plus 2 tablespoons marmalade
- ¼ cup finely ground almonds
- ¼ cup vegan butter, softened
- 1 navel orange, peeled and sliced into ⅛-inch-thick rounds
- 1½ teaspoons baking powder
- 1 teaspoon pure vanilla extract
- ¾ teaspoon salt

Directions:

1. Lightly oil a baking tray that will fit in the steamer basket of your Instant Pot.
2. Sprinkle a tablespoon of sugar over the base of the baking tray and top with the orange slices.
3. In a bowl combine the flour, cornmeal, baking powder, almonds, and salt.
4. In another bowl combine the remaining sugar, the butter, 1/3 cup of marmalade, and vanilla and mix well. Slowly stir in the almond milk.
5. Combine the wet and dry mixes into a smooth batter.
6. Pour the batter into your baking tray and put the tray in your steamer basket.
7. Pour the minimum amount of water into the base of your Instant Pot and lower the steamer basket.
8. Seal and cook on Steam for 12 minutes.
9. Release the pressure quickly and set to one side to cool a little.
10. Warm the remaining 2 tablespoons of marmalade and brush over the cake.

657. Peanut Butter & Chocolate Cheesecake.

Preparation Time: 30 Minutes
Servings: 8

Ingredients:

- 16 ounces vegan cream cheese
- 8 ounces silken tofu, drained
- 1½ cups crushed vegan chocolate cookies
- ¾ cup natural sugar
- ½ cup creamy peanut butter, at room temperature
- ¼ cup unsweetened cocoa powder
- 3 tablespoons vegan butter, melted
- 2 tablespoons hazelnut milk

Directions:

1. Lightly oil a baking tray that will fit in the steamer basket of your Instant Pot.
2. Combine the chocolate crumbs and the butter.
3. Press the chocolate base into your tray.
4. Blend the cream cheese and tofu until smooth.
5. Add the peanut butter, cocoa, hazelnut milk, and sugar to the cheese mix and fold in well.
6. Pour the cheese onto your base and put the tray in your steamer basket.
7. Pour the minimum amount of water into the base of your Instant Pot and lower the steamer basket.
8. Seal and cook on Steam for 15 minutes.
9. Release the pressure quickly and set to one side to cool a little.

658. Blueberry Brownies.

Preparation Time: 20 Minutes
Servings: 8

Ingredients:

- 1 cup cooked black beans
- ¾ cup unbleached all-purpose flour
- ½ cup unsweetened cocoa powder
- ½ cup blueberry jam
- ½ cup natural sugar
- 1½ teaspoons baking powder
- 1 teaspoon pure vanilla extract

Directions:

1. Lightly oil a baking tray that will fit in the steamer basket of your Instant Pot.
2. Blend together the beans, cocoa, jam, sugar, and vanilla.
3. Fold in the flour and baking powder until

the batter is smooth.

4. Pour the batter into your tray and put the tray in your steamer basket.
5. Pour the minimum amount of water into the base of your Instant Pot and lower the steamer basket.
6. Seal and cook on Steam for 12 minutes.
7. Release the pressure quickly and set to one side to cool a little before slicing.

659. Pumpkin Spice Oat Bars.

Preparation Time: 25 Minutes
Servings: 10

Ingredients:

- 2 cups old-fashioned rolled oats
- 1 cup non-dairy milk
- 2/3 cup canned solid-pack pumpkin
- ½ cup chopped toasted pecans
- ½ cup sweetened dried cranberries
- ½ cup packed light brown sugar or granulated natural sugar
- 6 ounces soft or silken tofu, drained and crumbled
- 2 teaspoons ground cinnamon
- 1½ teaspoons baking powder
- 1 teaspoon salt
- 1 teaspoon pure vanilla extract
- ¼ teaspoon ground nutmeg
- ¼ teaspoon ground allspice

Directions:

1. Lightly oil a baking tray that will fit in the steamer basket of your Instant Pot.
2. Stir together the oats, cinnamon, nutmeg, allspice, sugar, baking powder, and salt.
3. Blend together the tofu, pumpkin, milk, and vanilla until smooth and even.
4. Stir the wet and dry ingredients together before folding in the pecans and cranberries.
5. Pour the batter into your tray and put the tray in your steamer basket.
6. Pour the minimum amount of water into the base of your Instant Pot and lower the steamer basket.
7. Seal and cook on Steam for 12 minutes.
8. Release the pressure quickly and set to one side to cool a little before slicing.

660. Tutti Frutti Cobbler.

Preparation Time: 30 Minutes
Servings: 6

Ingredients:

- 1¼ cups unbleached all-purpose flour
- 1 cup fresh blueberries, rinsed and picked over
- 1 cup fresh blackberries, rinsed and picked over
- ¾ cup natural sugar
- ½ cup unsweetened almond milk
- 2 large ripe peaches, peeled, pitted, and sliced
- 2 ripe apricots, peeled, pitted, and sliced
- 1½ tablespoons tapioca starch or cornstarch
- 1 tablespoon vegetable oil
- 1 teaspoon baking powder
- ½ teaspoon pure vanilla extract
- ¼ teaspoon salt
- ¼ teaspoon ground cinnamon

Directions:

1. Lightly oil a baking tray that will fit in the steamer basket of your Instant Pot.
2. Toss the fruit in the tapioca and ½ a cup of sugar and put in the tray.
3. Put the tray in your steamer basket.
4. Pour the minimum amount of water into the base of your Instant Pot and lower the steamer basket.
5. Seal and cook on Steam for 12 minutes.
6. In a bowl stir together the flour, remaining sugar, cinnamon, baking powder, and salt.
7. Slowly combine with the almond milk, vanilla, and oil until soft dough is formed.
8. Release the Instant Pot's pressure quickly, give the fruit a stir, and cover with the dough.
9. Seal and Steam for another 5 minutes.
10. Release the pressure quickly and set to one side to cool a little.

661. Pear Mincemeat.

Preparation Time: 35 Minutes
Servings: 6

Ingredients:

- 4 firm ripe Bosc pears, peeled, cored, and

chopped

- 1 large orange
- 1½ cups apple juice
- 1¼ cups granola of your choice
- 1 cup raisins (dark, golden, or a combination
- 1 cup chopped dried apples, pears, or apricots, or a combination
- ½ cup packed dark brown sugar or granulated natural sugar
- ¼ cup brandy or 1 teaspoon brandy extract
- 2 tablespoons pure maple syrup or agave nectar
- 2 tablespoons cider vinegar
- ½ teaspoon ground cinnamon
- ½ teaspoon ground allspice
- ½ teaspoon ground nutmeg
- ¼ teaspoon ground cloves
- Pinch of salt

Directions:

1. Zest the orange, then peel it, deseed it, and quarter it.
2. Blend the orange flesh and zest and put in your Instant Pot.
3. Add the pears, dried fruits, juice, sugar, brandy spices, vinegar, and salt.
4. Seal and cook on Stew for 12 minutes.
5. Release the pressure naturally, take out some of the juice, then reseal and cook another 12 minutes.
6. In a bowl mix the granola and syrup.
7. Release the pressure of the Instant Pot naturally and sprinkle the crumble on top.
8. Seal the Instant Pot and cook on Stew for another 5 minutes.
9. Release the pressure naturally and serve.

662. Brown Betty Bananas Foster.

Preparation Time: 15 Minutes
Servings: 4

Ingredients:

- 6 cups cubed white bread, a little stale helps
- 4 ripe bananas, peeled and chopped
- ⅓ cup chopped toasted pecans
- ⅓ cup pure maple syrup
- ⅓ cup packed light brown sugar or granulated natural sugar
- ¼ cup unsweetened almond milk
- 2 tablespoons brandy
- ½ teaspoon ground cinnamon
- ¼ teaspoon ground nutmeg
- ¼ teaspoon ground ginger
- ⅛ teaspoon salt

Directions:

1. Lightly oil a baking tray that will fit in the steamer basket of your Instant Pot.
2. In a bowl combine almond milk, maple syrup, and the spices.
3. Roll the bread cubes in the milk mix.
4. In another bowl mix the bananas, pecans, brandy, and sugar.
5. Layer your two mixes in the tray: half bread, half banana, half bread, half banana.
6. Pour the minimum amount of water into the base of your Instant Pot and lower the steamer basket.
7. Seal and cook on Steam for 12 minutes.
8. Release the pressure quickly and set to one side to cool a little.

663 Bread & Butter Pudding.

Preparation Time: 25 Minutes
Servings: 8

Ingredients:

- 3 cups nondairy milk, warmed
- 2 cups cubed spiced bread or cake, stale is better
- 2 cups cubed whole-grain bread, stale is better
- 1 (16-ouncecan solid-pack pumpkin
- ¾ cup packed light brown sugar or granulated natural sugar
- 3 tablespoons rum or bourbon or 1 teaspoon rum extract (optional
- 1 teaspoon pure vanilla extract
- 1½ teaspoons ground cinnamon
- ¼ teaspoon ground nutmeg
- ¼ teaspoon ground allspice
- ¼ teaspoon ground ginger
- ¼ teaspoon salt

Directions:

1. Lightly oil a baking tray that will fit in the steamer basket of your Instant Pot.
2. Put the bread cubes in the tray.
3. Mix the pumpkin, sugar, vanilla, rum, spices, and salt.
4. Slowly stir in the milk.
5. Pour the mix over the bread.
6. Pour the minimum amount of water into the base of your Instant Pot and lower the steamer basket.
7. Seal and cook on Steam for 20 minutes.
8. Release the pressure quickly and set to one side to cool a little.

664. Custard Bread Pudding.

Preparation Time: 45 Minutes
Servings: 6

Ingredients:

- 6 cups cubed white bread
- 3 cups unsweetened almond milk
- 2 cups fresh raspberries or sliced strawberries, for serving
- ½ cup vegan white chocolate chips
- ½ cup packed light brown sugar or granulated natural sugar
- ½ cup dry Marsala
- Pinch of salt

Directions:

1. Melt your white chocolate into a cup of the almond milk. If using your Instant Pot, keep the lid off, stir throughout.
2. Add the Marsala, sugar, and salt.
3. Clean your Instant Pot.
4. Press half the bread cubes into the insert.
5. Pour half the Marsala mix on top.
6. Repeat.
7. Seal and cook on low for 35 minutes.
8. Release the pressure naturally.
9. Serve warm with fresh berries.

665. Chocolate Bread Pudding.

Preparation Time: 40 Minutes
Servings: 6

Ingredients:

- 4 cups white bread cubes
- 2 cups unsweetened almond milk
- 2 cups vegan semisweet chocolate chips
- ½ cup chopped pecans or walnuts
- ¾ cup granulated natural sugar
- ¼ cup unsweetened cocoa powder
- 1 tablespoon vegan butter
- 1 teaspoon pure vanilla extract
- ½ teaspoon salt

Directions:

1. Oil a baking tray that will fit in your Instant Pot.
2. Melt 1 and 2/3 of the chocolate chips with 1.5 cups of the almond milk.
3. Spread the bread cubes in your Instant Pot, sprinkle with nuts, and the remaining chocolate chips.
4. Warm the remaining almond milk in another saucepan with the sugar, cocoa, vanilla, and salt.
5. Combine the cocoa mix with the chocolate chip mix and pour it over the bread.
6. Seal your Instant Pot and cook on Beans for 30 minutes.
7. Depressurize naturally.

666. Mango Rice Pudding.

Preparation Time: 35 Minutes
Servings: 6

Ingredients:

- 2 (14-ouncecans unsweetened coconut milk
- 2 cups unsweetened almond milk, plus more if needed
- 1 cup uncooked jasmine rice
- ½ cup granulated natural sugar, or more to taste
- 1 large ripe mango, peeled, pitted, and chopped
- 1 teaspoon coconut extract
- 1 teaspoon pure vanilla extract
- ¼ teaspoon salt

Directions:

1. Spray the Instant Pot insert with cooking spray.
2. Add the milks and bring to a boil.
3. Add the rice, sugar, and salt, seal, and cook on Rice.
4. Depressurize quickly and stir in the extracts and mango.

5. The pudding will thicken as it cools.

Tapioca With Apricots.

Preparation Time: 25 Minutes
Servings: 4

Ingredients:

- 2½ cups unsweetened almond milk
- ½ cup chopped dried apricots
- ⅓ cup small pearl tapioca
- ⅓ cup granulated natural sugar
- ¼ cup apricot preserves
- 1 teaspoon pure vanilla extract

Directions:

1. Spray the inside of your Instant Pot with cooking spray.
2. Put in the tapioca, sugar, almond milk, and apricots.
3. Seal and cook on Stew for 12 minutes.
4. Release the pressure fast.
5. In a bowl combine the preserve and vanilla.
6. Add the mixture to your tapioca and reseal your Instant Pot.
7. Leave to finish in its own heat.
8. Serve hot or cold.

668. Poached Pears In Ginger Sauce.

Preparation Time: 25 Minutes
Servings: 6

Ingredients:

- 2½ cups white grape juice
- 6 firm ripe cooking pears, peeled, halved, and cored
- ¼ cup natural sugar, plus more if needed
- 6 strips lemon zest
- ½ cinnamon stick
- 2 teaspoons grated fresh ginger
- Juice of 1 lemon
- Pinch of salt

Directions:

1. Warm the grape juice, ginger, lemon zest, salt, and sugar until blended.
2. Add the cinnamon stick and the pears.
3. Seal and cook on Stew for 12 minutes.
4. Take the pears out.
5. Add lemon juice and more sugar to the liquid.
6. Cook with the lid off a few minutes to thicken.
7. Serve.

669. "Baked" Apples.

Preparation Time: 35 Minutes
Servings: 6

Ingredients:

- 6 large firm Granny Smith apples, washed
- ½ cup naturally sweetened cranberry juice
- ⅓ cup sweetened dried cranberries
- ⅓ cup packed light brown sugar or granulated natural sugar
- ¼ cup crushed, chopped, or coarsely ground almonds, walnuts, or pecans
- Juice of 1 lemon
- ½ teaspoon ground cinnamon

Directions:

1. Core the apples most of the way down, leaving a little base so the stuffing stays put.
2. Stand your apples upright in your Instant Pot. Do not pile them on top of each other! You may need to do two batches.
3. In a bowl combine the sugar, nuts, cranberries, and cinnamon.
4. Stuff each apple with the mix.
5. Pour the cranberry juice around the apples.
6. Seal and cook on Stew for 20 minutes.
7. Depressurize naturally.

670. . Maple & Rum Apples.

Preparation Time: 25 Minutes
Servings: 6

Ingredients:

- 6 Granny Smith apples, washed
- ½ cup pure maple syrup
- ½ cup apple juice
- ⅓ cup packed light brown sugar
- ¼ cup golden raisins
- ¼ cup dark rum or spiced rum
- ¼ cup old-fashioned rolled oats
- ¼ cup macadamia nut pieces
- 1 teaspoon ground cinnamon
- ½ teaspoon ground nutmeg
- Juice of 1 lemon

Directions:

1. Core the apples most of the way down, leaving a little base so the stuffing stays put.
2. Stand your apples upright in your Instant Pot. Do not pile them on top of each other! You may need to do two batches.
3. In a bowl combine the oats, sugar, raisins, nuts, and half the nutmeg, half the cinnamon.
4. Stuff each apple with the mix.
5. In another bowl combine the remaining nutmeg and cinnamon, the maple syrup, and the rum.
6. Pour the glaze over the apples.
7. Seal and cook on Stew for 20 minutes.
8. Depressurize naturally.

671. Pumpkin & Chocolate Loaf.

Preparation Time: 15 Minutes
Servings: 8

Ingredients:

- 1¾ cups unbleached all-purpose flour
- 1 cup canned solid-pack pumpkin
- ½ cup packed light brown sugar or granulated natural sugar
- ½ cup semisweet vegan chocolate chips
- ¼ cup pure maple syrup
- 2 tablespoons vegetable oil
- 2 teaspoons baking powder
- 1 teaspoon pure vanilla extract
- ½ teaspoon salt
- ½ teaspoon ground cinnamon
- ¼ teaspoon ground allspice
- ¼ teaspoon ground nutmeg

Directions:

1. Lightly oil a baking tray that will fit in the steamer basket of your Instant Pot.
2. In a bowl, combine the flour, baking powder, baking soda, salt and spices.
3. In another bowl combine the pumpkin, maple syrup, sugar, vanilla, and oil.
4. Stir the wet mixture into the dry mixture slowly until they form a smooth mix.
5. Fold in the chocolate chips.
6. Pour the batter into your baking tray and put the tray in your steamer basket.
7. Pour the minimum amount of water into the base of your Instant Pot and lower the steamer basket.
8. Seal and cook on Steam for 10 minutes.
9. Release the pressure quickly and set to one side to cool a little.

672. Cheesecake

Preparation time: 45 minutes
Ingredients:
For the crust:

- 4 tbsp. butter
- 6 cups coconut, shredded
- Any sweetener you consider appropriate
- 8 Oz. cream cheese
- ½ cup stevia sweetener
- ½ maple syrup
- 16 Oz. can of pineapple in a syrup, crashed or whole, drained
- ¼ cup whipping cream
- 5 eggs

Directions:

1. After you mix all the crust ingredients press evenly and place it into the baking tray or pan and have it baked for at least 10 minutes. Let it cool.
2. In a blender mix well the cream cheese with sweeteners, the pineapple until blended.
3. Add the eggs gradually and pour this batter into the pan you have prepared.
4. Bake for 90 minutes. Remove from oven and let it cooled.

Tip: Can be served with additional pineapple on top and/or with whipped cream whatever topping you choose to your liking.

673. Gluten-Free Nutella Brownie Trifle

Preparation time: 60 minutes
Ingredients:
For the brownies:

- 6 Oz. hazelnuts
- ½ cup almonds
- ½ cup cashews
- 1 cup medjool dates, pitted
- ½ tsp. vanilla extract
- 2 tbsp. cacao powder
- 2 tbsp. hazelnut butter
- 1 tbsp. maple syrup or honey, to taste

- For the frosting:
- ½ cup avocado, fresh crushed
- 1 ½ tbsp. coconut oil
- ½ tsp. vanilla
- 2tbsp. coconut maple syrup
- 1 tbsp. cacao
- 1 tbsp. nut butter

Directions:

1. You will need some baking paper for lining the baking tray.
2. Dry the hazelnuts and almonds in a frying pan until toasted.
3. Add ¾ of all the nuts with the almonds into the food processor until they are broken to chunks.
4. Add the dates and process again, then all the rest ingredients until you have a sticky mass.
5. Pour it onto the baking tray lined with paper. Press the crumbly mixture you made with your fingers until the top of it is even. Place into the fridge while you are cooking the glaze.
6. For the glaze you will have to mix well all the ingredients in a bowl or process them all in a food processor until well combined. It should be smooth and creamy.
7. Remove your brownie from a fridge add the frosting on top spreading it evenly.
8. Top the brownie with the remaining nuts and place again into the fridge until you have it served.

674. Low-Carb Curd Soufflé

Preparation time: 45 minutes

Ingredients:

For the soufflé:

- 7 Oz. cream
- ½ cup condensed milk
- 1 pack (1 Oz.) gelatin for a dense soufflé
- 1 cup milk
- 5 Oz. cottage cheese

Directions:

1. Fill the gelatin with milk and set aside.
2. Mix the condensed milk with the cream and bring to boil on a low heat.
3. Pour the gelatin mass into the boiled mixture and mix it, then let it cool.
4. In a mixer, have all the mass combined well with the cottage cheese for at least 10 minutes.
5. Pour it into the silicone moulds for the cupcakes and let it freeze for a couple of hours and serve.

675. Cream Cheese Cookies

Preparation time: 40 minutes

Ingredients:

- 1 cup butter
- ¾ cup stevia or any sugar substitute
- 4 Oz. cream cheese, softened
- 1 egg
- 2 cups almond flour
- 1 cup coconut flour
- Sesame seeds
- Vanilla or any flavored extract to taste

Directions:

1. Mix the butter with the sweetener until fluffy.
2. Beat the cream cheese and add the egg, then flour and mix it with the flavor and seeds you have chosen.
3. Let it chill for 3-4 hours.
4. Roll the cookie mass into a log and have it sliced thus forming your cookies.
5. Bake until brown up to 15 minutes or more to make them crispy.

676. Chia Seeds Pudding with Berries

Preparation time: 60 minutes

Ingredients:

- 2 cups coconut milk, full fat
- 1 banana, sliced
- ½ cups chia seeds
- Honey or stevia for sweetening
- 5 Oz. at least any fresh berries

Directions:

1. Stir the milk, chia seeds and stevia (or honey) in a mixing bowl.
2. Add half of all the berries and let the mixture chilled for at least 1 hour.
3. Mix it up again and add the berries and banana before serving.

Tip: Chia seeds have omega-3 fatty acids, protein, fiber,

calcium and antioxidants.

677. Smoothie Bowl

Preparation time: 45 minutes

Ingredients:

- 6 Oz. berries, fresh or frozen
- 2 medium frozen bananas
- ½ cup Almond milk
- 1 cup jellified yoghurt
- 1 tbsp. Chia seeds
- 1 tbsp. Hemp seeds
- 1 tbsp. Coconut flakes
- Raspberry jam or any other, to taste

Directions:

1. In a blender mix the bananas with half of the berries until it has a puree consistency.
2. Organise your smoothie in a bowl decorating it in rows with the yogurt spot, the puree and fresh berries and with a pinch of seeds and flakes you have.

678. Coconut milk smoothie

Preparation time: 15 minutes

Ingredients:

- 1 cup Greek yogurt
- 1 cup coconut milk, full fat
- 1 banana, fresh or frozen
- 1 cup baby spinach, fresh
- 1 tbsp. honey
- 5 Oz. blueberries or other berries

Directions:

1. In a blender mix all the ingredients until smooth. Add the ice for a thicker smoothie.

679. Yogurt Smoothie with Cinnamon and Mango

Preparation time: 15 minutes

Ingredients:

- 4 Oz. frozen mango chunks, mango pulp or fresh mango
- 1 cup Greek yogurt
- 1 cup coconut milk, full fat
- 3-4 cups milk
- 3 tbsp. flax seed meal
- 1 tbsp. honey
- 1 tsp. cinnamon

Directions:

1. In a blender mix all the ingredients, except cinnamon until smooth. Sprinkle each smoothie with a pinch of cinnamon.

680. Lemon Curd Dessert (Sugar Free)

Preparation time: 35 minutes

Ingredients:

- ½ cup unsalted butter
- ½ cup lemon juice
- 2 tbsp. lemon zest
- 6 egg yolks
- Stevia for sweetening

Directions:

2. On a low heat melt the butter in a saucepan.
3. Whisk in the stevia or any other sweetener, lemon ingredients until combined, then add the egg yolks and return to the stove again over the low heat.
4. Whisk it until the curd starts thickening.
5. Strain into a small bowl and let cool.
6. Can be stored in a fridge for several weeks.

681. Chocolate Almond Butter Smoothie

Preparation time: 35 minutes

Ingredients:

- 2 tbsp. chocolate protein powder
- ½ tbsp. cacao powder
- 1 cup almond milk
- 2 tbsp. almond butter
- 1 fresh banana
- ½ cup fresh strawberries
- 1 tbsp. chia or hemp seeds
- Maple syrup or stevia for sweetening

Directions:

Put all the ingredients into the blender and mix until it has creamy consistency.

682. Berry and Nuts Dessert

Preparation time: 25 minutes

Ingredients for 2 portions:

- 10 Oz. yogurt or yogurt drink

- 7 Oz. strawberries, fresh
- Blueberries, raspberries or any berries you may like
- 1 banana, sliced
- Pinch of Pistachio
- Pinch of cashews
- 4 walnuts, shelled
- Pinch of pumpkin seeds
- Pinch of sunflower seeds
- Several fresh mint leaves

Directions:

In a serving dish pour the jellied yogurt and top it with all the fresh ingredients.

683. Pastry with Nuts, Mango and Blueberries

Preparation time: 45 minutes

Ingredients:

For the pastry:

- 1 cup whole wheat flour
- ½ cup whole wheat almond flour
- ½ cup butter
- 2 eggs yolks
- 2 Oz. water
- 12 Oz. blueberries or any berries to your liking
- 2 Mangoes
- 1 pinch of pumpkin seeds
- Sesame and sunflower seeds
- Peanuts, dried
- For the filling:
- 8 Oz. cream cheese
- 1 mango, chopped
- ½ icing sugar
- 2 tbsp. lemon juice

Directions:

1. In a bowl mix the flour ingredients with the butter, add the egg yolks and some water until combined and forms a ball.
2. Knead the dough a little until it is smooth and refrigerate for half an hour covered with a napkin.
3. Mix all the ingredients of the pastry filling in a blender.
4. Grease your baking tray or a cooking tin and dust with some flour.
5. Pour the dough into the tin and bake for 30 minutes (200 grades) until lightly brown.
6. Pour the filling onto the pastry and top it with berries and nuts. Add some dessert sauce for serving.

684. Keto Vegan Pumpkin Mousse

Preparation time: 15 minutes

Ingredients:

- 15 oz. firm Tofu
- 15 oz. organic Pumpkin
- 1 tbsp. Cinnamon
- ½ tsp. Ginger
- Stevia for sweetening

Directions:

Mix all the ingredients in a blender until smooth. Taste and add more stevia for sweetening.

685. Keto Flax Seed Waffles

Preparation time: 20 minutes

Ingredients for 4 portions:

- 2 cups Golden Flax Seed
- 1 tbsp. Baking Powder
- 5 tbsp. Flax Seed Meal (mixed with 15 tbsp. Water)
- ⅓ cup Avocado Oil
- ½ cup Water
- 1 tsp. Sea Salt
- 1 tbsp. fresh Herbs (thyme, rosemary or parsley) or 2 tsp. cinnamon, ground

Directions:

1. Preheat the waffle-maker.
2. Combine the flax seed with baking powder with a pinch of salt in a bowl. Whisk the mixture.
3. Place the jelly-like flax seed mixture, some water and oil into the blender and pulse until foamy.
4. Transfer the liquid mixture to the bowl with the flax seed mixture. Stir until combined. The mixture must be fluffy.
5. Once it is combined, set aside for a couple of minutes. Add some fresh herbs or cinnamon. Divide the mixture into 4 servings.
6. Scoop each, one at a time, onto the waffle maker. Cook with the closed top until it's

ready. Repeat with the remaining batter.
7. Eat immediately or keep in an air-tight container for a couple of weeks.

686. Keto Lemon Fat Bombs

Preparation time: 60 minutes

Ingredients (for approx. 30 fat bombs):

- 1 cup Coconut Oil, melted
- 2 cups Raw Cashews, boiled for 10 minutes, soaked
- ½ cup Coconut Butter
- 1 Lemon Zest
- 2 Lemons, juiced
- ¼ cup Coconut Flour
- ⅓ cup Coconut, shredded
- A pinch of salt
- Stevia for sweetening

Directions:

1. Mix all the ingredients in a food processor and blend until combined.
2. Place the mixture to a bowl and have it cooled up in the freezer to 40 minutes.
3. Remove from freezer and make the balls.
4. Place them onto the cooking tray and again place into the freezer for hardening.
5. Remove from the freezer and store in an air-tight container for up to a week. Let them thaw before serving.

687. Candied Pecans

Preparation time: 60 minutes
Ingredients for 4 portions:

- 6 oz. Whole Pecans
- ½ cup Aquafaba
- 1 oz. Palm Sugar
- 1 oz. whole Green Cardamom Pods
- ¼ tsp. Salt
- 1 tsp. Allspice

Directions:

1. Pre-heat oven to 350°F/180°C.
2. Prepare a baking tray with a piece of parchment paper.
3. Remove the cardamom seeds from the pods. Crush the seeds and lay them onto one side of the tray.
4. Chop the sugar or grind it in a food processor.
5. Whisk the aquafaba until frothy, stir in the sugar and salt. Fold in the nuts, allspice, cardamom, until everything is coated.
6. Spread the mixture evenly over the baking tray for about 15 minutes and replace it onto the cooling rack.
7. When cooled, pecans can be enjoyed as a topping or as they are.

688. Rice and Cantaloupe Ramekins

Preparation time: 10 minutes
Cooking time: 30 minutes
Servings: 4

Ingredients:

- 2 tablespoons flaxseed mixed with 3 tablespoons water
- 2 cups cauliflower rice, steamed
- 1 cup coconut cream
- 2 tablespoons stevia
- 1 teaspoon vanilla extract
- ½ cup cantaloupe, peeled and chopped
- Cooking spray

Directions:

1. In a bowl, mix the cauliflower rice with the flaxseed mix and the other ingredients except the cooking spray and whisk well.
2. Grease 4 ramekins with the cooking spray, divide the rice mix in each and cook at 360 degrees F for 30 minutes.
3. Serve cold.

Nutrition: calories 180, fat 5.3, fiber 5.4, carbs 11.5, protein 4

689. Strawberries Cream

Preparation time: 10 minutes
Cooking time: 0 minutes
Servings: 2

Ingredients:

- 1 cup strawberries, chopped
- 1 cup coconut cream
- 1 tablespoon stevia
- ½ teaspoon vanilla extract

Directions:

1. In a blender, combine the strawberries with the cream and the other ingredients, pulse well, divide into cups and serve cold.

Nutrition: calories 182, fat 3.1, fiber 2.3, carbs

3.5, protein 2

690. Almond and Chia Pudding

Preparation time: 10 minutes
Cooking time: 15 minutes
Servings: 4

Ingredients:

- 1 tablespoon lime juice
- 1 tablespoon lime zest, grated
- 2 cups almond milk
- 2 tablespoons almonds, chopped
- 1 teaspoon almond extract
- ½ cup chia seeds
- 2 tablespoons stevia

Directions:

1. In a pan, mix the almond milk with the chia seeds, the almonds and the other ingredients, whisk, bring to a simmer and cook over medium heat for 15 minutes.
2. Divide the mix into bowls and serve cold.

Nutrition: calories 174, fat 12.1, fiber 3.2, carbs 3.9, protein 4.8

691. Dates and Cocoa Bowls

Preparation time: 2 hours
Cooking time: 0 minutes
Servings: 6

Ingredients:

- 2 tablespoons avocado oil
- 1 cup coconut cream
- 1 teaspoon cocoa powder
- ½ cup dates, chopped
- 3 tablespoons stevia

Directions:

1. In a bowl, mix the cream with the oil, the cocoa, the cream and the other ingredients, pulse well, divide into cups and keep in the fridge for 2 hours before serving.

Nutrition: calories 141, fat 10.2, fiber 2.4, carbs 13.8, protein 1.4

692. Berries and Cherries Bowls

Preparation time: 10 minutes
Cooking time: 0 minutes
Servings: 4

Ingredients:

- 1 cup strawberries, halved
- 1 cup blackberries
- 1 cup cherries, pitted and halved
- ¼ cup coconut cream
- ¼ cup stevia
- 1 teaspoon vanilla extract

Directions:

In a bowl, combine the berries with the cherries and the other ingredients, toss, divide into smaller bowls and serve cold.

Nutrition: calories 122, fat 4, fiber 5.3, carbs 6.6, protein 4.5

693. Cocoa Peach Cream

Preparation time: 10 minutes
Cooking time: 0 minutes
Servings: 4

Ingredients:

- 2 cups coconut cream
- 1/3 cup stevia
- ¾ cup cocoa powder
- Zest of 1 lime, grated
- 1 tablespoons lime juice
- 2 peaches, pitted and chopped

Directions:

1. In a blender, combine the cream with the stevia, the cocoa and the other ingredients, pulse well, divide into cups and serve cold.

Nutrition: calories 172, fat 5.6, fiber 3.5, carbs 7.6, protein 4

694. Nuts and Seeds Pudding

Preparation time: 10 minutes
Cooking time: 20 minutes
Servings: 4

Ingredients:

- 2 cups cauliflower rice
- ¼ cup coconut cream
- 2 cups almond milk
- 1 teaspoon vanilla extract
- 3 tablespoons stevia
- ½ cup walnuts, chopped
- 1 tablespoon chia seeds
- Cooking spray

Directions:

1. In a pan, combine the cauliflower rice with the cream, the almond milk and the other ingredients, toss, bring to a simmer and cook over medium heat for 20 minutes.
2. Divide into bowls and serve cold.

Nutrition: calories 223, fat 8.1, fiber 3.4, carbs 7.6, protein 3.4

695. Cashew Fudge

Preparation time: 3 hours
Cooking time: 0 minutes
Servings: 6

Ingredients:

- 1/3 cup cashew butter
- 1 cup coconut cream
- ½ cup cashews, soaked for 8 hours and drained
- 5 tablespoons lime juice
- ½ teaspoon lime zest, grated
- 1 tablespoons stevia

Directions:

1. In a bowl, mix the cashew butter with the cream, the cashews and the other ingredients and whisk well.
2. Line a muffin tray with parchment paper, scoop 1 tablespoon of the fudge mix in each of the muffin tins and freeze for 3 hours before serving.

Nutrition: calories 200, fat 4.5, fiber 3.4, carbs 13.5, protein 5

696. Lime Berries Stew

Preparation time: 10 minutes
Cooking time: 20 minutes
Servings: 6

Ingredients:

- Zest of 1 lime, grated
- Juice of 1 lime
- 1 pint strawberries, halved
- 2 cups water
- 2 tablespoons stevia

Directions:

1. In a pan, combine the strawberries with the lime juice, the water and stevia, toss, bring to a simmer and cook over medium heat for 20 minutes.
2. Divide the stew into bowls and serve cold.

Nutrition: calories 172, fat 7, fiber 3.4, carbs 8, protein 2.3

697. Apricots Cake

Preparation time: 10 minutes
Cooking time: 30 minutes
Servings: 8

Ingredients:

- ¾ cup stevia
- 2 cups coconut flour
- ¼ cup coconut oil, melted
- ½ cup almond milk
- 1 teaspoon baking powder
- 2 tablespoons flaxseed mixed with 3 tablespoons water
- ½ teaspoon vanilla extract
- Juice of 1 lime
- 2 cups apricots, chopped

Directions:

1. In a bowl, mix the flour with the coconut oil, the stevia and the other ingredients, whisk and pour into a cake pan lined with parchment paper.
2. Introduce in the oven at 375 degrees F, bake for 30 minutes, cool down, slice and serve.

Nutrition: calories 221, fat 8.3, fiber 3.4, carbs 14.5, protein 5

698. Berry Cake

Preparation time: 10 minutes
Cooking time: 30 minutes
Servings: 6

Ingredients:

- 2 cups coconut flour
- 1 cup blueberries
- 1 cup strawberries, chopped
- 2 tablespoons almonds, chopped
- 2 tablespoons walnuts, chopped
- 3 tablespoons stevia
- 1 teaspoon almond extract
- 3 tablespoons flaxseed mixed with 4 tablespoons water
- ½ cup coconut cream
- 2 tablespoons avocado oil

- 1 teaspoon baking powder
- Cooking spray

Directions:

1. In a bowl, combine the coconut flour with the berries, the nuts, stevia and the other ingredients, and whisk well.
2. Grease a cake pan with the cooking spray, pour the cake mix inside, introduce everything in the oven at 360 degrees F and bake for 30 minutes.
3. Cool the cake down, slice and serve.

Nutrition: calories 225, fat 9, fiber 4.5, carbs 10.2, protein 4.5

699. Dates Mousse

Preparation time: 30 minutes
Cooking time: 0 minutes
Servings: 4

Ingredients:

- 2 cups coconut cream
- ¼ cup stevia
- 2 cups dates, chopped
- 1 teaspoon almond extract
- 1 teaspoon vanilla extract

Directions:

1. In a blender, combine the cream with the stevia, dates and the other ingredients, pulse well, divide into cups and keep in the fridge for 30 minutes before serving.

Nutrition: calories 141, fat 4.7, fiber 4.7, carbs 8.3, protein 0.8

700. Minty Almond Cups

Preparation time: 10 minutes
Cooking time: 10 minutes
Servings: 4

Ingredients:

- 1 cup almonds, roughly chopped
- 1 tablespoon mint, chopped
- ½ cup coconut cream
- 2 tablespoons stevia
- 1 teaspoon vanilla extract

Directions:

1. In a pan, combine the almonds with the mint, the cream and the other ingredients, whisk, simmer over medium heat for 10 minutes, divide into cups and serve cold.

Nutrition: calories 135, fat 4.1, fiber 3.8, carbs 4.1, protein 2.3

701. Lime Cake

Preparation time: 10 minutes
Cooking time: 40 minutes
Servings: 4

Ingredients:

- ½ cup almonds, chopped
- Zest of 1 lime grated
- Juice of 1 lime
- 1 cups stevia
- 2 tablespoons flaxseed mixed with 3 tablespoons water
- 1 teaspoon vanilla extract
- 1 and ½ cup almond flour
- ½ cup coconut cream
- 1 teaspoon baking soda

Directions:

1. In a bowl, combine the almond with the lime zest, lime juice and the other ingredients, whisk well and pour into a cake pan lined with parchment paper.
2. Introduce in the oven at 360 degrees F, bake for 40 minutes, cool down, slice and serve.

Nutrition: calories 186, fat 16.4, fiber 3, carbs 6.8, protein 4.7

702. Vanilla Pudding

Preparation time: 10 minutes
Cooking time: 40 minutes
Servings: 4

Ingredients:

- 2 cups almond flour
- 3 tablespoons walnuts, chopped
- 1 and ½ cups coconut cream
- 3 tablespoons flaxseed mixed with 4 tablespoons water
- 1 cup stevia
- 1 teaspoon vanilla extract
- 1 teaspoon baking powder
- 1 teaspoon nutmeg, ground

Directions:

1. In a bowl, combine the flour with the

walnuts, the cream and the other ingredients, whisk well and pour into 4 ramekins.
2. Introduce in the oven at 350 degrees F, bake for 40 minutes, cool down and serve.

Nutrition: calories 399, fat 39.3, fiber 4.7, carbs 11.2, protein 7.2

703. Cinnamon Avocado and Berries Mix

Preparation time: 5 minutes
Cooking time: 0 minutes
Servings: 4

Ingredients:

- 1 cup blackberries
- 1 cup strawberries, halved
- 1 cup avocado, peeled, pitted and cubed
- 1 cup coconut cream
- 1 teaspoon cinnamon powder
- 4 tablespoons stevia

Directions:

1. In a bowl, combine the berries with the avocado and the other ingredients, toss, divide into smaller bowls and serve cold.

Nutrition: calories 162, fat 8, fiber 4.2, carbs 12.3, protein 8.4

704. Raisins and Berries Cream

Preparation time: 5 minutes
Cooking time: 0
Servings: 4

Ingredients:

- 1 cup coconut cream
- 1 cup blackberries
- 3 tablespoons stevia
- 2 tablespoons raisins
- 2 tablespoons lime juice

Directions:

1. In a blender, the cream with the berries and the other ingredients except the raisins, pulse well, divide into cups, sprinkle the raisins on top and cool down before serving.

Nutrition: calories 192, fat 6.5, fiber 3.4, carbs 9.5, protein 5

705. Baked Rhubarb

Preparation time: 10 minutes
Cooking time: 20 minutes
Servings: 4

Ingredients:

- 4 teaspoons stevia
- 1 pound rhubarb, roughly sliced
- 1 teaspoon vanilla extract
- 2 tablespoons avocado oil
- 1 teaspoon cinnamon powder
- 1 teaspoon nutmeg, ground

Directions:

2. Arrange the rhubarb on a baking sheet lined with parchment paper, add the stevia, vanilla and the other ingredients, toss and bake at 350 degrees F for 20 minutes.
3. Divide the baked rhubarb into bowls and serve cold.

Nutrition: calories 176, fat 4.5, fiber 7.6, carbs 11.5, protein 5

706. Cocoa Berries Mousse

Preparation time: 10 minutes
Cooking time: 0 minutes
Servings: 2

Ingredients:

- 1 tablespoon cocoa powder
- 1 cup blackberries
- 1 cup blueberries
- ¾ cup coconut cream
- 1 tablespoon stevia

Directions:

1. In a blender, combine the berries with the cocoa and the other ingredients, pulse well, divide into bowls and keep in the fridge for 2 hours before serving.

Nutrition: calories 200, fat 8, fiber 3.4, carbs 7.6, protein 4.3

707. Nutmeg Pudding

Preparation time: 10 minutes
Cooking time: 20 minutes
Servings: 6

Ingredients:

- 2 tablespoons stevia
- 1 teaspoon nutmeg, ground
- 1 cup cauliflower rice

- 2 tablespoons flaxseed mixed with 3 tablespoons water
- 2 cups almond milk
- ¼ teaspoon nutmeg, grated

Directions:

In a pan, combine the cauliflower rice with the flaxseed mix and the other ingredients, whisk, cook over medium heat for 20 minutes, divide into bowls and serve cold.

Nutrition: calories 220, fat 6.6, fiber 3.4, carbs 12.4, protein 3.4

708. Lime Cherries and Rice Pudding

Preparation time: 10 minutes
Cooking time: 25 minutes
Servings: 4

Ingredients:

- ¾ cup stevia
- 2 cups coconut milk
- 3 tablespoons flaxseed mixed with 4 tablespoons water
- Juice of 2 limes
- Zest of 1 lime, grated
- 1 cup cherries, pitted and halved
- 1 cup cauliflower rice

Directions:

1. In a pan, combine the milk with the stevia and bring to a simmer over medium heat.
2. Add the cauliflower rice and the other ingredients, stir, cook for 25 minutes more, divide into cups and serve cold.

Nutrition: calories 199, fat 5.4, fiber 3.4, carbs 11.5, protein 5.6

709. Chocolate Pudding

Preparation time: 10 minutes
Cooking time: 20 minutes
, fiber 0, carbs 3, protein 4
Servings: 4

Ingredients:

- 2 tablespoons cocoa powder
- 2 tablespoons coconut oil, melted
- 2/3 cup coconut cream
- 2 tablespoons stevia
- ¼ teaspoon almond extract

Directions:

1. In a pan, combine the cocoa powder with the coconut milk and the other ingredients, whisk, bring to a simmer ad cook over medium heat for 20 minutes.
2. Divide into cups and serve cold.

Nutrition: calories 134, fat 14.1, fiber 0.8, carbs 3.1, protein 0.9

710. Coffee and Rhubarb Cream

Preparation time: 10 minutes
Cooking time: 20 minutes
Servings: 4

Ingredients:

- ¼ cup brewed coffee
- 2 tablespoons stevia
- 2 cups coconut cream
- 1 teaspoon vanilla extract
- 2 tablespoons coconut oil, melted
- 1 cup rhubarb, chopped
- 2 tablespoons flaxseed mixed with 3 tablespoons water

Directions:

In a bowl, mix the coffee with stevia, cream and the other ingredients, whisk well and divide into 4 ramekins.
Introduce the ramekins in the oven at 350 degrees F, bake for 20 minutes and serve warm.

Nutrition: calories 300, fat 30.8

365-DAY MEAL PLAN

DAY	BREAKFAST	MAINS	DESSERT
1	Avocado Smoothie	Vinegar Cucumber, Olives and Shallots Salad	Maple-Walnut Oatmeal Cookies
2	Asparagus and Avocado Bowls	Creamy Brussels Sprouts Bowls	Banana-Nut Bread Bars
3	Avocado and Pomegranate Bowls	Green Beans and Radishes Bake	Apple Crumble
4	Oregano Peppers Bake	Avocado and Radish Bowls	Chocolate-Cranberry Oatmeal Cookies
5	Coconut Green Smoothie	Celery and Radish Soup	Cashew-Chocolate Truffles
6	Pesto Tomato Bowls	Lime Avocado and Cucumber Soup	Banana Chocolate Cupcakes
7	Scallions Zucchini Bake	Avocado and Kale Soup	Minty Fruit Salad
8	Leeks and Arugula Salad	Spinach and Cucumber Salad	Sesame Cookies
9	Spinach Salad	Spinach and Broccoli Soup	Mango Coconut Cream Pie
10	Zucchini Butter	Curry Spinach Soup	Cherry-Vanilla Rice Pudding (Pressure cooker
11	Basil Zucchini and Cucumber Noodle Salad	Avocado, Spinach and Kale Soup	Chocolate Coconut Brownies
12	Creamy Cheese Soufflés	Arugula and Artichokes Bowls	Lime in the Coconut Chia Pudding
13	Chives Stuffed Tomatoes	Mushroom and Mustard Greens Mix	Melon Coconut Mousse
14	Capers Cauliflower Rice and Avocado	Greens and Vinaigrette	Ginger-Spice Brownies
15	Roasted Peppers Muffins	Tomato and Peppers Pancakes	Avocado and Pineapple Bowls
16	Mint Watermelon Bowl	Avocado, Pine Nuts and Chard Salad	Tangerine Stew
17	Tomato and Avocado Pizza	Grapes, Avocado and Spinach Salad	Pineapple and Melon Stew
18		Chard Soup	Cocoa Muffins
19	Spicy Bowls	Mushrooms and Chard Soup	Creamy Pineapple Mix
20	Vegetarian Keto Breakfast Frittata	Avocado Soup	Grapefruit Cream
21	Waffle/Cinnamon Roll	Coconut Zucchini Cream	Coconut and Almond Truffles
22	Scrambled Eggs with Cheddar & Spinach	Zucchini and Cauliflower Soup	Almond Balls
23	Creamy Zucchini Noodles	Greens and Olives Pan	Almond-Date Energy Bites
24	Keto Pumpkin Pancakes	Cauliflower and Artichokes Soup	Pecan and Date-Stuffed Roasted Pears
25	Sweet Cauliflower Rice Casserole	Grilled Veggie Mix	Chocolate And Walnut Farfalle
26	Avocado Oatmeal	Eggplant and Olives Stew	Peach-Mango Crumble (Pressure cooker
27	Zucchini Muffins	Hot Cabbage Soup	Zesty Orange-Cranberry Energy Bites
28		Tomato, Green Beans and Chard Soup	Mint Chocolate Chip Sorbet
29	Berry and Dates Oatmeal	Hot Roasted Peppers Cream	Pumpkin Pie Cups (Pressure cooker
30	Mushroom Muffins	Eggplant and Peppers Soup	Strawberry Parfaits With Cashew Crème
31		Vinegar Cucumber, Olives and Shallots Salad	Maple-Walnut Oatmeal Cookies
32	Tomato Oatmeal	Creamy Brussels Sprouts Bowls	Banana-Nut Bread Bars
33	Avocado Smoothie	Green Beans and Radishes Bake	Apple Crumble
34	Asparagus and Avocado Bowls	Avocado and Radish Bowls	Chocolate-Cranberry Oatmeal Cookies

35	Avocado and Pomegranate Bowls	Celery and Radish Soup	Cashew-Chocolate Truffles
36	Oregano Peppers Bake	Lime Avocado and Cucumber Soup	Banana Chocolate Cupcakes
37	Coconut Green Smoothie	Avocado and Kale Soup	Minty Fruit Salad
38	Pesto Tomato Bowls	Spinach and Cucumber Salad	Sesame Cookies
39	Scallions Zucchini Bake	Spinach and Broccoli Soup	Mango Coconut Cream Pie
40	Leeks and Arugula Salad	Curry Spinach Soup	Cherry-Vanilla Rice Pudding (Pressure cooker
41	Spinach Salad	Avocado, Spinach and Kale Soup	Chocolate Coconut Brownies
42	Zucchini Butter	Arugula and Artichokes Bowls	Lime in the Coconut Chia Pudding
43	Basil Zucchini and Cucumber Noodle Salad	Mushroom and Mustard Greens Mix	Melon Coconut Mousse
44	Creamy Cheese Soufflés	Greens and Vinaigrette	Ginger-Spice Brownies
45	Chives Stuffed Tomatoes	Tomato and Peppers Pancakes	Avocado and Pineapple Bowls
46	Capers Cauliflower Rice and Avocado	Avocado, Pine Nuts and Chard Salad	Tangerine Stew
47	Roasted Peppers Muffins	Grapes, Avocado and Spinach Salad	Pineapple and Melon Stew
48	Mint Watermelon Bowl	Chard Soup	Cocoa Muffins
49	Tomato and Avocado Pizza	Mushrooms and Chard Soup	Creamy Pineapple Mix
50		Avocado Soup	Grapefruit Cream
51	Spicy Bowls	Coconut Zucchini Cream	Coconut and Almond Truffles
52	Vegetarian Keto Breakfast Frittata	Zucchini and Cauliflower Soup	Almond Balls
53	Waffle/Cinnamon Roll	Greens and Olives Pan	Almond-Date Energy Bites
54	Scrambled Eggs with Cheddar & Spinach	Cauliflower and Artichokes Soup	Pecan and Date-Stuffed Roasted Pears
55	Creamy Zucchini Noodles	Grilled Veggie Mix	Chocolate And Walnut Farfalle
56	Keto Pumpkin Pancakes	Eggplant and Olives Stew	Peach-Mango Crumble (Pressure cooker
57	Sweet Cauliflower Rice Casserole	Hot Cabbage Soup	Zesty Orange-Cranberry Energy Bites
58	Avocado Oatmeal	Tomato, Green Beans and Chard Soup	Mint Chocolate Chip Sorbet
59	Zucchini Muffins	Hot Roasted Peppers Cream	Pumpkin Pie Cups (Pressure cooker
60		Eggplant and Peppers Soup	Strawberry Parfaits With Cashew Crème
61	Berry and Dates Oatmeal	Vinegar Cucumber, Olives and Shallots Salad	Maple-Walnut Oatmeal Cookies
62	Mushroom Muffins	Creamy Brussels Sprouts Bowls	Banana-Nut Bread Bars
63		Green Beans and Radishes Bake	Apple Crumble
64	Tomato Oatmeal	Avocado and Radish Bowls	Chocolate-Cranberry Oatmeal Cookies
65	Avocado Smoothie	Celery and Radish Soup	Cashew-Chocolate Truffles
66	Asparagus and Avocado Bowls	Lime Avocado and Cucumber Soup	Banana Chocolate Cupcakes
67	Avocado and Pomegranate Bowls	Avocado and Kale Soup	Minty Fruit Salad
68	Oregano Peppers Bake	Spinach and Cucumber Salad	Sesame Cookies
69	Coconut Green Smoothie	Spinach and Broccoli Soup	Mango Coconut Cream Pie
70	Pesto Tomato Bowls	Curry Spinach Soup	Cherry-Vanilla Rice Pudding (Pressure cooker
71	Scallions Zucchini Bake	Avocado, Spinach and Kale Soup	Chocolate Coconut Brownies
72	Leeks and Arugula Salad	Arugula and Artichokes Bowls	Lime in the Coconut Chia Pudding
73	Spinach Salad	Mushroom and Mustard Greens Mix	Melon Coconut Mousse

74	Zucchini Butter	Greens and Vinaigrette	Ginger-Spice Brownies
75	Basil Zucchini and Cucumber Noodle Salad	Tomato and Peppers Pancakes	Avocado and Pineapple Bowls
76	Creamy Cheese Soufflés	Avocado, Pine Nuts and Chard Salad	Tangerine Stew
77	Chives Stuffed Tomatoes	Grapes, Avocado and Spinach Salad	Pineapple and Melon Stew
78	Capers Cauliflower Rice and Avocado	Chard Soup	Cocoa Muffins
79	Roasted Peppers Muffins	Mushrooms and Chard Soup	Creamy Pineapple Mix
80	Mint Watermelon Bowl	Avocado Soup	Grapefruit Cream
81	Tomato and Avocado Pizza	Coconut Zucchini Cream	Coconut and Almond Truffles
82		Zucchini and Cauliflower Soup	Almond Balls
83	Spicy Bowls	Greens and Olives Pan	Almond-Date Energy Bites
84	Vegetarian Keto Breakfast Frittata	Cauliflower and Artichokes Soup	Pecan and Date-Stuffed Roasted Pears
85	Waffle/Cinnamon Roll	Grilled Veggie Mix	Chocolate And Walnut Farfalle
86	Scrambled Eggs with Cheddar & Spinach	Eggplant and Olives Stew	Peach-Mango Crumble (Pressure cooker
87	Creamy Zucchini Noodles	Hot Cabbage Soup	Zesty Orange-Cranberry Energy Bites
88	Keto Pumpkin Pancakes	Tomato, Green Beans and Chard Soup	Mint Chocolate Chip Sorbet
89	Sweet Cauliflower Rice Casserole	Hot Roasted Peppers Cream	Pumpkin Pie Cups (Pressure cooker
90	Avocado Oatmeal	Eggplant and Peppers Soup	Strawberry Parfaits With Cashew Crème
91	Zucchini Muffins	Vinegar Cucumber, Olives and Shallots Salad	Maple-Walnut Oatmeal Cookies
92		Creamy Brussels Sprouts Bowls	Banana-Nut Bread Bars
93	Berry and Dates Oatmeal	Green Beans and Radishes Bake	Apple Crumble
94	Mushroom Muffins	Avocado and Radish Bowls	Chocolate-Cranberry Oatmeal Cookies
95		Celery and Radish Soup	Cashew-Chocolate Truffles
96	Tomato Oatmeal	Lime Avocado and Cucumber Soup	Banana Chocolate Cupcakes
97	Avocado Smoothie	Avocado and Kale Soup	Minty Fruit Salad
98	Asparagus and Avocado Bowls	Spinach and Cucumber Salad	Sesame Cookies
99	Avocado and Pomegranate Bowls	Spinach and Broccoli Soup	Mango Coconut Cream Pie
100	Oregano Peppers Bake	Curry Spinach Soup	Cherry-Vanilla Rice Pudding (Pressure cooker
101	Coconut Green Smoothie	Avocado, Spinach and Kale Soup	Chocolate Coconut Brownies
102	Pesto Tomato Bowls	Arugula and Artichokes Bowls	Lime in the Coconut Chia Pudding
103	Scallions Zucchini Bake	Mushroom and Mustard Greens Mix	Melon Coconut Mousse
104	Leeks and Arugula Salad	Greens and Vinaigrette	Ginger-Spice Brownies
105	Spinach Salad	Tomato and Peppers Pancakes	Avocado and Pineapple Bowls
106	Zucchini Butter	Avocado, Pine Nuts and Chard Salad	Tangerine Stew
107	Basil Zucchini and Cucumber Noodle Salad	Grapes, Avocado and Spinach Salad	Pineapple and Melon Stew
108	Creamy Cheese Soufflés	Chard Soup	Cocoa Muffins
109	Chives Stuffed Tomatoes	Mushrooms and Chard Soup	Creamy Pineapple Mix
110	Capers Cauliflower Rice and Avocado	Avocado Soup	Grapefruit Cream
111	Roasted Peppers Muffins	Coconut Zucchini Cream	Coconut and Almond Truffles
112	Mint Watermelon Bowl	Zucchini and Cauliflower Soup	Almond Balls

113	Tomato and Avocado Pizza	Greens and Olives Pan	Almond-Date Energy Bites
114		Cauliflower and Artichokes Soup	Pecan and Date-Stuffed Roasted Pears
115	Spicy Bowls	Grilled Veggie Mix	Chocolate And Walnut Farfalle
116	Vegetarian Keto Breakfast Frittata	Eggplant and Olives Stew	Peach-Mango Crumble (Pressure cooker
117	Waffle/Cinnamon Roll	Hot Cabbage Soup	Zesty Orange-Cranberry Energy Bites
118	Scrambled Eggs with Cheddar & Spinach	Tomato, Green Beans and Chard Soup	Mint Chocolate Chip Sorbet
119	Creamy Zucchini Noodles	Hot Roasted Peppers Cream	Pumpkin Pie Cups (Pressure cooker
120	Keto Pumpkin Pancakes	Eggplant and Peppers Soup	Strawberry Parfaits With Cashew Crème
121	Sweet Cauliflower Rice Casserole	Vinegar Cucumber, Olives and Shallots Salad	Maple-Walnut Oatmeal Cookies
122	Avocado Oatmeal	Creamy Brussels Sprouts Bowls	Banana-Nut Bread Bars
123	Zucchini Muffins	Green Beans and Radishes Bake	Apple Crumble
124		Avocado and Radish Bowls	Chocolate-Cranberry Oatmeal Cookies
125	Berry and Dates Oatmeal	Celery and Radish Soup	Cashew-Chocolate Truffles
126	Mushroom Muffins	Lime Avocado and Cucumber Soup	Banana Chocolate Cupcakes
127		Avocado and Kale Soup	Minty Fruit Salad
128	Tomato Oatmeal	Spinach and Cucumber Salad	Sesame Cookies
129	Avocado Smoothie	Spinach and Broccoli Soup	Mango Coconut Cream Pie
130	Asparagus and Avocado Bowls	Curry Spinach Soup	Cherry-Vanilla Rice Pudding (Pressure cooker
131	Avocado and Pomegranate Bowls	Avocado, Spinach and Kale Soup	Chocolate Coconut Brownies
132	Oregano Peppers Bake	Arugula and Artichokes Bowls	Lime in the Coconut Chia Pudding
133	Coconut Green Smoothie	Mushroom and Mustard Greens Mix	Melon Coconut Mousse
134	Pesto Tomato Bowls	Greens and Vinaigrette	Ginger-Spice Brownies
135	Scallions Zucchini Bake	Tomato and Peppers Pancakes	Avocado and Pineapple Bowls
136	Leeks and Arugula Salad	Avocado, Pine Nuts and Chard Salad	Tangerine Stew
137	Spinach Salad	Grapes, Avocado and Spinach Salad	Pineapple and Melon Stew
138	Zucchini Butter	Chard Soup	Cocoa Muffins
139	Basil Zucchini and Cucumber Noodle Salad	Mushrooms and Chard Soup	Creamy Pineapple Mix
140	Creamy Cheese Soufflés	Avocado Soup	Grapefruit Cream
141	Chives Stuffed Tomatoes	Coconut Zucchini Cream	Coconut and Almond Truffles
142	Capers Cauliflower Rice and Avocado	Zucchini and Cauliflower Soup	Almond Balls
143	Roasted Peppers Muffins	Greens and Olives Pan	Almond-Date Energy Bites
144	Mint Watermelon Bowl	Cauliflower and Artichokes Soup	Pecan and Date-Stuffed Roasted Pears
145	Tomato and Avocado Pizza	Grilled Veggie Mix	Chocolate And Walnut Farfalle
146		Eggplant and Olives Stew	Peach-Mango Crumble (Pressure cooker
147	Spicy Bowls	Hot Cabbage Soup	Zesty Orange-Cranberry Energy Bites
148	Vegetarian Keto Breakfast Frittata	Tomato, Green Beans and Chard Soup	Mint Chocolate Chip Sorbet
149	Waffle/Cinnamon Roll	Hot Roasted Peppers Cream	Pumpkin Pie Cups (Pressure cooker
150	Scrambled Eggs with Cheddar & Spinach	Eggplant and Peppers Soup	Strawberry Parfaits With Cashew Crème

151	Creamy Zucchini Noodles	Vinegar Cucumber, Olives and Shallots Salad	Maple-Walnut Oatmeal Cookies
152	Keto Pumpkin Pancakes	Creamy Brussels Sprouts Bowls	Banana-Nut Bread Bars
153	Sweet Cauliflower Rice Casserole	Green Beans and Radishes Bake	Apple Crumble
154	Avocado Oatmeal	Avocado and Radish Bowls	Chocolate-Cranberry Oatmeal Cookies
155	Zucchini Muffins	Celery and Radish Soup	Cashew-Chocolate Truffles
156		Lime Avocado and Cucumber Soup	Banana Chocolate Cupcakes
157	Berry and Dates Oatmeal	Avocado and Kale Soup	Minty Fruit Salad
158	Mushroom Muffins	Spinach and Cucumber Salad	Sesame Cookies
159		Spinach and Broccoli Soup	Mango Coconut Cream Pie
160	Tomato Oatmeal	Curry Spinach Soup	Cherry-Vanilla Rice Pudding (Pressure cooker
161	Avocado Smoothie	Avocado, Spinach and Kale Soup	Chocolate Coconut Brownies
162	Asparagus and Avocado Bowls	Arugula and Artichokes Bowls	Lime in the Coconut Chia Pudding
163	Avocado and Pomegranate Bowls	Mushroom and Mustard Greens Mix	Melon Coconut Mousse
164	Oregano Peppers Bake	Greens and Vinaigrette	Ginger-Spice Brownies
165	Coconut Green Smoothie	Tomato and Peppers Pancakes	Avocado and Pineapple Bowls
166	Pesto Tomato Bowls	Avocado, Pine Nuts and Chard Salad	Tangerine Stew
167	Scallions Zucchini Bake	Grapes, Avocado and Spinach Salad	Pineapple and Melon Stew
168	Leeks and Arugula Salad	Chard Soup	Cocoa Muffins
169	Spinach Salad	Mushrooms and Chard Soup	Creamy Pineapple Mix
170	Zucchini Butter	Avocado Soup	Grapefruit Cream
171	Basil Zucchini and Cucumber Noodle Salad	Coconut Zucchini Cream	Coconut and Almond Truffles
172	Creamy Cheese Soufflés	Zucchini and Cauliflower Soup	Almond Balls
173	Chives Stuffed Tomatoes	Greens and Olives Pan	Almond-Date Energy Bites
174	Capers Cauliflower Rice and Avocado	Cauliflower and Artichokes Soup	Pecan and Date-Stuffed Roasted Pears
175	Roasted Peppers Muffins	Grilled Veggie Mix	Chocolate And Walnut Farfalle
176	Mint Watermelon Bowl	Eggplant and Olives Stew	Peach-Mango Crumble (Pressure cooker
177	Tomato and Avocado Pizza	Hot Cabbage Soup	Zesty Orange-Cranberry Energy Bites
178		Tomato, Green Beans and Chard Soup	Mint Chocolate Chip Sorbet
179	Spicy Bowls	Hot Roasted Peppers Cream	Pumpkin Pie Cups (Pressure cooker
180	Vegetarian Keto Breakfast Frittata	Eggplant and Peppers Soup	Strawberry Parfaits With Cashew Crème
181	Waffle/Cinnamon Roll	Vinegar Cucumber, Olives and Shallots Salad	Maple-Walnut Oatmeal Cookies
182	Scrambled Eggs with Cheddar & Spinach	Creamy Brussels Sprouts Bowls	Banana-Nut Bread Bars
183	Creamy Zucchini Noodles	Green Beans and Radishes Bake	Apple Crumble
184	Keto Pumpkin Pancakes	Avocado and Radish Bowls	Chocolate-Cranberry Oatmeal Cookies
185	Sweet Cauliflower Rice Casserole	Celery and Radish Soup	Cashew-Chocolate Truffles
186	Avocado Oatmeal	Lime Avocado and Cucumber Soup	Banana Chocolate Cupcakes
187	Zucchini Muffins	Avocado and Kale Soup	Minty Fruit Salad
188		Spinach and Cucumber Salad	Sesame Cookies
189	Berry and Dates Oatmeal	Spinach and Broccoli Soup	Mango Coconut Cream Pie

190	Mushroom Muffins	Curry Spinach Soup	Cherry-Vanilla Rice Pudding (Pressure cooker
191		Avocado, Spinach and Kale Soup	Chocolate Coconut Brownies
192	Tomato Oatmeal	Arugula and Artichokes Bowls	Lime in the Coconut Chia Pudding
193	Avocado Smoothie	Mushroom and Mustard Greens Mix	Melon Coconut Mousse
194	Asparagus and Avocado Bowls	Greens and Vinaigrette	Ginger-Spice Brownies
195	Avocado and Pomegranate Bowls	Tomato and Peppers Pancakes	Avocado and Pineapple Bowls
196	Oregano Peppers Bake	Avocado, Pine Nuts and Chard Salad	Tangerine Stew
197	Coconut Green Smoothie	Grapes, Avocado and Spinach Salad	Pineapple and Melon Stew
198	Pesto Tomato Bowls	Chard Soup	Cocoa Muffins
199	Scallions Zucchini Bake	Mushrooms and Chard Soup	Creamy Pineapple Mix
200	Leeks and Arugula Salad	Avocado Soup	Grapefruit Cream
201	Spinach Salad	Coconut Zucchini Cream	Coconut and Almond Truffles
202	Zucchini Butter	Zucchini and Cauliflower Soup	Almond Balls
203	Basil Zucchini and Cucumber Noodle Salad	Greens and Olives Pan	Almond-Date Energy Bites
204	Creamy Cheese Soufflés	Cauliflower and Artichokes Soup	Pecan and Date-Stuffed Roasted Pears
205	Chives Stuffed Tomatoes	Grilled Veggie Mix	Chocolate And Walnut Farfalle
206	Capers Cauliflower Rice and Avocado	Eggplant and Olives Stew	Peach-Mango Crumble (Pressure cooker
207	Roasted Peppers Muffins	Hot Cabbage Soup	Zesty Orange-Cranberry Energy Bites
208	Mint Watermelon Bowl	Tomato, Green Beans and Chard Soup	Mint Chocolate Chip Sorbet
209	Tomato and Avocado Pizza	Hot Roasted Peppers Cream	Pumpkin Pie Cups (Pressure cooker
210		Eggplant and Peppers Soup	Strawberry Parfaits With Cashew Crème
211	Spicy Bowls	Vinegar Cucumber, Olives and Shallots Salad	Maple-Walnut Oatmeal Cookies
212	Vegetarian Keto Breakfast Frittata	Creamy Brussels Sprouts Bowls	Banana-Nut Bread Bars
213	Waffle/Cinnamon Roll	Green Beans and Radishes Bake	Apple Crumble
214	Scrambled Eggs with Cheddar & Spinach	Avocado and Radish Bowls	Chocolate-Cranberry Oatmeal Cookies
215	Creamy Zucchini Noodles	Celery and Radish Soup	Cashew-Chocolate Truffles
216	Keto Pumpkin Pancakes	Lime Avocado and Cucumber Soup	Banana Chocolate Cupcakes
217	Sweet Cauliflower Rice Casserole	Avocado and Kale Soup	Minty Fruit Salad
218	Avocado Oatmeal	Spinach and Cucumber Salad	Sesame Cookies
219	Zucchini Muffins	Spinach and Broccoli Soup	Mango Coconut Cream Pie
220		Curry Spinach Soup	Cherry-Vanilla Rice Pudding (Pressure cooker
221	Berry and Dates Oatmeal	Avocado, Spinach and Kale Soup	Chocolate Coconut Brownies
222	Mushroom Muffins	Arugula and Artichokes Bowls	Lime in the Coconut Chia Pudding
223		Mushroom and Mustard Greens Mix	Melon Coconut Mousse
224	Tomato Oatmeal	Greens and Vinaigrette	Ginger-Spice Brownies
225	Avocado Smoothie	Tomato and Peppers Pancakes	Avocado and Pineapple Bowls
226	Asparagus and Avocado Bowls	Avocado, Pine Nuts and Chard Salad	Tangerine Stew
227	Avocado and Pomegranate Bowls	Grapes, Avocado and Spinach Salad	Pineapple and Melon Stew
228	Oregano Peppers Bake	Chard Soup	Cocoa Muffins

229	Coconut Green Smoothie	Mushrooms and Chard Soup	Creamy Pineapple Mix
230	Pesto Tomato Bowls	Avocado Soup	Grapefruit Cream
231	Scallions Zucchini Bake	Coconut Zucchini Cream	Coconut and Almond Truffles
232	Leeks and Arugula Salad	Zucchini and Cauliflower Soup	Almond Balls
233	Spinach Salad	Greens and Olives Pan	Almond-Date Energy Bites
234	Zucchini Butter	Cauliflower and Artichokes Soup	Pecan and Date-Stuffed Roasted Pears
235	Basil Zucchini and Cucumber Noodle Salad	Grilled Veggie Mix	Chocolate And Walnut Farfalle
236	Creamy Cheese Soufflés	Eggplant and Olives Stew	Peach-Mango Crumble (Pressure cooker
237	Chives Stuffed Tomatoes	Hot Cabbage Soup	Zesty Orange-Cranberry Energy Bites
238	Capers Cauliflower Rice and Avocado	Tomato, Green Beans and Chard Soup	Mint Chocolate Chip Sorbet
239	Roasted Peppers Muffins	Hot Roasted Peppers Cream	Pumpkin Pie Cups (Pressure cooker
240	Mint Watermelon Bowl	Eggplant and Peppers Soup	Strawberry Parfaits With Cashew Crème
241	Tomato and Avocado Pizza	Vinegar Cucumber, Olives and Shallots Salad	Maple-Walnut Oatmeal Cookies
242		Creamy Brussels Sprouts Bowls	Banana-Nut Bread Bars
243	Spicy Bowls	Green Beans and Radishes Bake	Apple Crumble
244	Vegetarian Keto Breakfast Frittata	Avocado and Radish Bowls	Chocolate-Cranberry Oatmeal Cookies
245	Waffle/Cinnamon Roll	Celery and Radish Soup	Cashew-Chocolate Truffles
246	Scrambled Eggs with Cheddar & Spinach	Lime Avocado and Cucumber Soup	Banana Chocolate Cupcakes
247	Creamy Zucchini Noodles	Avocado and Kale Soup	Minty Fruit Salad
248	Keto Pumpkin Pancakes	Spinach and Cucumber Salad	Sesame Cookies
249	Sweet Cauliflower Rice Casserole	Spinach and Broccoli Soup	Mango Coconut Cream Pie
250	Avocado Oatmeal	Curry Spinach Soup	Cherry-Vanilla Rice Pudding (Pressure cooker
251	Zucchini Muffins	Avocado, Spinach and Kale Soup	Chocolate Coconut Brownies
252		Arugula and Artichokes Bowls	Lime in the Coconut Chia Pudding
253	Berry and Dates Oatmeal	Mushroom and Mustard Greens Mix	Melon Coconut Mousse
254	Mushroom Muffins	Greens and Vinaigrette	Ginger-Spice Brownies
255		Tomato and Peppers Pancakes	Avocado and Pineapple Bowls
256	Tomato Oatmeal	Avocado, Pine Nuts and Chard Salad	Tangerine Stew
257	Avocado Smoothie	Grapes, Avocado and Spinach Salad	Pineapple and Melon Stew
258	Asparagus and Avocado Bowls	Chard Soup	Cocoa Muffins
259	Avocado and Pomegranate Bowls	Mushrooms and Chard Soup	Creamy Pineapple Mix
260	Oregano Peppers Bake	Avocado Soup	Grapefruit Cream
261	Coconut Green Smoothie	Coconut Zucchini Cream	Coconut and Almond Truffles
262	Pesto Tomato Bowls	Zucchini and Cauliflower Soup	Almond Balls
263	Scallions Zucchini Bake	Greens and Olives Pan	Almond-Date Energy Bites
264	Leeks and Arugula Salad	Cauliflower and Artichokes Soup	Pecan and Date-Stuffed Roasted Pears
265	Spinach Salad	Grilled Veggie Mix	Chocolate And Walnut Farfalle
266	Zucchini Butter	Eggplant and Olives Stew	Peach-Mango Crumble (Pressure cooker
267	Basil Zucchini and Cucumber Noodle Salad	Hot Cabbage Soup	Zesty Orange-Cranberry Energy Bites

268	Creamy Cheese Soufflés	Tomato, Green Beans and Chard Soup	Mint Chocolate Chip Sorbet
269	Chives Stuffed Tomatoes	Hot Roasted Peppers Cream	Pumpkin Pie Cups (Pressure cooker
270	Capers Cauliflower Rice and Avocado	Eggplant and Peppers Soup	Strawberry Parfaits With Cashew Crème
271	Roasted Peppers Muffins	Vinegar Cucumber, Olives and Shallots Salad	Maple-Walnut Oatmeal Cookies
272	Mint Watermelon Bowl	Creamy Brussels Sprouts Bowls	Banana-Nut Bread Bars
273	Tomato and Avocado Pizza	Green Beans and Radishes Bake	Apple Crumble
274		Avocado and Radish Bowls	Chocolate-Cranberry Oatmeal Cookies
275	Spicy Bowls	Celery and Radish Soup	Cashew-Chocolate Truffles
276	Vegetarian Keto Breakfast Frittata	Lime Avocado and Cucumber Soup	Banana Chocolate Cupcakes
277	Waffle/Cinnamon Roll	Avocado and Kale Soup	Minty Fruit Salad
278	Scrambled Eggs with Cheddar & Spinach	Spinach and Cucumber Salad	Sesame Cookies
279	Creamy Zucchini Noodles	Spinach and Broccoli Soup	Mango Coconut Cream Pie
280	Keto Pumpkin Pancakes	Curry Spinach Soup	Cherry-Vanilla Rice Pudding (Pressure cooker
281	Sweet Cauliflower Rice Casserole	Avocado, Spinach and Kale Soup	Chocolate Coconut Brownies
282	Avocado Oatmeal	Arugula and Artichokes Bowls	Lime in the Coconut Chia Pudding
283	Zucchini Muffins	Mushroom and Mustard Greens Mix	Melon Coconut Mousse
284		Greens and Vinaigrette	Ginger-Spice Brownies
285	Berry and Dates Oatmeal	Tomato and Peppers Pancakes	Avocado and Pineapple Bowls
286	Mushroom Muffins	Avocado, Pine Nuts and Chard Salad	Tangerine Stew
287		Grapes, Avocado and Spinach Salad	Pineapple and Melon Stew
288	Tomato Oatmeal	Chard Soup	Cocoa Muffins
289	Avocado Smoothie	Mushrooms and Chard Soup	Creamy Pineapple Mix
290	Asparagus and Avocado Bowls	Avocado Soup	Grapefruit Cream
291	Avocado and Pomegranate Bowls	Coconut Zucchini Cream	Coconut and Almond Truffles
292	Oregano Peppers Bake	Zucchini and Cauliflower Soup	Almond Balls
293	Coconut Green Smoothie	Greens and Olives Pan	Almond-Date Energy Bites
294	Pesto Tomato Bowls	Cauliflower and Artichokes Soup	Pecan and Date-Stuffed Roasted Pears
295	Scallions Zucchini Bake	Grilled Veggie Mix	Chocolate And Walnut Farfalle
296	Leeks and Arugula Salad	Eggplant and Olives Stew	Peach-Mango Crumble (Pressure cooker
297	Spinach Salad	Hot Cabbage Soup	Zesty Orange-Cranberry Energy Bites
298	Zucchini Butter	Tomato, Green Beans and Chard Soup	Mint Chocolate Chip Sorbet
299	Basil Zucchini and Cucumber Noodle Salad	Hot Roasted Peppers Cream	Pumpkin Pie Cups (Pressure cooker
300	Creamy Cheese Soufflés	Eggplant and Peppers Soup	Strawberry Parfaits With Cashew Crème
301	Chives Stuffed Tomatoes	Vinegar Cucumber, Olives and Shallots Salad	Maple-Walnut Oatmeal Cookies
302	Capers Cauliflower Rice and Avocado	Creamy Brussels Sprouts Bowls	Banana-Nut Bread Bars
303	Roasted Peppers Muffins	Green Beans and Radishes Bake	Apple Crumble
304	Mint Watermelon Bowl	Avocado and Radish Bowls	Chocolate-Cranberry Oatmeal Cookies
305	Tomato and Avocado Pizza	Celery and Radish Soup	Cashew-Chocolate Truffles
306		Lime Avocado and Cucumber Soup	Banana Chocolate Cupcakes

307	Spicy Bowls	Avocado and Kale Soup	Minty Fruit Salad
308	Vegetarian Keto Breakfast Frittata	Spinach and Cucumber Salad	Sesame Cookies
309	Waffle/Cinnamon Roll	Spinach and Broccoli Soup	Mango Coconut Cream Pie
310	Scrambled Eggs with Cheddar & Spinach	Curry Spinach Soup	Cherry-Vanilla Rice Pudding (Pressure cooker
311	Creamy Zucchini Noodles	Avocado, Spinach and Kale Soup	Chocolate Coconut Brownies
312	Keto Pumpkin Pancakes	Arugula and Artichokes Bowls	Lime in the Coconut Chia Pudding
313	Sweet Cauliflower Rice Casserole	Mushroom and Mustard Greens Mix	Melon Coconut Mousse
314	Avocado Oatmeal	Greens and Vinaigrette	Ginger-Spice Brownies
315	Zucchini Muffins	Tomato and Peppers Pancakes	Avocado and Pineapple Bowls
316		Avocado, Pine Nuts and Chard Salad	Tangerine Stew
317	Berry and Dates Oatmeal	Grapes, Avocado and Spinach Salad	Pineapple and Melon Stew
318	Mushroom Muffins	Chard Soup	Cocoa Muffins
319		Mushrooms and Chard Soup	Creamy Pineapple Mix
320	Tomato Oatmeal	Avocado Soup	Grapefruit Cream
321	Avocado Smoothie	Coconut Zucchini Cream	Coconut and Almond Truffles
322	Asparagus and Avocado Bowls	Zucchini and Cauliflower Soup	Almond Balls
323	Avocado and Pomegranate Bowls	Greens and Olives Pan	Almond-Date Energy Bites
324	Oregano Peppers Bake	Cauliflower and Artichokes Soup	Pecan and Date-Stuffed Roasted Pears
325	Coconut Green Smoothie	Grilled Veggie Mix	Chocolate And Walnut Farfalle
326	Pesto Tomato Bowls	Eggplant and Olives Stew	Peach-Mango Crumble (Pressure cooker
327	Scallions Zucchini Bake	Hot Cabbage Soup	Zesty Orange-Cranberry Energy Bites
328	Leeks and Arugula Salad	Tomato, Green Beans and Chard Soup	Mint Chocolate Chip Sorbet
329	Spinach Salad	Hot Roasted Peppers Cream	Pumpkin Pie Cups (Pressure cooker
330	Zucchini Butter	Eggplant and Peppers Soup	Strawberry Parfaits With Cashew Crème
331	Basil Zucchini and Cucumber Noodle Salad	Vinegar Cucumber, Olives and Shallots Salad	Maple-Walnut Oatmeal Cookies
332	Creamy Cheese Soufflés	Creamy Brussels Sprouts Bowls	Banana-Nut Bread Bars
333	Chives Stuffed Tomatoes	Green Beans and Radishes Bake	Apple Crumble
334	Capers Cauliflower Rice and Avocado	Avocado and Radish Bowls	Chocolate-Cranberry Oatmeal Cookies
335	Roasted Peppers Muffins	Celery and Radish Soup	Cashew-Chocolate Truffles
336	Mint Watermelon Bowl	Lime Avocado and Cucumber Soup	Banana Chocolate Cupcakes
337	Tomato and Avocado Pizza	Avocado and Kale Soup	Minty Fruit Salad
338		Spinach and Cucumber Salad	Sesame Cookies
339	Spicy Bowls	Spinach and Broccoli Soup	Mango Coconut Cream Pie
340	Vegetarian Keto Breakfast Frittata	Curry Spinach Soup	Cherry-Vanilla Rice Pudding (Pressure cooker
341	Waffle/Cinnamon Roll	Avocado, Spinach and Kale Soup	Chocolate Coconut Brownies
342	Scrambled Eggs with Cheddar & Spinach	Arugula and Artichokes Bowls	Lime in the Coconut Chia Pudding
343	Creamy Zucchini Noodles	Mushroom and Mustard Greens Mix	Melon Coconut Mousse
344	Keto Pumpkin Pancakes	Greens and Vinaigrette	Ginger-Spice Brownies
345	Sweet Cauliflower Rice Casserole	Tomato and Peppers Pancakes	Avocado and Pineapple Bowls

346	Avocado Oatmeal	Avocado, Pine Nuts and Chard Salad	Tangerine Stew
347	Zucchini Muffins	Grapes, Avocado and Spinach Salad	Pineapple and Melon Stew
348		Chard Soup	Cocoa Muffins
349	Berry and Dates Oatmeal	Mushrooms and Chard Soup	Creamy Pineapple Mix
350	Mushroom Muffins	Avocado Soup	Grapefruit Cream
351		Coconut Zucchini Cream	Coconut and Almond Truffles
352	Tomato Oatmeal	Zucchini and Cauliflower Soup	Almond Balls
353	Avocado Smoothie	Greens and Olives Pan	Almond-Date Energy Bites
354	Asparagus and Avocado Bowls	Cauliflower and Artichokes Soup	Pecan and Date-Stuffed Roasted Pears
355	Avocado and Pomegranate Bowls	Grilled Veggie Mix	Chocolate And Walnut Farfalle
356	Oregano Peppers Bake	Eggplant and Olives Stew	Peach-Mango Crumble (Pressure cooker
357	Coconut Green Smoothie	Hot Cabbage Soup	Zesty Orange-Cranberry Energy Bites
358	Pesto Tomato Bowls	Tomato, Green Beans and Chard Soup	Mint Chocolate Chip Sorbet
359	Scallions Zucchini Bake	Hot Roasted Peppers Cream	Pumpkin Pie Cups (Pressure cooker
360	Leeks and Arugula Salad	Eggplant and Peppers Soup	Strawberry Parfaits With Cashew Crème
361	Spinach Salad	Vinegar Cucumber, Olives and Shallots Salad	Maple-Walnut Oatmeal Cookies
362	Zucchini Butter	Creamy Brussels Sprouts Bowls	Banana-Nut Bread Bars
363	Basil Zucchini and Cucumber Noodle Salad	Green Beans and Radishes Bake	Apple Crumble
364	Creamy Cheese Soufflés	Avocado and Radish Bowls	Chocolate-Cranberry Oatmeal Cookies
365	Chives Stuffed Tomatoes	Celery and Radish Soup	Cashew-Chocolate Truffles

CONCLUSION

The Ketogenic diet is truly life changing. The diet improves your overall health and helps you lose the extra weight in a matter of days. The diet will show its multiple benefits even from the beginning and it will become your new lifestyle really soon.

As soon as you embrace the Ketogenic diet, you will start to live a completely new life.

On the other hand, the vegetarian diet is such a healthy dietary option you can choose when trying to live healthy and also lose some weight.

The collection we bring to you today is actually a combination between the Ketogenic and vegetarian diets. You get to discover some amazing Ketogenic vegetarian dishes you can prepare in the comfort of your own home. All the dishes you found here follow both the Ketogenic and the vegetarian rules, they all taste delicious and rich and they are all easy to make.

We can assure you that such a combo is hard to find. So, start a keto diet with a vegetarian "touch" today. It will be both useful and fun!

So, what are you still waiting for? Get started with the Ketogenic diet and learn how to prepare the best and most flavored Ketogenic vegetarian dishes. Enjoy them all!

Made in the USA
Coppell, TX
07 January 2020

14212820R00138